S0-DPJ-086

# THE Third PINK BOOK

A GLOBAL VIEW OF
LESBIAN AND GAY
LIBERATION AND OPPRESSION

Property of Jose E. Muñoz

edited by
## Aart Hendriks, Rob Tielman, and Evert van der Veen

PROMETHEUS BOOKS • BUFFALO, NEW YORK

Published 1993 by Prometheus Books

*The Third Pink Book: A Global View of Lesbian and Gay Liberation and Oppression.*
Copyright © 1993 by Aart Hendriks, Rob Tielman, and Evert van der Veen. All rights
reserved. No part of this publication may be reproduced, stored in a retrieval system,
or transmitted in any form or by any means, electronic, mechanical, photocopying, recording,
or otherwise, without prior written permission of the publisher, except in the case of brief
quotations embodied in critical articles and reviews. Inquiries should be addressed to
Prometheus Books, 59 John Glenn Drive, Buffalo, New York, U.S.A. 14228-2197, 716-
837-2475. FAX: 716-835-6901.

This book is a publication of the International Lesbian and Gay Association (ILGA).
For further information on the ILGA or any of the previous or forthcoming Pink Books,
please contact: ILGA Information Secretariat, Kolenmarktstraat 81, B-1000 Brussels, Belgium. Tel/fax: 32.2.502 2471.

Editors: Aart Hendriks, Rob Tielman, and Evert van der Veen

Editorial Board: Dennis Altman, Virginia Apuzzo, John Clark, Kurt Krickler, Lisa Power,
Grada Schadee, and Rebecca Sevilla

97 96 95 94 93     5 4 3 2 1

Library of Congress Cataloging-in-Publication Data

The third pink book : a global view of lesbian and gay liberation and oppression / edited
    by Aart Hendriks, Rob Tielman, and Evert van der Veen.
        p.    cm. — (New concepts in human sexuality series)
    Includes bibliographical references.
    ISBN 0-87975-831-7
    1. Gay liberation movement. 2. Homosexuality—Law and legislation. 3. Gays—Civil
rights. I. Hendriks, Aart, 1961–    . II. Tielman, Rob, 1946–    III. van der Veen, Evert,
1960–    IV. Series.
HQ76.5.T47     1993
305.9'0664—dc20                                                              93-398
                                                                              CIP

Printed on acid-free paper in the United States of America.

In memory of Jean Claude Letist and Frank Arnal

# Contents

PART TWO: A COUNTRY-BY-COUNTRY SURVEY

# Preface

## Aart Hendriks, Rob Tielman, and Evert van der Veen

Since its foundation in 1978, the International Lesbian and Gay Association (ILGA) has published two reports on the legal and social situation of lesbians and gay men throughout the world. This book is the third in what we hope will be a continuing series.

The first *Pink Book* was produced in 1984, the year of international lesbian and gay action. The second appeared in 1988, in commemoration of the tenth anniversary of the ILGA. We are proud that we are now, five years later, able to present a new and updated version of the *Pink Book,* in the hope that this edition will turn out to be at least as instrumental in achieving lesbian and gay goals as the first two editions have.

ILGA's *Pink Book*s have a twofold purpose: first, to describe the present legal and social situation for lesbians and gay men in various countries of the world in order to allow readers to assess the global picture, and, hopefully, to offer some concrete proposals for improving the current situation. To this end, our authors describe the public attitude in their respective countries toward homosexuality. For several nations, a careful and in-depth analysis of both formal regulations and other social value systems regarding lesbians and gay men is made. In addition, the interaction between changing public attitudes and the development of the lesbian and gay movement is assessed. Lesbians and gay men in many countries may learn from these valuable experiences and transform this vital information into local and national initiatives. Second, this volume seeks to strengthen international collaboration between lesbians and gay men. This book itself is the unique product of such cooperation.

The third edition of the *ILGA Pink Book* includes more contributions from non-industrialized countries than either of its predecessors. Moreover, this edition will likely be made available in other languages than English. Both these factors reflect the steeply rising interest in lesbian and gay issues all around the world as well as the important role the *Pink Book* plays as a source of information and inspiration.

The final result of our work is a colorful anthology offering unique inside information about the lesbian and gay movement in Australia, Argentina, Canada, the People's Republic of China, Denmark, France, Germany, Ireland, the Netherlands, the Philippines, the United Kingdom, the United States, West Africa, Zimbabwe, and several other nations. In addition, a country-by-country survey gives an up-to-date report on the legal and social position of lesbians and gay men in the vast majority of countries around the world.

Everyone who contributed to this enterprise did so without promise of any financial reward. In contributing to the *ILGA Pink Book,* be it by writing, editing, or translating manuscripts, we were all bound by concern for lesbians and gay men all over the world.

During the production of this volume, all three editors were affiliated with the Gay and Lesbian Studies Department of the University of Utrecht in the Netherlands. The fact that we all spoke the same language and shared the same work premisses considerably facilitated communication. Moreover, we could benefit from the in-house facilities, ranging from coffee machines to computer terminals and telecommunication equipment. We acknowledge the generous support offered by the Board of the Gay and Lesbian Studies Department, and are particularly indebted to the tireless assistance of its secretariat.

In addition, we gratefully acknowledge the input of the so-called "think-tank," a pool of independent experts established in order to assist the editing team and to secure a genuinely international outlook. This think-tank was composed of committed ILGA members from Australia (Dennis Altman), Austria (John Clark and Kurt Krickler), the Netherlands (Grada Schadee), Peru (Rebecca Sevilla), the United Kingdom (Lisa Power) and the United States (Virginia Apuzzo).

Those who assisted include numerous others who, in various ways, helped and inspired the authors in writing their articles. They gave the editing team ideas and information, and assisted in collecting and correcting available data or helped to translate manuscripts. In this respect, it was a relief to know that we could always fall back on Micha Ramakers of ILGA's Information Secretariat in Brussels.

It is only as a result of the tireless commitment of all those in the international lesbian and gay movement that this book could be compiled. Our poor thanks cannot begin to measure our gratitude for the inspiring help received from so many people.

Lastly, we would like to dedicate this book to all members the ILGA lost during the course of the last decade, mainly as the result of AIDS. Among them, there were ILGA members who made a valuable and unforgettable contribution to the *Pink Book* project. Just before the galleys of this book were ready, we learned that Frank Arnal, a contributor to this volume, had died. Without Frank's involvement, as well as the commitment of many others, it is very unlikely that this project would ever have seen the light of day. In this respect, we will never forget the input we received from Jean Claude Letist, Leen Meijboom, and Jehuda Sofer; we can only hope that their energy and optimism will equally inspire future editors of this fascinating project.

# Introduction

## John Clark, Aart Hendriks, Lisa Power, Rob Tielman, and Evert van der Veen

The publication of the first global report on lesbian and gay liberation and oppression in 1985 was a landmark in the history of the International Lesbian and Gay Association (ILGA), which had been founded in 1978 as the International Gay Association (IGA). The *Pink Books* began a new phase in the ILGA's efforts to promote and defend the interests of lesbians and gay men worldwide, and to strengthen international collaboration between them.

The title *Pink Book* refers to the close and often hostile links between the homosexual and heterosexual elements in society. Pink was the color designated by an intolerant political movement, the German National-Socialist (Nazi) Party, to label homosexuals, who were persecuted and rounded up for extermination. That same color has become the symbol both of deviance and self-respect for lesbians and gay men.

The aim of this book is to give a global overview of lesbian and gay liberation and oppression. It uncovers the legal and sociocultural situations of lesbians and gay men around the world, and reports the changes in their development. Like its predecessors, this edition of the *Pink Book* consists broadly of two parts. Part One contains articles describing the interaction between the development of the lesbian and gay communities and the various sociocultural elements operating within the country being discussed. The overriding theme is "self-organization"; the articles demonstrate that there is no uniform way of achieving self-empowerment. Our hypothesis, borne out by the contributions received, is that

15

sociocultural pluralism is reflected not only in our sexual and political preferences, but also in the way we organize ourselves.

Part Two is a country-by-country survey, which provides a succinct description of the legal and social situation of lesbians and gay men in almost all nations of the world, combined with an up-to-date review of the national and local lesbian and gay movements.

## THE WORLDWIDE STRUGGLE FOR LESBIAN AND GAY RIGHTS

Since the publication of the first *Pink Book,* much has changed both within and beyond the ILGA. The *Pink Book* itself was instrumental in widening our views and increasing knowledge about many aspects of the movement. The ILGA, as the only international federation for all types of lesbian, gay, and bisexual groups, has grown immensely and now includes more than four hundred groups from fifty countries, covering every continent. It has held fifteen world conferences and many regional ones, bringing together activists of many different beliefs and backgrounds to share, learn, and build.

The ILGA works both to support the lesbian and gay movements in each country and to represent their interests to international human rights and inter-governmental organizations. Because lesbians and gay men are nowhere mentioned in any of the international human rights documents, we must constantly promote and defend our position. Since the publication of the last *Pink Book,* there have been several notable victories for the ILGA in this area. In 1991, Amnesty International finally included lesbians and gay men as prisoners of conscience within its mandate after fifteen years of lobbying and direct action demonstrations. We continue to work with Amnesty to put their commitment into practice. The ILGA's other long-standing campaign to persuade the World Health Organization (WHO) to declassify homosexuality as a disease met with similar success. The ILGA now has official relations with both the Department of Public Information at the United Nations and WHO's Global Programme on AIDS (GPA). In 1993, the ILGA is attending the World Human Rights Conference in Vienna.

The ILGA is currently working to obtain Non-Governmental Organization (NGO) representative status with the UN's Economic and Social Council (ECOSOC) and with the Council of Europe. It has also undertaken studies on discrimination for international bodies such as the European Community. But it works as well on a more intimate level to protest individual or national injustices and here, too, there have been notable successes. Prisoners have been released, anti-homosexual decisions reversed, and governments embarrassed by exposure of their homophobic actions. These actions continue, and are publicized through the ILGA bimonthly bulletin as well as by ILGA's action secretariat, the San Francisco-based International Gay and Lesbian Human Rights Commission (IGLHRC), and through the global press.

Over the past five years, AIDS and HIV have become a growing reality for lesbians, gay men, and bisexuals throughout the globe. Bangkok, Mexico City, Rio de Janeiro, and Johannesburg now face the same problems as San Francisco, New York, London, Amsterdam, and Sydney. Although it is important to acknowledge that the virus affects a wide and growing number of people outside our communities, there is no doubt that it has had an unparalleled impact upon our particular attempts at self-help and organization. The epidemic has claimed many of our leading and most loved members, including former ILGA secretary general, Jean Claude Letist; yet, at the same time, it has stimulated the growth of many more groups, often bringing lesbians and gay men together for the first time in a particular town or country. In some areas, it has meant the growth of identity and self-respect as lesbian, gay, or bisexual groups have demonstrated their ability to provide care and prevention services to fight the epidemic; sometimes it has even meant governmental recognition and funding. This growth in the work of ILGA members, many of whom are in the vanguard of the fight in their own countries, has been reflected in the increasing importance given to AIDS-related issues both at international conferences and within the ILGA bulletin itself. Sadly, this is certainly one aspect of our work that will continue to grow.

The world is changing fast in many ways. When we began preparations for the third update of our country-by-country survey, we would never have envisaged the massive and sudden political changes that lead to a redrawing of the world map, with many new countries proudly proclaiming themselves independent. While Western Europe slowly harmonized and Germany became one again, the Eastern part of the continent fragmented. The former Soviet Union is now a dozen separate countries and the Yugoslav Federation is undergoing a violent disintegration. The two Koreas and El Salvador have come to peace, while upheavals continue in the Middle East. No doubt, by the time this third edition is published, there will be many more changes, each of them with legal and social implications for lesbians and gay men.

With each new edition, the *Pink Book*'s country-by-country survey becomes more complete and more thorough. The first book contained information on 88 countries, the second on 124 countries. As the direct result of a more extensive international network and by collaboration with the ILGA Information Secretariat in Brussels (as well as boundary changes), the number of countries covered by the 1993 survey has risen dramatically to 202.

The increased visibility of lesbians, gay men, and bisexuals, supported by a strong movement, has proved to be a successful formula for confronting and fighting homophobic tendencies in all types of society. Well-organized groups in many countries have succeeded in at least partially improving our human rights. Yet there is still no nation in the world that can claim to fully respect the rights and dignity of its homosexual citizens. Moreover, legal and sociocultural mechanisms are still exclusively or predominantly based on the "assumption of hetero-sexuality," which generally implies and condones discrimination against non-heterosexuals. While some, primarily in the Northern Hemisphere and Australasia, are beginning to bridge the gap in legal protection between homosexuals and hetero- sexuals, in the vast majority of countries our rights are denied in many ways.

Unfortunately, over the past five years the situation in some countries, notably those in the grip of fundamentalist governments, has deteriorated. Judicial exe- cutions of lesbians and gay men have been reported from Iran and threatened elsewhere, matched by the action of unofficial death squads in a number of Latin American countries and homophobic violence throughout the globe. AIDS has also provided an excuse for repressive legislation in a number of countries. The rise both of fundamentalism in the U.S.A. and fascism throughout Europe is a continuing threat to many minorities. Yet, in the vast majority of countries, the situation continues to improve; the international lesbian and gay movement has been a major contributor to this process.

## PRODUCING THIS BOOK

At the 1989 annual ILGA world conference in Vienna, the decision was made to focus on one special theme for this edition of the *Pink Book*. In the majority of accepted articles, the ways in which female and male same-sex lovers organize and gain political power in the countries concerned is the prime target of analysis.

The various contributions confirm our hypothesis that there is no general model that applies to the effective organization of same-sex lovers throughout the world. The ways in which they organize themselves depend on various sets of circumstances, not least the role models society has prescribed for its members. There is no such thing as *the* lesbian or *the* gay man. Same-sex lifestyles differ from place to place and from time to time, each with its own advantages and disadvantages. The articles—each from its own perspective—look at how same- sex lovers use the tools available to improve the living conditions for lesbians and gay men. More or less successful efforts to change unfavorable circumstances are described.

Each contributor has written from a different point of view and a different part of the world. In countries where the level of self-organization of lesbians and gay men is still relatively low, the situation of the country as a whole is described. In those countries where an established, well-organized lesbian and gay movement exists, a specific item or group has been highlighted. Together these give an insight into many aspects of the worldwide lesbian and gay movement.

If we can draw a conclusion at all from the articles, it seems that aware- ness of a country's particularities is a condition of success in overcoming op- pression. Moreover, the various articles clearly demonstrate the importance of international collaboration and the key position the ILGA fills as an interna- tional platform where representatives of lesbians and gay organizations can meet to plan international actions.

## THE CONTENTS OF THIS BOOK

Preparations for this edition began immediately after the publication of the second *Pink Book*. With the help of the think-tank and many other ILGA members, and building on our experience from the second book, we asked over one hundred women and men to submit an abstract for possible contributions to a new edition. We aimed especially at achieving an equal share of lesbian and gay items as well as a reasonable geographical distribution of authors. Furthermore, for obvious reasons, we attempted, as a rule, to solicit native authors to describe conditions in their own countries. However, in several cases we had to fall back on others to perform this task. These were usually recommended to us by local lesbian or gay activists.

As usual in large-scale projects like this, despite frenetic efforts we did not totally succeed in achieving our goals. In the five years we worked on this book, we wrote more than 1,000 letters, made innumerable phone calls, and spoke to countless prospective authors as well as to many other people. We regret that some authors were unable to finish their contribution in time, generally for very legitimate reasons. To a considerable extent this reflects the unequal distribution of communication facilities and financial resources in the world, which also discriminates disproportionately against women. This goes some way to explain the imbalance between women and men, predominantly from industrialized countries, who eventually contributed to this volume.

Because of the diversity of issues being addressed, we decided to list the articles merely by alphabetical order of authors' surnames. In this way, we hope that the reader will experience the same sensation we had, when we read the first drafts of the articles, of how many different ideas and ways there are to strive for a similar goal.

Barry Adam opens with a description of the struggle for lesbian and gay legal rights in Canada. This is followed by an analysis by Frank Arnal of the importance of the gay media in organizing gay men in France. Vern Bullough and Fang Fu Ruan describe the almost complete denial of lesbians and gay men in the Chinese People's Republic. John Clark explores the question of whether or not the international lesbian and gay movement should remain grassroots or become highly professionalized from an historical perspective. In this respect developments and trends within the lesbian and gay movement in different parts of the world are compared. Mark Coutinho (pseudonym) describes the emergence of a lesbian and gay movement in Zimbabwe, which cuts across historical racial dividing lines. Jomar Fleras analyzes the old traditions of his home country, the Philippines, and the rise of the new lesbian and gay movement. Ilse Fusková-Kornreich and Dafna Argov describe the recent history of lesbian activism in Argentina and the ways lesbians support each other.

Bent Hansen and Henning Jørgensen describe how the Danish national lesbian and gay movement eventually achieved what it had been working for for decades:

a law that protects and grants to same-sex cohabitants privileges similar to those of heterosexual married couples. The importance of the registered partnership law is without precedent and has global implications, now that Denmark is the first country in the world that explicitly recognizes lesbian and gay couples as both a legal entity and as a family in their own right. John Hart follows with a critical assessment of how the Australian lesbian and gay movement achieved integration of lesbian and gay-specific issues within Australian immigration policy and the degree to which immigration barriers to foreign-born lovers of Australian gays, lesbians, and bisexuals were eventually lifted. Aart Hendriks and Willemien Ruygrok make a similar analysis of efforts by the Dutch lesbian and gay movement to guarantee to alien lesbians and gay men equal access to all human rights observed by the Dutch government. Didi Khayatt illustrates the deplorable situation of young lesbians at school. While she restricts herself to Canada, we assume that the same mechanism applies to many other industrialized and probably non-industrialized countries.

Ilse Kokula describes the features and special role of the Berlin state bureau for gay and lesbian emancipation in the reuniting German capital. David Norris describes the struggle for gay rights in Ireland both from a personal perspective and as a member of the Irish Senate. Gerben Potman and Huub Ruijrok describe the situation of male homosexuals in West Africa, building on their experience as visiting students in Senegal and Burkina Faso. Lisa Power and Tim Barnet explain the paradox of the British system: the answer to lesbian and gay oppression is greater freedom which, at the same time, requires better self-organization. Svend Robinson gives a description of his own experiences as an openly gay member of Parliament in Canada. Petra Schedler compares the organizational models of two gay and lesbian humanist organizations in the U.K. and the Netherlands. Christina Schenk describes the process of lesbian emancipation in the former German Democratic Republic, both before and after unification. Andrzej Selerowicz had the difficult task of describing the rapidly changing situation in Central and Eastern European countries, and the development of the lesbian and gay movements in these countries. Chris Smith describes his personal coming out and commitment to the movement as a member of Parliament in the U.K.

In the final two articles, the effects of long-term campaigning for equal rights are analyzed. Carmen Vázquez passionately describes the dreams and reality of lesbians and gay men in the U.S.A. and what this means for their movement. Evert van der Veen, Aart Hendriks, and Astrid Mattijssen analyze the evolution of the concept of lesbian and gay rights from a European perspective.

Part Two of the volume is a country-by-country survey of gay and lesbian liberation and oppression compiled by Rob Tielman and Hans Hammelburg.

We hope that this book makes a further contribution to the improvement of the human rights of lesbians and gay men throughout the world and strengthens international cooperation between lesbians and gay men. We acknowledge the important role that the ILGA plays in achieving both these aims, aware that without ILGA's input it would have been impossible to produce this version of the *Pink Book* as it is.

John Clark
Lisa Power*

Aart Hendriks
Rob Tielman
Evert van der Veen

ILGA Secretaries General

Editors

---

*ILGA Secretary General until July 1992

# Part One

# Fighting for
# Lesbian and Gay Rights

# 1

# Winning Rights and Freedoms in Canada

## Barry D. Adam

The history of homosexuality in Canada shares many of the traits of gay history in the United States and western Europe. There exists fragmentary evidence of such public venues as urban streets, bars, baths, and beaches being frequented by men with sexual interests in other men, in the early twentieth century and perhaps earlier. Evidence for lesbian gathering places is even sketchier, but women do appear in mixed-sex gay bars in reports from the 1950s. Certainly in the early post-war period, there was already a sizeable gay "underground" and same-sex bonding in Canada shared the gay and lesbian patterns that had been emerging over the last two centuries in other countries (Adam 1987). In the following decades, lesbians and gay men have come to have a profound impact upon Canadian society.

### THE 1950S AND 1960S: LONE VOICES

Canada shared the reactionary climate pervasive in the advanced capitalist societies during the 1950s. In the wake of the insecurity and trauma of World War II, much of Europe and North America seemed intent on reconstructing itself according to the orderly mythos of family, church, and nation. Indeed, some of the impetus for McCarthyism began in Canada in the late 1940s with the Gouzenko affair, which revealed that Soviet spy networks had been initiated in North America. The ascendant social ethos, which sought to "restore" an old order (which never really existed as such), provided no place for gays and lesbians. Official discourse denied homosexual life; its existence was acknowledged only in the yellow press, police action, and psychiatry (Adam 1987: ch. 4).

In the 1950s, the Royal Canadian Mounted Police began a project, in line with the McCarthyite witchhunt sweeping the United States at the time (Sawatsky 1980), to track "known homosexuals" on the grounds of their being "security risks." Local police offered the crime-and-scandal press of Toronto and Montreal numerous titillating incidents about sexual "perversion," which they tended to describe in the shocked tones of a Christian missionary stumbling into a tribe of cannibals (see Higgins 1986). But in the midst of this reign of vilification, a lone persistent letter writer, Jim Egan, appeared primarily in the pages of Toronto's *Justice Weekly,* to defend gay rights and to argue for the decriminilization of homosexual relations. In letter after letter, written from 1950 through the mid-1960s, Egan offered a passionate and articulate view of the gay world to readers of the scandal sheets that thrived on exposing the "underside" of urban life (Champagne 1987).

It is noteworthy that Egan's letter to mainstream dailies and monthlies received only disdainful rejections. "Respectable" opinion was thus immunized against change. When the Royal Commission on Criminal Law relating to Criminal Sexual Psychopaths met between 1954 and 1958, another lone voice, Axel Olson, came to complain about the anti-homosexual law being used for purposes of blackmail (Kinsman 1987a:127). The Commission received his testimony without comment, synthesizing instead police and psychiatric discourses into a warrant for the imposition of indefinite sentences upon those whom the judiciary would label "criminal sexual psychopaths."

In the post-McCarthy thaw of the 1960s, which was impelled by the growing civil rights, anti-war, and student movements, the first signs appeared of formal organization among gay men and lesbians in Canada. In the early 1960s, a Toronto gay bar, the Music Room, sponsored a regular discussion group which resulted in a short-lived publication called *Two,* in 1964. Also in 1964, Canada's first homophile organization formed in Vancouver under the name of the Association for Social Knowledge (ASK). ASK was inspired by contemporary homophile groups in California; it founded a social center through the initiative of two Dutch former members of the national Dutch Lesbian and Gay Organization (COC)* who were cognizant of the longstanding success of the Amsterdam clubhouse for lesbians and gay men (Kinsman 1987a). It lasted until 1969.

In 1969, the federal parliament amended the Criminal Code to exempt from prosecution the private sexual activity of two consenting adults. Two events of the mid-1960s precipitated law reform. The first was the 1966 conviction of a man from the Northwest Territories, Everett Klippert, as a habitual sexual offender simply for having had sex with several consenting adult men. The confirmation

---

*Cultuur en Ontspannings Centrum

of his indefinite sentence (essentially a life term) by the Supreme Court in 1967 opened a public debate on the effects of the anti-homosexual law. The second event was the 1967 British decision to discriminalize consensual homosexual acts between adults following a decade of public discussion after the Wolfenden Report (Adam 1987:67).* In the 1960s, many governments in western Europe and North America were liberalizing a series of laws concerning abortion, obscenity, and contraception at the behest of popular movements. In Canada, Pierre Trudeau, then Justice Minister, introduced decriminalization of homosexual acts between consenting adults as part of a comprehensive reform of the Criminal Code, announcing that the "state had no place in the bedrooms of the nation." The law passed with the approval of the Liberal and New Democratic parties. Many Conservatives and the rural Québécois Parti Créditiste voted against it (Sylvestre 1979; Kinsman 1987a; Adam 1987).

## 1969–1977: GAY LIBERATION, LESBIAN FEMINISM

The New Left movements of the 1960s revolutionized the language and tactics of protest. Nationalist movements in the third world along with civil rights and anti-war movements at home challenged the imperial order of the great powers established in the post-war era. The cautious and defensive strategies of oppressed groups in the 1950s gave way to a renewed self-assertion and pride in the 1960s (Adam 1978, 1987). Labor, black, and student actions showed how the ostensibly smooth workings of the dominating machines of state and capital could be upset, interrupted, and reworked. In 1967, a feminist group formed in Toronto: between 1969 and 1971, gay and lesbian people mobilized across the country, at first in major cities and campuses, but soon after in almost every city of more than 100,000 inhabitants.

In 1969, a small University of Toronto Homophile Association formed; in 1970, the Vancouver Gay Liberation Front met for the first time; and by 1971, Montreal and Ottawa had groups which mounted a first march on Parliament Hill. Like the movement elsewhere, Canadian organizations debated and split over issues of adopting militant tactics and forms of leadership and participation. Toronto Gay Action took the liberationist stance articulated in the journal *The Body Politic,* while the Community Homophile Association of Toronto organized a social center and pressed for civil rights. In Vancouver, the Gay Liberation Front was rapidly succeeded by the more moderate Gay Alliance toward Equality. The 1971 march in Ottawa forwarded an agenda which set the course of gay and lesbian efforts for many years to come:

---

*Wolfenden, J., et al., Report of the Committee on Homosexual Offences and Prostitution. London, 1957.

- abolition of the gross indecency law

- a uniform age of consent

- protection through human rights codes

- equal rights for same-sex couples

- the destruction of police files

- the right to serve in the Armed Forces

- an end to discrimination in immigration, employment, custody and adoption, and housing (Jackson and Persky 1982:217–220; Adam 1987; Kinsman 1987a).

Like its counterparts in other countries, the Canadian movement also experienced tensions over the frequent subordination of the concerns of lesbians in organizations dominated by gay men. Such groups as Gays of Ottawa flourished through the 1970s by assuring parity representation of both men and women, as well as of anglophones and francophones, in its leadership. However, many lesbians left gay groups to pursue their agenda within the women's movement. The struggle for the recognition and integration of lesbian issues in the feminist program often proved difficult and disheartening; but by the mid-1970s most women's organizations had embraced lesbian demands (Creet 1990).

In 1977, movement work began to show results. The federal (Liberal party) government dropped "homosexuals" from its list of persons banned from integrating into Canada, following an incident where a U.S. citizen was stopped at a land crossing but then brought into the country by air through movement sponsorship. The participation of many gay and lesbian activists in the nationalist movement in Québec resulted in the addition of "sexual orientation" to a provincial human rights code ("the Québec Charter of Human Rights and Freedoms") a year after the Parti Québécois came to power (Sylvestre 1979).

## 1976–1984: REACTION AND REPRESSION

In the late 1970s and 1980s, corporate and state elites moved to restabilize their control of the economy and policy, and to dampen the gains made by labor and new social movements (Adam 1987, 1991b). In the United States, the reactionary shift took the form of a formidable alliance of corporate interests, evangelical churches, and traditionally conservative rural white Protestants and Southerners, along with lobby groups opposing gun control, women's rights, pornography, and abortion. This New Right alliance culminated in the Reagan-Bush presidency, which breathed new life into U.S. military and imperial traditions and renewed reactionary discourses in the mass media (Adam 1990, 1991a). Never immune from the omnipresent U.S. media net, the rightward shift of public discourse in Canada emboldened two conservative governments, which had been in power for well over a generation, to attempt to push gay people back into the closet (Adam 1987:118).

The Drapeau administration in Montreal, which had come to power in the 1950s on a plank of Roman Catholic moral restoration, began with a "cleanup" campaign in the months preceding the opening of the 1976 Olympic Games, descending on seven bars and a bathhouse in four raids. The repressive offensive stalled in 1977 with the mass mobilization of a new Association pour les Droits des Gai(e) du Québec,* which resisted in the streets and in the courts by fighting the cases of several hundred men who had been arrested. It is in this context that the new Parti Québécois provincial government, a leftist-nationalist political formation with no political connections to the Drapeau old guard, introduced "sexual orientation" into the provincial human rights code.

In Toronto, the media panic generated over the 1977 murder of a fourteen-year-old shoeshine boy by four men, revived public stereotypes of gay child molesters and set the stage for the police seizure of *The Body Politic,* which had addressed pedophilia in an article called "Men Loving Boys Loving Men." The 1979 acquittal of the paper on obscenity charges was appealed by the Conservative administration through four more years of court appearances before its ultimate acquittal. In 1981, Toronto police arrested 286 "found-ins" and twenty "keepers" in a massive raid on city bathhouses during a provincial election campaign. As in Montreal, police attacks stimulated new gay mobilization, this time in the form of The Right to Privacy Committee, in a movement that had been losing energy in the mid-1970s.

In the late 1970s and early 1980s, then, the gay and lesbian movement was forced to take defensive action against a series of assaults initiated by police and governments. Not until the mid-1980s did the movement begin again to make gains in the consolidation of civil rights for gay and lesbian people.

## 1984–: CIVIL RIGHTS AND ELECTORAL POLITICS

Some fifteen years after the first march on Ottawa, a series of law reforms began to realize several aspects of the 1971 program with the momentum of change shifting back in favor of the gay and lesbian movement. The 1982 Canadian Constitution had failed to include "sexual orientation" in its Charter of Rights due to Liberal and Conservative intransigence in the face of a New Democratic amendment. "Sex" was added to the charter only at the last moment when women's organizations mobilized an effective national protest against its omission. The legacy of the new constitution had been to force litigants, through lengthy court

---

*Association for the Rights of Lesbians and Gays of Québec (Ed.)

battles, to attempt to establish that gay and lesbian people are indeed protected by Section 15 of the charter, which proscribes discrimination against people not specifically named in the nondiscrimination clause. But in 1986, the Ontario government added "sexual orientation" to its human rights code, and Manitoba and the Yukon Territory followed in 1987. With the Québec law already on the books, a majority of Canadians now received human rights protection through provincial legislation.

These changes came about not so much as the result of any change of heart on the part of existing governments, but because of the election of new reformist parties. In Ontario, the 42-year-old Conservative dynasty collapsed in favor of a minority Liberal government dependent on the New Democratic Party (NDP) to remain in office. When the Liberals introduced a bill to amend the human rights law to protect the disabled, they could not ignore an amendment by NDP member Evelyn Gigantes to add "sexual orientation." Rather than risk a split with their junior partner over such an issue, the Liberals agreed to adopt it into the government bill. The leader of the Conservatives, who, unlike the majority of his party, was urban and Jewish, also threw his support behind the bill. This did not deter the remaining Conservative members from a heated campaign of anti-gay vilification in concert with the province's Roman Catholic hierarchy and evangelical preachers. In the end, however, the NDP, the Liberals (minus four members), and four Conservatives voted for the measure (Rayside 1988; Ross 1990). In Manitoba and the Yukon, law reform was generated by NDP governments (Barnholden 1987; Kinsman 1987b).

In municipal politics, several openly gay candidates proved that voters had confidence that gay people could represent their interests. In 1986, Raymond Blain rode into the Montreal city council on a socialist wave which swept the aged Drapeau administration from power (Courte 1987). In 1988, Gordon Price, in a departure from the usual pattern, came to the Vancouver city council with a right-wing reform movement intent on controlling prostitution in the city's downtown residential district. Glen Murray's 1989 election in Winnipeg came about as part of an eight-candidate progressive challenge to entrenched business interests (King 1989). In 1991, Kyle Rae came to the Toronto city council on an NDP ticket representing a heavily gay and lesbian downtown ward. And in 1992, Michael Phalt was elected in Edmonton.

At the federal level, Vancouver-area NDP Member of Parliament, Svend Robinson, came out publicly in 1988 (Joyce 1989). With an already well-established reputation as a tireless defender of gay and other human rights and a vocal opponent of U.S. imperialism in Central America, Robinson quickly became the best known "face" of gay politics in the country. His coming out proved to be no liability with the electorate. In the following election, Robinson was returned to Parliament with an increased majority. Apart from a national gay and lesbian coalition which existed for a few years in the early 1970s, Robinson quickly became the most prominent voice for gay and lesbian issues on the federal scene.

In 1986, a group of Ottawa residents formed Égale (Equality for Gays and Lesbians Everywhere), and in 1987 a National Lesbian Forum formed within the National Action Committee for the Status of Women to help fill the need for a national lobby.

As part of a general reform to remove gender-discrimination from criminal law, the federal (Conservative) government in 1988 changed the age of consent for sexual activity to fourteen, but retained a last vestige of homophobia by establishing eighteen as the age of consent for anal intercourse. (The previous law had specified twenty-one as the age of consent for all homosexual relations.) A court challenge in Nova Scotia to the eighteen minimum age rule failed in 1990 (Metcalfe 1990). The same reform did, however, eliminate the crime of "gross indecency," an inherently vague label which had been used to net gay men for a wide range of supposed indiscretions.

With sexual orientation legislation covering most Canadians, movement attention began shifting toward gaining legal recognition of lesbian and gay couples for the rights and benefits already presumed by heterosexual marriage (Bell 1991; Ryder 1990). In several provinces, the claim for domestic partners' rights has been assisted by existing legislation recognizing nonmarital, common-law (heterosexual) relationships. A conference held in Toronto on the issue in 1989 revealed that many union contracts and at least ten insurance companies had already conceded some form of spousal benefits for gay and lesbian couples.

Several challenges were placed before the courts. In 1988, Toronto library worker Karen Andrews's application for provincial health insurance coverage for her lover and her lover's child was turned down by the courts (Eaton 1990:123). In 1988, Jim Egan, the pioneering gay activist, then 65, went to court to win for his partner of thirty-nine years, John Nesbit, the spousal allowance available to heterosexual couples under the Canada Pension Plan (Hill 1989). The case is still pending. In 1989, Brian Mossop appealed to the Canadian Human Rights Commission when his employer, the federal government, refused to allow him a day off to attend the funeral of his lover's father (Goliger 1989). The Commission ruled in his favor, but the Federal Court of Appeal struck down the ruling in 1990 (Robb 1990). It is noteworthy that the government's case against Mossop was joined by the anti-feminist women's organization, R.E.A.L. Women, and by evangelical, pentecostal, and Salvation Army churches. Finally, a 1989 federal court ruled that Les Beau must be permitted to visit his lover, Tim Veysey, in prison under the Private Family Visiting Program or "conjugal visit" program of Corrections Canada. The Federal Court of Appeal upheld this decision against the crown challenge (Goliger 1990b). In this case, the law had already provided for a range of eligible visitors extending well beyond the category of spouse.

The record of court challenges has, then, been mixed at best, with consistent opposition to domestic partners' rights being wielded by government prosecutors. Change will almost certainly have to come about through trade union pressure and, ultimately, legislative reform. Recently the very first steps have been taken in this process. In 1990, Toronto and Vancouver extended spousal benefits to city workers (Popert 1990; Morrison 1991), and in 1991 the new NDP government of Ontario granted spousal benefits to provincial employees (Ogilvie 1991). This has been followed by a 1992 ruling of the Ontario Human Rights Commission recognizing spouses of either gender which opens the way to challenging more than seventy provincial statues defining "spouse" in traditional heterosexual terms. Overall, however, gay and lesbian relationships still remain without state support, and very often face effective destruction by relatives and courts in such areas as inheritance and immigration. The record of lesbian and gay parents attempting to secure custody of their own children is a sorry one indeed. They are frequently subjected to various closet rules: no political activity or public organization to support their rights; a lover must be absent or sleep in a separate bed; the child cannot stay overnight; or the parent will lose visiting rights if he or she lives with someone of the same sex (Ryder 1990). As Mary Eaton (1990:118) remarks, the message of the courts seems to be: "The good lesbian mother is a woman who teaches her child that she is a freak, that there is absolutely nothing positive about what she is in terms of her lesbianism, that she is something to be ashamed of."

While the state has always been an important arena of struggle, movement concerns and activities have always arisen in many other areas. One of the issues that received the greatest amount of public attention in the late 1980s was the ordination of gay or lesbian clergy. In Canada, the issue dominated several conferences of the country's largest Protestant denomination, the United Church of Canada. Gay and lesbian members of the church had long pressed this traditionally liberal denomination for recognition of its concerns and, in 1984, the church assembly resolved to oppose discrimination against gay people; but, rather paradoxically, it refused to hire them as clergy. This ambivalence resulted in the decision of the 1988 convention to extend the right of ordination to openly gay and lesbian members (MacFarlane 1988). (Needless to say, as in every other church, there were already many closeted gay and lesbian clergy. This hard-fought resolution provoked the secession of some of the evangelical wing of the church, which called itself the Community of Concern. Over the following two years, about ten percent of congregations broke away rather than accept gay or lesbian clergy (Riordan 1990).

Another persistent problem faced by gay people everywhere has been anti-gay violence. All too often the response of the courts to the assault or murder of lesbians or gay men has been to accept as mitigating circumstances the assailants' allegations that their victims made sexual advances to them. In 1985, a gang of high school youths murdered Kenn Zeller, a Toronto librarian, in a park and received very light sentences by a judge who considered the murderers middle-class and otherwise well-behaved. In 1988, the entry staircase into Vancouver's Little Sisters bookstore was firebombed; no suspects were identified. In 1989, Joe Rose, a young AIDS activist, was killed outside a Montreal subway stop near the gay Village de l'Est area (Jones 1989). While young white males typically perpetrate street violence against gay men and lesbians (as they do against other women and visible minorities), the police and military, who are often drawn from the same constituency, remain another source of anti-gay repression. A 1990 Montreal police raid on a punk queer party resulted in fifty-six persons arrested in two weeks of subsequent protest (Smith 1990). While these incidents have attracted the greatest amount of attention from the gay press in recent years, state and street violence directed against gay men and lesbians remains pervasive and ongoing. A 1992 court decision, however, has struck down the anti-gay policies within the Canadian Armed Forces, impelling the federal government to introduce new training procedures to facilitate the integration of lesbian and gay military personnel.

## IMPACTS OF AIDS ON GAY AND LESBIAN RIGHTS

AIDS struck first among gay men in Canada, and this population comprised more than eighty percent of people with AIDS in Canada into the 1990s. In the face of the torpid response by governments and traditional social service agencies to the spreading epidemic, community-based groups sprang up out of gay movement networks both to meet the immediate practical needs of those already ill and to warn others of the risk inherent in unsafe sex (Adam 1991; Adam forthcoming). By the mid-1980s, community-based AIDS organizations had developed in every urban area across the country; in 1986, they were federated as the Canadian AIDS Society. Unlike the gay and lesbian movement, many AIDS organizations became rapidly institutionalized with full-time staff funded through government grants in several provinces. As the public hysteria around AIDS abated after 1985, many AIDS organizations expanded well beyond their roots in the gay community, as nongay volunteers and professionals became incorporated into them and as charitable funding became available. In many ways, AIDS organizations have quickly outstripped the human and financial resources of their gay and lesbian counterparts, as well as co-opted many of their most active members. But the full history of AIDS issues and organizing exceeds the scope of this article: suffice it to say that AIDS issues became directly involved in shaping at least four areas of gay and lesbian rights.

The first area concerns border-crossing bans imposed by the U.S. government. "Homosexuals" had been included among persons prohibited from entering the United States since the McCarthy era; in 1987, HIV-positive people were added to the list. As the majority of Canadians live within one hundred kilometers (approximately 160 miles) of the United States border and more Canadians than any other nationality cross into the United States every year, these regulations had an inordinate impact upon Canadian lesbians and gay men. In practice, they provided warrant for arbitrary harassment of gay people by U.S. border guards who, for example, annually accosted lesbians going to the Michigan Women's Music Festival. In practice, the AIDS ban proved to be just one more method of harassing suspected gay people at border crossings. In 1990, James Saccary was interrogated and banned from the United States when found to be carrying a safer sex pamphlet, and Ross Waddell was refused entry to see the Names Project quilt in Washington, D.C. (Goliger 1990a). In the same year, Canadian AIDS organizations joined an international boycott of the world AIDS conference in San Francisco to protest the discrimination against people with AIDS. New legislation, won partly through the efforts of openly gay congressmen Barney Frank and Gerry Studds, dropped the anti-gay ban and transferred the anti-HIV-positive ban to the U.S. Public Health Service in October 1990. In 1991, the Bush administration intervened to reimpose the ban on seropositive people, which was revised in 1993 by President Clinton.

The second area has been that of state censorship. Canada Customs regularly seizes books, journals, videos, and movies which concern gay and lesbian topics (Ross 1988). Continued seizures—even when most or all materials are subsequently released and despite the supposed exemption of AIDS-related materials—function to strangle the gay and lesbian bookstores operating in the three largest cities by impounding expensive inventories for months and by rendering topical magazines obsolete. A Customs directive which suppresses depictions of anal sex has jeopardized AIDS education materials and continues to provide warrant for the arbitrary meddling of Customs bureaucrats in the flow of gay and lesbian ideas and images into the country. Even after clearing Customs, local retailers still remain vulnerable to prosecution under obscenity laws. With the 1992 *Butler* decision of the Supreme Court of Canada, won by the feminist Legal Equality Action Fund (LEAF), the new standard for identifying "obscenty" has been set as "what the community would tolerate others being exposed to on the basis of the degree of harm that may flow from such exposure" (Bearchell 1993:38). Intended by LEAF as a measure to curb male violence against women by controlling the propagation of degrading images of women, the ruling led within weeks to two police raids on Toronto's Glad Day bookstore. The first resulted in the conviction of the store and the banning of a wide range of gay male erotica widely available in the United States and Europe. The second led to the prosecution of the U.S. lesbian erotic magazine, *Bad Attitude*. Ironically, due to a quirk in the judicial interpretation of the Charter of Rights, many U.S. citizens cross to Canada to see nude male and female strippers (banned in many U.S. states) while many Canadians go to the United States for representations of sexuality which are blocked by Customs.

The third area concerns AIDS and gay rights. These two issues became mixed in the case of Eric Smith, a Nova Scotia teacher dismissed from his post in a rural town following the illegal revelation of his serostatus. The Nova Scotia government responded to national publicity by appointing Smith to a new provincial Task Force on AIDS which, in turn, recommended among other things that the government add "sexual orientation" to its human rights code. The provincial human rights commission subsequently announced that despite a lack of legal authority to do so, it would recognize "sexual orientation" discrimination anyway. Chastened by a national critique of its AIDS phobia, the rural town still refused Smith's reinstatement as a teacher in 1991—this time because he is gay (Elliott 1991). The dénouement of the affair was the provincial government's decision to include "sexual orientation" in the human rights code, making Nova Scotia the fourth (of ten) provinces to do so. Most remarkable about this is that it is the first time that a Conservative government has taken such a step. Subsequent reform has proven to be uncontroversial, with New Brunswick following suit in 1992 and British Columbia in 1993.

The final area where AIDS has directly impacted on gay and lesbian rights has been in organizing itself. In 1988, AIDS Action Now! formed in Toronto, inspired by New York's ACT-UP (AIDS Coalition to Unleash Power), to forward an urgent agenda of AIDS issues which were not being vigorously pursued by community-based AIDS organizations (Barnholden 1988). These included demands for faster approval of new drugs, anonymous (not simply confidential) HIV testing, and representation of people with AIDS in the direction of AIDS policy. The more militant street activism of AIDS Action Now! in turn, engendered the founding of Queer Nation in 1990 (Visser 1990a, 1990b), whose more anarchic, anti-hierarchical, and direct-action approach to gay and lesbian issues recalled the early days of gay liberation "zaps" upon homophobic institutions and authorities. In its brief existence, Queer Nation invaded straight bars with anti-gay reputations, patrolled downtown streets against gay-bashers, held kiss-ins in suburban shopping malls, joined pro-choice (on abortion) demonstrations, and confronted far-right political parties (Collins 1991). By 1992, it had disintegrated through internal dissension.

## CONCLUSION

In recent years, the Canadian gay and lesbian movement, like its counterparts elsewhere, has continued to proliferate in new sites as lesbians and gay men assert their presence in more and more spheres of life. In 1989, aboriginal people organized as the Toronto Gays and Lesbians of the First Nations, developing an AIDS program from native Indian communities (Charles 1990). Aboriginals joined already active organizations of people of Asian and African descent.

Canadian culture was marked by such celebrated gay and lesbian writers as Michel Tremblay (Courte 1990), Thomson Highway (Ogilvie 1989), and Jane Rule (Brooks 1988/89), though Tremblay and Highway were better known as exponents of Québécois and aboriginal culture, respectively, then as "gay writers." Famed country and western singer k. d. lang came out publicly in 1992. On a more regional level, gay and lesbian film festivals became regular events in Toronto and Montreal as have Toronto Queer Culture festivals devoted to film, theater, visual arts, music, readings, and dance. Organized fund-raising in Toronto through the Lesbian and Gay Appeal has succeeded in collecting more than $100,000 each year for the promotion of a wide variety of cultural and political projects. Gay and lesbian scholarship has become more formalized through the Concordia University Lesbian Studies Coalition (Gammon et al. 1990) in Montreal and the Toronto Centre for Lesbian and Gay Studies founded in 1990. Vancouver hosted some 7,000 athletes and 2,000 artists from twenty-four countries in the 1990 Gay Games (Morrison 1990).

Gay and lesbian networks, culture, and organization, then, show increasing vitality in the 1990s and, after decades of struggle, are making headway in achieving rights and recognition in Canadian society.

## REFERENCES

Adam, Barry. 1978. *The Survival of Domination*. New York: Elsevier/Greenwood.
———. 1987. *The Rise of a Gay and Lesbian Movement*. Boston: G. K. Hall/Twayne.
———. 1989. "The State, Public Policy, and AIDS Discourse." *Contemporary Crises* 13:1–14.
———. 1990. "Television News Constructs the 1990 Nicaragua Election." *Critical Sociology* 17(1):99–109.
———. 1991. "Nicaragua, the Peace Process, and Television News." *Canadian Journal of Communication* 16(1):19–30.
———. 1992. "Sex and Caring among Men." *Modern Homosexualities*. Edited by Kenneth Plummer. London: Routledge.
———. Forthcoming. "Post-Marxism and the New Social Movements." *Canadian Review of Sociology and Anthropology*.
Barnholden, Patrick. 1987. "Manitoba NDP Finally Does It." *Rites* 4(4):5.
———. 1988. "AIDS Action Group Forms." *Rites* 4(9):5.
Bearchell, Chris. "Cut That Out!" *This Magazine* 26(6):376–40.
Bell, Laurie. 1991. *On Our Own Terms*. Toronto: Coalition for Lesbian and Gay Rights in Ontario.
Brooks, Brenda. 1988/89. "To Be Able to Last the Course." *Rites* 5(7):14–15.
Champagne, Robert, ed. 1987. *Jim Egan, Canada's Pioneer Gay Activist*. Toronto: Canadian Lesbian and Gay History Network.
Charles, Claude. 1990. "G.L.F.N.—A Short History." *Rites* 7(4, Supp):3.
Collins, David. 1991. "Fabulous Fighting Queers." *Xtra!* 164:5.
Courte, Bernard. 1987. "Gay Councillor Elected in Montreal." *Rites* 3(8):9.
———. 1990. "Gripping Reconciliation." *Xtra!* 161:23.
Creet, M. Julia. 1990. "A Test of Unity." In *Lesbians in Canada*. Edited by Sharon Stone. Toronto: Between the Lines.
Eaton, Mary. 1990. "Lesbians and the Law." In *Lesbians in Canada*. Edited by Sharon Stone. Toronto: Between the Lines.
Elliott, Kevin. 1993. "A Despised Local Hero." *Xtra!* 174(Supp 21):5.
Gammon, Carolyn, et al. 1990. "Organizing Lesbian Studies at Concordia." In *Lesbians in Canada*. Edited by Sharon Stone. Toronto: Between the Lines.

Goliger, Gabriella. 1989. "Victory for Equal Rights." *Xtra!* 123:7.

———. 1990a. "Undefended Border?" *Xtra!* 148(Supp 7):1, 3.

———. 1990b. "Veysey Wins Appeal." *Xtra!* 152(Supp 10):3.

Higgins, Ross. 1986. "Montreal Gays and Lesbians in the Yellow Press of the 1950s." *Canadian Lesbian and Gay History Network Newsletter* 2:9–11.

Hill, Harry. 1989. "BC Couple Launch Charter Challenge." *Rites* 5(8):13.

Jackson, Ed, and Stan Persky. 1982. *Flaunting It!* Vancouver: New Star.

Jones, Emma. 1989. "AIDS Activist Murdered in Montréal." *Rites* (May):1.

Joyce, Rob. 1989. "Personal and Political." *Xtra!* 119:5.

King, Ian. 1989. "Winnipeg Elects Open Gay Man to City Council." *Xtra!* 136:3.

Kinsman, Gary. 1987a. *The Regulation of Desire*. Montreal: Black Rose.

———. 1987b. "Yukon Says Yes, Military Says No." *Rites* 3(10):5.

MacFarlane, Mary Anne. 1988. "Victory in Victoria." *Rites* 5(5):4.

Metcalfe, Robin. 1990. "Charter Challenge Loses." *Xtra!* 149(Supp 8):3.

Morrison, Sheila. 1990. "Triumph for 'Sodom North.' " *Xtra!* 156(Supp 12):5.

———. 1991. "Another Triumph in Sodom North." *Xtra!* 164:5.

Ogilvie, Dayne. 1989. "Reviving the Trickster." *Xtra!* 119:9.

———. 1991. "Getting in a Family Way." *Xtra!* 164:1.

Popert, Ken. 1990. "Gay Spouses Recognized." *Xtra!* 159:13.

Rayside, David. 1988. "Gay Rights and Family Values." *Studies in Political Economy* 26:109–147.

Riordan, Michael. 1990. *The First Stone*. Toronto: McClelland.

Robb, Kevin. 1990. "We Aren't Family." *Xtra!* 156(Supp 11):4.

Ross, Becki. 1988. "Launching Lesbian Cultural Offensives." *Resources for Feminist Research* 17(2):12–13.

———. 1990. "Sexual Dis/orientation or Playing House." In *Lesbians in Canada*. Edited by Sharon Stone. Toronto: Between the Lines.

Ryder, Bruce. 1990. "Equality Rights and Sexual Orientation." *Canadian Journal of Family Law* 9(1):39–97.

Sawatsky, John. 1980. *Men in the Shadows*. Toronto: Doubleday.

Smith, Neil. 1990. "Montreal Lesbians and Gays Protest." *Xtra!* 156(Supp 11):5.

Sylvestre, Paul François. 1979. *Les homosexuels s'organisent*. Ottawa: Éditions Homeureux.

Visser, Andy. 1990a. "Queer Notions." *Xtra!* 156:1.

———. 1990b. "Queer Direct Action." *Xtra!* 157:1.

# 2

# The Gay Press and Movement in France

## Frank Arnal

One might wonder why, in France in the 1990s, there are so few community services on offer for gay men. Paris is a capital which today still has no gay center worthy of the name,[1] the city's mayor ignores the gays who live there, and the rare attempts by the Socialist government to assist gay activists have failed lamentably. We remember a budget allocation intended by the Ministry of Culture for the purchase of gay libraries for all the gay centers that were trying to get off the ground between 1981 and 1983. The centers were short-lived and the books disappeared. I mention this story because books play a fundamental role in the lives of French homosexuals—writing is the transmitter of an ideology which is of prime importance for anyone who wants to understand the specific Frenchness of the French gay movements.

The historian of homosexual literature in France can trace its origin to the beginning of the eighteenth century, just at the time when, in Paris, the Jardin des Tuileries was opened to the public and the sodomites of the age were about to acquire the habits that Parisian homosexuals still display between the Seine and the rue de Rivoli. The Marquis de Sade was already preaching tolerance toward those who *should never be insulted* but should rather be pitied as victims of a *fault of nature.* At the same time, he glorifies sodomy with both sexes, while condemning any specialization!

The following century saw the simmering of intellectual questioning of the concepts of gender and sex, but the answers given by psychiatrists codified a medicolegal attitude that was to immobilize their inquiries for a century. It is therefore on the literary side that one must look for any "movement." Émile Zola had in his possession the testimony of an admirer which he intended to use in his series of novels on the Rougon Macquart. (The Rougons are a family illustrating the scientific theories of degeneration.) An Italian francophile sent him the account, and Zola contemplated writing a book on the subject. Happily for French gays, but unfortunately for historians, he abandoned the project, which would have placed homosexuality alongside the other "social evils." The text was nevertheless published in the French psychiatrists' magazine *Annales médico-légales* by Raffalovitch, the poet of Russian origin who contributed to the magazine and compiled the papers he had written for it in a book on "uranism" and "unisexuality" in 1896.

It is the eve of the twentieth century, and Paris is the beacon city. It is ignorant of the gay nightlife of Berlin, known only to a few specialists. Nevertheless, condemnation of the "German vice" is rife in the work of many cartoonists, for example in the satirical paper *l'Assiette au beurre*. The French, defeated in the Franco-Prussian War in 1871, are plotting their revenge. From now on it is via the poetic movements that the challenge to bourgeois family values is expressed, both by the Symbolists—is there anyone who is unaware of Verlaine's and Rimbaud's relationship and writings?—and by such *fin de siècle* decadents as Jean Lorrain, Rachilde, and Joseph Péladan.* The year 1890 marks the start of a debate on homosexuality which in France, unlike other countries, is not psychiatric in content but is in the main the concern of literary circles.

Before 1914 André Gide had already written *Corydon,* a defense and celebration of homosexuality, which he would publish after the war. Baron Fersen, in addition to writing poems, was editing the magazine *Akademos.* Before his lifestyle became known and caused a scandal, Fersen wanted to stamp his age with the seal of decadence and affectation. *Akademos* (1907) was in a sense the first homosexual magazine to be published in France. There is nothing militant about its contents, and it contained nothing comparable to what could already be read in Germany. Nevertheless, we can find in an issue of 1909 an article signed G. Delbrouze on "moral prejudice" ("le préjudgé contre les moeurs"). The general tone of the magazine is that of the homosexual "scene" of the time.

From that time onward, a sharp distinction can be drawn between the discussion of French intellectuals and writers in general on the question of homosexuality, and what was being written in the rest of Europe, especially in Germany. Characteristically, female homosexuality was disregarded, despite the presence of the "américaines" who set up house on the left bank of the Seine; the writings of Renée Vivien aroused no response. Books formed part of a male milieu and after 1918, titles on male homosexuality were legion. Marcel Proust broke the silence in 1921 with *Sodom and Gomorrah,* Gide took advantage of the opening,

---

*Jean Lorrain was the pseudonym of the French writer Paul Duval (1855–1906). Joseph Péladan (1859–1918) was a novelist and playwright who also had a reputation as a mystic. (Ed.)

and Jean Cocteau was to widen it. In France in the twenties, the novel with a homosexual theme was the prime mediator of discussion on homosexuality.

The magazine *Inversions*[2] first appeared on November 15, 1924; it was swiftly banned by the courts, and after a few issues changed its title, in imitation of a famous German gay magazine, to *L'Amitié* (*Friendship*). The editors were prosecuted under the 1920 law against contraception and Malthusianism.* Between its covers were to be found most of the names who had already distinguished themselves by their interest in male homosexuality. It was the first real organ of the French homosexual press, the ancestor of *Gai Pied*.

The story of *L'Amitié* is recounted by Gilles Barbedette and Michel Carassou, who trace the history of this period in their *Paris Gay 1920*. Literary issues occupied a prominent position in the journal. One of its most regular contributors, Axieros (the pseudonym of Guyolot-Dubasty) is typical of pre-1914 sensibility: the cult of ideal beauty, an idealization of love, and nostalgia for Greek mores. It is interesting to note the lack of a real response to its publication or to the trial that followed. Even André Gide seems to have been unaware of it. This may be explained by the social origin of *L'Amitié*'s creators, who were ordinary white-collar workers with no important connections. What is more, they published writers whose style is very old-fashioned for the period. The age of surrealism was just beginning, and the homophobia of that movement's head, André Breton, is well known.

It was not until the start of the Fourth Republic that there were new attempts by homosexuals to make their voices heard. The publication *Futur* (1952), a large-format magazine, and later the short-lived *Juventus,* battled for a few years against the re-adoption of a Petainist law which the Church and the French fascists had succeeded in having adopted during the Occupation. This law created a different age of sexual consent if the partners were of the same sex. Despite Sartre's *Genet* and the importance of Cocteau, the issue aroused no interest in left-wing intellectual circles, which were often hostile to love between men. The magazine *Arcadie,* founded in 1954 by André Baudry, would last for twenty-eight years. It sought to be academic in both tone and format: no photos, few contributions from women, an ethic of procrastination on the place of male homosexuals in French society and of misgiving with regard to their promiscuous habits, and a minute and systematic record of anything written or exhibited having to do with homosexuality. The situation remained static for a long time. *Arcadie,* which had problems at its inception, was banned from sale to minors. (The ban was lifted only in 1974.) To understand the meaning of this restriction and the novelty of the situation opened up for homosexual self-expression after 1974, it is necessary to know something of the peculiar features of the French press after 1945.

In France, newspapers and magazines are distributed nationally by a single

---

*Sic (translator's note)

company, the NMPP, which, by its articles of incorporation, is obliged to respond to any request for supply of a title. Thus, *Arcadie* could have been present on all newsstands on French territory. The liberal operation of the NMPP is limited by only one law, on the protection of young people's reading, and they can refuse any publication subject to restriction under that law. Therefore, the legal prohibition placed on *Arcadie* meant it could only be sold by subscription. Its print run may have amounted to some 6,500 copies in its best years. Its manager and owner, André Baudry, who retired to the Naples area in 1982, gives a figure six times that, but it seems that this represents the total of readers of the magazine since its creation in addition to the members of an Arcadie club, whose rules did not require subscription to the magazine.

After 1974, a few gay magazines took advantage of the removal of the ban on *Arcadie* and tried their luck on the newsstands. Leaving aside the attempts of J. Coquelle, they were more geared to erotic content than to serious discussion of homosexuality; in this they were imitating, with fewer resources, the "Filipacchi" press which was already very widely known and read in France, and whose publications, such as *Lui* and *Union,* were intended to gratify the fantasies of "new" heterosexual men.

The gay groups that were coming into being had no part in this phenomenon. FHAR (Front Homosexuel d'Action Révolutionnaire = Homosexual Revolutionary Action Front) was part of the left. Its press, with short-lived titles like *Le fléau social* (*The Social Scourge*) and *L'antinorm,* was private, and could only be purchased in a few bookshops in the center of Paris. A special issue of the Spontaneist monthly *Tout* (*Everything*) which was available on newsstands, was banned by the Ministry of the Interior in 1971 because it was entirely devoted to the FHAR Manifesto. It could perhaps be said that in the seventies there was a cat-and-mouse game being played between gays who wanted to put their ideas on the newsstands and the authorities who tried to contain this development. Note that discussions and literature on homosexuality continued to flourish in book production in an uninterrupted line since 1920. Since publications sold in bookshops were not covered by the press law, they were rarely prosecuted. Two major exceptions were the special issue of the social science journal *Recherches* devoted to homosexuality (March 1973) and P. Guyotat's novel *Eden, eden, eden,* the trials over which roused the left-wing intelligentsia.

This is the context in which the birth of *Gai Pied* needs to be placed. Its essential features were formed by a very specific past history characterized by the predominance of discussions solely concerned with male homosexuality and the facilities offered by the NMPP distribution system set up in 1945.

In 1975, taking over from FHAR and rather on the lines of the English Gay Liberation Front, the GLH (Groupes de Libération Homosexuels = Homosexual Liberation Groups) was formed in France. In Paris, one branch of the GLH was GLH-PQ (Politique et Quotidien = Politics and Daily Life), whose prime mover was Jean Lebitoux and in which Gérard Vappereau and I were involved. This was the seedbed of the monthly *Gai Pied*. For four years, the founders of GLH-PQ were to explore various aspects of a militant activism that was not focused on challenging the law as in northern Europe, but on the ideological bases of the repression of homosexual reality.

In 1979, Jean Lebitoux was ready to launch his monthly. His group abandoned GLH-PQ, which subsequently disappeared; the same year, provincial GLH activists and some Parisian gays set up CUARH (Comité d'Urgence Antirépression Homosexuelle = Emergency Committee Against Homosexual Oppression). This split between the gay movement and the gay press was to be a lasting one. It probably explains the enduring success of *Gai Pied* as well as the eventual disappearance of the CUARH. The latter experienced a short-lived success: close to 10,000 people took part in its demonstrations prior to 1981. Its determination to be a mixed organization cut across French habits of single-sex action. To be sure, FHAR had been set up by women and lesbians,* but they soon abandoned the organization to gay men. The conflict between French lesbians and gay men immediately crystallized around their relationship to the affirmation of sex as pleasure. Lesbians, much influenced by feminists, challenged gay men's macho sexuality, while gay men questioned the puritanism and moralism concealed behind feminist propagandizing.

The *Gai Pied* created under these circumstances was thus a periodical addressed to a gay male readership interested in all aspects of gay issues, both political and erotic, with no bar on any facet of gay reality. This position, which has remained unchanged since the first issue of *Gai Pied* in April 1979, formed the basis for the magazine's success. It corresponded to the expectations of a very diverse readership which found nothing to buy on the newsstands except the babblings of an erotic gay press with little visual appeal (the three titles published by SAN: *OFF, Jean Paul,* and *Hommes*) and the magazine *Arcadie* which, in fact, continued to be sold on subscription. *Gai Pied*'s subtitle, *Magazine homosexuel d'information politique et générale* (*Homosexual Magazine of Political and General Information*), represents an ambition that will never be abandoned. The implicit references to the kind of journalism created by the daily *Libération* and its supplement of the time, *Sandwich,* run by J. L. Hennig and M. O. Delacour, are obvious, especially in the style adopted and the large number of free small ads.

*Gai Pied* monthly very rapidly acquired a wide readership and fame. It is bought by an average 25,000 readers and read by two to three times that number. Its success, in my opinion, comes from an intelligent connection with the French intellectual tradition (the interview with Sartre in *Gai Pied* shortly before his death caused a sensation), the talents that were developed in it, and its rejection of militant propaganda. Every gay group or initiative could find there a reflection of its action, CUARH more than any other, but the handling of news was first

---

*Sic* (translator's note)

and foremost professional, or moving toward being so. In this sense, *Gay Pied* invented gay journalism in France. Important names like Tony Duvert, Renaud Camus, Yves Navarre, Dominique Fernandez, and Guy Hocquenghem contributed to its reputation. On the other hand, Jean Lebitoux, Gilles Barbedette, Hugo Marsan, René de Ceccaty, and I built our reputations there. Today Gilles Barbedette, editor of the publisher Rivages' foreign list, is regarded as the most talented person in his field. René de Ceccaty contributes to the celebrated literary pages of the daily newspaper, *Le Monde.*

*Gai Pied* thus built its image as a medium of discussion and knowledge, while CUARH was the vehicle of gay action. In the first year after the Socialists took power in 1981, they had some remarkable successes (including the abolition of the difference between gay and straight ages of consent, and the Deferre circular instructing the police to avoid discriminatory attitudes). Where the leaders of CUARH went wrong was in being fascinated by the success of *Gai Pied.* They wanted a monthly magazine, too—*Homophonies,* which represented the mixed organization of CUARH, being aimed at gay men and lesbians equally, but which had great difficulty especially in the publication of small ads, where the magazine wanted to maintain parity; however, demand came overwhelmingly from gay men. *Homophonies* did find its own small readership (with around 5,000 copies sold, at most), but exhausted its energies and sparked internal conflicts. In my view, this was responsible for the rapid disappearance of CUARH, which was dying from 1984 onward.

*Gai Pied,* on the other hand, in response to the arrival of *Homophonies* and plans for another monthly, *Samouraï,* transformed itself into *Gai Pied Hebdo* (*Weekly*) in November 1982. The decision to become a weekly magazine was crucial. Despite its success, *Gai Pied* had few employees: it was structured as a collective consisting of management, associations of editors and employees, and the editors were unpaid. The move to 45 rue Sedaine, large premises in Paris's XIth Arondissement,* further influenced this decision: it was necessary to move forward and become more professional. The new format was a complete success. The weekly sold almost as many copies as the monthly, but four times a month, which considerably increased the readership, estimated in 1985 to be between 60,000 and 100,000 for an average print run of 45,000 copies and a sale of 27,000 copies per week, with subscriptions representing only 8 percent of the total.

This development did not take place without major difficulties, however: the departure in 1981 of Jacky Fougeray, who left to found the short-lived monthly *Samouraï* (and who has recently inaugurated a good-quality, free gay monthly, *Illico*); the break in 1983 with Jean Lebitoux, who disagreed with the professionalization brought about by weekly publication; and the abolition in 1988 of the management co-managed by Hugo Marsan and me since 1981. In 1991, a

---

*Today the area has doubled but the address is the same, and the telephone number has remained unchanged since 1979, evidence of durability!

complete reshuffling of the editorial team was made to produce a less ambitious weekly, and at the same time a new and expanded monthly magazine.

These problems, while related to the well-known decline in impetus experienced by the gay movement worldwide at that time, were magnified at *Gai Pied Hebdo* by its very success and by the creation of Minitel (see below). In 1985, the magazine achieved its maximum sales in a market with no competition. It had about thirty reasonably paid employees and a large number of freelance contributors paid by the column. But behind this apparent good health lay a crisis in the French gay movement. CUARH had disappeared; Fréquence Gaie, the Paris gay radio station set up in 1981, was doing badly; and AIDS had begun its deadly work. *Gai Pied Hebdo* was obliged to take responsibility for the totality of information services provided for gays: it doubled the size of its premises; took the gay radio station under its wing; and made its premises available to the AMG (Association des Médecins Gais = Gay Doctors' Association), and an association of gay psychologists (SOS-Écoute Gaie = gay helpline). All gay activism seemed to be contained in the rue Sedaine, with the exception of the lesbian monthly (*Lesbia*), the Socialist gay group (GPL), the Christian group (David et Jonathan), and the work of Pastor Doucé (CCL). Together with Doucé, we were the only French association represented in ILGA throughout this entire period.

All this may have helped to create the illusion that French homosexuals formed a community that was going to integrate into the wider society. Not so, however. The Socialist government evaded the gay issue, refused to support specific protection for gays, and refused to repeal laws forbidding the advertisement of condoms and the over-the-counter sale of syringes. At the same time, there appeared Minitel, the electronic data service that France Télécom was to install in half of all French homes, which would open the way to electronic cruising. This was a fantastic success and made a fortune for the better-known services. *Gay Pied Hebdo* took advantage of the new phenomenon. Indeed, it was to earn a great deal of money from its cruiseline service on Minitel.

This money arrived just when the decline of sales began; it served in part to make up for the shortfall of sales of the weekly, which grew steadily worse after 1988. Today *Gai Pied Hebdo*[3] survives only because of the Minitel revenue. The paper has lost two-thirds of its readers and its manager is seriously considering, if not doing away with the present format, at least making major changes and reducing the number of pages. Since 1987, glossy American erotic publications translated into French (e.g., *Honcho* and *All Man*) have been available on the newsstands. The Minister of the Interior, Charles Pasqua, had tried to stem the tide by attempting to ban these imports; but by doing so, he also attacked *Gai Pied Hebdo*. Public reaction was vigorous and Pasqua retreated. This gave legitimacy to the American publications, and the NMPP now has to distribute them everywhere. Freedom of the press gained a new kind of "pin-up" magazine but, in a sense, *Gai Pied Hebdo,* being too generalized, has lost its readership to the attraction of pictures of cowboys with a hard-on.

To conclude, let us bear in mind the impossibility in France of a mixed gay press. Founded five years ago, *Lesbia,* run first by Christiane Jouve and later by Catherine Gonard, is on sale at newsstands. It is the only lesbian magazine and virtually the only lesbian organization. With a small print run and unpaid contributions, *Lesbia* cannot be compared with *Gai Pied Hebdo,* except that, like the latter, it serves as a catalyst for a large part of the lesbian movement. Therein lies both the strength and the weakness of the French gay system.

## NOTES

1. The *Maison des Homosexualités* is a recent attempt whose success remains to be confirmed. It is run by Jean Lebitoux. LMH, 25 rue Michel de Comte, 75003 Paris. Tel: 42 77 72 77.

2. Most of the articles from this magazine have been reprinted in Gilles Barbedette, *Gay Paris 1920.* For more information, consult the publications of GKC, BP 36, 59009 Lille, France.

3. No attempt has been made in this article to spell out *Gai Pied*'s leading role in the prevention of AIDS among homosexuals and its links with the AFLS since 1989. See on this subject the collection of articles from the round table *Sida et homosexualité–avril 1991 (AIDS and Homosexuality–April 1991)* published by GKC in December 1991. For additional bibliography on the period, see: *Les lois de l'amour (The Laws of Love)* by Janine Mossuz-Lavou (Pavot 1991), and the documentation centers of *Gai Pied* and Lesbian Archives, both located on the rue Sedaine.*

*Editor's note: In October 1992, *Gai Pied* ceased to exist. Frank Arnal died on January 11, 1993. Frank was unable to revise and update this article himself.

# 3

# Same-Sex Love in Contemporary China

## Vern L. Bullough and Fang Fu Ruan

Male and female homosexuality traditionally has been a feature of Chinese life,[1] and on this basis one would expect to find evidence of same-sex love in modern China.[2] Matters, however, are not so simple. This is because discussions of sexuality per se in China are still not regarded as a proper subject for public discussion. Lenore Norrgard, for example, in her search for lesbians in China, had to go to Hong Kong to find information she could not find on the mainland. Indeed, those attempting to examine homosexuality or lesbianism in China mostly end up reporting on Hong Kong.[3]

Another observer, N. D. Kristof, wrote in 1990:

> Homosexuality is rarely discussed in China's press or in routine conversations. Most Chinese assert that they have never known a homosexual and that there must be extremely few in Chinese society. In large cities, particularly in the southern city of Canton, same-sex lovers meet in certain bars or parks. They sometimes refer to each other in the Cantonese dialect as *geilor,* or gay guy. There are no advocacy groups for same-sex lovers in China. But if the nation lacks an outspoken gay community, it also lacks the invective and bitter hostility that is sometimes directed toward same-sex lovers in the West. There are no common insults in Chinese related to sexual orientation. Most Chinese frown on homosexuality, but characterize it as improper or in poor taste rather than a sin. The police generally are oblivious to signals of homosexuality, in part because it is common for Chinese of the same sex to hold hands as a sign of friendship. But same-sex lovers are occasionally arrested and sentenced to brief jail terms.[4]

Kristof is perhaps too optimistic. Technically there is no specific law against same-sex love in the current Criminal Law of the People's Republic of China. Instead, Article 106, which refers broadly to "hooliganism," is used.[5] It was not unusual in the period between 1955 and 1985 for homosexuals to receive five-year prison terms, although the situation seems to be improving in the 1990s. Moreover, silence about homosexuality and lesbianism might well be a silence based on repression and enforced ignorance, and not of approval or even tolerance. One of the more prominent attorneys in China today, when asked in 1985 to express his opinion on same-sex love, said that, although homosexuality

> exists in different societies and cultures, with some minor exceptions [it] is considered abnormal and disdained. It disrupts social order, invades personal privacy and rights, and leads to criminal behavior. As a result, same-sex lovers are more likely to be penalized administratively and criminally.[6]

In 1987, Zheng Zhanbei, a leading forensic psychiatrist, asserted that homosexuality was against social morality, interfered with social security, damaged the physical and mental health of adolescents, and should be officially made a crime.[7] The Chinese are not unaware that their attitudes are somewhat different from those in the west. Z. Liu, a well-known newspaper reporter and editor of a popular magazine, who spent some two years of study in Chicago, described his American experience with same-sex love in 1984:

> One group on campus, calling itself the gay and lesbian Illini, met every week. I was enormously curious about this group, which concerned itself with issues of homosexuality, but I never ventured to go to any of their meetings. I inquired of friends, however, to find out who these people were and what they did. One of my friends argued that love between those of the same sex is natural and has existed throughout history—during the Roman Empire, it was even made legal, he said. I disagreed, saying that it wouldn't be good for society to open up this issue. In ancient China, homosexuality was practiced by a few rich people, but the general public didn't approve.[8]

Richard Green, who lectured on human sexuality at Beijing Union Medical College in 1988, reported:

> I described my research on the nonsexual behaviors of young boys that predicted later homosexuality. I asked the physicians in the audience whether comparable childhood behaviors were found among Chinese boys. I was told that there were no homosexuals in China.[9]

Earlier, one of the authors of this article had visited and lectured to health professionals in China, and found the same denial, although, when pressed, some of the Chinese professionals would admit that "such people" existed but that they were mentally ill.

However, there are some indications of change beginning to take place. In September 1991, officials of Shanghai, the largest city in China, reluctantly admitted that there were perhaps 10,000 homosexuals in the city, although others felt that the officials were deliberately underestimating and that the total numbers were closer to 200,000.[10] Unfortunately, one of the factors bringing about a change in attitudes is the growing concern over sexually transmitted diseases (STDs). Officials at Changzheng Hospital in Tianjin, the third-largest city in China, recently reported that out of the 366 cases of STDs which they had examined, 61 resulted from male homosexual activity. Of these, 80 percent involved anal sex, 10 percent oral sex, and 10 percent both anal and oral. Emphasizing the lack of organization of the gay community in China was the fact that 80 percent of the sexual activity took place in public toilets between strangers. The age of the participants ranged from sixteen to sixty, with the median age being between twenty to thirty years old.[11] This is the closest approach to an accurate figure that we have on any kind of homosexual activity in China.

Interestingly, one of the reactions of the Chinese to such statistics is to equate homosexuality and lesbianism with "Western social diseases" derived from Western ideology and thoughts.[12]

Another reaction is to demand that such Western imports be severely punished, as Ruixiong Wan recommended in 1988.[13] Some, however, regard homosexuality and lesbianism as a mental illness, for which one of the common treatment modalities is aversion therapy for both males and females.

When same-sex lovers are treated for what most Chinese doctors regard as their "mental illness," they are sometimes given painful electric shocks to discourage erotic thoughts. An alternative approach is to offer herbal medicines that induce vomiting. In either case, the idea is to stimulate an extremely unpleasant reaction that will be associated thereafter with erotic thoughts and thus reduce the patient's ardor. Both approaches are hailed by doctors in China as remarkably successful in "curing" homosexuality.[14]

For the most part, individuals subjected to this treatment had been sent by family members.

At this writing, the best descriptions of homosexuality in China come from personal contacts made by Fang Fu Ruan and by a Hong Kong journalist, Hui Fu, who spent ten months traveling in China in search of information on gays. Ruan's contacts, dating from 1985, were responses to an article titled "Homosexuality: An Unsolved Puzzle" in a widely circulated Chinese health magazine.[15] The article attracted enough attention to be reprinted in the most widely distributed magazine in China, a Chinese version of *Reader's Digest*. Since it was the first article to appear in a popular press, it encouraged readers to respond to what had formerly been a forbidden topic.

Some sixty Chinese men (no women) wrote to the editors, fifty-six of whom identified themselves as homosexual. Two of the letters by non-homosexuals were hostile—one from a faculty member at a medical college, and the other from a teacher in a factory training center. Interestingly, most of the homosexual letter-writers revealed their identities, believing that their letters would remain confidential. They also gave considerable information about themselves.

It is from their descriptions that the only information we have about homosexuality can be garnered, a far cry from the desirable statistical sampling. Thirty-four, for example, indicated their age, with most (25) being between twenty-one and thirty; three were under twenty, and one was over sixty. The largest number lived in Shanghai, although letters came from all over the country. Of the twenty-two who mentioned marital status, eight were married, two divorced, and the rest were single. The wives of the married men had no knowledge about their husband's homosexuality; although several had children, they regretted having to live with such hypocrisy. Most feared arrest and punishment if their homosexuality became known. One of the respondents, a physics teacher in a high school, had already been arrested and sentenced to five years for his homosexual activity.

Since Ruan had given brief descriptions of two actual cases of gay life in Hubei and Shanghai, many of the letter writers expressed interest in contacting them, indicating a real sense of isolation. One letter writer (letter no. 43) wrote:

> The greatest pain for us, the same-sex lovers, is our inability to express our deepest inner sorrow. We have to hide our feelings in front of others. I therefore beg you to fulfill my wish by giving me the names and addresses of other same-sex lovers. This may help me find the will to go on living.

Another (letter no. 10) wrote, "I hope to contact other same-sex lovers through your magazine," while still another (letter no. 25) wished that Ruan could become the "go-between for homosexuals and provide a bridge for the great many same-sex lovers" to contact each other.

One writer (letter no. 8) went into some detail about his hope for some sort of organization or club where gays could meet:

> I fantasized that there would be a place where same-sex lovers can converse and interact freely. I fantasized having a lover. But fantasy is not real. In reality, same-sex lovers do not automatically love all other same-sex lovers. They choose their partners just like heterosexuals. But where can I find them? . . . We should provide ways for exclusive same-sex lovers to contact one another.

Some appeared much more knowledgeable about the existence of other gays. One letter writer (no. 26) had traveled to eighteen different cities and provinces throughout China in his hunt for homosexual partners, finding them everywhere he went. Unfortunately, he did not indicate how he located them but only reported that they came from every walk of life.

A more detailed description comes from the effort of Hui Fu to locate gays.[16] He found that gays were heavily closeted but that they did meet in a limited number of places such as public restrooms, parks, shopping centers, and public baths which had acquired a reputation, at least among the homosexual community, for being meeting places. Cruising time uniformly was in the early evening, after 6:00 P.M. In Beijing, gays picked each other up in two of the city's major shopping centers, in Tienanmen Square, and in Jih-tan Park. In Shanghai, the favorite gathering spot was in front of the Central Post Office. In Sian, an ancient walled city, Fu could not locate any gays after two days of searching; however, just before he left the city, he went into a public restroom located near the city wall. This turned out to be a meeting place.

Apparently, a few chosen public restrooms were the key meeting-places elsewhere in China, in part because of the acute housing shortage and real lack of clubs or other places where individuals could meet outside the work place. Since few Chinese have any chances for privacy in their own home and hotels and motels for the ordinary person are almost nonexistent, the restrooms and baths serve not only as contact places but scenes of homosexual activity as well.

If China lacked any gay male organizations, lesbians were even more closeted. Lenore Norrgard reported in 1990:

> In nearly ten years of visiting, studying, working, and living in China and Hong Kong, I had never managed to meet any women who identified as lesbians. It wasn't because I didn't look: Whenever I got on a conversational basis with someone who seemed relatively open or enlightened, I would ask about homosexuality.[17]

While Norrgard found what she called a refreshing lack of homophobia, she attributed this to a general lack of sexual knowledge about the existence of homosexuality. Perhaps the best illustration of this innocence among large segments of the Chinese population was the case of the two young lesbian women who went to the marriage bureau to register their bond to each other. Much to their surprise, they found themselves arrested. They were apparently so naive that they were not even aware that what they were doing was regarded as unusual. We are not sure what to make of this case, since two contradictory explanations are possible—either that lesbianism is more common than it appears although few are aware lesbians exist and perhaps do not even know about lesbianism as such, or that lesbianism is extremely rare. The only thing that can be stated with certainty is that lesbians keep a low profile. One of her Hong Kong respondents told Norrgard:

In China they're especially naive about lesbianism. Homosexuality among men they can understand more, because it's more often represented in stories. You never read about women having relationships with women.[18]

Though Fang Fu Ruan never received letters from lesbians as he did from gay men, he did meet and interview three lesbians in 1985, all inmates in the Shanghai Women Delinquents Correctional Institution. Two had been jailed for prostitution and one as a sex criminal.

One of the women, Ms. Za, had never known about lesbianism until during one of her jail terms. There she met a woman who had been arrested and jailed for lesbian behavior. The two women became friends, and after her initial surprise about what lesbianism entailed, Ms. Za decided that she really was a lesbian herself and actively seduced other women. After being released, she still earned her living as a prostitute but also continued to engage in lesbian activities when the opportunity presented itself.

Another case was that of a Ms. Jia, who had been a constant companion of another woman, Ms. Yi. Jia was married but only reluctantly had intercourse with her husband. If it had been possible, she would have always had sex with Yi. Unfortunately, Yi herself got engaged, and Jia became desperate, fearful that she and Yi would lose contact. Jia promised to divorce her husband and move in with Yi; but when Yi disagreed, Jia decided that it was better to kill her lover than give her up to a man. Inevitably the murder story made the news, even in China.

Much of our information about lesbianism, in fact, comes from court cases reported in the news media, in which one of the lesbian partners became jealous over the activities of the other. Cheng He and Qian Fang report several cases like this.[19]

Perhaps because almost all of the cases of lesbianism to be reported in the Chinese popular press involved some kind of violence, the image of the lesbian is worse than that of the male homosexual. Almost anything derogatory can be written about them. Shui Shui in a 1989 story, which seems to have been entirely based on the author's imagination, describes a secret "lesbian company" of women who engage in murder and other crimes because they have been hurt and rejected by men.[20] Apparently, the public imagination about lesbians was such, that the story was widely believed to be true.

Usually unrecorded are other incidences of lesbian love, such as the one told to Ruixong Wan. This was the case of a woman who had just recently married when her husband, accused of "rightism," was sent off to a forced labor camp. Soon after his departure she gave birth to a son and her economic circumstances worsened. Still, even though she was told her husband had died of starvation in the forced labor camp, the woman never remarried, and continued to eke out a minimal living. One day, another woman visited her, bringing food. Gradually the friendship blossomed, and two became lovers, and continued to enjoy a close relationship over the years without interference of the police or the community leaders.[21] It might well be that the fact that one of the lovers had a child, saved them from being discovered.

In conclusion, it seems that pressures remained so great and government control was so omnipresent, that it is difficult for homosexuals and lesbians to organize. Homosexuals and lesbians existed and they survived, but they did not flourish. It is a sad commentary that our sources remain either official ones such as prison records, arrests, and sexually transmitted disease reports, or result from incidental and haphazard contacts. Homosexuals, in spite of this, seem to have found places where they can meet and contact each other but meetings remain secretive and furtive. Even though there is a long tradition of tolerance of lesbianism in Chinese society, lesbians remain even more closeted than gay males, and those who do surface have a rather violent image. No national or local reliable statistics are available about Chinese gays and lesbians, and even anecdotal evidence may be misleading, since the majority of those who supply it do so only because they are being coerced by legal authorities. As of this writing, it seems that it will take rather radical changes to allow Chinese homosexuals and lesbians to live any kind of "normal" and fulfilling life.

## NOTES

1. See Bret Hinsch, *The Male Homosexual Tradition in China* (Berkeley and Los Angeles: University of California Press, 1990); R. H. van Gulik, *Sexual Life in Ancient China* (Leiden: E. J. Brill, 1961); E. Chou, *The Dragon and the Phoenix* (New York: Arbor House, 1971); L. E. Girchner, *Erotic Aspects of Chinese Culture* (privately printed, 1957); Fang Fu Ruan and Y. M. Tsai, "Male Homosexuality in the Traditional Chinese Literature," *Journal of Homosexuality* 14 (1987): 21–33.

2. One of the few examples of any effort to do so, however, is F. F. Ruan and Y. M. Tsai, "Male Homosexuality in Contemporary Mainland China," *Archives of Sexual Behavior* 17 (1988): 189–99.

3. L. Norrgard, "Opening the Hong Kong Closet," *Out/Look* (*National Lesbian and Gay Quarterly*) 2 (Winter 1990): 56–61. This was also the case of F. Lieh-Mak, K. M. Hoy, and S. L. Luk, "Lesbianism in the Chinese of Hong Kong, *Archives of Sexual Behavior* 12 (1983): 21–30.

4. N. D. Kristof, " 'Curing' Homosexuals in China," *San Francisco Chronicle,* January 31, 1990.

5. Chun-ie Fang, *Law Annual Report of China 1982/3* (Chinese) (Hong Kong: Kingsway International Publications Ltd., 1982).

6. Fang Fu Ruan, writing under the pseudonym J. M. Hua, "Homosexuality: An Unsolved Puzzle," *Zhu Nin Jiankang (To Your Good Health)* 3 (1985): 14–15. See also the section on homosexuality in Fang Fu Ruan, ed., *Xing zhishi shouce (Handbook of Sexual Knowledge)* (Beijing: Scientific and Technological Literature Publishing House, 1985).

7. Ruixion Wan, "The Major Variations of Sex and Love—About the Problems

of Homosexuality in China," *Nu Shi Ren Tan (The Ten Women's Tales),* Wen Bo, ed. (Beijing: China Social Sciences Press, 1988), pp. 78–109.

8. Z. Liu, *Two Years in the Melting Pot* (San Francisco: China Books and Periodicals, Inc., 1984).

9. See the introduction by Richard Green to Fang Fu Ruan, *Sex in China: Studies in Sexology in Chinese Culture* (New York: Plenum, 1991), p. v.

10. *World Weekly,* September 1, 1991.

11. *World Journal,* September 13, 1991.

12. This was the conclusion of a 1987 article in the *Beijing Daily News,* which was the subject of a press release by United Press International on February 4, 1987, and which ran in a number of American newspapers.

13. Wan, "The Major Variations of Sex and Love."

14. Kristof, " 'Curing' Homosexuals."

15. Fang Fu Ruan (J. M. Hua), "Homosexuality: An Unsolved Puzzle."

16. For the results of Hui Fu's efforts, see Fang Fu Ruan and K. R. Chong, "Gay Life in China," *The Advocate* 470 (April 14, 1987): 28–31.

17. Norrgard, "Opening the Hong Kong Closet."

18. Ibid.

19. Cheng He and Qian Fang, "The Sex-Love of Yin-Yang Inversion: An Inquiry into Homosexuality in China" (Chinese), *Qinhai Quncong Yishu (Art and Literature of Qinhai Provinces)* No. 103 (April 1989): 2–23.

20. Shui Shui, "Lesbians' Company" (Chinese), in *Junlu Yanqing (The Love Story in the Military Tour)* (Shengyang: Lianoning Mingzu Press, 1989), pp. 66–95.

21. Wan, "The Major Variations of Sex and Love."

# 4

# The Global Lesbian and Gay Movement: Mass Movement, Grassroots, or by Invitation Only

## John Clark

The Lesbian and Gay Rights Movement is the struggle to achieve equality, freeing lesbian and gay people from the oppressive standards of a homophobic culture. In isolation if necessary, the homosexual minority will adopt its own set of standards. Lesbians and gays will live constructive and satisfying lives with or without the "approval" of others, while continuing to promote social reform. Because change does not occur on its own, some pressure must be applied. Woodrow Wilson observed: "If you want to make enemies, try to change something." But homosexuality already has its enemies. The Lesbian and Gay Rights Movement was therefore created out of necessity, not out of desire, and it will continue until the oppression which fuels it is exhausted. Lesbians and gay men will simply no longer excuse their enemies; they will no longer tolerate the intolerance; and they will no longer patronize their own persecution.

Roger E. Biery (1990)

The lesbian and gay movement worldwide has taken on many different faces in the course of our relatively short history. Often contemporary thinking and events in mainstream society have influenced the advancement and development of our movement. However, over the years, groups of lesbians and gay men have, in general, taken on either a grassroots structural concept or that of a selective membership/special interest group. Both forms have in their own way booked success and failure.

Does one of these forms present an advantage over the other? Will the movement in the year 2000 have a place for both? In which directions will the international lesbian and gay movement have to move in order to remain an effective force? How can we best gain and *deal with* "power?"

The founding of the Wissenschaftlich-Humanitäres Komitee (Scientific-Humanitarian Committee) on May 15, 1897, by Magnus Hirschfeld, Max Spohr, and Erich Oberg in Berlin marked the beginning of the lesbian and gay liberation movement. Other countries followed later (Britain and the Netherlands in the early 1900s, and Sweden in the 1930s). In France, where the Napoleonic Code meant an absence of specific criminal sanctions, the period saw a flowering of gay life, but no specifically political movement (Altman 1982). The rise of homophile groups in the United States had to wait until after World War II, when the Mattachine Society (1951) and Daughters of Bilitis (1955) were founded.*

Although wartime events brought about a major restructuring of society and its processes, the end of the war brought pressures to restore earlier social order. In the Netherlands, for example, the Roman Catholic Church, having welcomed the persecution of homosexuals during the Nazi era, called for recriminalization of homosexuality after the war (Adam 1987). McCarthyism, although not a single nor isolated phenomenon, would stand vicariously for reactionary forces in the post-war Western World; forces which would do everything possible to quell the budding search for a purpose and an identity.

Yet the post-war homophile movement continued to develop: the homophile group Levensrecht, the predecessor of the Cultuur en Ontspannings Centrum (COC), was revived in the Netherlands in 1946, Forbundet af 1948 in Denmark, Riksforbundet for Sexuellt Likaberattigande (RFSL) in Sweden, and Det Norske Forbundet av 1948 in Norway. The Netherlands COC sponsored five international conferences for sexual equality between 1951 and 1958, offering support and, most important, hope for lesbian and gay organizations in Europe (Adam 1987).

The early homophile organizations differed greatly from later ones. Some were science and law-reform oriented, and most of them remained small and select. They typically adopted a cautious and secretive approach to social change, which made it inherently difficult to raise awareness and reach the masses. Secrecy among members, concerning both meetings and membership, was often a life-preserving necessity. The times before the war and immediately after were marked by a level and breed of homophobia that few of us today can imagine. Especially in the United States, the "witch hunts" of the McCarthy era deeply affected the lives and organizing efforts of homosexual men and women. Although many

*There were earlier attempts, most notably the Chicago Society for Human Rights, founded by Henry Gerber in 1924 and Bachelors for Wallace in 1948. However, the Mattachine Society and Daughters of Bilitis were the first organizations in the United States of the homophile era to have a distinct influence on the development of a lesbian and gay liberation movement.

early organizations were striving to become mass movements, inherent secrecy, that built-in human attribute of self-preservation, hampered these attempts. Indeed, the Mattachine Society established from the very beginning a strict hierarchical structure, which is one of the reasons why it was able to survive the repression of the '50s and early '60s. But, this very logistic inflexibility contributed to the organization's gradual crumbling in the late '60s. As Roger Biery notes: "The very survival of these organizations would ultimately cripple their effectiveness."

These attributes, although quite representative for the time, applied mainly to the homophile movement in the U.S. In the Netherlands especially, the situation was not so bleak. Barry Adam (1987) provides the following analysis:

> In the Netherlands, a peculiar balance of political forces that has guaranteed a more genuinely pluralistic society than other liberal democracies combined to allow more direct participation of the 1950s homophile movement in the political process and less direct confrontation between the state and homosexuality than in Germany or the English-language countries. The result has been considerable continuity in the national gay and lesbian federations of the Netherlands (as well as Denmark, Norway, and Sweden), all of which have worked well and survived from their founding in the late 1940s and early 1950s. Gay liberation, although provoking a rethinking of the political agenda, never overturned the early organizations but instead became largely integrated into them.

Beginning in the mid-1960s, the pot started to boil over. All over North America and Western Europe, civil rights and counterculture activism began to take hold, shaking the very roots of mainstream society. At Columbia University and at the Sorbonne, radical gay caucuses were formed; in the Netherlands the Socialist Youth organization formed a gay caucus. But it was the Stonewall Rebellion in New York, in June 1969, that marked the transition from the homophile era to the lesbian and gay liberation movement.*

The Gay Liberation Front (GLF) was founded on July 31, 1969, just one month after Stonewall. But the split between the homophiles and the liberationists were followed in the U.S. by the split between the liberationists (cultural reformers) and the radicals (revolutionaries).

As the radicals became more and more dogmatic, the cultural reformers tried to rally homosexuals and, at the same time, confront political candidates and make gays influential in the political system. This aroused the revolutionary suspicion and the radical antagonism that led some activists to leave GLF and organize the Gay Activist Alliance (GAA) in fall 1969, a group that was to become one of the most prominent organizations of the time (Marotta 1981). Its structure was grassroots; its membership was militant but not violent. Like many groups

---

*Stonewall was not the first case of riots. Already in 1967, police raids on gay bars in Los Angeles sparked public protests. Still, June 1969 has been designated the turning point in lesbian and gay politics and the "birthday" of the modern liberation movement.

of the liberation era, the GAA borrowed its tactics from the black civil rights movement (Biery 1990). The National Gay Task Force* followed in 1973, the year in which the GAA was already in contact with over 1,100 lesbian and gay groups in North America.

A wave of change overcame Germany in the late 1960s and early 1970s. In the former GDR (1968) and in the Federal Republic of Germany (1969), homosexuality was decriminalized. In 1970, there were attempts in Hamburg, Wiesbaden, and Munich to form large organizations, which all failed after a short time. Rosa von Praunheim's landmark film, *Nicht der Homosexuelle ist pervers, sondern die Situation in der er lebt* (*It is not the homosexual, but the situation in which he lives, that is perverse*), was first shown in 1971, the year in which the glf-Köln was founded, a grassroots organization that still exists today. But in Germany, too, the first conflicts between the "Integrationisten" and the "Radikalen" were already beginning in 1972 (Frieling 1985).

The mass movement with its beloved unilevel hierarchy and decision-making structures was going full force when, on August 8, 1978, a meeting in Coventry, England, decided to found the International Lesbian and Gay Association (ILGA).†

The founding of the ILGA was also based on the concept of grassroots organizational logistics and membership involvement. The first constitution did not foresee any persons in office, only secretariats with limited authority; a headquarters office was out of the question. In fact, the ILGA's grassroots structure at the beginning of its history was so loosely knit that its effectiveness in acting on current matters was greatly hampered. Many members refused to let the ILGA "exist" outside of annual conferences. "Decisions" could be made only during the annual conference, leaving the ILGA in limbo fifty-one weeks of the year. Decision making at the conference was also limited to those matters that could find an 80 percent majority approval.

But "Baby ILGA," for all its shortcomings, was something unique, a structure within the lesbian and gay liberation movement that would greatly influence the development of that movement, especially in those countries and regions where "the seed had not yet been sown."‡ It may also have been the ILGA's uncomplicated

---

*The National Gay Task Force changed its name to the National Gay and Lesbian Task Force in 1986.

†The ILGA was founded as the International Gay Association and changed its name to the International Lesbian and Gay Association in 1986. The ILGA was not the first attempt to establish international cooperation. From 1951 to 1958, the International Committee for Sexual Equality existed. For more information, see H. Holtmaat and R. Piastor, "Ten Years of International Gay and Lesbian Solidarity: Ten Years of ILGA," in the *Second ILGA Pink Book* (1988), pp. 33–45.

‡Besides the support the ILGA has lent to the movement in Asia, Africa, and South America, it has been instrumental with its Eastern Europe Information Pool in the development of a visible lesbian and gay liberation movement in most of the countries of the former Eastern bloc. For more information about the history of the movement in Eastern Europe, see *Out in Europe, Second ILGA Pink Book, Rosa Liebe unterm roten Stern,* and the annual publications of the Eastern Europe Information Pool, HOSI Wien.

networking structures that appealed to lesbians and gay men from different cultures, offering them a very open platform and enabling them to meet and communicate in a constructive way.

The 1970s were marked by the drive for all lesbians and gay men to come out and work together in the open mass movement, tackling the entire sphere of lesbian and gay issues. "Out of the closets and into the streets" was GAA's big slogan. According to Toby Marotta (1981), "the 1970s will be recorded as the decade in which gay life won legitimacy."

But the liberation movement era faded away with the counterculture. The "one-for-all, all-for-one" euphoria began to sour as platforms and agendas grew out of proportion, often cluttered with nongay issues, and as lesbians and gays began to realize that they did not form a homogeneous entity. Indeed, they had to come to the conclusion that they belonged to one of the most nonhomogeneous minorities in the world.

Lesbians also discovered that their interests were not being reflected in the "gay" movement. Women were also greatly influenced by the New Left and civil rights movements of the 1960s. In the U.S., they initiated contemporary feminist political activity in 1966 by forming the National Organization for Women (NOW). But in the early days of the gay liberation movement, lesbian activists were often still working within mixed organizations. "Yet however precociously they appreciated their status as women and their stake in feminism, lesbians . . . characterized themselves as homosexuals and gay political activists until lesbian emigrés from women's groups persuaded them to attach more significance to their identities as women and their political callings as feminists" (Marotta 1981). And thus began a further ramification of the movement: the formation and evolution of Radicalesbians.*

The 1980s (but also the 1970s in some organizations) saw the breakdown of the post-Stonewall movement into subgroups with ethnic, regional, social, and even job-related interests. The yuppie professionalism and *savoir faire* of mainstream society began to infiltrate the lesbian and gay movement, replacing the revolutionary "flower power" atmosphere of the liberation era. Activists tired of the energy-draining processes of grassroots groups, preferred to join up with professional organizations. Political diversity was replaced with close peer decision making; group consciousness raising, with methodical lobbying efforts.

Dennis Altman, in his book *The Homosexualization of America* (1982), provides the following analysis:

> There is a basic division within the gay movement between those people who argue that homosexuals can organize like other minorities and win their goals through the system, and those who contend that in a society permeated with

---

*Radicalesbians, centered around Rita Mae Brown, was started in May 1970 after the Second Congress to Unite Women and drew heavily on lesbians from GLF.

heterosexism only a radical social transformation can achieve genuine equality and acceptance. This division outlines two sorts of disagreement, one over mass tactics versus elite organizing, and the other over separatism versus particaption in a general radical coalition. What Edmund White characterized as a clash between assimilationists and radicals, and what John Mitzel described as a conflict between the good gays and the bad gays, is a constant theme of gay politics, both in the United States and elsewhere.

The homophile era started the ball rolling, with men and women first considering the idea of a homosexual identity. Although they were not able to exhibit a high visibility profile or "excite the masses," they did set the stage for the liberationists to make their big breakthrough after Stonewall.

The mass movement of the 1970s brought about changes within ourselves, within the lesbian and gay community. Come out, become visible, demand your rights, and through this process we developed a desire to change society. This movement, however, did not provide the avenues to gain the power to make these changes. The revolutionaries refused to tread these paths, preferring instead to bypass them completely. Assimilationists, on the other hand, often faded into appeasement on their way down the road.

Many see the hope of attaining our goals through the more structured, subject-oriented, professional and elite organizations. They give our movement a focus and work intensity that cannot be attained within other organizational structures. Other people, however, see these as too elitist, as reflecting only the negative aspects of mainstream patriarchal society, as a sellout to the heterosexualism. Appeasement will be the ultimate downfall of the movement. Without radical actions there will be no reactions.

We should also not forget perhaps one of the largest segments of the lesbian and gay population. Those who are "not interested in politics" feel that we should not make waves, believing that if we are nice people, others will like us or at least leave us alone, arguing that "whatever we do in our bedrooms and behind closed doors is nobody's business," etc., ad nauseam.*

So the question remains, which direction should, will, must the international lesbian and gay movement take for the 1990s and beyond? The answer is not a cop-out, but an objective assessment of historical development and contemporary necessity. The diversity of the "fronts" we must fight on demands a diversity in the structural forms with which we model our community, gain power, and fight discrimination and intolerance. Rather than faulting unilevel decision-making bodies for their sluggishness and inefficiency or faulting select membership structures for their lack of democratic processes, we should support parallel activities.

We must promote a diversity and power at the grassroots level, for therein

---

*Of all the problems facing the lesbian and gay movement, self-discrimination and apathy within our own ranks may be one of our largest hindrances. But this is the topic of another article.

lies our community strength. There are also situations, especially in the fight against AIDS, when all of our efforts with logical discourse fail to bring any success or reaction. In such instances, direct action tactics and sometimes even civil disobedience remain our only course of action. In order to mobilize and educate lesbians and gay men and improve our visibility, we must continue to spin the thread of the mass movement and thus cement the effectiveness of grassroots.

But in order to add efficiency to this effectiveness, we must further the work of special interest groups. The financial and legal resources for legal reform and lobbying will remain with professional and select-membership organizations that have specialized in such enterprises. As society in general, and discrimination against lesbians and gay men specifically, become more and more technically perfected,* so, too, must these advances be reflected in our own activities. We must learn not only to act but also react with speed, efficiency, and professionalism. We must also recognize the diversity of homosexuals and the desire of many to form groups with a single ethnic, religious, professional, or political interest.

In some countries, especially in northern Europe, wide-reaching, national umbrella organizations are able to cover the focused work of specialized groups, incorporating them into the general structure of the organization, and at the same time allowing them to act independently. However, this fortunate form of "both worlds under one roof" structure is not available in many countries. Its roots can often be traced to the long history of national organizations in these countries.

We cannot sit back and wait for the structures established by mainstream heterosexual society to consider and take up our interests. We would be waiting a long time! These are *our* rights, and we are the ones who will have to secure them. Human rights conventions have been created to protect the rights of all people, including the population that is homosexual. Therefore, it is our right— our responsibility—to confront society with our concerns. Homosexuality is not a sickness, but homophobia is, and homosexuality is being defined by a society that does not understand this concept. When the power of definition resides somewhere else, then it must be regained, because self-definition is its only legitimate form.

Such a basic form of power is, however, too complex and elusive to be readily and easily attainable. Our future as lesbians and gay men will depend on our ability and willingness to effectively claim our rights in a unified and concerted effort. At the same time, we must have the courage to recognize and accept—yes, even promote—our diversity. We demand that mainstream society accept our diversity; that same demand we can make on ourselves.

---

*Many of the forces and groups that promote discrimination against homosexuals are well managed and use well-perfected technical and office facilities and large sums of money to further oppression.

## REFERENCES AND BIBLIOGRAPHY

Adam, Barry. *The Rise of a Gay and Lesbian Movement.* Boston: Twayne Publishers, 1987.

Altman, Dennis. *The Homosexualization of America.* Boston: Becaon Press, 1982.

*The Alyson Almanac.* Boston: Alyson Publications, 1989.

Biery, Roger E. *Understanding Homosexuality—The Pride and the Prejudice.* Austin, Tex.: Edward-William Publishing Company, 1990.

Bullough, Vern. *Homosexuality: A History.* New York: New American Library, 1979.

Gough, Jamie, and Mike Macnair. *Gay Liberation in the Eighties.* London: Pluto Press, 1985.

Katz, Jonathan. *Gay American History.* New York: Avon Books, 1976.

———. *Gay-Lesbian Almanac.* New York: Harper & Row, 1983.

Marotta, Toby. *The Politics of Homosexuality.* Boston: Houghton Mifflin, 1981.

*Rosa Liebe unterm roten Stern (Pink Love under the Red Star).* Homosexuelle Initiative (HOSI). Wien Auslandsgruppe Collective. Hamburg: Frühlings Erwachen, 1984.

*Schwule Regungen—schwule Bewegungen (Gay Motions—Gay Movements).* Edited by Willi Frieling. Berlin: Verlag Rosa Winkel, 1985.

*Second ILGA Pink Book.* ILGA Pink Book Editing Team. Utrecht: Interfacultaire Werkgroep Homostudies, 1988.

Tatchell, Peter. *Out in Europe.* London: Rouge, 1990.

# 5

# Lesbian and Gay Life in Zimbabwe

## Mike Coutinho

In September 1990, Gays and Lesbians of Zimbabwe (GALZ) was born. The organization grew out of two decades of social organizing within the white and coloured* gay and lesbian community. Although GALZ is predominantly a white organization, it may provide a framework within which black gay men can establish a forum for exploring their own experiences and identities.

In trying to form GALZ, gay and lesbian activists had to recognize that the gay community was affected by the deep class and racial divisions which still plague Zimbabwean society. In the meeting that declared GALZ's formation, five young black men from Harare's townships argued the point that a white organization that was geared toward tennis games and pool parties was not going to meet the needs of youthful and politicized black gays and lesbians.

In 1988, there were only a handful of black gay men who participated in gay community social events. Most of these men either had white lovers or were from middle-class backgrounds. Things started to change when a series of safer sex workshops were conducted. The two white gay facilitators made a special effort to tap into the informal networks of black gay men in the townships. Through the forum of the workshops, black gay men came together and talked about being gay and African. The very presence of poor black gay youths challenged many of the assumptions behind organizing within the gay community. The impli-

---

*"Coloured" refers to Zimbabweans of mixed racial heritage, usually African-European but also mixes of South Asian and South East Asian. Although the term "coloured" was once a part of apartheid ideology, it is now being reclaimed to identify a distinct African experience and a particular ethnocultural community.

cations of this revolutionary situation can only be understood within the context of Zimbabwean history.

## HISTORICAL BACKGROUND

Zimbabwe became independent in 1980 after a fifteen-year armed struggle against the racist state of Rhodesia. Despite a policy of racial reconciliation on the part of Robert Mugabe's ruling ZANU (PF) party, many whites in Zimbabwe have never learned to respect their black compatriots. Although young whites go to multiracial schools in multiracial neighborhoods, they still tend to think of themselves as a race apart. This mentality, combined with the reality of the social and economic inequalities that still exist between the majority of whites and most blacks, keeps Zimbabwe a divided society.

The history of gay life in Zimbabwe parallels the larger historical experience. There has long been a gay life in Zimbabwe. Older white gay men tell tales of dodging the police while cruising Cecil Square (now Africa Unity Square) as far back as the early 1950s. Older black gay men recall tales of romance and hardships on the other side of town in the single-sex hostels for migrant laborers.

When the Liberation War came in the 1960s and 1970s, many white and coloured men were able to expand their circle of gay friends through the Rhodesian military structures. There were even bars and nightclubs that catered to the white gay and lesbian community.

By the end of the war, coloured gay men, many of whom had served in the Rhodesian forces, began insisting on their right to enter "whites only" gay bars. After some shoving matches and sharp words, that right was established, linking white and coloured gay men in an uneasy social alliance.

## BLACK GAY ZIMBABWE

The black gay history of Zimbabwe is rooted in the culture of township hostels and prisons. Hidden from public discussion, homosexuality was defined as a sexual necessity under unnatural conditions. Homosexuality is still illegal in Zimbabwe due to the Roman-Dutch statutes established under Rhodesian rule. Although GALZ has discussed the issue of legal reform, it is very unlikely that legislators would consider the issue important enough to address. The only known cases of men being prosecuted under the sodomy laws since independence were all in conjunction with other crimes, such as extortion. In traditional (Shona* and Ndebele) law, homosexuality is not recognized at all.

---

*Eighty percent of Zimbabwe's population is Shona-speaking. Fifteen percent speak other African languages, the largest of which is Ndebele. Five percent of the population is white, coloured, or Asian in origin.

Yet African cultures in Zimbabwe are diversifying. As the national economy moves into the industrial and post-industrial age, new lifestyle options are developing in the urban areas. This has provided a space for individuals to become fully conscious of their homosexuality. Presently, black gay men are asserting their collective identity and are attending gay community events in ever-growing numbers.

Throughout the townships small networks of gay men are emerging. The emergence of black lesbian consciousness, however, is constrained by women's lack of the economic and social independence which is available to men. Some women do manage to connect with the gay male networks; and if they are lucky, they are able to link up with other lesbians in the townships.

Though some black gay men are from privileged backgrounds, most live in the economically underdeveloped townships. Some black gay youths are homeless and illiterate. Many are struggling to make enough money to eat, and so prostitution with tourists has become a common method of economic survival.

The struggle of black gays and lesbians in Zimbabwe is a battle on two fronts. One struggle is against racism in the established gay community. The other is against the invisibility of gays within heterosexual African cultures.

## SAFER SEX WORKSHOPS

Until 1989, there had been no forum for lesbians and gay men to come to gether and talk about being gay in Zimbabwe. Finally, after two successful lesbian and gay video festivals, two members of the gay community decided to organize a series of safer sex workshops to deal with the ever-growing AIDS epidemic.

For the first time, outreach was made to the networks of black gay men in the townships. The response was enthusistic. Each of the three workshops included black, coloured, and white young gay men. Although dealing with the issue of AIDS, much of the discussion revolved around defining a gay identity and the nature of "community" in a multiracial gay context. From the start a number of preconceptions were challenged.

Black gay youths are eager to challenge the myth about how heterosexual Shona culture really is. "I think all African men are bisexual," exclaimed Farai during one workshop. Farai is a Shona man in his late twenties. Although wageless and with little formal education, he is politically aware and committed to helping black gays and lesbians organize themselves.

During a workshop, Farai tells of his experiences of contemporary township nightlife. In most of the urban beer halls there are a few men who service the patrons in much the same way the women prostitutes do. Sex is exchanged for a beer or a few dollars, or sometimes for free. The sexual partners are almost exclusively married men. The gay men are frequently physically assaulted.

Farai travels the beer hall circuit, networking and counseling men about their identity and their health care. He hopes that the safer sex workshops will become a forum for bringing these isolated individuals together in a supportive and affirmative context.

Farai has also challenged the myth that African families always reject their gay children. He came out to his family as a teenager and, after living on the street for a while, was accepted back into his sister's home, gay identity and all. This acceptance includes the fact that Farai will not get married and have children. Many African gay men and most, if not all, lesbians usually give way to the overwhelming social pressure to marry and have children.

Ntuli, another gay male, tells a workshop of his journey home to a village near Shurugwe to tell his grandmother that he was going to marry an Australian man. Once the matriarch gave her approval, the rest of his family members were bound to respect her decision.

## GALZ (GAYS AND LESBIANS OF ZIMBABWE)

The response to the workshops by the white gay community has been mixed. The white lesbian activists and a few white men have been supportive within the context of the newly formed GALZ. In other quarters, black gay men (invisible as always) have had to listen to white gay men say such things as, "Ja, I'd go, but they let all those blacks in." Ntuli, who has experienced this attitude, says angrily before a workshop begins, "You know they call us bloody kaffirs when they think we are not listening."

Despite the significant prevalence of racism among some of the white gays, the overall feeling within the community is that if GALZ intends being a responsible gay organization, it must have a multiracial approach. Such an approach necessitates an awareness of the class contradictions within the society and within the gay community itself. A simple statement of antiracialism will not be sufficient to bring the different parts of the community together.

When GALZ held its first annual Halloween party in 1990, the effects of the networking and workshops were clearly demonstrated. There were more black gay men present than there had been at any previous event. The men came mostly from the Harare area but also from smaller cities, such as Mutare.

With its limited and apolitical agenda, GALZ is treading a cautious path designed to break down the isolation of lesbians and gays in Zimbabwe without drawing unwanted attention from the police. Though committed to a bigender, multiracial, and multiclass ethos, GALZ remains predominantly white. Whether it manages to adjust to allow for increased black involvement and to attend to the needs of gays and lesbians in the townships, will partly determine the future of gay unity in Zimbabwe.

# 6

# Reclaiming Our Historic Rights: Gays and Lesbians in the Philippines

## Jomar Fleras

Rise up, Sisters!
This is not a moment for mourning.
The earth may rumble, the sky turn dark,
but Heaven a legacy for the brave!

Now is the time to sing
Our song of Liberation!

—Nick Deocampo, Filipino gay poet

June 1991. The Philippines. After more than six hundred years of silence, Mount Pinatubo awakened and unleashed its pent-up, seething fury. From the bowels of hell, the angry volcano spewed tons and tons of sulphuric ash, burying the twin cities of Angeles and Olongapo, sites of two of the largest American military installations and infamous centers of the flesh trade. The doomsday moralists likened this calamity to the destruction of Sodom and Gomorrah—signs of the Armageddon—and consequently called for repentance for past sins.

In defiance of the apocalyptic warnings, the first gay Mass was celebrated in Manila. In a booming recalcitrant voice, a gay ex-priest narrated the Old Testament love story of David and Jonathan and preached the virtues of homosexual love. Witnessing the event were twenty brave Filipino gay men who dared possible excommunication by the Catholic Church and the threats of fire and brimstone. Later on, seven gay men were elected to the Board of Directors of the Metropolitan Community Church Manila, the only Christian church in the Philippines which advocates that homosexuality is not a sin.[1]

Earlier, Reachout AIDS Education Foundation held its world premiere of *Poisoned Blood,* the first documentary on the social impact of AIDS in the Philippines.[2] This video documentary analyzed the sexual make-up of the Filipino and blamed the sexual hypocrisy resulting from three hundred years of Catholic indoctrination under the Spanish colonizers as a contributor to the spread of AIDS in the country.[3] Not surprisingly, the religious right condemned the documentary as blasphemous. (This was partly because the opening sequence showed a man dancing naked with a rosary around his neck.)

In another part of the city, the organization Katlo (Third Sex) was being formed by gay men from different walks of life. Initiated by the politicized theater artists of the Philippine Educational Theater Association (PETA), Katlo dared to tackle highly sensitive issues of gay consciousness and gay pride. Another group composed mainly of young "butch" gay customers of the Library Sing-Along Bar started getting involved in issues concerning "coming out" and self-esteem.

On the other hand, the feminist movement, which had been initially preoccupied primarily with the anti-prostitution, anti-U.S. bases movement, started confronting lesbian issues. The lesbian faction of the feminist movement opposed a definition of lesbianism based primarily on sex, and reasserted that lesbian women, too, could desire and shape sexual experience. During the sixth International Women and Health Meeting in Manila, lesbianism was redefined as a form of resistance to patriarchy and male oppression.

It was amazing that all these unorchestrated "awakenings" of homosexual men and women were happening with a volcanic eruption as a dramatic background. Nick Deocampo, internationaly acclaimed alternative filmmaker and gay poet, whose gay film *Oliver* shocked the world with its Marxist dialectical exposé of a gay prostitute, used the imagery of the volcano as his poetic metaphor: "The awakening of lesbian and gay consciousness is like the awakening of a volcano. We have long been dormant. It's now about time that lesbian women and gay men come out with a bang."[4]

## HOMOSEXUALITY AS SUPERSTRUCTURE

The Philippines is a neocolonial, multicultural society with a population of over 60 million. About 85 percent of the population is Catholic. Philippine history may be summarized as follows: an Indo-Malayan tribal culture from A.D. 500 to the mid-sixteenth century, 333 years of Spanish colonial rule, forty-five years of American colonial rule, four years of Japanese occupation, ten years of democracy, twenty years under the dictatorship of Ferdinand Marcos, and a democratic government from 1986.

In analyzing the historical struggle of homosexuals in the Philippines for sociopolitical organization at the macro level and for personhood at the micro level, we must first realize that homosexuality is part of the socioeconomic and political superstructure of society.

Robert Padgug, an expert on sexuality and classical history writes: "The important comprehension that sexuality, class, and politics cannot easily be disengaged from one another must serve as the basis of a materialist view of sexuality in historical perspective as well. . . . The history of sexuality is therefore the history of a subject whose meaning and contents are in continual process of change. It is the history of social relations."[5]

In this article I will trace the evolution and metamorphosis of homosexuality in the Philippines vis-à-vis the histories of the powers that be—the economic, religious, and social realities and world developments. In order to reconstruct our homosexual past, I have extensively used not only chronicles of Filipino and Western writers but also oral accounts. In the absence of unprejudiced written materials on gay and lesbian history in the Philippines, oral history is critical in recovering our homosexual history.


## THE PRE-HISPANIC SHAMANS

Before the Spanish conquistadores came, the Philippines were populated by Indo-Malayan scattered tribes known as *balangays*. At the head of the tribe was the village chieftain. But exercising more de facto power than the chieftain was the *babaylan* or *catalonan*, who was the shaman, the medicine man, the high priest, the overseer of sacred functions, and adviser to the chieftain. Power among tribal people is not perceived as political or economic, but supernatural and paranormal.

In most cases, a "man whose nature inclined toward that of a woman," called a *bayoguin*, was assigned the role of the *babaylan*.[6] The ancient tribes believed that the godhead consisted of the interaction of male and female components, and that bisexuality or androgyny represented immortality. Thus, the male priest who dressed as a female symbolized bisexuality and, therefore, immortality.[7]

A 1738 chronicle of Fray Juan Francisco de San Antonio reports that *hombres maricones* (effeminate men), who were "inclined to be like women and to all the duties of the feminine sex," were "ministers of the devil" or "served as priests to a hermaphrodite god" of the Tagalogs (a Philippine ethnic grouping) prior to the Spanish arrival.[8]

Religious transvestism was not unique to the Philippines. In fact, the practice was probably inherited from immigrants from the Indonesian empires of SriVijaya and Madjapahit.[9] Parallelisms exist with the religious transvestism of the *tadu mburake* shamans of the Toraja Pamona tribe of Central Sulawesi (Celebes), the *bisu* of the Makassarese tribe of Southern Sulawesi, and the *basir* of the Ngaju Dayak tribe of Kalimantan (Borneo).[10]

Animism was widely practiced before the Spanish came. Our ancestors worshiped a hermaphrodite god called *Bathala,* which literally means "man and woman in one."[11]

The effeminate *babaylans* were also known to have married men and to have lived with them.[12] It was considered a great honor for a family to have its young son cohabit with the elderly *babaylan.* However, the man-boy relationship would be terminated when the boy was ready to marry; after all, men were still needed to repopulate the tribe. Again, this practice of pederasty was prevalent in Indonesian tribal cultures, such as in the Minangkabau society of West Sumatra.[13] We do not have colorful accounts of sex between women during pre-Spanish times. But ethnographic accounts and folk legends record the existence of female warriors, chieftains, and shamans. The most famous of them was Queen Urduja, legendary not only for her beauty but also for her strength. It was said that she could do battle with any man.

Whether these women were lesbians was never mentioned. They could have indulged in sex with each other, or they could have merely been Amazons who were forced to do the work of men for the preservation of the tribe. With the dearth of written documents, we can only conjecture.

What we may conclude from the available documents, is that before the Westernization of the Philippines, sex between people of the same gender was considered normal. Like most ancient societies, the *balangays* did not discriminate on the basis of sexual orientation. Effeminate men and masculine women enjoyed powerful and respected positions in society. Like the berdache of the Native American tribes, they were not only accepted but revered for their ability to assume both male and female roles.

## CHRISTIAN INTOLERANCE

Since the twelfth century, Christian Europe has had made illicit all sexual relations between two persons of the same gender. In the sixteenth century, Catholic reformations in Europe brought about a growing concern with legislating moral conduct and curbing heresy, an offense traditionally associated with homosexuality.[14]

Saint Thomas Aquinas' *Summa Theologiae* listed the following as lustful vices against nature: masturbation, bestiality, coitus in an unnatural position, and copulation with one's own sex.

In Spain, Gregorio Lopez' *Las Siete Partidas* (1256) decreed, "Women sinning in this way [lesbianism or what he termed "the silent sin" (*peccatum mutum*)] are punished by burning according to the law of their Catholic Majesties, which orders that this crime against nature be punished with such a penalty, especially since the said law is not restricted to men, but refers to any person of whatever condition who has unnatural intercourse."[15]

When the Spanish began colonizing the Philippines in the early sixteenth century, the homophobia that was fast spreading throughout Europe was transplanted. The Spanish repressed and labeled immoral the homosexuality that Filipinos had taken so casually before then.[16]

The conquistadores did to the Philippines what they did in Central America: they tried to destroy the native culture and the old religion. In Colombia, Gonzalo de Oviedo y Valdes boasted of destroying a gold relief depicting "a man mounted upon another in that diabolic and nefarious act of Sodom."[17] In the Philippines, they destroyed the *anitos* (the gods of flora and fauna) and they stripped the transvestite shamans of their authority.

To enable the Spanish empire to strengthen its control of the colony, the Catholic faith was instituted and pagan beliefs were destroyed. The *babaylans* were persecuted not so much because of their homosexuality but, rather, because they represented the old religion. According to John Silva, "The Spanish priests were not only assiduous in writing about 'disgusting sodomites and servants of the devil'; they proceeded to crucify, burn at the stake, and savagely kill large numbers of *babaylans* who were men-lovers."[18]

Male transvestism was especially condemned because it struck at the very heart of European ideas of gender power relations. Male transvestism defied not only the moral but also the social order. Unlike the pre-Spanish tribes which had a more flexible social organization, the new feudal structure introduced by the Spanish had rigid hierarchies: men and women were assigned specific, inflexible roles.

Sodomy was also being practiced during that time. Early Spanish historians claimed that sodomy was introduced to Filipinos by the Chinese, when the Chinese started immigrating as a result of the galleon trade. Archbishop of Manila Miguel de Benavides wrote to the king of Spain, Felipe III, in 1603: "The continual sodomy which the Chinese practice in these islands is so great in extent that they communicate these to the Indians [the term for early Filipinos]."[19]

Although lesbianism was recognized as a sin, it did not receive the attention given to male homosexuality. The waste of male seed was considered a worse offense against the laws of God and nature than the misuse of female seed.[20] Lesbian sex was more tolerated than sex between men partly because of that era's perverse fetish with female chastity. In Agnolo Firenzuola's *Ragionamenti amorosi* (1548), the women argue that it would be better for them to love each other to avoid risking their chastity.

What is also ironic is that the Spanish clergy during that time was known to get enmeshed in not only heterosexual but also homosexual scandals. Friars flaunted openly their native mistresses and altar boys. Even in Spain, as early as the twelfth century, Muslim writers considered the Spanish clergy peculiarly prone to homosexuality.[21] Lesbian sex in monastic orders was also known to exist as early as A.D. 423. The councils of Paris (1212) and Rouen (1214) went to the extent of prohibiting nuns from sleeping together.[22] What is also interesting to note is that effeminate men did not completely abandon their traditional roles as priests.

They became actively involved in Church rituals. Some even went to the extent of entering the priesthood. Effeminate men and even misogamist women found refuge and immunity from persecution behind the hallowed walls of the Almighty Church; they found new freedom to express their "homosexualities" as priests and nuns. Even to this day, when parents observe that a son has pronounced effeminate traits, he is encouraged to enter the priesthood.

We do not have written accounts of homosexual practices among the laity during the Spanish era. However, we do know that passionate but chaste emotional intimacies between men and between women, patterned after classical models of *amicitia,* or friendship, were considered honorable. Pair-bonding was practiced in the all-boy and all-girl schools introduced by the clergy. Once again, we suspect that, just as in European boarding schools, homosexual love and even sex found discreet gratification in these exclusive schools.

To escape social ridicule and to conform with family pressures, many men and women who loved their own sex were forced into marriage and procreation. Still, we do have, in almost all families, the presence of maiden aunts and genteel bachelor uncles.

An historical twist proved fortunate in that when the Napoleonic Code was introduced in Europe in the early 1800s, we were under the rule of Spain, which was part of the empire of Napoleon. Thus the code, which did not fix penalties for sodomy, was adapted as part of our laws. Homosexuality was then decriminalized. In any case, during the last years of Spanish colonial rule, as more and more homosexual men and women infiltrated the clergy and religious orders, the Catholic Church became more tolerant toward gays and lesbians.

## AMERICAN LIBERALISM

Before the last century, there was no concept of the homosexual as a person; homosexuality was simply regarded as a sinful perverse behavior which anyone might choose to indulge in. The word "homosexual" was not introduced into English until 1892. The turn of the century witnessed the "invention of the homosexual," that is, "the new determination that homosexual desire was limited to certain identifiable individuals for whom it was an involuntary sexual orientation of some biological or psychological origin."[23]

Although identification not only of "deviance" but also of the "deviant" may in some ways be liberating and a legitimizing of social relations, it can also be stigmatizing. This was clearly the case in America at the turn of the century, when the seeds both of homosexual liberation and of homophobia were planted. American men and women learned to love each other in both verbal and physical forms, and attempted to locate that expression of love in tradition and social order.[24]

Freed from moralistic Victorian norms, the turn of the century witnessed the sexualization of America and its exploration of its colonial might. America focused its erotic fantasies and greed for conquest on the South Seas. "The noble savages of these exotic lands provided both sexual excitement and cultural difference." Love for the young men of the South Seas became not only a personal affection for the exotic but also a political statement: America stretching its erotic muscles and discovering its imperial and sexual hold over its colonies.[25]

At the end of the nineteenth century, America procured the Philippines as a spoil of its war with Spain. The new colonial power introduced new concepts of sexual liberalism primarily through the U.S. military, which was notorious as a haven for homosexuals.[26]

The relaxing of three centuries of sexual repression opened the proverbial floodgates. The newfound sexual freedom slowly encouraged gay men and lesbian women to express themselves. The introduction of capitalism and the subsequent industrialization of the Philippines pulled men and women from the bondage of the home and land into the marketplace and the factories. Under these conditions, men and women were given the opportunity to seek self-identity, and to discover their sexual and emotional attractions. Slowly, subcultures of gay men and, much later, of lesbian women, grew as homosexuals rediscovered themselves and each other. Gay men were the first to be liberated because they were less bounded than women by social norms; also, since industrialized centers had traditionally been male spaces, gay male life developed significantly faster than the lesbian subculture.

This era witnessed as well the rebirth of the cross-dressers. Understandably, the lower classes were the first to be sexually liberated since they were not as constrained by demands of society as the upper classes, who were expected to exhibit proper decorum in public.

According to oral accounts, lower-class transvestites working as laundry "women" inside the American military bases would service the sexual needs of the GI's. They were not particularly pretty, but the Americans claimed, "We just cover their faces with the flag and fuck their asses." Oral accounts also claim that the Americans introduced fellatio.

Upper-class gay men found their own sexual expression within exlusive schools operating on the buddy and best friend system. Later on, since there were no gay bars then, moneyed gay men began holding clandestine private parties, which turned into orgies.

Just as in America, cross-dressing was being practiced by working-class women for a variety of economic, sexual, and adventure-seeking reasons, and to rebel at the male order. These mannish lesbians drank, smoked, and worked in traditionally macho occupations.[27] On the other hand, girls belonging to the new bourgeoisie discovered the joys of lesbian sex as interns of exclusive schools for girls. They became best friends with other girls their own age, shared secrets, and developed infatuations for an older student or a teacher.

However, society rejected the personhood that homosexual men and women were discovering, and tried to quash the homosexual's struggle for self-identity by creating the stereotypes.

As early as the 1920s, gay men were being portrayed as comic screaming queen characters and lesbian women were ridiculed as mannish, offensive dykes in stage-show vaudevilles. This trend would continue in the movies and, later, on television.[28] What is interesting to note is that cross-dressing was only shown as a physical manifestation of a social deviance; the deeper sexual meaning of the phenomenon, i.e., attraction to the same sex, was never even implied. Cross-dressing (homosexuality itself was not really discussed) was also portrayed as merely a passing fancy—the effeminate hero would turn straight in the end when he found the right woman, or the butch heroine would turn into a princess, once kissed by the handsome hero.

But perhaps the worst stigmatization that homosexuals suffered during this era was the belief that it was "bad luck" for a family to have a homosexual son or daughter. In response, homosexuals strove hard to prove their worth. They excelled in school, in the creative arts, and even in athletic competitions. They made money, sent their siblings to school, and took care of their parents during their old age.

The end of World War II, the end of American occupation, and the beginning of the Republic witnessed the continuing struggle of homosexual men and women to forge their own subculture.

## NEOCOLONIAL MACHO FEUDALISM

Four centuries of white supremacy in the Philippines conceived a people enchained by a neocolonial feudal structure that, even today, dictates sexual prejudices. The deeply ingrained macho feudal structure, introduced by the Spanish and encouraged by the Americans as part of its complicity with the ruling capitalist class, molded the psychology and sexuality of homosexual men and women.

The feudal mode revolves around the myth of the macho. Men assume leadership roles while the women are subservient. Men are expected to be virile, libidinous, and even promiscuous, while women are, like the Virgin Mary, chaste, docile, and servile. The strong are idolized while the weak are held in contempt. Those who dare to contest these feudal roles are ridiculed and treated like outcasts.

Homosexual men are called *bakla,* a condescending term that connotes physical and mental weakness, indecisiveness, frailty, unreliability, impotency, and emasculation. Lesbian women are called by the more innocuous term "tomboy," which carries imagery of boyish young girls who are able to outrun their brothers.

Human sexuality is viewed as phallocentric: the penis is considered necessary in the sexual act. People regard it as normal for women to be attracted to men, and even understandable for men to be attracted to other men, but illogical for women to be attracted to women. Men do not consider lesbian women as a serious threat to their own access to women's sexual favors.

Even homosexual relations are affected by the neocolonial structure. Sexual colonialism has fostered the view of the lower class as sexual trade. These class and gender interactions have played an important role in the rise of male prostitution. Colonial fantasies have also given rise to a fixation with the huge penis and, as a result, a preference for *meztizos* (Eurasians or Amerasians) as well as for white men. According to Doreen Fernandez, "Many of the gay relationships are composed of couples of quite unequal social or intellectual standing. More frequently, one sees the patron-ward model, with one the dispenser of bounty and the other in some form of dependent role, be it social or financial."[29]

## THE MARCOS YEARS

The twenty-year conjugal dictatorship of Ferdinand and Imelda Marcos (1965–1985) created a perverse culture that further reenforced macho feudalism. It was the height of decadence and conspicuous consumption set in the midst of economic deprivation.

As Deocampo has stated, "The Marcos years were characterized by the general complicity of homosexual men and women with the dictatorship. This era was the height of gay sexuality, the emergence of the homosexual subculture, and the insidious rise of prostitution."

While the Stonewall riots gave birth to gay liberation in the U.S., in the Philippines, homosexual men and women were still perpetuating the feudal stereotypes. Gay men portrayed themselves in the media as "screaming queens" who did nothing but gossip, act silly, and lust after men. Even the sexual revolution of the late 1960s did not free homosexuals but only made sure that women were available for the use of men.

To legitimize their existence, homosexual men and women came out with the concept of gender dysporia: The gay man thought of himself as a woman trapped in a man's body while the lesbian woman envisioned herself with a trapped male soul that phallicized her. Thus, homosexuals were considered neither male nor female, but members of a "third sex."

Homosexual men were the first to create their own subculture: fashion and lifestyle, bars, cruising areas, language, and organizations. Transvestism, sex changes, hormonal injections, and silicon implants became the most convenient ways for gay men to assert their own identities.

Female impersonation became popular when a group called the Paper Dolls did the rounds not of only gay bars but of TV shows and private parties. This group was famous for its realistic impersonation of such famous stars as Liza Minnelli, Dionne Warwick, Diana Ross, and Julie Andrews.

Gay men even had their own lingua franca, popularly known as swardspeak. Gay men invented new words and new expressions as a means to communicate discreetly with one another.

Gay organizations were formed during this era. Two of the first gay organizations were Manila 500 and Sining Kayumanggi Royal Family based at Mehan Garden, a park which was transformed into a cruising area. Other gay groups that formed were primarily trade-related (fashion designers and hairdressers), religious, and social. These groups organized fashion shows, May flower festivals where transvestites would spend fortunes for their gowns, and beauty contests.

Gay bars offering diverse forms of entertainment—macho dancing, sex shows, discos, and drag shows—began sprouting in major urban centers. The earliest gay bars were Talipapa, 690, and Coco Banana.

Unfortunately, at the height of the Marcos regime, sex tourism was encouraged by the government as a means to raise the dollars needed to finance the "edifice complex" of Imelda. With the influx of tourists looking for cheap sex, male, female, and child prostitution became rampant. Men, women, and children discovered that by selling their bodies to sex-starved heterosexual men, rich gay men, and pedophiles, they would be able to buy their next meal.

Lesbian women in general were "unobtrusive." They did not scream their identities as gay men did. They did not have their own macho contests or lesbian bars. They did not even have their own organization.

Filipina author Arlene Babst writes: "There is a relieving thought that tomboys are easier to handle than boys, less socially shattering than male homosexuals, less expensive than a pregnant daughter, and easier to live with than whores. The lesbian is saved by default, by the Filipino's tendency to think of the worst and then thank God that, bad as things are, the worst has not yet befallen them."[30]

General tolerance of homosexuals increased during the Marcos regime. Gay men became the court jesters. Imelda herself was said to be very fond of gay men; after all, these gay men came out with entertaining shows and antics that, like an "opium," made society forget the bigger social realities of moral decay, poverty, and corruption.

Families even started thinking of their homosexual son or daughter as good luck, for they contributed to the family income. Gay men and women saved their families from starvation by working as hairdressers, manicurists, fashion designers, peddlers, or even as prostitutes.

However, there were homosexual men and women who dared to confront, question, and defy the status quo. We know of several of our brother and sisters who have gone up to the mountains to wage an armed revolution against the oppressive ruling class. Their battle, however, was against the whole political system and not against the sexual feudalism that still enchained gay men and lesbian women.

There were those who planted the seeds of gay and lesbian liberation. Filmmaker Lino Brocka came out with *Tubog sa Ginto* (*Dipped in Gold*), his first serious gay film which tackled the sensitive issue of male prostitution. Playwrights produced serious works dealing with issues of "coming out," homosexual relationships, and human rights abuses against gay men and lesbian women.

## HUMAN RIGHTS ABUSES

Homosexuality is not illegal in the Philippines. Homosexual men and women are tolerated but not accepted; they are still very much marginalized. The general attitude is patronizing.

Leni Marin, a lesbian Filipina from the Commission on the Status of Women in California, explains, "Homophobia could range from outright bashing saying 'these people are sick and should be shot' to saying 'let's just forgive them because they're human beings, too.' "[31]

Human rights abuses against homosexuals range from fathers who beat up their gay sons, gay bashings, police entrapment, exploitation by prostitutes, inequality in the workplace, theft, and even murder. But when they do happen, people just think of them as isolated cases, believing that "they deserve it because they have been promiscuous."

One can be overtly gay as long as he is in the arts or as long as he practices stereotypical professions like hairdressing or design. No gay man is welcome in traditionally cloistered, macho-dominated business or in military service.

One executive said, "I have been told that homosexuals are easily influenced. So they should not be in security jobs or jobs involving secret or sensitive data. We are also very particular about jobs that entail cash handling." (The executive probably thought that a homosexual person would embezzle company funds to give to his or her lover.)

There are laws which protect homosexuals from discrimination but in a country where justice, if not denied, is often delayed, these laws are never really enforced. There is no systematic oppression of lesbian women and gay men. Thus, the seeming lack of systematic homophobia has resulted in the lack of a systematic homosexual response.

## GAY LIBERATION AND THE FEMINIST MOVEMENT

When Ferdinand Marcos declared martial law in 1972 and imprisoned his political rivals and critics, many politicized homosexuals went into exile to America. There they became involved in the gay and lesbian liberation movement. When Marcos was ousted by the People's Power Revolution in 1986, many of these exiled homosexuals returned with fresh ideas and new concepts of gay and lesbian liberation.

Gay men and lesbians started deconstructing and breaking away from the feudal stereotype imposed upon them by society. Now, it has become acceptable for gay men to be "butch" or for lesbian women to be "feminine." Closet queens and dykes have slowly started to come out in the open. Relationships that are non-feudal and between persons of equal social status have become fashionable.

We are also witnessing the emancipation of women in general. The new woman has gotten involved in the movement to obtain equality in rights, duties, freedom, responsiblities, and employment. The new woman has become a social and a political actor. The rise of the new woman is now helping in the lesbian woman's struggle for self-identity.

Fernandez writes, "Considering the circumstances of Philippine society and the mechanism of acceptance presently existing, gay liberation in the Philippines will come with women's liberation and indeed with the liberation of society. It will come with the throwing off of the shackles of feudal thinking, in which male dominance means female subservience and relegation to nonpersons in charge of child-bearing; and not being male/macho means being somewhat less of a person, remembered mainly for a sexual orientation and not for personhood."[32]

## THE SPECTER OF AIDS

The late 1980s created a new monster that is stalking the homosexual community: AIDS. Homosexual transmission officially makes up only 10 percent of the known HIV cases in the country but 49 percent of the known clinical AIDS cases are gay men. No extensive HIV testing has been done on gay men (less than 7 percent of the total of 165,514 HIV tests already done in the country). Gay men are being diagnosed only when they are confined in hospitals with AIDS symptoms.

The spread of AIDS among homosexual men is mainly due to ignorance. Many still believe that AIDS is transmissible through donating blood, sharing utensils, casual contact, mosquito bites, public toilets and swimming pools. The majority practice unprotected anal sex; few have even tried using condoms.[33]

In the event of a major epidemic in the gay community, there is a great possibility that gay men will become scapegoats of society, with the result that whatever progress has been made toward gay liberation will certainly be set back, if not undone completely.

## CONCLUSION

The 1990s will continue to witness the emergence of politicized homosexual men and women in the Philippines. Slowly, the individual and fragmented efforts of gay men and lesbian women are being collectivized. Solidarity of gays and lesbians will catalyze the centuries of struggle for social acceptance and political power.

Plans are even under way for a Gay Pride week, which will feature an international lesbian and gay film festival, a theater festival, mardi gras, and a symposium. Soon there will be a gay press. Gay men are even now banding together to battle the spread of AIDS in the Philippines. Just as in the West, gay men here are poised to be at the forefront of the AIDS activist movement.

Gay and lesbian activism is, in practical terms, just starting. But society can no longer deny the homosexual community's right to be heard. Gay men and lesbian women will assert their personhoods. They will fight and eventually win their historic rights as leaders and as healers.*

## NOTES

1. Metropolitan Community Church Manila was founded in June 1991. It is a member of the Universal Fellowship of Metropolitan Community Churches, a Christian denomination with a predominantly lesbian and gay ministry founded in Los Angeles in 1968.

2. The Reachout AIDS Education Foundation is composed primarily of gay and lesbian artists, who are committed to using arts and culture in stopping the spread of AIDS in the Philippines.

3. Jomar Fleras, *Poisoned Blood* (June 1991).

4. Interview with Nick Deocampo, October 1991.

5. Robert Padgug, "Sexual Matter: Rethinking Sexuality in History," *Hidden from History: Reclaiming the Gay and Lesbian Past* (Meridian Books, 1990), pp. 55, 58.

6. Juan de Plasencia O.S.F., "Customs of the Tagalogs" (1589).

7. Justus M. van der Kroef, "Transvestism and the Religious Hermaphrodite in Indonesia," *Journal of East Asiatic Studies* 3, no. 8 (April 1954): 257-58.

8. Juan Francisco de San Antonio, "The Native People and their Customs" (1738).

9. The hypothesis that the ancient Philippines were once a part of the Sri Vijayan empire (A.D. 670) was formulated by Prof. Otley Beyer of the University of the Philippines in 1921.

10. Doreen Fernandez, "The Gay," in *Being Filipino* (GCF Books, 1981), p. 259.

11. Ibid., p. 263.

12. Padgug, "Sexual Matter."

13. Dede Oetomo and Bruce Emond, "Homosexuality in Indonesia," unpublished paper.

14. Arlo Karlen, "The Homosexual Heresy," *Chaucer Review* 6, no. 1 (1971): 44-63.

15. Chronicle found in "Las siete partidas del sabio rey Don Alfonso el Nono, nuevamente glosadas por el licenciado Gregorio Lopez" (Salamanca 1829-31; reprint of 1565 ed.), 3: 178.

16. de Plasencia, "Customs of the Tagalogs."

17. Peter Webb, *The Erotic Arts* (Boston: New York Graphic Society, 1975), pp. 103-136.

18. John Silva, *A Photograph of a Gay Ancestor* (Lavender Godzilla).

19. Miguel de Benavides, "Letters from Benavides to Felipe III," in Blair and Robertson, op. cit. 12. pp. 101-126. The traditional belief that sodomy was introduced by the Chinese is reflected in the local English term "Chinese kick" for anal intercourse. (Donn V. Hart, "Homosexuality and Transvestism in the Philippines: The Cebuano Filipino Bayot and Lakin-on," *Behavior Science Note* [1968]: 231). This is not surprising since in Chinese Buddhism, the sublimely gentle Bodhisattva is represented as a hermaphrodite god. Documented homosexuality was being practiced in Imperial China as early as the third century B.C. in the "Chronicles of Warring States" (Vivien W. Ng, "Homosexuality and the State in Late Imperial China," in *Hidden From History*).

---

*Jomar Fleras has produced a documentary film based on this essay.

20. Judith C. Brown, "Lesbian Sexuality in Medieval and Early Modern Europe," *Hidden from History*, p. 71.

21. John Boswell, *Christianity, Social Tolerance and Homosexuality: Gay People in Western Europe from the Beginning of the Christian Era to the Fourteenth Century* (Chicago: University of Chicago Press, 1980).

22. de Benavides, "Letters from Benavides to Felipe III," in *Hidden from History*, p. 69.

23. George Chauncey, Jr., "Christian Brotherhood or Sexual Perversion? Homosexual Identities and the Construction of Sexual Boundaries in the World War I Era," in *Hidden from History*, p. 312.

24. Robert K. Martin, "Knights-Errant and Gothic Seducers," in *Hidden from History*, p. 170.

25. Ibid., p. 171.

26. A notorious lesbian from San Francisco, called Babe Bean, who disguised herself as Jack Garland, probably even made it to the Philippines as a lieutenant during the Spanish-American war (San Francisco Gay History Project, in *Hidden from History*, p. 191).

27. Esther Newton, "The Mythic Mannish Lesbian," in *Hidden from History*, p. 282.

28. Dolphy, a Filipino heterosexual comedian, came out in a series of "gay" films titled *Facifica Falayfay* and *Fefita Fofonggay*.

29. Fernandez, "The Gay," in *Being Filipino*.

30. Arlene Babst, "The Lesbian," in *Being Filipino*, p. 94.

31. Lani T. Montreal, "Pars & Mars," *Sunday Inquirer Magazine*, November 25, 1990, p. 17.

32. Fernandez, "The Gay," in *Being Filipino*, p. 90.

33. These findings are based on figures released by the National AIDS Prevention and Control Program dated October 1991. A Knowledge-Attitudes-Practices survey among gay men was done in 1989 by the Department of Health in collaboration with AIDSCOM.

# 7

# Lesbian Activism in Argentina: A Recent but Very Powerful Phenomenon

## Ilse Fuskóva-Kornreich and Dafna Argov

*This is a personal account by two women. Ilse, 62, has been a lesbian since 1985 after being married for thirty years. She is the mother of three children with whom, as with her husband, she maintains a warm relationship. Her main interest in lesbian feminist activism, which she regards as "the liberation of women's energy from 5,000 years' imprisonment under patriarchy." The second author is Dafna, 30, who chose lesbian activism in Argentina as the subject of her social anthropology degree thesis at the National University of Buenos Aires.*

### DAFNA

Ilse was asked by ILGA (the International Lesbian and Gay Association) to contribute to this book, and we got to know each other shortly after that. A feminist friend had given me her phone number. I spoke to her and asked if I could interview her for my research, which was still in its very early stages. We met twice. The first time, I asked her a series of questions and noted down her answers. The second time, I brought her the transcript of what she had said at our previous meeting.

In the transcript, Ilse discovered significant facts from her past, which she had recounted to me herself, but which had never before taken on such a concrete existence. Since Ilse felt comfortable with this method of working, she asked me to help her draft this article.

That's why most of it is a first-person account of Ilse's own experiences in relation to activism—experiences that we reconstructed together using the method described.

The personal history told by each activist or group of activists sheds light on the history of the social movement under study. There is no place for the kind of individualism that would seek to shift reality away from nonhierarchical forms of interpersonal experience. So Ilse's story represents one facet of lesbian activism in Argentina.

In this country, after a long period of dictatorship (1976–1983) in which any kind of activism was out of the question, an awareness is slowly developing of the need to be politically active around the issues of being a woman and sexual choice. In the report that follows, Ilse identifies 1985 as the crucial year in which the desire of gay women to come together and do something as Argentinian lesbian feminists began to be felt. It was that same year that the Comunidad Homosexual Argentina (CHA) was created; both men and women have been active in CHA since its inception.

So we see here the two major social movements which function as reference points for Argentinian lesbians: the feminist movement on the one hand and the human rights movement on the other. Some lesbians commit themselves more to one movement than the other, but all are working to bring about social change.

Another important date in the growth of lesbian activism in our country comes, in my opinion, in 1990, when the Fifth Latin American and Caribbean Feminist Gathering (V Encuentro Feminista Latinoamericano y del Caribe) was held here in Argentina. Ilse will speak about the period from 1985 to 1990.

At the time when the gathering took place, there were two organized forms of lesbian activism in Buenos Aires: (1) the publication *Cuaderno de Existencia Lesbiana* (*Notebook of Lesbian Existence*), founded in 1987 (to be discussed below), and (2) the lesbian feminist group called "Las Lunas y las Otras" ("The Moons and the Others"). This group was formed some five months before the gathering, and continues in operation to this day with about ten members.

Another attempt at lesbian organization before 1990 was GAL (Grupo Autogestivo de Lesbianas = Self-Managed Lesbians' Group), an open group run on premises loaned by a feminist organization. However, tensions within the group itself and with the organization led to the group's dissolution.

So at the time of the Fifth Gathering, lesbian activism in our country was somewhat "dormant." But such was the impact of the gathering that *Cuaderno de Existencia Lesbiana* and "Las Lunas y las Otras" were joined afterwards by some interesting new initiatives. On the one hand, the "Grupo de Reflexión de Lesbianas" (Lesbian Discussion Group) was formed, a very strong feminist group of some ten members which is still in existence today. On the other hand, the women who were active in CHA created a space in which specifically to address lesbian issues. It is fair to say that between then and now, the role of women within the organization has greatly increased in importance.

Indeed, my own research work, which represents an act of political commitment to lesbians, was the result of the impact made on me personally by the Fifth Gathering.

Finally, I would like to say that we live in a country in which people still find it very difficult to accept anything that is different. There are sections of society in Argentina which are strongly opposed to homosexuality and women's liberation. After experiencing repressive authoritarianism of the kind that used to exist here, many women are afraid to be known publicly as lesbians. Many stages need to be worked through before they can come out. There are very few Argentinian lesbians who dare appear in the media. Ilse is one of them. So, although we know that social movements function through the combined action of an infinite number of participants, all active and indispensable but invisible, we have to recognize the courage of those who are able to "be up-front" for the rest.


## ILSE

I've taken part in feminist discussion and action groups since 1981, but the first time we had the opportunity of thinking of ourselves as lesbians was after the Third Latin American and Caribbean Feminist Gathering (III Encuentro Feminista Latinoamericano y del Caribe), held in Bertioga, Brazil, in 1985.

After the gathering, Empar Pineda, a Spanish lesbian feminist, came to Buenos Aires to give a couple of talks that turned out to be a real "bombshell." People were virtually hanging from the light fittings; we just couldn't pack more in. She gave us ideological material, in particular Adrienne Rich's pamphlet "Compulsory Heterosexuality and Lesbian Existence," which the Spanish women had translated, and material on the international Round Table on the Feminist Movement and Lesbianism (Mesa Redonda Internacional sobre Movimiento Feminista y Lesbianismo), which they had organized in Madrid in June 1984.

It was the first time that we had been able to conceive of ourselves from a standpoint other than that of "official" sexuality, and it gave us great strength and courage. The following year, we set up a study group here in Buenos Aires on lesbianism. There were about eight to ten women in the group. Among other things we worked on Adrienne Rich's essay. Working with this text was decisive for us.

In November 1986, after a year of weekly study meetings, Adriana Carrasco, who was 26, and I organized the first discussion workshops on lesbianism in Buenos Aires. These were held as part of the sessions of ATEM (Asociación de Trabajo y Estudio de la Mujer – Association for Work and Study on Women), an independent feminist association formed in 1981. This group was set up by about ten women, some heterosexual and some lesbian. The commitment of our heterosexual sisters to feminism is such as to lead them to define themselves as political lesbians. The implication is that lesbianism goes far beyond sexual practice. It is a challenge to the patriarchal prohibition that prevents us from having deep and positive relationships between women.

Some eighteen women of all ages, young and old, attended, and they were quite shy and fearful when they arrived. At the start of the workshop, a form was circulated with thirteen questions which each woman was requested to answer anonymously in writing. These were questions like: what attracts you to a woman? If you have had sex with women, have you spoken about it to your friends? Participants were asked to put the forms in a box, then each woman was asked to pick a form at random and read the answers aloud. The idea was to respect anonymity, making allowance for the inhibitions of those present. Nevertheless, when the first form was read, the author said, "I wrote that." Coque's courage to "be up-front" spread to the others and, as the remaining replies were read, the women acknowledged authorship of their "confessions." This generated such excitement and interest that the time flew by without our realizing it. One thing that happened, which took on anecdotal status, was when one of the Madres de Plaza de Mayo who was there said: "Girls, I have to go or my husband is going to lose me!"

After that workshop, we felt the need to make more widely known the thinking and the consciousness raising that had been born there. Adriana and I had the idea of bringing out a publication which, without any disagreement or doubt, we decided to call *Cuaderno de Existencia Lesbiana* (*Notebook of Lesbian Existence*). The answers given in the workshop were so moving in their candor that we wanted to include some of them in the first issue. In addition, we published the life stories of six lesbians.

On International Women's Day 1987, Adriana and I went to the meeting held in the Plaza Congreso with the first issue of our publication. When we reached the square where the women had gathered and started selling our magazine, some feminists and other women in political parties reacted with fear. "You can't sell this material," they said, "it will 'burn' (compromise) us all." But the members of ATEM supported us and invited the other women to discuss the subject. It was a short and very animated discussion. In the end, it was recognized that Adriana and I, working actively in the feminist movement, had the right to raise the specific issue of lesbianism. In two hours we had sold all fifty of the copies we had produced and financed ourselves. The demand was so great that we had to go back and photocopy another hundred, which were sold in the next few days.

On International Women's Day 1988, there were eight of us who "came out" for the first time with a large pink banner that read "Notebook of Lesbian Existence." There we stood underneath it, eight women, each with a flower on her lapel and a headband saying "passionately lesbian." We also brought our magazine, which by that time had already reached Issue 4.

On that march, we were the women most photographed by reporters, but none of the photos was published. At that time (1988), positive images of lesbians were still nowhere to be seen. We appeared either in the gutter press or nowhere at all. Any photo showing women happy and proud to be lesbians was intolerable to the system.

Something I regard as tremendously important is the fact that since 1987, at all the National Women's Gatherings (Encuentros Nacionales de Mujeres), which are held in a different province each year, workshops on lesbianism are unavoidable.

Now, I would like to say a little bit about lesbianism in the media. In September 1990, after having spent five months in San Francisco, I was invited to take part in a midday TV program with a large viewing audience. It was called "A cara limpia" ("With an Open Face") and hosted by Fernando Bravo. The subject was homosexuality, and I was to speak about lesbianism. But, full of the lively joy and pride of the San Francisco lesbians, I decided to talk not about "lesbianism" but about "me, a lesbian." After the program, the reaction of people in the street was positive. Some came up to me to thank me for appearing publicly as a lesbian.

The fact that I am able to appear publicly as a proud lesbian is due in part to a five months' stay in Berlin in 1987 and my contacts with German lesbians, and in part to the period I spent in San Francisco. There were two things that impressed me with the women I met in Germany and the United States: their personal pride in being lesbian and the social space they have secured for themselves. These realities boosted my energy; I didn't have the least doubt that I wanted to take part in this struggle, which for me consist in liberating the female energy imprisoned during 5,000 years of patriarchy.

Two months later, I and a friend from the Frente Safico (Sapphic Front, formed for a short time before the Fifth Latin American and Caribbean Feminist Gathering) were invited to take part in a rather provocative radio program, "Rock and Pop," which was broadcast at midnight and listened to mostly by young people. Jorge Lanata, a well-known Argentinian journalist, interviewed us for an hour, covering both personal and activist topics.

In October 1991, I was invited onto the program with the highest rating for its time slot, "Almorzando con Mirta Legrand" (Lunch with Mirta Legrand"). Legrand is a film star who now enjoys a prominent role as a social communicator. The panel was to talk about homosexuality, and consisted of two sexologists, the President of CHA, and myself, a lesbian activist. The program lasts an hour and a half, and is seen in Buenos Aires and the other provinces as well as the nearby Republic of Uruguay.

During the program the ratings went up substantially. The host said she was going to have it broadcast again. But that didn't happen, because the next day the bishop of the province of San Luis published a press release saying the harm done by the program to Argentine society was so great that in no way could it be reshown.

For a full week all the media were talking about the program and the battle between Ms. Legrand and the Catholic Church. In the end she gave in, and there was no more talk of rebroadcasting it.

During the show, however, I gave out our postbox number for the readers of *Cuaderno de Existencia Lesbiana.* As a result, we started to receive large numbers of letters. In some of them, women spoke of their isolation and their surprise on discovering that another woman could feel proud to be a lesbian.

For months afterward, people would recognize me and come up to me in the supermarket, in cafes, or on the street to thank me for my bravery. I only had three abusive phone calls; in every case they were older women, who called me "a tramp" ("atorranta") and "shameless" ("desvergonzada").

Because of the number of letters we received and their very moving tone, one of my friends suggested we organize a meeting with all the women who had written asking for help. A feminist organization called "Taller Permanente de la Mujer" ("Ongoing Women's Workshop") lent us the space to put this into effect. The first meeting was attended by about forty women, some of them old friends, some new. We introduced ourselves and recounted briefly our personal histories. It was very moving. One woman said she had waited thirty years for something like this to take place. The meeting lasted from six in the afternoon to ten in the evening, and then carried on until midnight in the bar around the corner. It was decided that we would meet again in the same place and at the same time every next-to-last Saturday of the month.

At that first meeting we also sketched out a plan to publish an announcement in a large-circulation daily newspaper, reading roughly as follows: "The lesbians of Buenos Aires greet the lesbians of the whole country and wish them a very happy Christmas." It would be a good way of signaling our visibility. It remains to be seen which newspaper will accept or dare to publish that kind of announcement.

In the written media, the subject of lesbianism used to appear only in the gutter press. But since the Fifth Latin American and Caribbean Feminist Gathering, which took place in Argentina with a massive and pugnacious lesbian presence, the subject was soon covered in magazines regarded as progressive. For example, in *El Porteño,* in spite of the photographs, which I thought were repulsive, the groups of lesbians interviewed came across as thinking people with a challenging ideology.

Our publication, *Cuaderno de Existencia Lesbiana,* continues to be distributed in the Women's Movement, and has now reached Issue 12, thanks to the constant help and contributions of six lesbians.


ILSE AND DAFNA


Having worked today for twelve consecutive hours to finish this work in one go, we end this report with the hope that we have succeeded in giving you some idea of the situation of lesbianism in Argentina.

# 8

# The Danish Partnership Law: Political Decision Making in Denmark and the National Danish Organization for Gays and Lesbians

## Bent Hansen and Henning Jørgensen

### INTRODUCTION

This article will concentrate on the influence the organized gay and lesbian movement has had on the adoption of the law on registered partnership in Denmark, and the kind of political setting in which it has been possible to carry through such a law.

We shall discuss the requirements which had, of necessity, to be satisfied before the law could be passed and also the public debate which took place, and is still taking place, on both marriage and the institution of partnership. There will be a brief description of the political and parliamentary system in Denmark as well as of the general social conditions. The political importance of the partnership legislation on the national and international level will be described. Finally, the working methods of the National Danish Organization for Gays and Lesbians (LBL) in the current Danish political atmosphere will be discussed.

## OUTLINE OF THE DANISH POLITICAL SYSTEM

Officially, Denmark upholds human rights, and respects the right of citizens to support various ideologies and to organize themselves in political parties and interest groups. But even in Denmark there is, in many cases, a gulf between the words of the constitution and their implementation. Like all marginal groups in society, gay men and lesbians know that rights are not equally distributed and that it is, therefore, necessary to struggle for them. But in most major matters, there is a broad consensus in Denmark or—put more negatively—perhaps there is a simple acceptance of things as they are. One of the most important reasons for this support for the basic lines of the Danish political system is undoubtedly one's upbringing in the system, and the faith in that system, which is solidified in the home, in schools, in the church, and through the mass media. No less in the many popular voluntary organizations, of which Denmark has so many, have the members experienced democracy and pragmatic compromise in practice. These organizations are an inseparable part of Danish democracy.

The church has never adopted a position of opposition to democracy and pluralism. The Danish state church is itself democratic, with popularly elected parish councils and characterized by a popular tradition of freedom which has, historically, given great support to democracy and pluralism. "Human being first and then a Christian," as Nikolai Grundtvig, perhaps the most influential popular Christian thinker in nineteenth-century Denmark, expressed it.

Danish culture is built on a solid humanist foundation, which provides considerable support for tolerance. As conscious humanists, Danes have to accept, to a greater or lesser degree, other ways of life. It would be difficult for the Danish ideological and historical tradition of Christian humanism to adopt a completely hostile attitude to homosexuality—at least in the long run, because there will always be an element of benevolence and tolerance, perhaps of indulgence. If Danes were to deny gays and lesbians a life on their own conditions, it would require a cutting of the ideological lifeline. This is not the image which Danes wish to have of themselves.

Political decision making in Denmark is far from being just a question of the relationship between citizens and parliament. Civil servants in the ministries and elsewhere have a considerable influence on public opinion; members of Parliament are influenced not only by the voters, but also by interest groups such as LBL and by the mass media. It is a complicated network, with various forms of interaction between the parties involved: government, civil service, parliament, the courts, interest groups, mass media, political parties, conflicting interests, the electorate, and groupings within the electorate.

With the constantly growing role in the decision-making process played by the interest groups and the decreasing role played by ideologies (and, therefore, political parties), the Danish political system increasingly becomes one concerned with single issues. The organizations that succeed in raising and justifying an issue in the media, in presenting it clearly to the public and politicians, have a relatively good chance of getting their views accepted.

## THE NATIONAL DANISH ORGANIZATION FOR GAYS AND LESBIANS (LBL)

LBL was founded in 1948 with great public interest, and also amid much prejudice and victimization. However, LBL achieved a considerable membership from the start, with local branches being set up throughout the country. Since then, developments have had their ups and downs: an absolute low point was reached in the 1950s' atmosphere of "McCarthyism," with victimization and denigration of all dissenters.

The major political goal of LBL is, and always has been, to work for equality of social status and rights—neither more nor less—for gays and lesbians. It is now a national organization with local branches at nine locations in Denmark. LBL has long since achieved social acceptance as the interest organization of Danish gays and lesbians.

While LBL is much more than this, we concentrate in this article on that aspect of the organization's functions which makes it an interest organization in Danish society, and the possibilities the organization has, as an idealistic, principled, and outgoing group, in the Danish political system.

## MARRIAGE AND PARTNERSHIP

### Some General Features

The Marriage Act and a whole series of other laws determine the meaning of marriage. As long as the couple remain together, the legal effects of the Marriage Act are few. The main principle is that the married couple are regarded as independent individuals, each of whom has rights over his/her own property and income, and that neither of them is responsible for obligations entered into by the other. They have, however, mutual maintenance obligations—that is to say, no matter who the breadwinner is, there exists equality between man and woman. But there is an exception to this equality, in that the woman, to a certain extent, may purchase everyday necessities at the expense of the man, although he may not act in a similar way. In homosexual circles, this rule has been used as an important argument against marriage, since it is seen as discriminating against the woman and making her dependent on the man.

Apart from the Marriage Act itself, the legal effects of marriage are felt chiefly in the areas of social services, housing, inheritance, and the administration of estates.

Since the Second World War, there has been a change in sexual roles, particularly on account of the much improved methods of birth control, but also because large numbers of women have entered the labor market. While puberty occurs at an increasingly early age, more young people receive a longer education, thus postponing the time given to full-time parenting and careers. Both the number of unmarried mothers and the divorce rate increased in the 1970s. In direct consequence of the arrival of the Pill, the number of births has fallen since the end of the 1960s.

The institution of the family changed in step with the fact that the welfare state took over a number of responsibilities, which has directly affected both child-rearing and the satisfaction of material needs. Nevertheless, the nuclear family remains the major social unit.

Denmark is a country with one of the largest percentages of women at work; at the same time, it has many day care centers to look after children and young people. This, together with the mechanization of housework, improved birth control, and an expanding service sector, explains why so much has happened in family life, in so short a time, since the mid-1960s. It is, perhaps, not accidental that Denmark was the first country to introduce partnership. It is important, though, to distinguish between changing relationships between the sexes and the willingness to try more unconventional forms of cohabitation, and the majority pattern of family life with its traditional sexual roles. However, much has actually happened in the general population regarding changing sexual roles. The experiments with forms of cohabitation made perhaps a little more headway among homosexuals in the 1970s than among heterosexuals. In any case, there was a strong ideology connected with the new ways of living.

Collective living, communes, and group families were attempts to break with the two-person nuclear family and traditional patriarchal supremacy. The media were interested in the new lifestyles, thus possibly exaggerating their importance. They did not, in many cases, lead the great majority into new family forms or ways of living. But these new lifestyles did raise the question of whether the nuclear family was the only correct form.

### A Proposed Law to Establish Forms of Cohabitation

In 1968, the Socialist People's party (SF), seeking to provide for the new forms of cohabitation, presented a bill to revise the Marriage Act. The basis of the proposal was that people arranged their lives in many different ways, many of which were far removed from the traditional pattern of the nuclear family; for example, group families or partnerships between gays or lesbians. It was not the task of the legislators to prescribe what was right, but rather to protect the weak.

Although the bill was not adopted, in a typically Danish consensus fashion, a committee was appointed to look into the broader consequences of, and the ideas behind, the SF proposal.

In 1973, to the great regret of LBL, the committee rejected the idea of marriage for gays and lesbians, because it would mean a breach with the traditional view of marriage and could have an unfortunate effect on the evaluations in other countries of the validity of Danish marriages. However, willingness was shown to consider the amending of certain relevant laws at a later date. This willingness did not achieve practical expression until 1980; during the 1970s, however, LBL had changed its position on marriage. In 1976, LBL reported that the interest in a heterosexual-type marriage was no longer present among gays and lesbians. In 1978, at a meeting with the chairman of the committee on marriage, LBL introduced instead the concept of a "partnership" having certain legal effects and including "public registration of . . . lasting cohabitation," i.e., a parallel to marriage.

The committee report, "Cohabitation without Marriage," published in 1980, revealed that the committee did not wish to create a framework of cohabitation for gays and lesbians through registration, but wished exclusively to solve isolated legal problems concerning cohabitation.

### The Discussion within LBL of Marriage and Partnership

Since the end of the 1960s, under the influence of developments in the rest of society, there has occurred an escalation of LBL activity in connection with the cohabitation problems of gays and lesbians. Internally, study groups were set up and seminars were held. Externally, attempts were made by various means to influence the attitude of the committee on marriage. The question of cohabitation became a permanent part of the internal discussion, as well as of the external activities of LBL.

About 1970, three points were laid down as a basis for approaches to the authorities, and were discussed with politicians and the then Minister of Justice: (1) equality with heterosexuals (i.e., marriage or the complete abolition of marriage); (2) a special framework of cohabitation giving the same legal rights as heterosexuals enjoyed; and, finally, (3) certain of the legal effects of marriage to be made to apply to the cohabitation of gays and lesbians.

The third point was raised on ideological grounds. In order to avoid the mutual maintenance obligations and to treat partners as independent individuals, one could not just demand "all" the legal effects of marriage. But, on the other hand, it involved a somewhat random list of demands concerning the legal effects.

These three points, in various ideological guises and with varying priorities, depending on developments in the homosexual community during the 1970s, became in reality the basis for LBL's policy on cohabitation until 1981, when the partnership proposal was adopted by the appropriate bodies in LBL.

During the 1970s, attempts were made on various occasions to influence various ministries and municipalities on minor problems. In several cases, it was not until politicians, civil servants, the media, and others had gotten involved that LBL's policy began to have an impact on the authorities. This emphasizes how, as an interest organization, LBL had to call upon a broad range of decision makers and put further pressure on them, through a public discussion about "discrimination" and "equality," in order to have its opinions "justified" and carried through. The combination of politicians and the press proved especially effective.

The ideological discussion in gay and lesbian circles, contributing to LBL's change of view in the 1970s, is still going on in the 1990s, although the discussion has, of course, somewhat changed its character with time.

"Family indoctrination" was an often-used expression. The priority given by society to the nuclear family involved an attitude among heterosexuals, the essence of which was a contempt for gays and lesbians, while gays and lesbians themselves felt unworthy and unsure about their own emotions.

On the other hand, gays and lesbians had a unique possibility to work for a disintegration and an undermining of the current patriarchal structure. There was no established method for the creation of social relationships and love affairs by gays and lesbians. If they wished to live a decent life and not be indifferent to the conditions which society offered, they had to stand together and thereby construct social relationships on their own conditions and maintain their right to do this even in the face of societal disapproval. Gays and lesbians had a duty to create an alternative to the traditional nuclear family.

There were also discussions about the extent to which the church should be involved in the marriage ceremony, in the case that "marriage" or partnership should be adopted. This discussion, however, was only sporadic.

Arguments made against legally recognized gay partnerships during the mid-1970s were worded in a more homophobic and chauvinist manner than they probably would be today. They had no great effect among the broad membership of LBL, or among the nonorganized gays and lesbians, although they probably did affect members of the new political organizations in gay and lesbian circles of the 1970s. However, the effect on public opinion overall was not especially striking.

The debate for and against official partnership or marriage for gays and lesbians was thus carried on in a relatively limited circle both within and outside LBL, while most gays were interested merely in obtaining recognition from society and in having their practical, legal, and economic problems of cohabitation solved. It was this majority attitude that made itself felt in the LBL proposal for partnership in 1981. The continuing ideologically based opposition was met by the argument, among others, that entry into a legal partnership was voluntary and that one could simply abstain from it, if one was against it.

## The Partnership Proposal

In light of the fact that the committee on marriage had made it known in 1980 that it would not propose a comprehensive framework of cohabitation for gays and lesbians but merely patch up individual laws, LBL decided to frame its own proposal for a partnership law. A committee prepared a carefully worded proposal which was adopted by the appropriate LBL organs in 1981.

During its detailed preparation of the proposal, LBL realized that marriage in Denmark has an effect on more than one hundred different laws. This discovery gave rise to a wish for thorough preparatory work to be done by a commission of experts. The purpose of the proposal was to regulate as many as possible of the legal and economic problems which could arise for gays and lesbians living as couples. On most points, the proposal involved the same legal effects as did marriage, although LBL did not attempt to deny heterosexuals their monopoly on marriage. In spite of criticism of certain aspects of the legal effects of marriage, LBL considered these effects overall to be so sensible that they should be included in its own proposal for partnership.

In respect of some of the legal effects of marriage, LBL adopted its own special position. The purpose of this was to make clear that it was not marriage that was being demanded, the committee on marriage having made it clear in 1980 that it would not accept a "second-class marriage" or a relationship that resembled marriage. At the same time, LBL could calm the fears of the Christians, who thought of marriage exclusively as a relationship between a man and a woman.

However, no one doubted that, if and when the proposal became a reality, LBL would have to accept some compromises. But at the time, the wording of the proposal satisfied all concerned. Giving, as it did, a clear view of the problems and providing models for their solution, the proposal was an expression of a pragmatic balancing act between friends and enemies, internal and external. Principally because of this, the proposal, with strong backing from LBL members, could become the object of serious discussion with the political decision makers. The proposal would determine the form of the debate on cohabitation for gays and lesbians in the years ahead, both among politicians and in the press.

Nothing, however, happened at once; there were to be two years of pressure, lobbying, and public meetings before LBL succeeded in persuading the Danish parliament to set up a "Commission to Elucidate the Social Circumstances of Homosexuals." The proposal to set up the commission was prepared in close collaboration between LBL and representatives of the political parties which together had a majority in Parliament.

## THE COMMISSION TO ELUCIDATE THE SOCIAL CIRCUMSTANCES OF HOMOSEXUALS IN DENMARK

The proposal was approved by Parliament in May 1984; but as the Minister of Justice was in no hurry to appoint the members of a commission which he regarded as unwelcome, it was not set up until the end of November 1984. LBL had two representatives in the commission. The commission's mandate was prepared in close collaboration between LBL and the parliamentary proposers; it was, however, broader than the government and civil servants wished, and therefore broader than what they would accept. The minister refused to grant sufficient funds for the carrying out of the proposed—and, even today, still necessary—cultural and social investigations mentioned in the commission's mandate. Indeed, it was not until the commission began its work that Parliament even dared to use the words "gays and lesbians" instead of "homosexuals." Parliament worded the commission's mandate as follows:

> Recognizing that homosexuals ought to have the possibility of living in accordance with their identity and of arranging their lives in society thereafter, and recognizing that adequate possibilities of doing this are not present, the commission shall collect and present available scientific documentation on homosexuality and the homosexual way of life as well as institute investigations to elucidate the legal, social, and cultural circumstances of homosexuals.
>
> In this connection, the commission shall propose measures aimed at removing the existing discrimination within all sectors of society and at improving the situation of homosexuals, including proposals making provision for permanent forms of cohabitation.

It was considered desirable that, parallel with the commission's work, there should be a public debate on gays and lesbians and on the conditions governing their lives. It was thought that the commission should help to further and arrange such a debate. In this, however, it only succeeded to a limited extent by the publication of interim reports.

In an international context, it might seem affected to be disappointed over not seeing the fulfillment of all one's wishes as an interest organization for gays and lesbians. But this is not the main point. It is of much greater interest to assess why we were not successful. This was because the then Minister of Justice was an old political hand, who knew what action to take when faced with a decision with which he disagreed.

He had most likely read the following, written about 1970 by a member of his own party who was Minister of Finance and who, after his departure from office, wrote a somewhat bitter but instructive book about his experience in government, from which we offer the following excerpts:

> . . . [T]his is the greatest risk in setting up a commission. You run the risk that it will arrive at unwanted conclusions. But in composing the commission, the wise minister can almost always . . . protect himself against this risk.
>
> If it is intended that the commission should shelve a matter, a prominent person known to be lacking in efficiency and who is a pedant should be appointed as chairman. He should also be so submissive and loyal to his minister that it will not occur to him to conclude the commission's work before the minister . . . has given the go-ahead. . . . [A] certain presenility is excellent. . . . But every commission has to have a secretary. . . . It is therefore a question of finding

a clever young civil servant who is known for the fact that paper sticks to his hands like adhesive tape. . . . The minister must ensure that the secretary is not granted leave of absence from his normal work [so that he does not have time to attend to his work as commission secretary]. When the minister has settled the matter of the chairman and the secretary . . . he shall make sure that the commission is incapable of coming to an agreement.

There are other political machinations that might be brought to bear on the composition of a commission, including giving places to opposing political parties and then leaving it to them to make a mess of it all. The Minister of Justice used all these tactics to some extent in composing the commission, at the same time as he secured a majority on the commission through a sufficient number of civil servants who were bound to him by their loyalty. Most of the commission's decisions were thus minority decisions; unfortunately for the minister, they were approved by a majority in Parliament. But it is obvious that it made great demands on LBL's lobbying activities.

In spite of the minister's dislike of the commission and his tactical dodges in the appointment of members, the interim reports on gay and lesbian culture published by the commission succeeded in starting an internal debate in gay and lesbian circles, although the effect on public opinion was not great.

After some discussion, a gay researcher, Henning Bech, and a lesbian researcher, Karin Lützen, were appointed. They produced a report reviewing a number of major problems and conclusions from the scholarly literature on homosexuality as well as gay and lesbian lifestyles. In addition, the two researchers made proposals for further work and investigations, which the commission was unfortunately unable or unwilling to follow up.

The two researchers also conducted in-depth interviews with twenty gay men and twenty-five lesbians, as the commission's contribution to a description of the lifestyle and culture of gays and lesbians in Danish society today. The final report includes a chapter intended to give a broad impression of the circumstances of gays and lesbians in modern Denmark. There is an appendix on the main trends in the culture and organization of Danish gays and lesbians.

While the commission was sitting, it had direct influence on some legislative initiatives through its interim juridical reports. For example, the anti-discrimination legislation was extended to include a prohibition against discrimination on grounds of "sexual orientation" as well as sex, race, and religion.

Finally, the commission discussed the LBL proposal of a law on "registered partnership for two persons of the same sex." Although a majority of the commission (including its chairman) rejected the proposal, the LBL successfully lobbied a parliamentary majority to vote for it. The LBL succeeded as well in breaking the hold of the parties on their members, so that the latter were allowed a free vote in accordance with their consciences, provided they had the courage and the will to vote against the party line. This resulted in a decisive majority for the measure in the Danish parliament in May 1989. The law came into effect on October 1 of that year, and the first "registrations" took place at the town hall in Copenhagen on the same day.

## THE MEANING OF PARTNERSHIP

Basically, the Danish law on registered partnership for gays and lesbians has the same legal effect as heterosexual marriage. For example, there are now solutions to such practical problems such as housing, pension, inheritance, and other rights in cases where one partner has died, just as there is provision for the division of a joint estate in the case of a "divorce." But partnership does not grant the right to adopt children, neither a partner's children nor nonrelated children.

It must be emphasized that the law on partnership is primarily a law for Danes. This means that *at least one of the partners must be a Danish citizen, resident in Denmark.* On the other hand it does not matter where the other partner lives or comes from. Partnership can be entered into only in Denmark and has legal effect only while the partners are in Denmark. It is not recognized by other countries, and when in other countries, the partners will be regarded as unmarried.

Partnership is registered by the municipal authorities at the town hall with the same ceremony as is used in the case of civil weddings for heterosexuals. There is no possibility of a church wedding for homosexual couples in Denmark.

In the course of the first two years after the law came into effect, almost 2,000 partnerships were entered into, of which about thirty were again dissolved. The law is still so new and experience so limited that it would not be reasonable to begin to interpret the meager statistical material so far available. But there is a not unexpected tendency for partnerships to be entered into by persons between thirty and forty years of age, and by more gay men than lesbians. That the law seems to be less popular among lesbians may be due to the inability of registered partners to adopt either nonrelated or a partner's children, as well as to the provisions in the law for mutual maintenance obligations between the partners.

A careful guess would be that the annual number of partnerships entered into will stabilize and, in time, will come to correspond proportionately to the number of marriages contracted. All parts of Danish society, including gays and lesbians, are only now beginning to accustom themselves to the existence of the law and to the fact that partnership has become a real possibility. This process of adjustment will take time, especially for many gays and lesbians who, almost automatically and, by dint of circumstances, have adopted a very independent and individual lifestyle.

During the work on the introduction of the partnership law, LBL has always refused to justify their desire for such a law. The principle of equality has been the main argument—and justification. When two adult members of a society wish to marry, they should be given this opportunity, whatever their sex.

The adoption of the partnership legislation has been of great importance both in Denmark and abroad. In Denmark, it has meant much greater visibility for gays and lesbians, an acceptance of gay and lesbian cohabitation, and an initiation of a broad debate on conditions for lesbians and gays. Take, for example, the fact that all official forms must now include partnership as well as marital status.

Internationally, the law has already affected and inspired similar legislative initiatives in other countries, especially in Scandinavia. Other European Community countries have expressed an interest in the Danish partnership legislation as well.

The law providing for partnership for gays and lesbians has broken new ground. But it will not be fully satisfactory until it has established real equality. The law must also include the right to adopt and the possibility of a church wedding or registration for those who wish it.

The years ahead will show whether the gay and lesbian movement and its organization have the political strength to achieve real equality and a decent legislative framework for the homosexual community.

## LBL'S POSSIBILITIES IN THE POLITICAL SYSTEM

### LBL as an Interest Organization

Like other interest organizations, LBL seeks, along with the political parties and decision makers, to affect the distribution of the spiritual and material benefits in society. This LBL does by trying to influence Parliament, the political parties, civil servants, the press and public opinion. Since it is a Danish tradition to include the interest organizations in the political process, it was natural that LBL be included in the consideration of partnership legislation.

When an agreement is reached between a majority in Parliament and LBL, this is a guarantee that LBL will support the question among its own members and homosexual circles, so that the majority does not have difficulties later. The whole system is dependent upon LBL appearing as a reliable negotiating partner, which has its membership behind it. Thus, LBL becomes a valuable ally for the Danish authorities. In a case such as partnership, where LBL is able to convince all parties that it is safeguarding "justified" interests, that it is demanding "equality," and that it feels "discriminated against," the organization is in a strong position. It is a prevailing norm that a government must take account of all "justified" interests in society. If it does not do this, there will always be an opposition in Parliament ready with allegations that a one-sided, or unjust, or wrong policy is being followed. This, of course, LBL can make use of.

When does LBL begin to intervene, if it is to have any influence? As early as possible in the decision-making process. LBL always tries to be consulted or—if it is a question of committee or commission work—to be represented on the committee. When a legislative proposal is presented or a parliamentary committee is considering a concrete issue, LBL often applies to be heard by the committee. This happened many times in connection with the partnership measure.

Since LBL, as an idealistic organization, does not have the same contacts with the decision-making, administrative authorities as do, for example, trade unions and business organizations, LBL makes a point of having good formal and informal contacts with single members of Parliament, in order to exercise influence. Here, of course, it can be an advantage if some of the members belong to LBL or are homosexual. But LBL has good relations with many MPs who sympathize with the organization.

Members of Parliament can, for example, ask questions of the minister or get the backing of the party to present a legislative proposal, as was the case with the proposal on partnership. In other cases, LBL can request a meeting with the minister with a view to presenting concrete proposals or to discussing individual cases.

Probably just as important is the general "understanding" between the political parties and LBL. In Denmark, LBL has usually had its best contacts with the liberals and leftists. The greatest opposition, of course, has come from parties and single members with a fundamentalist Christian view. However, Denmark has never had a large Christian party, as has been the case in some other European nations.

But there are no clear demarcations; therefore, it is important for LBL constantly to maintain good contacts with as many parties and members of Parliament as possible. Parties and members may sympathize with LBL on single issues, but LBL need not sympathize with other aspects of their policies. Since lobbying has such great importance for LBL, the organization has developed a tradition of inviting leading politicians and civil servants to discuss LBL's general policy— or single issues—at its headquarters in Copenhagen. Many good contacts have been created in this way.

## LBL AND THE MASS MEDIA

It is questionable whether, in the short run, the mass media can change the minds of the public or the politicians; nevertheless, the fact that the decision-making authorities actually believe that newspapers, radio, and TV have an important influence on the formation of public opinion is of great importance. Danish democracy is typified by decision-making processes that are greatly influenced by the single issues raised in the media.

By and large, the mass media mirror the general opinions of society, and this, in turn, influences the choice of copy and its presentation. Over a period of years, this cannot but have an impact on the formation of political opinion in Denmark. And it also makes its mark on the presentation of gay and lesbian views in the media. They do not get there by themselves; it requires a conscious press strategy on the part of LBL to achieve objective and positive coverage.

LBL's strategy toward the media has been marked by a wish to build a network of journalists who are reliable; in whom the organization has faith; and with whom, where possible, there is a confidential and personal contact. LBL has emphasized its own reliability and impartiality in the content of its statements to the press, and has ensured that its press releases, for example, are clear and unambiguous, and do not send out varying signals regarding any one issue. In order to secure continuity and uniformity in relation to the press, it is usually only the leadership of the organization which undertakes this function.

LBL has always found it more useful to be represented in various contexts and to influence the story in a sensible direction than to be too selective and refuse to participate if, for example, the journalist's idea and approach seem too pop and superficial.

## LBL AND THE ACCOMPLISHMENT OF PARTNERSHIP

Parliamentary practice in Denmark requires that, in principle, a government shall be given a vote of "no confidence" before it needs to resign. That is to say, it does not need to have a majority behind it on all issues. During the 1980s, this principle was extended by the Conservative government, which accepted a majority vote against it on single issues to a much greater extent than previous Danish parliaments.

This has extended the possibilities for maneuvering by the opposition and for the opposition parties to collaborate with interest groups on the carrying out of single issues. It was thus possible to have a commission set up and have the partnership proposal adopted without the support of a reluctant Conservative government—although the minister was able to make the work of the commission on partnership difficult in the way described above.

Thus, it was possible, again and again, to get the recommendations of the commission's minority carried through to a decision by a parliamentary majority without the support of the government.

But the parliamentary situation alone, although it was a good starting position, was not an adequate explanation of the accomplishment of partnership. The law on partnership for gays and lesbians is proof that even a homosexual, idealistic organization can get its policy carried out—by making use of the parliamentary rules, by lobbying members of Parliament, by a conscious press strategy which provided backing in the media, by a clear formulation of the proposal, by a strong membership backing, and by its cogent arguments for equality. LBL's achievement is all the more remarkable given the fact that it was fighting against lukewarmly supportive public opinion, a hostile government, and leading civil servants who were bound by loyalty to political decisions they had already made.

The accomplishment of partnership in Denmark, ultimately, is due not only to the nature of a liberal country with a developed consensus culture, where religious antagonisms do not play an important role, but also to the changes of the last decade in the pattern of democratic decision making. These changes have given greater room to interest organizations for the carrying out of individual cases in close cooperation with the mass media and influential politicians. But we must acknowledge as well the changes in sexual roles which have taken place during the last twenty to thirty years, and the more accepting attitudes to homosexuality among the general public.

# 9

# Gay and Lesbian Couple Immigration to Australia: Pressure Group Compromises and Achievements

## John Hart

Australia, although the world's largest island, is inhabited by only 17 million people. Since the first (often unwilling) European settlement in the eighteenth century, immigration has remained a major source of political and personal concern within and outside the continent. Since the end of the Second World War, Australia has had an immigration program that has attempted to balance the need for skilled and unskilled labor with a commitment to family reunion. In discussing homosexual immigration, unions, and reunions, two important factors should therefore be noted at the outset: first, almost uniquely in the world, an Australian migration program does exist, second, the policy of the Australian government has been to encourage not only primary migrants to settle but also those persons' families to join them in their new land.

This article is about the maneuvers by the government and gay and lesbian people since 1983 to try and ensure that same-sex partners be included in the family reunion policy. Between 1983 and 1989, over 500 partners from overseas were allowed to join their Australian lovers as residents. While this is an important achievement, compromises have had to be made in order that the ideology of the family not be seen to be weakened by same-sex partnerships. Provisions were made by pressure groups and government without an official category of "homosexual partner" becoming part of the migration quota.

The following is an outline of the developments made during this period:

## Chronology of Major Events during the Arrangement

**1983**  The Hawke Labour government is elected. The first Immigration Minister, Stewart West, receives applications from same-sex couples but makes no decisions.

**1984**  Second Immigration Minister, Chris Hurford. The Gay and Lesbian Immigration Task Force (GLITF) is formed to achieve equality in the Australian immigration system for gay and lesbian couples.

**1985**  The minister agrees to meet the Task Force. An arrangement is made in which the minister will personally use his discretion under the Migration Act of 1958 to decide on applications on a case-by-case basis. A four-year duration of relationship requirement is placed on same-sex relationships.

**1987**  The next Minister for Immigration, Mick Young, appears reluctant to make case decisions.

**1988**  Still another Minister for Immigration is appointed. The new incumbent, Clyde Holding, faces hostile questioning in Parliament. Same-sex migration is linked with AIDS in Parliament and the media.

**1989**  The Labour government's fifth Labour Minister for Immigration, Robert Ray, takes over and announces his determination to restrict ministerial discretion under the Migration Act. In September, the duration requirement is reduced to thirty months. In December, the Migration Act is amended. Restrictions on ministerial discretion aimed at removing abuses of the general migration program have the effect of stopping the use of ministerial discretion to enable same-sex couples to be "quietly" approved by the minister.

**1990**  Transitional arrangements are made by the Immigration Department while awaiting the decision of yet another new minister, Gerry Hand. Same-sex applicants can apply for extensions of their temporary entry visas when in Australia. The Immigration Department confirms that there is "no class of visa for homosexual partners of Australian citizens or residents."

**1991**  On April 15, the federal government introduces a new regulation for Nonfamilial Relationships of Emotional Interdependency, which provides a new visa and permit category that can be used by same sex-partners to achieve residency. A six-month length of relationship is required before an application for conditional residency can be made. A two-year waiting period for permanent residency is still required, with the minister remaining the primary decision maker. The GLITF views this as a major victory, although its aim of a migrant entry category similar to heterosexual couples is not realized.

## THE GAY AND LESBIAN IMMIGRATION TASK FORCE

The GLITF was formed in 1984 by gay activists and some couples then involved in making an application to the Department of Immigration. Previously, applications had been made and approved on a case-by-case basis by the government, most frequently after a politician had made recommendations to the minister on the couple's behalf. It was judged in 1984 that the political moment was right for changing this unsatisfactory situation. The new Labour government would hopefully be more tolerant of sexual difference than its predecessors; there were also some gay couples prepared to be open in their applications in terms of government and media identification.

The aims of the GLITF are to achieve equality in those applications where one partner is not Australian, and to ensure that changes in immigration policy take into account the needs of people who are lesbian or gay. There are groups who meet to provide an advising service and to lobby in Sydney, Melbourne, and Adelaide, and to maintain contacts in other places in Australia.[1]

The government was reluctant to include homosexuals in the migration program. To do so has been judged by the successive ministers to be a source of political problems. Since 1984, the gay and lesbian pressure group set up to concentrate on this issue has been successfully involved with Immigration Department policy makers and bureaucrats in acting as advocates for the individual couples who wanted to unite or reunite in Australia. The group was also helping thereby to ensure that applications to the department were fulfilling the official criteria relating to the type of couple relationship appropriate for migration purposes. Above all, homosexual applicants had to demonstrate a "genuine" relationship. This was really little different from the demand placed on the heterosexual relationships which formed the basis for concessionary migration; that is, residence in the country allowed on the strength of a relationship with a primary migrant, resident, or citizen. Internationally, governments are concerned to ensure that "sham" or fraudulent marriages do not figure in migration applications. However, unlike heterosexual partnerships, same-sex relationships approved as genuine had to undergo a probationary period, first of four and then of two years, to prove that they were "successful." A breakdown in the partnership carried with it the possibility that the foreign partner would be required to leave Australia. Part of the arrangement for homosexual couples, therefore, required a marriage-type relationship, even down to the structural inequality of one person being able to dictate the country of residence of the other.

The standards of what constituted a genuine relationship were met by the applicants' showing evidence of joint holdings of accommodation, household bills, and other objective evidence; for example, joint bank accounts and wills made out to each other. Less tangible evidence included legal statements about the feelings each partner held for the other. Relatives and friends were also required to provide supportive legal declarations. The expectation was that such declarations would contain descriptions of partners meeting and falling in love, being mutually dependent emotionally, and feeling devastated by the possibility that one partner could not enter or remain in Australia as a legal resident. The stated commitment to the other person was to be lifelong.

The GLITF has remained very active in its involvement with gay migrants to Australia. While holding the status merely of a self-help group, the GLITF has an over 90 percent success rate; indeed, it has functioned as a de facto administration arm of the Department of Immigration.

It was this fascinating interrelationship of public policy, pressure group politics, and personal adaptations that I set out to research. The majority of the couples who participated were contacted through the GLITF. I conducted interviews by mail with over ninety couples living in different parts of Australia, and of these thirty granted personal interviews. These interviews were conducted over a two-year period, 1988 and 1989. The experiences I had may be reasonably generalized to apply to all same-sex applicants to date. However, subsequent changes, for example, the reduction in the duration requirements, may well alter the experience for couples who have applied more recently.

## A PROFILE OF THE GAY AND LESBIAN COUPLES APPLYING FOR MIGRATION

We should now profile the homosexual men and women who found themselves part of this unique arrangement with the government. Obviously, they were required, under the arrangement, to be "out" at least to themselves and some friends, and preferably to relatives. It is not a usual experience for lesbians and gay men to have to declare their sexual orientation in order to achieve government benefits. Many of the overseas partners came from countries where same-sex behaviors are subject to persecution. They then had to face uncertainty in the exercise of Australian governmental power in their favor before they would be granted the right to immigrate. Additionally, those partners who have applied since mid-1989 must be tested for HIV. Seropositive status will almost certainly result in the denial of an application.

A profile of the participants in my study indicates a number of gender-related differences, first in age. The ages of the women ranged from 20 to 45. There were no large discrepancies in the age of partners. The men ranged in age from 23 to 67, with significant age differences in age between partners being common. These were especially marked when the overseas partner came from Southeast Asia. The Australian partner in these couples was frequently between ten and twenty years older. The reasons for these differences are speculative. When I asked these men about their choices, answers included the economic, the erotic, and the situational. A common reason given for the partnership by both genders was, "I fell in love." Such feelings were viewed by the women and men as being beyond national boundaries.

Significant differences were also observable in respect to the countries of origin of the overseas partners. Generally the women chose lovers from English-speaking countries while the men were about equally divided into those who also had English-speaking partners and those whose partners came from Australia's close neighbors: Indonesia, Singapore, Malaysia, Thailand, and Japan. These overseas partners generally were younger, had known their partners for a shorter time, were less educated, and had problems speaking English.

In summary, the group of same-sex partners who became available for study included men who belied many of the assumptions that are made from the available research on homosexual couples. That is, they were apparently lovers chosen because of their differences rather than for their homogeneous qualities. In the case of men with partners from Southeast Asia, the initial inequality imposed by different residential status was reinforced by age, education, English language proficiency, and employment prospects in Australia. The relationships themselves may also have been constructed on personal differences which involved a celebration of inequality.

How have these couples survived the significant life events of migration, structural discrimination involving bureaucratic regulation, and the prescription of at least external conformity to a dependent pair model of relationship? Perhaps not surprisingly, a major theme emerging from my research was that of the stress felt by (almost) everyone involved in this arrangement. This also included the Minister for Immigration who first met with the gay and lesbian pressure group. In an interview I conducted with this politician in 1987, he described his decision, made, it was suggested, by the GLITF against the advice of certain departmental policy makers, in these words: "It was the most politically sensitive area of immigration for me. I always expected it to blow up."

For those at the receiving end of the government ministers' personal discretion, the results of living under such close scrutiny ranged from anxiety to physical and mental symptoms requiring medical help. The partners I interviewed were united in naming the department's inefficiencies or policies as the main cause of their stress. It was those couples who, in fact, most conformed to a model gay couple—based on the departmental requirements outlined above—who appeared to suffer the most. The well-established couples, who may have felt that they had a great deal to lose if their applications failed, experienced a comparatively greater amount of stress because of their awareness of the costs of failure.

Only for some people was the stress element also connected to the outcome of their relationships. For most women and men the stress remained independent of their "success" or "failure" as an intimate couple. At the time of my contact with the study group, the "failure" rate of around 20 percent was not excessive as compared with heterosexual partnerships; nor was it made known to the department. While considering the effects of stress, we should also note that the marriage-type structure imposed by government, for example, having to cohabit, was responsible for some couples' restructuring their relationships in certain ways, thereby also helping to keep some of the couples together—at least as long as was required by the government.

For many of us, observing this group of people is of great interest, not only because of the sometimes apparent attraction of inequality, but also as they appear to have had to conform to a patterning of same-sex relationships which is outside of that taken to be ideologically correct in the lesbian and gay movements. One woman in my study, who, by the time of the one-year follow-up, had left her partner for another relationship, described her situation in a way that may apply to many same-sex couples:

> I feel the Department of Immigration is basing the elements of a relationship on heterosexual standards and is trying to validate and contain lesbian and gay relationships on the same pattern, e.g., living together, lifelong commitment, sharing bank accounts, and loss of individuality. Does it have to be like this to be genuine?

If we now turn our attention to this woman's question, we should develop it to ask what strategies were available to the pressure group in the arrangement that was made with the Australian government in 1985, and that still forms the basis of the requirements for same-sex partners to live together here.


## BACKGROUND TO THE MIGRATION POLICY

In 1983, Australia saw the beginnings of the Labour government of Bob Hawke. The issue of nondiscriminatory migration policy, in terms of sexual orientation or race, was held to in theory, but in practice was fraught with ambivalence. For example, although anti-discrimination legislation existed in some states, in others there were still laws outlawing male homosexuality. Moreover, a White Australia Policy had been in operation until 1973. In the most highly populated state, New South Wales, the anti-homosexual laws were only repealed in 1984; and by that time, the media began to be filled with "AIDS and Gay Men" stories. It was, therefore, a time of uncertain opportunity for social reform.

The pressure group formed to deal with this single issue was initially discouraged by the failure of the first, left wing, Labour Minister to act in the immigration cases. When the second minister, apparently more politically and personally conservative than his predecessor, took over and acted favorably, the group was surprised and made aware of how it had to carefully nurture relationships with a particular minister and his department in order to cope with one overarching political fact: gay and lesbian people were relegated to the margins of a family migration policy and likely to remain in that uncomfortable position. Throughout the 1980s, the immigration question proved to be a difficult one for political careers, resulting in six different Immigration Ministers in seven years, and a continual effort having to be made by the pressure group to achieve good relationships with a new decision maker. The 1958 Migration Act did provide the minister with a good deal of personal discretion to grant a change of status from visitor to permanent resident. When this situation was tightened in 1989, for a while same-sex partners were, apparently unintentionally, left without a way of changing their status to permanent resident. This remained the case until 1991, when the new regulation, "Emotional Interdependency," was introduced by a sympathetic minister. Yet all these developments required continual political lobbying by gays and lesbians and their supporters. The GLITF is still faced with the possibility that after another election the Labour party will be removed from office. Hence the need to lobby the opposition who are usually seen as even more conservative in the area of sexual politics.

The traditional attitude of the Australian government decision makers has been that immigration is always a contentious issue, dependent on the need to balance the social good, including family reunion and refugee commitments, with the demands of the economy. The land is seen as dangerously empty compared with nearby countries that have small land mass and large populations. Such countries are also poorer economically than Australia. Social anxiety results when Australian men choose heterosexual partners from such countries, who are then granted concessional migrant status. In addition to anxiety about race, there is also the problem of gender relations in Australia. For reasons that have emerged since the first overwhelmingly male European settlement 200 years ago, Australia is a homosocial society with rigid gender roles and consequential anxiety about male homosexuality and the undervaluing of women's sexuality. The negative publicity about same-sex migration in the press and Parliament has concentrated on male couples; although these do represent the majority of applicants, the existence of lesbian women has been ignored. To such factors has been added a high rate of HIV positive status among male homosexuals. It can therefore be assumed that there would not be general political support for including same-sex partnerships in migration provisions. The Australian experience differs from the possibilities that currently exist in Europe for nondiscrimination as to the gender of a migrant partner. Given the political situation of gay men and lesbians in Australian society, the answer to that question concerning conformity in sexual roles would appear to be that there is little room for official approval of alternative lifestyles.

All the players in this scenario have striven to create a situation where same-sex migration would be under a large amount of control. The first agreement in 1985 was made with a minimum of publicity. The result was that anyone inquiring at an Australian government bureau or embassy overseas would have been told there was no homosexual migration. This was and is understandable given the discretion of the minister until 1989; moreover, the inclusion of gay and lesbian partners in the emotionally interdependent category was not generally publicized. This was part of the agreement made between the minister and the pressure group. Each case was then individually decided upon by the minister personally. The first to initiate the arrangement told me that he actually read through each file to make his own assessment, rather than rely on the summary or recommendations of his staff. The fact that each application was usually so well presented and hence successful was the result of the efforts of the GLITF. Each couple was instructed how to fill in the very complex documentation and encouraged to appear spontaneous in their stories of meeting and falling in love, within a formula approved by the department. This formula was inevitably based on heterosexual models.

The policing of the relationships first occurred in the lack of general publicity given to the provision. This was followed by the informal use of the GLITF in the socialization of the applicants and the filtering of applications from only "genuine" couples. Next came the individual case decisions by the minister. Later there was the need to prove the relationships were successful over a period ranging from four to two years. By this time the scrutiny of Task Force and government was less intense; my research indicates that neither was aware of the developments of the relationships. This is an appropriate situation for a democratic society. Even though there is a duration test for the couples, the requirements of the department are met by statements about the durability of the relationship. Again the first minister made the point to me: "My intuition is that about half of them will stay together over the four years—but that would not change the decision I made. After all, look at the divorce rate." The GLITF has deliberately not extended its activities beyond political lobbying and advocacy for individuals as well as assistance in the application process.

We need, however, to consider the effects on the individuals of participating in a relationship experience which has not previously been discussed in lesbian and gay research. My own study has shown the costs of the uncertainty of such a discretionary policy. To blame the government's immigration department for the stress many gay and lesbian couples feel is certainly valid; but this same pressure gives strength to many of these men and women, both to process their own applications and to be a resource for others. The GLITF's experience also focuses on the values attached to long-term relationships. A requirement of lifelong commitment reminds us that people grow in same-sex relationships and are not usually constrained within that relationship by the formalities of heterosexual pairings. It may be that when the individuals in this study have benefited from their migratory relationships, the intimate forms of their primary relationships will change. People form intimate pairs for a diversity of reasons—sexual, social, economic, and emotional. It may take two lifetimes to achieve some relationship goals.

## CONCLUSION

Over 1,000 people in Australia have, since 1985, been directly involved in a unique agreement with the government based on the dubious achievement of being able to prove that, in less than favorable circumstances, they can prove heterosexual look-alikes, and demonstrate genuine and successful intimate relationships for the purposes of migration. The work of the GLITF continues to aim toward total equality with heterosexual couples for "genuine" same-sex relationships in the migration program. I would conclude that the achievement of a "successful" couple relationship depends on who is making such an evaluation.

## NOTE

1. Current information is available from the Task Force: GLITF, GPO Box 2622, Sydney NSW 2001. Please include a donation if you are asking for information.

# 10

# "Strangers" in the Netherlands: Dutch Policy toward Gay and Lesbian Aliens

## Aart Hendriks and Willemien Ruygrok

## INTRODUCTION

Many people regard the Netherlands as heaven on earth for gay men and lesbians. The common myth is that Dutch law recognizes homosexual marriages and that gay men and lesbians coming from less enlightened countries can easily obtain refugee status in the Netherlands. In reality, however, Dutch society is somewhat less permissive. In 1990, the Dutch Supreme Court stated that according to the civil code, marriage is accessible exclusively to two persons of the opposite sex, although it openly questioned the rationale of this restriction. As yet, same-sex couples are only allowed to inscribe their relationship, at least in some cities, in a "public register," an act having merely emotional and ceremonial importance and without any legal significance. Regarding the provision of a permit allowing a gay or lesbian alien to stay in the country, it should be noted that Dutch immigration policy is anything but liberal. It is extremely difficult to obtain refugee status. Criteria for other permits granting resident status in the Netherlands have been considerably restricted.

Despite all this, the Netherlands has, at least abroad, the image of being a country with a very liberal approach toward minorities, including homosexuals. However, the degree of liberalism in Dutch immigration and asylum policy is in direct proportion to various immigration fluxes and the success of attempts to regulate this process in combination with such variables as employment and housing. During the last decade, Dutch authorities have frantically tried to design a policy commensurate with Dutch economic interests, while at the same time fulfilling Dutch obligations under international law. Dutch aliens' policy was never intrinsically hostile toward homosexual aliens; the biggest problems turned out to be making politicians aware of the issue of homosexuality as it bears on requests for immigration, refuge, or asylum. This article gives an overview of the efforts made by the Dutch gay and lesbian movement during the last fifteen years to urge Dutch authorities to respond fairly and adequately to homosexual aliens applying for residence in the country.

In this article we will critically analyze the official Dutch immigration policy, particularly assessing to what extent this policy corresponds with the needs and interests of gay men and lesbians coming from abroad. We will restrict ourselves to two situations we have been most frequently been confronted with: (1) a homosexual alien having affective bonds with a Dutch citizen (of the same sex), and (2) a homosexual alien having been persecuted in his or her country of origin because of sexual orientation. We will build upon our experience as volunteer and staff member of the Dutch Association for the Integration of Homosexuality COC, which is for many foreign gay men and lesbians the first organization they address immediately before or after arrival in the Netherlands, or when they are considering settling in that country.

We will show that we have been relatively successful extending the category of people eligible for the dependent residence permit (*afhankelijke verblijfsvergunning,* i.e., the permit that allows an alien to join his or her Dutch partner). With respect to homosexual asylum seekers, it was only in 1992 that the refugee status was granted because of persecution on the ground of sexual orientation (Metz 1993). In a larger number of cases, homosexual asylum seekers, all of them male, have obtained the asylum status "for pressing humanitarian reasons."

## DUTCH ALIENS' POLICY: LEGAL FRAMEWORKS AND APPLICABLE STANDARDS

Dutch society has always been a small melting pot with people of different social, denominational, ethnic, and cultural backgrounds living together in a relatively small geographical area. Instead of pursuing a policy of forceful integration, Dutch politicians opted for giving individuals and groups freedom to develop according to their own values, although not allowing one group to dominate another. This attitude, a pragmatic solution to the problem of clashes between certain groups, probably also explains why the Netherlands could easily serve as refuge to large numbers of expelled and persecuted people, such as the Huguenots and Portuguese Jews in the Middle Ages, and Jews from Nazi Germany during the 1930s.

Since the Dutch are a pragmatic people, aliens are welcome to come and stay as long as the benefits outstrip the costs. This can be clearly demonstrated by a look at the adaptations made to Dutch immigration policy during the last five decades. In this period, the country experienced several influxes of both political and economic immigrants. Thanks to the post-war economic boom, initially the country could easily absorb a large number of immigrants; Dutch companies were even forced to actively recruit staff in countries with a surplus of (mostly unskilled) workers. In the 1970s, however, the world economic recession resulted in numerous corporate bankruptcies and caused an increasing number of people to lose their jobs. In response to growing unemployment, disproportionately affecting people from ethnic minority groups, the Dutch authorities tightened the immigration provisions in an effort to curtail the number of aliens trying to settle in the Netherlands.

Dutch policy regarding refugees and asylum seekers, however, is somewhat different. International treaties clearly define the category of persons who should be regarded as refugees with inalienable rights. Concerning those asylum seekers not fulfilling this strict definition, there is less international consensus as to the treatment these people should receive.

Modern Dutch alien's policy is based upon a system of permits (Goethart 1991). The kind of permit an alien needs depends in particular on his or her nationality and the intended period of stay. The conditions for obtaining such a permit become stricter the longer a non-national wishes to reside in the Netherlands. A notable exception concerns citizens from other EC (European Community) countries. According to supranational EC legislation, EC citizens have the privilege of free access to the labor market and to freely offer their services throughout the territory of the EC. These rights include the right to freely settle in the place where a paid activity is being performed. As a result, gay and lesbian citizens from other EC countries can relatively easily settle in the Netherlands provided they are working there. We will, therefore, focus mainly on gay and lesbian aliens from non-EC countries.

The general rules of Dutch aliens' policy can be summarized as follows: toward short-term visitors (no more than three months), it is rather permissive and can be described as "yes, unless." On the other hand, Dutch policy toward applicants for a long(er)-term residence permit follows the device "no, unless" (Boeles 1984).

The system of permits is embedded in special laws and other legal and administrative provisions. As mentioned above, the Dutch authorities are not completely free to determine the terms of such legislation, since in some cases they are already bound by internationally agreed-upon regulations. According to Article 94 of the Constitution, Dutch national legal provisions should give way to binding international provisions in case of a conflict between the two.

Besides numerous international treaties, covenants, conventions, and, more recently, "accords" and "agreements,"[1] the basis of Dutch aliens' policy can be found in national legislation. The following laws and regulations form the policy's legal framework: the Constitution, the Aliens' Act (*Vreemdelingenwet*[2]), the Aliens'

Decree (*Vreemdelingenbesluit*[3]), the Aliens' Regulation (*Voorschrift Vreemdelingen-gen*[4]), and the Aliens' Circular (*Vreemdelingencirculaire*[5]). In February 1989, a proposal of law to review the Aliens' Act was introduced in Parliament (*Algehele herziening Vreemdelingenwet*[6]), but as yet it is uncertain when Parliament will deal with this issue.

From this legal framework can be derived a number of standards that apply to Dutch immigration and asylum policy. The four most important principles, which may also play a role in case of a homosexual alien wishing to settle down in the Netherlands, read as follows:

1) The *nondiscrimination* principle, as laid down in Article 1 of the Dutch Constitution as well as numerous international documents.[7] According to standing Dutch jurisprudence, this principle applies to all people who reside in the Netherlands, independent of their nationality, ethnic origin, sex, sexual orientation, or any other stand. (Hendriks et al. 1990).

2) The principle of *legal security,* as embedded in Article 2 of the Constitution. Legislation should prevent practices of arbitrary admission and expulsion of aliens (Simon et al. 1990).

3) The *non-refoulement* principle, as laid down in Article 33 of the Convention relating to the Status of Refugees. The Netherlands has agreed that no one can be compelled to return "to any country where he or she may have reasons to fear persecution or danger of life, liberty, or freedom because of reasons pertinent to the refugee status."[8]

4) The principle of *minimum interference* (Hendriks 1990). This principle implies that all states, including the Netherlands, shall introduce as few hindrances as possible that may impede international mobility.

While this runs outside our main focus (although very relevant to many gay/lesbian groups and persons), it should be noted that the Dutch authorities have not restricted the minimum interference with travel principle in view of the number of people infected with HIV. AIDS has not induced the Dutch government to introduce travel restrictions against those actually or supposed to be HIV-positive. In contrast with many other countries, the Dutch government, with the almost unanimous support of Parliament, has consequently advocated the right of all people to travel and migrate, independent of their HIV-status.

## ALIENS WITH A DUTCH PARTNER

We are regularly addressed by homosexual aliens, most of them males, who wish to settle in the Netherlands with a same-sex partner. Though in some exceptional cases, the partner himself may not be a Dutch national (which can cause additional problems), we will restrict ourselves to analyzing the legal and practical barriers homosexual aliens may encounter when applying to join their Dutch partners.

As mentioned above, as long as their stay does not extend beyond three months, aliens in general do not encounter any problem in staying with their Dutch partner, regardless of their sexual orientation. Entrance and stay will depend on the general conditions of the Aliens' Act, Aliens' Decree, and Aliens' Regulation being fulfilled, including the following criteria:

1) Aliens should meet with all requirements for transborder movement (notably, possession of a valid travel document, including a visa for nationals of certain countries).

2) Aliens should possess sufficient financial means to support themselves while in the Netherlands as well as the resources to pay for the journey to a place outside the Netherlands where access is secured.

3) Aliens should not pose a threat to public order or to national security, including public morals and public health (Boeles 1984). With respect to the latter requirement, it should be noted that the Dutch government does not consider homosexuality "immoral" or "a psychohormonal disease." We do not have any evidence of Dutch custom and immigration authorities discriminating against incoming aliens on the basis of their (presumed) sexual orientation.

It becomes somehow more difficult in case aliens wish to stay with their Dutch partners for more than three months. As a general rule an alien, not being an EC citizen, would need a residence permit, which is generally issued for a specific purpose for a maximum period of one year. After this period, an alien may apply for renewal of the residence permit. Alternatively, aliens may seek permission to stay indefinitely in the country. For that they would need a settlement permit (*vestigingsvergunning*). The requirements for a such a permit are even more severe than those for a resident permit, corresponding with the Dutch "no, unless" mentality. An alien will only be granted a settlement permit on the basis of at least one of the following criteria being fulfilled:

1) The Netherlands complies with an international obligation by admitting the alien involved (notably in the case of a refugee).

2) The alien serves an essential Dutch interest (the skills he/she possesses are not [sufficiently] available in the Netherlands).

3) There is a pressing humanitarian reason for allowing the alien to stay (notably in cases where the person involved has bonds with the Netherlands that oppose expulsion).

In cases where an alien has a steady Dutch partner, it is generally easier to obtain one of the warranted permits. "Family reunification" is recognized as one of the "pressing humanitarian reasons" that should allow an alien to settle in the Netherlands. In view of this, a system of "dependent residence permits" has been developed, meaning that aliens are welcome to stay in the Netherlands as long as they have a Dutch partner with suitable housing and a minimum income, and the alien does not pose a threat to public security.

Probably no one will be surprised to learn that the dependent residence permit was originally introduced to enable the reunification of married couples. Since marriage is restricted to people of the opposite sex, this meant in practice that same-sex couples were totally excluded from this favoring system. Being confronted with several cases of an alien denied a dependent residence permit, the COC began lobbying the Dutch government, while at the same time seeking the support of friendly organizations. This effort has been successful: since the beginning of the 1980s, the nonmarried foreign partners of Dutch citizens have also been eligible for a dependent residence permit. In 1982, this principle, explicitly prohibiting discrimination based on the sexual orientation of the applicant's relationship, was inserted in the Aliens' Circular.

One year later, we formulated the precise terms of a Dutch aliens' policy that would not discriminate on the basis of sexual orientation. These terms were laid down in a policy paper called "Discrimination in Aliens' Policy," copies of which were forwarded to all members of Parliament. This paper contained a description of the existing Dutch policy toward gay and lesbian aliens, an analysis of discriminatory practices, and a list of recommendations for policy adaptations to be made. Probably as a result of this paper and the consequent alteration of the Aliens' Circular, all homosexual aliens who wanted to join their Dutch partners and who could fulfil the general requirements (in the areas of housing, minimum income, and public security) have been granted a dependent residence permit since 1984.

The Dutch authorities have also sought to find solutions to the other problems pointed out in our policy paper, resulting in a number of proposed amendments of law. However, these have not yet induced further adaptation of the aliens' law. It was the Dutch judiciary who explicitly granted protection to a Dutch-U.S. lesbian couple with a child in accordance with Article 8 ECHR (the right to private life and family life). According to the judge, settling the case in summary proceedings, the State of the Netherlands would injustifiably interfere with the right to family life by expelling the U.S. woman.[9]

Despite the fact that the position of homosexual aliens with a Dutch partner has improved considerably, we are as yet not completely satisfied. Nonmarried couples still suffer from several forms of discrimination in the provision of dependent residence permits. For example a "waiver" is routinely given to the foreign spouse of a Dutch citizen in case the latter is unable to fulfil the requirement of financial means sufficient to support two persons. On the other hand, such "waivers" are systematically denied to nonmarried partners under similar circumstances. This practice conflicts with the nondiscrimination principle. Despite the fact that judicial procedure is still in a state of flux,[10] there are now signs of this practice soon being changed and expanded to apply to nonmarried partners as well. We shall continue to advice aliens about their rights as well as strive for further improvements in the current Dutch immigration policy.

Moreover, we have set ourselves the task of ensuring that our 1983 recommendations become fully incorporated in Dutch aliens' policy. Last but not least, the COC should remain prepared to take action in case the application of a homosexual alien is being unfairly dealt with by some bureaucrat adhering to reactionary views. We consider it our task to remind these functionaries of the general rules and to make sure that homosexual aliens receive the treatment they are entitled to.

As a courtesy to our gay and lesbian alien friends, the COC has produced informative brochures on Dutch aliens' policy. These brochures, available in various languages, succinctly explain how and under what conditions an alien with a Dutch partner may obtain a residence permit (*vergunning tot verblijf*).[11]

## HOMOSEXUAL REFUGEES AND ASYLUM SEEKERS

Refugees and asylum seekers share the desire or the necessity to seek refuge in a foreign country. Homosexual refugees or asylum seekers may be defined as persons who are obliged to leave their country of origin because of their sexual orientation.

There are, of course, various reasons why a persecuted homosexual chooses to settle in the Netherlands. We will not further explore this question, although we should mention that if refugees' choices are being determined by the fact that they already have partners in the Netherlands, they should seriously consider applying first for dependent residence permits. As we will see, despite years of lobbying, political pressure, and promises made by distinct administrative bodies, it was only in 1992 that the first homosexual alien was granted refugee, or "A," status, because of his or her homosexuality. The importance of a refugee status is that it offers the individual involved the most complete guarantees with respect to residence and against extradition, as compared with any other legal status an alien can obtain in the Netherlands. This also explains why so many aliens are eager to obtain refugee status, and only alternatively will apply for another permit that authorizes them to stay.

The COC has always maintained that the general definition of a refugee, as formulated in the Convention relating to the Status of Refugees (Article 1) and the Dutch Aliens' Law (Article 15), covers persons persecuted on the ground of their sexual orientation. According to these documents, a refugee is a person who has well-founded fears "of being persecuted for reasons of race, religion, nationality, membership of a particular social group or political opinion, is outside the country of his nationality, and is unable, or owing to such fear, is unwilling, to avail himself of the protection of that country . . ." (Article 1 [A under 2] Convention).

Although neither the convention nor the Dutch Aliens' Act (which gives a slightly different definition of a refugee, but, according to standing jurisprudence, refers to the same group of people[12]) may have foreseen granting refugee status on the basis of sexual orientation, neither of the two documents seems explicitly to exclude homosexual refugees as a special category within the broad category of "membership of a particular social group." The COC has accordingly been lobbying vigorously to get homosexual refugees recognized as a specific social group, in full conformity with the terms laid down both in the convention and the act.

Those who do not fulfil the refugee criteria are not automatically returned to their country of origin. In some cases, by way of favorable exception, they may alternatively be granted asylum status. This will be given to those aliens who, for "pressing humanitarian needs," cannot be sent back to their country of origin. One may imagine that sexual orientation can lead to such a situation, leaving aside the fact that one has established affective bonds with a Dutch citizen. The advantage of obtaining asylum, or "C," status, is that this entitles refugees to somewhat better safeguards than do ordinary permits under Dutch aliens' law.

## Case Histories

In 1979, a Polish asylum seeker addressed the COC, stating that his reason for leaving Poland was directly related to the hostility he met with as a homosexual. Within a period of months, the COC received similar requests for legal advice from a Chilean and a South African. All claimed to be "refugees," in that they alleged that they were victims of persecution because they belonged to the social group of homosexuals. Moreover, all three were prepared to explain their cases to the court, a unique event in our history of advising and counseling gay and lesbian aliens. Apparently the time was ripe for a change.

More than ever before, we realized that neither the Dutch refugee law nor the legal provisions touching upon the granting of asylum status refer to sexual orientation. Therefore, we were aware of the importance of the litigations by the Pole and the Chilean (the South African decided to go into exile in Sweden later on), knowing that these would result in landmark decisions.

While these cases were still pending, the COC took the initiative first of starting a broad campaign around the issue of gay and lesbian asylum seekers. A special working group (*werkgroep homoseksuele vluchtelingen*) was set up, which also involved the Dutch Section of Amnesty International; the Dutch Association for Refugees (VVN); and the Schorer Foundation, an institution that offers psychosocial counseling to homosexuals. Second, the COC established contacts with gay and lesbian groups within all Dutch political parties—a common phenomenon in this country—to inform them about this issue and to involve them in further activities. Third, the COC began to lobby members of Parliament, government ministers, and other persons in high positions in order to make them aware of how gay men and lesbians were being persecuted in many countries, a situation that might eventually result in their having to leave their native country.

This policy of operating concurrently at three different levels turned out to be very effective in getting the issue of gay and lesbian asylum seekers on the political agenda, and contributed to the (partial) success of our campaign.

Thanks to the massive pressure thus put upon politicians, we induced Parliament to discuss this issue even before the Judicial Commission of the Council of State came to its verdicts in the cases of the Chilean and the Pole. On February 28, 1980, the Second Chamber of Parliament adopted a motion ("Motion Beckers")[13] on the issue of homosexuality and refuge. The motion stated that "in several countries people are persecuted because of their homosexuality, not rarely resulting in long-term deprivation of liberty or even the death sentence." The motion requested "the government to apply legal regulations in such a way that persons who are exposed to oppression or persecution because of their homosexuality can claim the refugee status."

The government, by way of the State Secretary of Justice, Mrs. Haars-Berger, reacted hesitantly but not negatively. Mrs. Haars-Berger stated that she would not automatically grant all gay and lesbian asylum seekers with "A" or "B" status;[14] instead, each case would, as a rule, be assessed individually. This suggested that at least some applicants could become eligible for refugee status.

More than a year later it was ruled, in the case of the Chilean, that persecution on the grounds of homosexuality could indeed be a reason for according refugee status: "[A] reasonable interpretation of persecution for reasons of membership of a particular social group could also include persecution on the grounds of sexual orientation."[15] In spite of this promising interpretation, however, both the Chilean and the Pole were denied refugee status. In the case of the Chilean, the Judicial Commission of the Council of State found that "in Chile there is no *systematic persecution* of persons with a homosexual orientation by the authorities. The allegation made by the applicant that expressing feelings of homosexuality is forbidden by the Penal Code is, as such, insufficient to justify such a far-reaching decision."[16] Both were however, after years of litigation and tension, granted asylum status "for pressing humanitarian reasons."

It may be obvious that we were not wholly satisfied with the result of our intensive lobby. Despite the fact that by the beginning of the 1980s, Parliament, government, and the judiciary had explicitly expressed the view that persons who are persecuted because of their sexual orientation are eligible for refugee status, these promising statements were not reflected in actual Dutch refugee policy. We therefore had to continue our campaign to ensure that these perspectives became truly transformed and fully incorporated into real refugee policy.

Since the mid-1980s, the goal of the COC in the matter of asylum for gay and lesbian refugees has been threefold. First, we have continued our efforts to make it possible for those who are persecuted because of their sexual orientation to apply successfully for refugee status in this country. Benefiting from the work of the human rights organizations named above, we have, at regular intervals, annoyed Dutch politicians with cases of gay men who had been refused refugee status on debatable grounds. We learned that the best way of convincing politicians was to be well documented. It was even better to suggest directly how similar practices could be avoided in the future. This obliged us to amass a case file of abuses by Dutch immigration officials, as well as to study the legal and social position of gay men and lesbians in other countries. In this regard, we have benefited from the generous support received from individual researchers and some university institutions.

Second, the COC considers it its task to provide homosexuals seeking asylum in the Netherlands with accurate information about their legal and social status. To that end, readily accessible information material has been produced in the languages spoken by most homosexual asylum seekers. In addition, we have organized a range of support services for those in need. Since then, the local branches of the COC have provided individual care to asylum seekers and played a role in facilitating social contacts. The Amsterdam headquarters of the COC has remained primarily responsible for the more incidental and structural problems, including the development of a national policy.

Third, since we realize that our success ultimately depends on the (moral) support we receive from others, we have regularly informed our members, sympathizers, and the public at large about our activities and the obstacles we have met when advocating gay and lesbian asylum seekers' rights. To publicize our views, we have made use of the media, including gay and lesbian magazines as well as refugee-specific publications.

### COC's Work with Refugee Centers and Lawyers of Gays Seeking Asylum

The COC has regularly negotiated with administrators of centers for asylum seekers in cases where homosexuals have been harassed by other residents because of their sexual orientation. In such cases, the COC would strive to obtain separate accommodations for the homosexual residents involved, usually outside the center, to protect their* mental and physical integrity against harassment and other forms of unwarranted intimidation. We learned that the Dutch policy of placing asylum seekers of the same nationality together in the same center can work very much against the best interest of gay and lesbian refugees.

From the mid-1980s, the COC has approached lawyers known to defend or to have defended homosexual asylum seekers. We felt that some of these lawyers did not possess adequate knowledge of the legal and social position of homosexuals in their clients' respective countries of origin. The COC offered up-to-date information that could be used in legal proceedings.

In 1989, the COC launched a new initiative to educate some 250 sympathetic

---

*All cases of harassment to date have involved gay men only.

lawyers after another denial of a request for refugee status, this time from a British citizen. We sent around a circular letter asking the lawyers to describe their own experiences in the fields of asylum seekers and homosexuality. Their responses confirmed our assumptions: while homosexuality plays a role in many asylum cases, this issue is hardly ever looked at as part of the asylum procedure. This encouraged the COC to produce a small brochure, "Homosexuality and Asylum," containing practical information and recommendations for all concerned with the rights and well-being of homosexual asylum seekers.

The present State Secretary of Justice, Mr. A. Kosto, was willing to receive a copy of the brochure. On this occasion, however, he merely repeated the famous words of his predecessor, Mrs. Haars-Berger: each case would be looked at individually. To show, however, that these were not just empty words, but that he was indeed willing to recognize homosexual asylum seekers who fulfilled the refugee criteria, the state secretary brought the issue of homosexuality again to the attention of his personnel. Probably as a result of this instruction, an increasing number of homosexuals seeking asylum has since then been allowed to stay in the country to await the final decision on their application. By the beginning of 1993, however, it became known that the Ministry of Justice had indeed been granting the refugee status to a number of gay asylum seekers. This means that it took twelve years before the Motion Beckers finally gained the desired results!

## CONCLUSION

The COC aliens' policy developed at a time when Dutch immigration and asylum policy had become more and more aloof as a result of the economic recession and increasing unemployment, notably among ethnic minorities. The tightening of the immigration and asylum admittance criteria may be one of the reasons that not all our complaints and suggestions for policy adaptation are being heard.

Our first experiences with Dutch immigration officials taught us that the aliens' policy was constructed on the (probably unconscious) assumption that all people are heterosexual. We undertook numerous activities to convince the officials that the scope their policy ignored the needs of homosexual aliens and that this urgently needed readjustment.

Our campaigns have been relatively successful: We have made it possible for homosexual aliens who want to join their Dutch partners to now obtain a dependent residence permit relatively easily. However, the present Dutch system still favors married couples, which means that we must still work to broaden the public's concept of a "partner."

Our lobbying in behalf of homosexual asylum seekers has been very successful in word, but only at a very late stage in practice. In spite of the broad political consensus in favor of considering homosexual persecution as valid grounds for refugee status, it is only recently that the first homosexual was actually being recognized as a refugee on the grounds of his or her sexual orientation. It remains to be seen whether the few cases accepted so far are exceptions, or whether they reflect a more permanent change of policy.

An evaluation of our own work shows that we would not have been even half as effective and successful without the support of other persons and institutions, both within and outside the COC. We foresee that we will only succeed in breaking down the last bits and pieces of a policy that originally focused exclusively on heterosexual "family" reunification and "real" refugees, by remaining in close contact with our allies and convincing our politicians of the injustice of some of the present practices.

Also, even after the "de-heterosexualization" of Dutch aliens' policy, that is, the formulation and implementation of a policy that does not discriminate on the basis of heterosexual orientation, we do not expect the COC's work in this area to end. Homosexual aliens coming to the Netherlands will continue to need information about their legal rights and the way they should present their application. As a result of their often traumatic experiences, some may also need psychosocial counseling and other forms of support. It is not to be expected that homosexual aliens, particularly those coming from countries openly engaging in homophobic terror, will easily inaugurate contacts with Dutch officials. The role the COC can continue to play is that of a bridge between incoming aliens and numerous domestic services and institutions.

The target we set for ourselves is to learn more about the experiences and obstacles lesbian aliens encounter in their efforts to leave their country of origin and to settle in the Netherlands. So far, there have only been a few lesbians applying for a dependent residence permit and, as far as we know, none for refugee status on grounds of their sexual orientation. Despite massive evidence of practices of sexual abuse of women (e.g., in the case of Bosnia),[17] the entire asylum seekers policy remains attuned to the experiences and needs of men. The fact that all cases of homosexual asylum have concerned males probably reflects the distinct forms of homosexual persecution abroad, in combination with the generally better possibilities men have to flee. It may also have to do with the thresholds we pose to lesbian asylum seekers and our sensitivity to their experiences and needs.

## NOTES

1. I.e., the Schengen Accord of June 14, 1985, and the Agreement on the implementation of the Schengen Accord of June 19, 1990.

2. Act of January 13, 1965, *Staatsblad* (*Official Journal*) 40.

3. Decree of September 19, 1966, *Staatsblad* 387, and December 9, 1987, *Staatsblad* 558.

4. *Nederlandse Staatscourant*, 1966, 188.

5. *Nederlandse Staatscourant*, 1982, 208.

6. *Tweede Kamer*, vergaderjaar 1988–1989 (*Second Chamber of Parliament,* parliamentary year 1988–1989), 21 018, nrs. 1–3.

7. Art. 2 Universal Declaration on Human Rights (UDHR); Art. 2 and 26 International Covenant on Civil and Political Rights (CCPR); Art. 2 International Covenant on Economic, Social, and Cultural Rights (CSECR); Art. 14 European Convention for the Protection of Human Rights and Fundamental Freedoms (ECHR); and Preamble European Social Charter (ESC).

8. Report of the UN High Commissioner for Refugees, UN Doc.E/–1988/53, no. 24.

9. President of Court of Justice The Hague, November 20, 1991, *Kort Geding* 1992, No. 21.

10. Judicial Commission of the Council of State, December 1990, *Gids Vreemdelingenrecht,* D6–66.

11. In February 1990, we produced the third edition of the brochure under the title "Resident Permits and Relation(s)."

12. Judicial Commission of the Council of State, October 16, 1980, *Rechtspraak Vreemdelingenrecht,* 1981, No. 1, and Judicial Commission of the Council of State, February 2, 1982, *Gids Vreemdelingenrecht,* D12–66.

13. *Tweede Kamer*, vergaderjaar 1979–1980, 15649 016, nr. 20. This motion was later called the "motion Beckers," named after the radical member of Parliament, Mrs. Ria Beckers, who had introduced the motion.

14. The "B" status was created by Royal Decree in 1974 as a special settlement permit without restrictions and prescriptions (KB January 10, 1974, No. 38, *Rechtspraak Vreemdelingenrecht,* No. 1, 1974). With the decision of the Judicial Commission of the Council of State of February 29, 1988, the "B" status was de facto abolished (*Rechtspraak Vreemdelingenrecht,* No. 3, 1989).

15. Judicial Commission of the Council of State, August 13, 1981, *Rechtspraak Vluchtelingenrecht* No. 5, 1981.

16. Judicial Commission of the Council of State, July 28, 1983, *Gids Vreemdelingenrecht,* D12–85.

17. The issue of sexual abuse is completely ignored by the Geneva Conventions.

## REFERENCES

Bestuurscommissie Politiek N.V.I.H COC. *Homoseksualteit & asiel* (*Homosexuality and Asylum*). Amsterdam: Board Committee on Politics N.V.I.H. COC, 1990.

Boeles, Pieter. *Vreemdelingenrecht en Nederlanderschap* (*Aliens' Law and Dutch Citizenship*). Zwolle: Tjeenk Willink, 1984.

———. "Vrij verkeer van personen: mensenrechten aan de buitengrenzen" ("Free Movement of Persons: Human Rights beyond the Borders"). In *Sociaal-Economische Wetgeving* 38, no. 11 (November 1990): 686–765.

Fernhout, Roel. *Erkenning en toelating als vluchteling in Nederland* (*Recognition as and Admission of a Refugee in the Netherlands*). Deventer: Kluwer, 1990.

Goethart, Rutger. *Internationaal verkeer van personen en HIV-infectie* (*International*

*Movement of Persons and HIV Infection*). Interuniversitair samenwerkingsverband Universiteit van Amsterdam, Instituut voor Sociale Geneeskunde, Sectie Gezondheidsrecht en Rijksuniversiteit Limburg, Vakgroep Gezondheidsrecht. Maastricht: Rijksuniversiteit Limburg (Inter-university cooperation, University of Amsterdam, Institute of Social Medicine, Section Health Law, and University of Limburg, Department of Health Law), 1991. Report.

Hendriks, Aart. "The Right to Freedom of Movement and the (Un)lawfulness of AIDS/ HIV Specific Travel Restrictions from a European Perspective." *Nordic Journal of International Law* 59, nos. 2–3 (1990): 186–203

———. *AIDS and Mobility.* Copenhagen: World Health Organization/Regional Office for Europe, 1991. Report EUR/ICP/GPA 023, EUR/HFA Target 4

Hendriks, Aart, and Astrid Mattijssen. "Discriminatie op grond van seksuele voorkeur" ("Discrimination on the Ground of Sexual Orientation"). *Noord Nederlands Tijdschrift voor Mensenrechten,* No. 1 (1991).

Metz, Eric. "Justitie verleent A-status aan homovluchtelingen" ("Justice Grants Refugee Status to Gay Asylum Seekers"), *XL,* No. 3 (1993): 26–27.

Simon, Henk J. "Onmenselijke behandeling en asiel" ("Inhumane Treatment and Asylum"). *Nederlands Juristenblad* 65, no. 37 (October 25, 1990): 1437–46.

Simon, Henk J., and Aart Hendriks. "Vreemdelingenrecht en AIDS" ("Aliens' Law and AIDS"). In J. K. M. Gevers et al. (eds.), *AIDS in het recht (AIDS in the Law),* pp. 85–113. Nijmegen: Ars Aequi Libri, 1990.

Willems, Erwin. "Vluchtelingenstatus wegens homoseksualtiteit" ("Aliens' Status due to Homosexuality"). Utrecht: University of Utrecht, 1991 (unpublished).

# 11

# Proper Schooling for Teenage Lesbians in Canada*

## Madiha Didi Khayatt

At the end of grade 10, after I had come to the realization [that I was a lesbian], I would spend a lot of time in the chapel praying. That's what I thought I should do. I got to the point where I was so depressed with it and feeling so incredibly guilty about it. I was causing this evil, because I had just been nominated "Catholic Student of the Year" for Ontario, and I just couldn't deal with these two [realizations] kind of together. So I tried to kill myself in the chapel we had in school. One of the teachers came in and took me to the guidance office and made me call the stress line. I talked to them. They kept me there all day. I begged them not to tell my parents that I had tried to do this—and [all along] I was waiting for somebody to ask me why, but they never did. (girl, age 13)[1]

The recent *Report of the [Health and Human Services] Secretary's Task Force on Youth Suicide* from the United States claims that gay and lesbian youth are overrepresented in adolescent suicide statistics. The report suggests that homosexual youth are two to six times more likely to commit suicide than heterosexual youth.[2] In England, the London Gay Teenage Group reports that one out of

*This research was funded by the block transfer grant from the Ontario Ministry of Education to the Ontario Institute for Studies in Education. I am indebted to Bob Tremble, Tony Gambini, Laurie Bell, Kim Mistysyn, and Krysten Wong for assisting with the recruitment of informants; and to Nicole Groten for transcribing interviews. I would like to thank SMR and Marian McMahon for their helpful comments.

every five of the 416 lesbian and gay young people they surveyed, "at some point [had] felt under such intolerable pressure that they attempted suicide."[3] In Canada, a Winnipeg study of gay and lesbian youth revealed that of the 45 young people surveyed, two thirds had contemplated committing suicide and one quarter of them had actually attempted it.[4] Likewise, of the twelve young lesbians I interviewed in Toronto, four mentioned at least one attempt to kill themselves. The tragic recurrence of the findings revealed by the above-mentioned surveys comes as no surprise when one becomes aware that, for the most part, lesbian and gay adolescents lack public support systems; frequently sense a need to hide their sexual preference from their parents; and often feel isolated, guilty, and lonely within the context of the school system.

In 1990, George Smith and I undertook a study to investigate the barriers to the provision of quality education for lesbian and gay youth in the area of Toronto. We conducted a parallel research: he worked with young men, while I interviewed young lesbians.[5]

Although, in 1986, Ontario added "sexual orientation" to its list of those areas where discrimination is prohibited, it does not necessarily guarantee equal rights of access to quality education for lesbian and gay youth, in the same way that sexism and racism have not been eliminated through legislation—or even curricular changes. It does, however, leave school districts in Ontario open to human rights complaints. Despite Bill 7, the sexual orientation clause in the Ontario Human Rights Code, no board of education in Ontario recognizes publicly the needs of lesbian and gay youth; none has made any provisions to allow them adequate support or created a positive and safe environment in which to come out.

For the purposes of this investigation, and because we believe that the experiences of lesbians and gay men may have common features, but are essentially and fundamentally different, George Smith and I divided the research according to our respective genders. Consequently, this paper will address only the problems of lesbian adolescents[6] within the school system; it will describe their experiences and provide an analysis of the social relations of schooling, of their families, and of the dominant heterosexual society, all of which shape and determine these experiences.

From the beginning, our decision not to incorporate young women and young men into the same research proved valid. Once we began our interviews, it became increasingly evident that not only did their stories and experiences prove different, but such factors as the age at which they recognized their homosexuality, where they found support, and how they expressed their sexuality, all had enough profoundly dissimilar elements that it would have done justice to neither sex to present them together. For instance, young men tended to name and express their sexuality, on the average, at a younger age than young women.[7] This is immediately apparent when confronting the very high proportions of gay males to lesbians in youth organizations. An added factor is that male sexuality is often evident in the public sphere: men, in general, claim and conduct much of their experiences (including sexual ones) in public spaces. Lesbians are more likely to self-identify and act out their sexuality later than gay males. The reasons for this may include, I suggest, the fact that women, in general, are expected by society not to express sexual needs, nor is it appropriate for them to initiate sexual activity at a young age. This often leads many young women not to make conscious decisions early in their lives regarding their sexual preference. In addition, compulsory heterosexuality, although also applied to men, is more strongly prescribed and enforced by society on women. This is evident in such practices as the enormous social pressures to marry, to please men, and to be appealing and available to them.

Of the twelve young women who participated in my part of the research, seven were white, two had a parent of different race or ethnicity from the other, and three were Asian.[8] They were either middle-class or came from low income families. None lived on the streets.[9] All were living in Toronto at the time of the interviews; two, however, were from the Maritime Provinces; two others went to schools in small communities close to Toronto; and one was from Ottawa; the rest had been born, raised, and gone to school in Toronto. Three students attended Catholic schools. These schools are provincially funded but retain a proviso in the Education Act of Ontario that they: "may establish and maintain programs and courses of study in religious education for pupils in all schools under [their schoolboards'] jurisdiction.[10]

When I first began interviewing the students, one of my first insights was to note how they recognized that their visibility, while it was rarely acknowledged, was often due to their particular situation in the school system:

> But I think I was also very lucky, because I was in this position where I'd done a lot of work for school . . . so I knew a lot of people. I'd already earned respect that could not be taken away just because I was gay. (girl, age 16)

> But the thing is that being in the "gifted program" was really wonderful because, unlike a lot of other people that I've met since then, who talk about what a really rough time they had in high school because they had to go out on all these fake dates and stuff like that, there was no pressure on us to go out on dates if we didn't want to. (girl, age 16)

However, when asked to suggest ways that could make school more gay-positive for other students who might be coming out, the respondents often were clear regarding the subtle (and not so subtle) ways in which their schools failed them, despite positive acknowledgment of the girls' academic and other abilities.

Twelve young women produced twelve different stories: some of their experiences were difficult but bearable, others terrifying or lonely. However, their reports had many factors in common, most of which will become evident later in this essay. But, depending on the context of their particular school, the circumstances and the age of their first "coming out," whether they disclosed their sexual identity, and the environment of their particular school or school board, some had it easier than others. For instance, almost without exception, those interviewees who were enrolled in the Catholic system had a much more difficult time than their public school counterparts. One of the reasons may be that sex education in Catholic schools is often taught under the rubric of religion, whereas in the public system it may be included under health, among other subjects. The significance of learning about sexuality as part of religious instruction is that sexual behavior is regarded as a moral issue, expressed, for example, in terms of "sin" and "purity."

The coming-out processes are seldom easy. Each incident depends on the social context, the emotional and political awareness of the person coming out, and the openness of those being informed. As Gloria Krysiak points out: "The 'coming out' process for adolescents is particularly difficult because, as minors, adolescents are dependent on their families, lack access to good information, have little mobility and no legal rights in the area of sexual preference."[11] It is the way each individual handles her own special events, given the lack of safety surrounding her at school, but also taking into consideration the need to disclose, that goes into producing the particular events of each account. This young woman's experience was frightening:

> I guess in grade 10 was the first time I actually kind of said to myself: I'm homosexual. I was thirteen, because I had skipped some grades. They were giving a lecture at the church on the evils of sexuality and they were giving only the various things that you could do wrong, like having premarital sex or masturbating, and they went through the list. Amongst that they made a statement that the [Catholic] church had recently done investigations and decided that homosexuals were homosexual because of birth, then it was something that they necessarily had to accept, [but] it's against the laws of the church to practice homosexuality. (girl, age 13)

This next one seemed to have a relatively positive beginning:

> In grade 9 my best friend and I wrote notes back and forth a lot. One day I wrote to her saying, "I love you and I hope you don't think that's gay or anything because it's not." She took it really well, I guess. She said, "Oh yeah, I love you, too. You're such a good friend." And homosexuality wasn't an issue. Then, in grade 10, we both had a crush on the same boy in grade 13; we talked a lot on the phone. I guess it started that we masturbated over the phone, and we talked about our bodies a lot and we spent a lot of time at each other's houses, sleeping over on the weekends. Then we became sexually involved with each other; but we didn't consider it a lesbian relationship at all—it was just experimenting and we were both having fun. I don't remember when I started feeling that "lesbian" described me. (girl, ages 14 to 15)

Confusion and initial denial marked the experience of this next student:

It didn't dawn on me until after my second homosexual experience. Then I started to doubt my sexuality. I was, at that point, 15. I believed myself to be heterosexual and had no homosexual inclinations of any sort. I got involved in two relationships with other women and it made me think for a while. I went through a period of denial, came to terms with it, and then started dating men again. Then, back to women. I wavered [because] I wasn't really comfortable with it until a year and a half ago. Now I can confidently say that I am a lesbian. (girl, ages 15 to 17)

If the following student was confused, the advice she got, when forced to see a therapist, enraged her:

I saw a psychiatrist at that time, on OHIP [provincial health insurance] and I said, "Oh, I've been [hanging around] with lesbians and I still don't have a label for myself, and I don't know if I'm a lesbian. It's the not knowing that upsets me," and he said to me: "I don't think you're a lesbian." And that was it. As if it was his place to know. As if he could know. As if that was what I was asking. (girl, age 19)

One young woman came out to herself at the same time as a friend of hers did. On the one hand, she chose to remain quiet about her sexuality and was able to finish her schooling. On the other hand, her friend came out to all their friends at school, all of whom seemed to react negatively to her news. "It's hard for her," the young woman explained, "because she still hangs out with them, and she's been through an awful time, she's an alcoholic and just can't deal with it." (age 17) As Alan Malyon suggests: "The majority of openly lesbian and gay adolescents are alienated from their peers as well as from the larger heterosexual culture. In addition, they have little access to the gay or lesbian communities, since most such social activities and establishments are adult-oriented.[12]

Each one of these young women dealt with her process differently. For three of the interviewees, it was relatively easier than for the rest because they were well established in their schools, or because they belonged to strong (or high profile) cliques (in two cases, marginalized cliques), which provided each with a semblance of safety and/or support. For others, the process was isolating, lonely, and terrifying. On the whole, even for those in cliques, it was a difficult experience—for some, an experience that did not end with their graduation from high school. For those young women who found it less difficult, it was generally because some lesbian or gay male adolescent before them in school had already paved the way:

It was kind of fashionable to be bisexual. There was a group of people, maybe two or three years ahead of me and they were known bisexuals—it was kind of considered really cool. But I didn't know them personally. (girl, age 14)

This next respondent described the gay/lesbian clique in her school as "very tough." She gives an example:

In terms of [straight] people walking down the hall, if they went, "you're a dyke"— like my friends would have just gone, "Well, and you're a het!" It wasn't a big deal. (girl, age 17)

However, for those students who were surviving on their own, their process at school was full of anguish. One interviewee described how she attempted to sublimate the urgent demands of her young body:

I was on the Cross Canada running track team and so when I was running, that was when I would deal with it. In my head I would visualize myself counting the pavement to kind of get rid of it, that every step would be a step away from these feelings. It was like a visual enactment. Every time I went running, (every day we did ten kilometers), I would enact this when I was running. (girl, age 16)

Another young woman became particularly self-conscious about her every move. She portrays her school days as being very lonely, a time when she did not have or want friends in case they suspected, as she put it, her "condition." She put all her energies into her studies instead. She analyses her feelings in the following quote:.

I was 13 when I became self-conscious. I didn't worry about it [lesbian attractions] till actually my period started when I was 13. I suddenly lost a certain amount of innocence when my period started. I think that's one of the things. I got suddenly a feeling of guilt about being a woman, and that's when I remember first really feeling [self-conscious]. I remember these thoughts of "I hope that person doesn't think I'm a lesbian" for doing this gesture, or saying that thing. Especially physical contact, like if I brush against a woman, it would be like: "Oh gee, I hope she doesn't think something of that." (girl, age 13)

Extraordinary loneliness characterizes this next student's experiences at school. She had chosen to come out publicly, and even when I was interviewing her, she had no regrets about her action (she is still attending school), despite her current feelings of isolation:

[Before others at school knew], people loved me, students loved me and I was nominated for Student Council. Then, in grade 11, everybody knows that I'm a lesbian, because I told some of my friends and they told everyone, but most people seem to back off and don't want to talk to me or say "hi," but, like it's not the same any more. (girl, age 15)

Later, she added, "I feel like I'm a misfit, you know—it really doesn't get to me. I forgot about it and I don't deal with it."

Of the three lesbian students who mentioned attempting to run away from home, one did not succeed. She said: "I actually ran away from home three times, and used to come back with the police and nobody asked me why. My parents didn't ask why. The school didn't ask why." The two others succeeded in staying away. They were both older (16 and 18, respectively). One left because of the extraordinary violence she was experiencing in her family, the other because of her sexual orientation:

> My parents and I had a falling out when I came out to them. I moved in right away with my girlfriend at the time—which was not a good idea, because we were still very young and we didn't know exactly how long this relationship would last, but I needed a place. She had a place because she'd moved out already because of telling her parents. So both of us were stacked into this room because we both told our parents and were living in this [tiny] room. It was horrible. (girl, age 17)

Alan Malyon, writing about gay and lesbian adolescents, remarks that they often have few options. Not only are they frequently alienated from their peers but, in many cases, from their families as well. Moreover, these youths have no access to counseling outside the school because laws often require parental consent for psychological treatment of minors. According to Malyon, "most parents will accept only conversion (to heterosexuality) treatment goals."[13] Therefore, self-acknowledged lesbian and gay adolescents either come out in a "hostile and psychologically impoverished heterosexual social environment," or they may have to depend on finding a supportive homosexual community.[14] Neither alternative is satisfactory, according to Malyon. The former leaves the adolescents to deal with their confusions and questions alone; the latter often separates them from their families—their traditionally presumed basic framework of financial and/or emotional support. Since it is particularly difficult to find a job because of their youth and lack of marketable skills, Malyon points out: "A frequent adaptation to this set of problems is street prostitution."[15]

Within the social and academic context of the school system, homosexuality was not often visible. It did not appear as a topic covered by most school curricula, but it was certainly mentioned often enough on school grounds, and not always pleasantly:

> . . . [I]t was talked about just in derogatory terms—calling someone a "fag." There was nothing about lesbians at all.

> . . . [S]ome of the stuff [I heard] is outrageous: [gayness] is just a phase, there is something wrong with their chromosomes, poor conditioning, because they are raised by gay parents—all sorts of things.

. . . [N]othing but verbal bashing, like "fag" or "dyke." . . .

I remember there was this snowshoeing contest; it was [the school's] winter carnival and I had my favorite plaid jacket and jeans, and I was doing quite well
in the contest, and someone yelled out "fucking dyke," and I remember that
comment, you know, because I felt vulnerable enough as it was. . . .

You would hear a lot of names in the school yard: "Oh, he's a faggot." You
know, or "fag." I didn't hear about the word "dyke" until I came out. . . . I
remember one day, the first time I heard it [faggot], I ran home. It was like,
"God! I have to find out what this word is. I think it's my identity!" And I
looked up "faggot," and it said: "a bundle of sticks," or something, in the Webster's
dictionary. I thought, no, I guess it doesn't identify me. Nor does it identify
anyone they'd been calling "faggot."

It was seldom much better in the classroom. When I asked one young woman
whether she would have considered confiding in any of her teachers, she replied:

No. Definitely not. [Q. Why?] Because it was not talked about [in school]. When
kids would call other kids names, they [the teachers] would just ignore it. A
lot of times they would ignore it and let it go and just say, "You get back to
your seat," but they wouldn't address why they should not be using that word
or calling someone a "fag." They never went into that. No, I don't. I definitely
don't think so.

One of my interviewees, in her late twenties, lived with a lover older than
herself. She reported an incident that occurred in 1991:

I remember one day my lover's daughter came home from school and told me
that in her health class her teacher had made disparaging remarks about lesbians,
and when [my lover's daughter] said, "What is wrong with lesbians?"—because,
of course, at home she has her mother and myself—her teacher said: "Oh, well,
maybe you are [one too]!" I couldn't believe that a teacher, no matter what
his prejudices, would say something like that to a very impressionable thirteen-
year-old.

For the most part, the great majority of the interviewees described, on the
one hand, silence in the classroom. For instance, one student commented that
while her class was studying the American poet Audre Lorde, it was never mentioned
that she is a lesbian, although the fact that she is black was discussed. Another
young woman, who was enrolled in the gifted program, insisted that in spite
of the excellent teachers she had, regardless of the outstanding program she was
attending, there was absolutely no instance where teachers initiated the subject
of homosexuality. She added that if a student was interested, teachers were often
able to refer her or him to some sources.

On the other hand, misinformation often prevailed when teachers did allude to the subject of homosexuality. This frequently took the form of teachers telling students that homosexuality was a sin, a sickness, or a perversion. This was not restricted to Catholic schools, but was mentioned by two other women, one from a very religious family, and the other from a very conservative area of Toronto. Several students reported that some teachers represented lesbians stereotypically, saying "that [they] are supposed to be male-looking butches, into athletics of all sorts, and not very attractive from males' point of view," as one twenty-year-old lesbian reported. Interestingly, that image provided this young woman (as well as two other respondents) with a good rationale for denying their initial suspicions regarding their homosexual orientation. In her words: "One of my problems in dealing with it was that I was always dressed in skirts and wore makeup and long hair, very feminine-looking. [Therefore], I didn't understand how someone as feminine as I was could be attracted to another female."

Silence is a form of discrimination. It renders individuals or groups invisible because they are not part of the norm. The silence that enveloped the schools regarding the subject of homosexuality affected the students in myriad ways: Some reported feeling terrified about what was happening to them amidst what seemed like universal reticence to mention the topic; for others, it resulted in a "chilling effect," where they themselves hesitated or refused to bring up the subject for fear of being "branded." A number mentioned that the silence itself reinforced their suspicions that the topic was taboo, that what they were undergoing was, in some way, bad. One young lesbian, still attending school, said: "I don't know, sometimes I feel like I'm the only lesbian in the world." Finally, another young woman (age 23), when asked if lesbians were mentioned, even negatively, in her school, summed up the situation with her comment: "No, sadly, not even that sort of a taboo way."

Silence is not the only form of discrimination suffered by lesbian (and gay male) students in the school system. Frequently, it is the violent expressions of disfavor coupled with subtle exclusions from their peers that combine to make lesbian (and gay male) students feel like misfits. Although girls and women do not suffer the same incidence of gay bashing that boys and men do, we do live with our share of violence in our lives. Many of my young respondents described examples of this violence, both to their gay male friends and to themselves. The exchange is particularly relevant because of the response of the administration, from the point of view of the student:

    **Q.** [Since you came out at school] have you ever been approached by anybody who was curious or who had questions for you?

    **A.** Not questions, but a comment like: "We all know who you are, so you don't have to hide it." I go, "Oh, shit!" and I beat her up. No, I didn't. I just put a garbage can on her head.

    **Q.** Was she provoking you? Was she being mean?

**A.** Well, she was discriminating against me and everything—calling me names, and so on.

**Q.** That does not sound pleasant.

**A.** No, it wasn't. It was a bad experience.

**Q.** Was it at school?

**A.** Yes, it was in school.

**Q.** Did anybody say anything?

**A.** No. Nobody. Well, the principal got upset with me. He didn't get upset with her, I don't know why. That makes me wonder. The principal always likes sticking to the person that I'm fighting with, and it's very hard, actually. (girl, age 15, still in school)

Those students who came out publicly, whether of their own choosing or not, were often the butt of unnecessary comments, taunts, or harassment. One young lesbian and her lover came out inadvertently at their respective schools. She described what her lover went through at her school: "She would be walking down the hall and they'd say 'Dyke, here comes the dyke!' She lost a couple of friends because of that." (age 17) Another lesbian student, who willingly disclosed her sexuality at her school, poignantly expressed her hurt: "The funny part is, when I sit down [in the auditorium], no one will sit around me. That's the worst." But then she added, "I mean, that's hurting me inside, but I chose to come out and that's what you get if you come out."

Yet it is not the overt baiting so much as the subtle manifestations of disapprobation which particularly disturbed most of the interviewees. Perhaps, in some way, they almost expected harassment, but not having to tolerate or excuse the constant visibility and flagrant representation of heterosexuality with which they had to deal daily. It was overwhelmingly present in the curriculum; it was expressed implicitly in such nonacademic elements of school life as dances, assemblies, proms, and athletic events. It was as explicit in the classroom and hallways as it was implicit in the discernible lives of the teachers and administration.

Nevertheless, many of the students I interviewed did not remain passive. Some challenged the curriculum by insisting on mentioning lesbian or gay-related topics. Others wrote essays on the subject and asked embarrassing questions to teachers who either made homophobic remarks or else did not defend them in the face of a hostile classmate. Two (of the twelve) took their girlfriends to a school dance and danced openly with them. On the one hand, those who reported coming out publicly said it was worth it to them, despite the harassment. In fact, some had very pleasant experiences at school—teachers who congratulated them on their courage; peers who, surprisingly, accepted them; and even individual members of the administration who were reported to have sometimes tacitly endorsed them. One young lesbian who came out gave her reasons:

The fact is that I was already very visible [active in student council and athletically] in high school, and when I came out it was just another thing—a big additional thing, but just an addition. But I know a lot of lesbian and gay youth who go through high school thinking their life is worth shit, always thinking: "God, I'm so alone, I wanna die." I hear a lot of this and I get so angry that there isn't anybody to help them.

On the other hand, there were those students who remained silent, concealed, and invisible. They did not suffer overt hassles, but they had to put up with the anguish, the confusion, and the loneliness of not being able to disclose their secret. The longer they were silent, the more that hiding affected their confidence, fragmented their lives, and inhibited their self-expression. I know. I was silent for a long time. Because of jobs. Because of family. Because of friends and/ or colleagues who could have rejected me.

Students complained most bitterly of attitudes about the teachers found in particular departments in the school, departments from which they expected support. The first was guidance counseling. Many felt there should have been, at least, information, leaflets, and posters, if not actual teacher support. But none of the women I interviewed ever thought of seeking reassurance from guidance counselors. Second, students complained about the health and physical education department. They expected many opportunities to arise during health lessons where teachers could mention alternatives to heterosexuality, but nothing was ever mentioned in classes attended by the twelve young respondents. A number were astonished that homosexuality was not mentioned in such departments as history, English, or sociology. Finally, some were appalled that there was so little (if any) information in the library.

When I asked the interviewees for suggestions for improvement in the situation of lesbian and gay male students in the school systems, they were not lacking ideas. They wanted to see information on homosexuality: addresses and telephone numbers of contact people and support systems. They demanded that facts on safe sex should be prominently displayed, mentioning specifically lesbian and gay sexual practices. They suggested that all their teachers and the administration be well versed in ways to help, advise, and support lesbian and gay male students with their processes of coming out. They required curriculum changes which would include, at the very least, mention of prominent lesbians and gay men (who may be currently studied but who are seldom identified); but also examples of politicians, professionals, athletes, stars, and common people whose lives could serve to indicate that we exist. They wanted to see books in the library on the topic of homosexuality, not just academic titles but fiction representative of our lives. They insisted that guidance counselors be particularly informed, and chosen specifically to be non-sexist, nonracist, and nonhomophobic. As Gloria Krysiak acknowledged when she suggested the importance of school counselors' acting as student advocates: "This support is particularly important because gay people are the only minorities that do not have a parent as a role model."[16] One interviewee wanted a ten dollar fine levied on every individual who makes a pejorative remark to or about lesbians or gay men! Most very clearly understood that we have a long way to go before seeing any real changes.

The stories of the twelve young lesbians I interviewed are a clear testimony that homophobia and heterosexism are solidly entrenched within the school systems and within the larger society. It comes as no surprise that many of the individuals who are presently working to improve conditions for lesbian and gay people in general, and students in particular, often say quite openly: "This oppression is going to be the toughest to overcome." Perhaps what they mean is that, because homosexuality was diagnosed, dissected, and described, yet paradoxically hidden and concealed in shame or sin; perhaps because it is still too threatening to the status quo; or perhaps because so many people deny its possibilities, it will require an enormous effort to recognize homophobia and put it on the table as a form of oppression that cannot be tolerated any longer.

However, the situation has not remained unchanged. Older students who had passed through the school system have, in recent years, begun to organize. Many, if not most, universities and community colleges in Canada have, at the very least, a social club, but often political organizations instituted by lesbian and gay students to meet young lesbians, gays, or bisexuals. Unfortunately, no such clubs or organizations exist, to my knowledge, at the high school level yet, although students of that age group may have access to board-instituted counseling services such as that offered by the Toronto Board of Education. However, according to one counselor with whom I spoke, students frequently seem reluctant to use such facilities, unless they can do so anonymously over the telephone. The reasons for this are not yet clear, since such facilities as those of the Toronto board are still relatively new. In contrast, rural students, or those who live in or near small towns, have to come to Toronto (or other large urban centers) to find the relative comfort of groups which provide support to young lesbians and gays.

Three questions come to mind: (1) How are homophobia and heterosexism located in the educational system? (2) What mechanisms keep them in place? and (3) Given what we know, what can be done under the circumstances? I shall attempt to answer all of these questions using a feminist analysis to explicate the social organization, and, in this way, provide a backdrop against which we can make sense of the experiences of the respondents.

Schools, as transmitters of official ideologies,[17] cannot afford to condone male or female homosexuality, even if the law demands that lesbians and gay men be protected from discrimination. In an article about lesbian teachers and Bill 7, I described how a particular board of education, which considers itself relatively progressive, preferred to bury the then new recommendation protecting the rights of lesbians and gay teachers.[18] Likewise, officially requiring teachers to include homosexuality within the curriculum, or even making readily available information about the topic, is tantamount to an acknowledgment that there might be an alternative to heterosexuality. To date, virtually all boards of education in

Ontario have a tacit (if not official) policy that proselytizing about homosexuality is forbidden in the schools. Certainly, under certain conditions, the topic may be dealt with but not presented as an alternative sexual option. Yet, the subject of homosexuality does appear informally in the classroom, even if it is not in the official curriculum. However, very often, even those teachers who are politicized, or who are themselves lesbian or gay, have to be careful in the way they deal with questions about homosexuality when and if these come up in class. Therefore, it is no coincidence that the students interviewed all remonstrated against the lack of information, and that whatever mention of homosexuality they reported was frequently a student-originated challenge to the status quo.

Lesbian or gay teachers are seldom inclined to bring up the topic of homosexuality in class for fear of exposing themselves. Every one of the twelve young women I interviewed affirmed that even if they recognized that a particular teacher was lesbian or gay, they would never "out" her or him because they realized that it would jeopardize their jobs. However, even if the sexual orientation of lesbian or gay teachers were to become known, they could not stand as role models because the subtextual information conveyed in the concept of "role model" is that it be publicly recognized as such. In other words, teachers would have to be hired officially as gay or lesbian or perceived to have succeeded despite or because of their sexual orientation before they could be appreciated as role models to emulate. Just suspecting or knowing about the homosexuality of teachers helps gay and lesbian students know that they are not alone, but does not provide an example to the rest of school or society that it is "OK" to be homosexual.

The literature generated by the helping professions[19] often reduces the reasons why there exist barriers to quality education for lesbian and gay students: it is either lack of knowledge on the part of homophobic society or the lack of school support systems for lesbian and gay youth. According to this rationale, then, providing services, changing attitudes toward homosexuality, and teaching compassion or respect for homosexuals will all stop discrimination against lesbian or gay youth. Of course, these changes would help. However, as we have seen in the case of racism and sexism, legislating anti-discriminatory policies, as well as adding people of color and women to the curriculum, has not necessarily changed the attitudes of those who enforce such policies. Likewise with homosexuality, legislating policies would not make homosexuality acceptable but merely tolerated. And, as with racism and sexism, it would render the discrimination more subtle. If we are truly looking to eliminate oppression on the basis of gender, race, and sexual orientation, we have to challenge the structure of power as it is presently composed and resist current hegemonic ideologies; in the case of homosexuality specifically, we have to call into question heterosexuality itself.

CONCLUSION

According to the lesbian students I interviewed, several options are open to lesbian and gay youth in the school system today: (1) concealing their sexuality and remaining invisible; (2) coming out publicly and putting up with the hassles; (3) seeking a gay/lesbian community outside the school—an option not often possible for rural youth;[20] or (4) leaving school. Evidently, none of these options provides for quality education, and most may, indeed, be an eventual cost to society in the long run.

The legislation of anti-discriminatory policies may help, yet to date, no lesbian or gay youth has challenged a school board for failing to provide her or him with quality education. Schools have to be made to deal with the issue of homosexuality, as well as sexism and racism, *systemically*. Changes should be incorporated in the curriculum, in every discipline. In the case of homosexuality, as with sexism and racism, this can be done by talking about the issue, by insisting on its existence and its importance as an issue, by discussing it, and by challenging stereotypical misconceptions. Only then can we normalize homosexuality. This suggestion may not eliminate discrimination against homosexuals, but it would make the issue visible, present, and nonexceptional. It would certainly deal with the current marginalization of lesbian and gay youth, and thus, possibly provide them with a chance for quality education.

NOTES

1. Ages given at the end of quotes refer to the age at which the incident occurred rather than the current age. This is in order to guarantee that no informant is recognized as a continuous presence.

2. Commissioned Paper, *U.S. Department of Health and Human Services,* National Institute of Mental Health: Task Force on Youth Suicide. National Conference on Prevention and Interventions in Youth Suicide, June 11-13, 1986, Oakland, California.

3. Hugh Warren and the London Gay Teenager Group, *Talking about School* (London: The London Gay Teenager Group, 1984), p. 16.

4. Prairie Research Associates Inc., *The Gay and Lesbian Youth Services Network Survey of Gay Youth and Professionals Who Work With Youth* (August 1989), p. iii.

5. We each used a feminist sociological methodology developed by Dorothy E. Smith, described in detail in her book *The Everyday World as Problematic* (Boston: Northeastern University Press, 1987). Specifically, George Smith and I each adopted the methodological procedures of institutional ethnography, which explicate the "institutional relations determining everyday worlds and how the local organization of the latter may be explored to uncover their ordinary invisible determinations in relations that generalize and are generalized." In other words, it was by investigating ethnographically a "section" of the social world from the standpoint of the organization of the practices and activities of those who, in various ways, are involved in its production—in this case, the work and

activities of students, teachers, guidance counselors, and administrators—that we could begin to comprehend how lesbian and gay youth are rendered invisible, and how, because of their invisibility, they are seldom in a position to break the relative silence which envelops their lives at school.

6. George Smith presented his findings in a separate paper, unpublished as of this writing.

7. See Robert Earl Powell, "Homosexual Behavior and the School Counsellor," *The School Counsellor* (January 1987): 203.

8. Various organizations and support systems in Metro Toronto were consulted in the search for potential interviewees. These include: Lesbian and Gay Youth of Toronto (LGYT); Central Toronto Youth Services; The Toronto Board of Education Student Support Services, Counseling, and Information on Human Sexuality; Lesbian Youth Peer Support (LYPS); and Street Outreach Support (SOS). All interviews were conducted between May 1, 1990, and April 30, 1991. Where George Smith worked with nineteen gay young men, I was able to reach twelve lesbians. Each respondent was self-selected. For this reason, most of our interviewees were already self-identified as lesbian or gay. Therefore, for my part, I did not interview anyone who was confused about her sexual orientation, or who was still going through the process of coming out. We both worked from a simple interview schedule served to focus the interview, but which permitted each to modify the questions to adapt to the situation at hand. We guaranteed complete anonymity to every participant, assuring each that we would change names and places to protect their identity, and that their stories were and are not meant to be a sample. They were young women and men who granted us an interview. They represented only themselves and no statistical generalizations can be made based upon their experiences. The generalizations that can be made when using an institutional ethnography are based on examining the everyday world of these students, making visible the determinants of the social relations of which they are a part, and uncovering the local organization of the schools, thus contextualizing their lives within the educational system.

9. Despite a year-long search, I was not able to interview any "street kids" for this research. The women who presented themselves at the agency which supports street youth (SOS) were often living off selling their bodies. They did not identify themselves as lesbian. For an excellent account of their lives across Canada, see: Marlene Webert. *Street Kids: The Tragedy of Canada's Runaways* (Toronto: University of Toronto Press, 1991).

10. Government of Ontario. The Education Act. Revised Statutes of Ontario, 1990: 104 (2).

11. Gloria J. Krysiak, "A Very Silent Gay Minority," *The School Counsellor* (March 1987): 305.

12. Alan K. Malyon, "The Homosexual Adolescent: Developmental Issues and Social Bias," *Child Welfare* 60, no. 5 (May 1981): 328.

13. Ibid.

14. Ibid.

15. Ibid., p. 329.

16. Krysiak, "A Very Silent Gay Minority," pp. 305–306.

17. To begin with, in a modern patriarchal Western capitalist society like Canada (this analysis is intended to situate and ground the experiences of the young women I interviewed. It is not meant to exclude other state formations, races, or creeds), white

male supremacy is contingent upon discernible differences being established between men and women, rich and poor, white people and people of color. These differences, although contentiously based on a physical reality, often on biologically "demonstrable" grounds, have to be maintained ideologically, socially, economically, and politically through institutional structures. The education system is governed and supported by the state in this country and can safely be said to reflect hegemonic ideology. What is taught at school is what is constructed as knowledge—defined by those in a position of power and serving to maintain the status quo.

Historically, as well as currently, one of the basic tenets of white male capitalist power (but not restricted to it) is that the distinctions between (white) males and the rest of society become common knowledge, perceived as "natural" or, in Gramsci's terms, as "common sense," a concept Chantal Mouffe interprets as that "which presents itself as the spontaneous philosophy of the man of the street, but which is the popular experession of 'higher' philosophies" (Chantal Mouffe, "Hegemony and Ideology in Gramsci," in Chantal Mouffe, ed., *Gramsci and Marxist Theory* [London: Routledge and Kegan Paul, 1979], p. 186). Once the distinctions are established, they are institutionalized, reproduced, and thus they become part of our everyday life. Consequently, since power in this society resides with (white) males, they prescribe the norms and they become the measure against which all others are compared. However, despite the neatness of this explanation, it is not as simple when applied to real people. Individuals and groups adopt their particular subversions, produce counterhegemonic ideologies (idid., p. 193), and live out their peculiar contradictions. Even though conformity is sustained and regulated through an entire ideological structure of laws and traditions, legitimized through institutions such as schools, churches, and the media, and rewarded economically and politically, many live their differences behind acceptable personae.

Although many hegemonic principles operate to maintain male supremacy, one of the most fundamental is heterosexuality. (See Adrienne Rich, "Compulsory Heterosexuality and Lesbian Existence," *Signs: Journal of Women in Culture and Society* 5, no. 4 [Summer 1980]: 631–60; Howard Buchbinder, Dinal Forbes, Varda Burstyn, and Mercedes Steedman, eds., *Who's On Top: The Politics of Heterosexuality* [Toronto: Garamond Press, 1987]; Sue Cartledge and Joanna Ryan, eds., *Sex and Love: New Thoughts on Old Contradictions* [London: The Women's Press, 1983], to name a few works which cogently argue this point.) However, heterosexuality itself depends upon the power differential which characterizes male/female relations, and therefore on the differences which justify this power. These differences are institutionalized in gender roles: masculinity becomes the measuring rod against which femininity is judged (and found wanting); it becomes the determinant, the relevant descriptor, and as such, the defining ingredient of power. Homosexuality, both in men and in women—but for different reasons—threatens the hegemony of masculinity. Gay men, stereotypically perceived as "effeminate," generally jeopardize the gender roles because they, often purposefully, blur the distinctions between masculinity and femininity. It must be understood that gay men do not necessarily reject masculinity; more likely, they manage it differently than heterosexual men, and they continue to enjoy male privilege, Lesbians threaten masculine hegemony as well. They challenge gender roles, they become financially independent, and they remove themselves from being sexually available to men—a prerogative that heterosexual men believe is rightfully theirs. Moreover, lesbians, as women, occupy a position in society different from that of gay men. But since more privilege is attached to masculinity than to femininity, tomboys, on the average, seem to have an easier time than the gentler males whose image defies traditional msculine prescriptions. (I elaborate this point more fully in my book *Lesbian Teachers: An Invisible Presence* (State University of New York Press, 1993).

18. Didi Khayatt, "Legalized Invisibility: The Effect of Bill 7 on Lesbian Teachers," *Women's Studies International Forum* 13, no. 3 (1990): 185–93.

19. Apart from the work already cited above, there are a number of books and articles that are useful on the subject of lesbian/gay youth. Among them are the following: The Gay Teachers' Group, *School's Out: Lesbian and Gay Rights in Education* (London: The Gay Teachers' Group, 1987); Ann Heron, ed., *One Teenager in 10: Writings by Gay and Lesbian Youth* (Boston: Alyson Publications, Inc., 1983); *Radical Teacher,* Issue No. 24: "Gay and Lesbian Studies"; *Radical Teacher,* Issue No. 29: "Teaching Sexuality"; Eric Rofes, "Opening Up the Classroom Closet: Responding to the Education Needs of Gay and Lesbian Youth," *Harvard Educational Review* 59, no. 4 (November 1989); *Now,* September 6–12, 1990, p. 13.

20. Lesbian and gay youth have been actively organizing and, consequently, have created support groups which extend a variety of services and counseling to lesbian and gay youth by lesbian and gay youth. In Toronto, two examples are: (1) Lesbian and Gay Youth of Toronto (LGYT), which is run by youth for youth. It is a place for meeting others, for organizing social and political events, and for simply coming out and sharing experiences with others of similar ages and needs; (2) Lesbian Youth Peer support (LYPS), which is an all-lesbian organization providing support and information to lesbians under twenty-five. In addition many colleges and universities in Ontario have student organizations that provide lesbian and gay students with a forum for expression and support in these preponderantly heterosexual institutions.

# 12

# The Lesbian-Gay Interface between East and West Germany

## Ilse Kokula

November 16, 1989 marks the day when, for the first time in Germany, a public office took up work that deals exclusively with the concerns of lesbian women and gay men, the *Referat für gleichgeschlechtliche Lebensweisen* (Center for Homosexual Lifestyles) of the Berlin Senat Department (equivalent to a Ministry) for Women's, Youth, and Family Affairs in Berlin.

## THE CENTER'S BEGINNING AND ORGANIZATION

The center was established by the AL (Alternative List)/SPD government (consisting of the Green party and the Social-Democratic party), which had been voted into office—to everyone's surprise—in the January 1989 elections, thus replacing the Christian Democratic government. In these elections, two gay men (Albert Eckert and Dieter Telge) won seats for the AL in the Berlin House of Representatives (Parliament of Land* Berlin). In the coalition negotiations with SPD, during which they succeeded in securing the creation of an equality office, they invited Berlin lesbians and gays to meet in order to discuss with them the

---

*Land* may be translated as "state," a subnational unit with far-reaching authority. Hamburg, Bremen, and Berlin are all such city-states.

establishment of such an office. Behind the scenes rather than openly, the experienced (heterosexual) AL member of Parliament, Dr. Hilde Schramm, who later became parliamentary vice-president, used her influence as well. Lesbians and gays were taken by surprise when confronted with the idea of a government office for the concerns of homosexual women and men, and hence somewhat at a loss in the discussion on aims and objectives, since they were not aware of experiences gained abroad.

For the Berlin Senat (i.e., the government of the federal state of Berlin) the establishment of that office meant breaking new ground, whereas other European countries had taken such a step years before. As early as a decade ago, several Dutch communities began setting up offices for *homo-emancipatie* (homosexual emancipation). Today there are twenty-eight towns, five provinces, and the Ministry of Welfare, Health, and Cultural Affairs in the Netherlands which stand for emancipation policy, and have created and staffed offices (of one person each) to this end. As far as the tasks and the organizational integration are concerned, our center may best be compared with the office created within the Dutch Ministry of Welfare, Health, and Cultural Affairs.

Britain, too, has taken a pioneering role in this respect. Since the end of 1986, there have been "gay and lesbian offices" or "gay rights workers" in communities and community associations. The National Lesbian and Gay Policy Conference, held in Newcastle in September 1989 under the heading of "Equality for All," was attended by representatives of thirty-four local governments. Many of them were women's, minority, or AIDS commissioners; but they, too, were obliged to defend the rights of lesbians and gays within their respective departments. At the conference "Aspects of Lesbian and Gay Emancipation in Local Governments," organized by the Center for Homosexual Lifestyles, British participants reported that the notorious Article 28 of the British Local Government Legislation, banning any deliberate promotion of homosexuality, has so far not had any direct impact on their activities. They fear, however, a detrimental effect on the general social climate and, as a consequence, on their work.

In the Netherlands, equality offices for homosexual women and men are located on three administrative levels: community, provincial, and national. In Great Britain, such offices are to be found at the community level only, whereas in Sweden and Norway they are found at the federal level only. In the United States there are a few administrative units and commissioners to represent the interests of lesbian women and gay men which are assigned to a local mayor's office or, in certain administrative areas, are charged with special tasks (such as the Commissioner for Homosexual Women and Men in the New York Police Department).

The Center for Homosexual Lifestyles in Berlin is located at the state level. Apart from being a city, Berlin is a state of the Federal Republic. There are no equivalent offices on the borough level, unlike the Women's and Foreigners' Commissioners, who are represented both at the borough and at the state levels.

In the State of Berlin, the "boroughs" are independent towns, twelve of which are located in the former West Berlin, and eleven in the former East Berlin, making a total of twenty-three towns. One of our aims in the years to come will be to set up similar offices in all of Berlin's boroughs.

Our center was affiliated with the section of the Senat Department responsible for family policy. The fact that our office is located in that section has conceptual implications. First of all, the emphasis is on what lesbians and gays have in common, rather than what divides them (while not ignoring that aspect). Second, family policy is conceived as one aspect of social policy rather than support for the traditional nuclear family. At a press conference the head of the family policy section and temporary head of the Center for Homosexual Lifestyles, Heinz-Günter Maassen, explained this concept as follows: the family policy section does not shape an image of the family but adapts to social developments. This encompasses the fact that many people choose not to live in a family. While the law accords to families a certain privacy which is recognized in society, this constitutional right should also be granted to alternative lifestyles.

At present, the Center for Homosexual Lifestyles has four staff positions, plus several trainee positions for social workers and law students. Additional positions are planned under national schemes to counteract unemployment; these, however, will be term positions only. It should be noted that within the Berlin administration an organizational unit called a *Referat* is staffed, on the average, by about forty persons. During the rather short time since its creation, our center has been treated very differently by the various politicians in Land Berlin. The two members of the House of Representatives of the Alternative List (i.e., the Green party), who had fought for the establishment of our center, were disappointed by its functioning during the first few months, as allegedly it had little to to show in the way of results and the first two employees (the two other positions were filled later) had, allegedly, adapted too much to administrative structures. As a a consequence, the House members advocated a reduction rather than an increase (as had been originally planned) of budgetary allocations.

In autumn 1990—almost one year after the foundation of the center—the Berlin state government underwent several crises, in the course of which the senator (minister) responsible for our center resigned. Following the outcome of the December 1990 elections, a government coalition was formed between the Social Democratic and Christian Democratic parties. During coalition negotiations the CDU (Christian Democratic Union) had demanded the abolition of the center on the following grounds: a general lack of funds, which was expected to worsen as a result of the unification of the two German states, and the arguments that no publicity should be given to homosexuality and that homosexual women and men were not covered by family policy. Lesbian and gay groups, initiatives, and projects; group initiatives and projects of the women's movement; concerned individuals; and the city administrations of Amsterdam (Netherlands) and Manchester (Great Britain) successfully appealed to the leadership of the Berlin SPD and CDU, thus assuring the survival of the center in its present form under the new government. Nor was the center affected by the restructuring of both the government and the administration, and remained in the same Senat Department, which was, however, pared down and stripped of Women's Affairs. It is now called the Senat Department for Youth and Family Affairs.

As one of their first activities—in accordance with the responsibilities of a state agency—the first two staff members of the center defined its tasks. In the course of the center's one-and-a-half-year existence, this definition had to be modified only in a few respects. It is the work of the center to:

1) undertake ministerial tasks. Chief among these are the participation in and influencing of laws, regulations, and guidelines to eliminate discrimination against homosexual women and men, their lifestyles, and forms of association.

2) enforce the principle that public administration in general, not just the center itself, is responsible for the concerns of lesbians and gay men.

3) educate the public and promote societal acceptance of gays and lesbians through events, publications, and education programs (e.g., to teachers and the police).

4) offer further training to special vocational groups: further education courses are intended, first of all, for the center's staff members. These persons are mainly social and educational workers.

5) work on precedents: in an improved political climate, lesbians and gays are increasingly claiming their civil rights from the state and organizations. Such precedents are to receive support if the people concerned approach the center or if the facts become known. In past months, there have been only a few (though time-consuming) cases concerning the right to asylum, the granting of residence permits, and appropriate counseling. The investigation into cases of discrimination within the administration, e.g., hiring, belongs in this area.

6) offer financial support to lesbian and gay projects and activities that deal with improving the social climate and informing the public: since only limited funds are available, priorities have to be agreed upon. In this field, contacts with lesbian and gay groups are closest.

Another conceptual decision had to be taken as a consequence of the center's limited staff: no social or psychological counseling is provided. This decision was also based on the following criteria: the center is located at a Senat Department (i.e., ministry) level and its tasks are, therefore, of a ministerial or planning nature. Social and psychological counseling do not fall within the sphere of a state authority. A promotion of lesbian and gay counseling agencies has been under discussion, but that aim has not yet been laid down in writing. The principle of subsidiarity, an important feature in German administration, also applies to the center. That principle stipulates that the state and its agencies only assume tasks in the social and cultural sectors, if these are not provided by voluntary organizations. (This, however, does not apply to the education sector which falls under the center's sphere of functions.) Only if no or insufficient advisory offices were available in this area, would the Senat Department have to offer such a counseling service. In addition, it was questioned whether it would be wise to file the names and addresses of individuals seeking advice, as long as there was still some political uncertainty about the future of the center.

The following are the center's target groups: they may be treated separately in analysis, although not always in routine practical work:

1) the general public, to whom acceptance of lesbians and gays is to be promoted

2) administrative staff

3) lesbians and gay men who do not yet or no longer feel part of the emancipation movement

4) those who are currently involved in the emancipation movement of lesbians and gay men.

## THE WORK OF THE CENTER DURING AND AFTER UNIFICATION

During the past twenty months, the center's work has covered a great range of activities, from the work on precedents, legal counseling for the foundation of associations, further education programs, and talks with parliamentarians to publicity schemes and lectures, both in Berlin and outside. A special field of activities was added as a result of the dramatic political changes in the two German states and, later, of unification. The city of Berlin grew bigger by the inclusion of the eastern part of the city, and the State of Berlin is now surrounded by the newly established Federal State of Brandenburg. Even before the Berlin Wall came down, there were contacts between the developing political and cultural subcultures of West and East Berlin (see Kokula 1988: 133–42). But these had been unilateral, for only West Berliners (West Germans and West Europeans) were allowed to travel to East Berlin and the former GDR (German Democratic Republic). All this changed abruptly, however, when the Wall was breached on November 9, 1989. Now the lesbians and gays from East Berlin and its surroundings poured into West Berlin.

From the start, the center for Homosexual Lifestyles has had a special relationship with the lesbians and gays in the former East Berlin and the new federal states. By its various activities the center has contributed significantly to the integration of a once divided city and state. Immediately after the Wall came down, the center's first two staff members were contacted by lesbians and gays from East Berlin and the former GDR. All interested visitors were informed of the functions of our center as well as of the West Berlin lesbian and gay movement with all its associated initiatives, groups, and projects. A great number of questions were asked: How many initiatives and groups are there? What do they offer? How is the work organized? What are the problems involved? There was hardly a day during the first few weeks after the center's opening when there were no visitors at all. These questions showed that contact among lesbians and gays in the former GDR had hardly been established. There were already groups in a number of East German cities, which, however, lacked the funds to build up a communication network. In the ensuing talks between East and West, the idea was put forward to organize a meeting in which lesbian and gay delegates from East Berlin and the GDR, and representatives of West Berlin groups and projects should meet and get to know each other. The addresses of committed individuals, initiatives, and groups within the GDR began to be collected. The addresses released for publication were distributed in a circular to which we asked for additions; these were then included in a second circular comprising an extensive list of addresses. Later we were informed of the usefulness of that list since it enabled gays in the former GDR to contact each other.

The first formal meeting between East and West took place in March 1990, at Schönberg Town Hall, then the seat of the Government of Land Berlin, and was attended by about seventy participants, representing twenty groups and initiatives form East Berlin and the GDR and sixteen from West Berlin. It was the aim of that meeting to enable participants to contact and get to know each other. In December 1990, there took place a second meeting, in which speakers from East Berlin and other cities of the former GDR reported on the history and situation of lesbians and gays in East Germany. The lectures were published in 1991.

During the first half of 1990, the majority of the people contacting us came from East Berlin and the GDR. They were interested in the lesbian and gay movement or had individual problems. Their questions dealt with issues of resettling in the West and of residence permits or asylum rights (in cases where one partner came from a socialist country). Many lesbians and gays who had met partners "from the West" in recent years, or who wanted to leave the GDR for political reasons, inquired about resettling possibilities. Between 1989 and October 3, 1990, when the two Germanies were united, so many East Berliners moved to the Western part of the city that all emergency reception camps were full. The Berlin Senat (i.e., the state government) ordered a resettlement to other West German camps. But most of the lesbians and gays who had come from East Berlin were interested primarily in the West Berlin lesbian/gay subculture. Therefore, they did not want to be sent to a transit camp in a small Bavarian town. On top of this there was political uncertainty and an unsettled legal situation, in which the old no longer applied and the new was not yet defined. At that time it was by no means clear whether the GDR would survive as an autonomous German state or whether it would be integrated into the Federal Republic. Many laws of the former GDR were no longer in effect during that transitional period, or else were no longer applied. It remained unclear what new laws, directives, and administrative regulations would become effective. This legal uncertainty was accompanied by a psychosocial one.

During the second half of 1990, when developments pointed increasingly to unification, our staff members would be increasingly approached for information concerning the creation of initiatives and groups, the foundation of associations, nd potential funding sources.

In March 1990, when the first "free elections" were held in the GDR, the transitional government of Prime Minister Modrow took office for a few months. In East Berlin as well, a new city parliament was elected, to which many members of the civil rights movements gained a seat. The East Berlin administration was reorganized, and there, too, members of the civil rights movement assumed political and administrative positions. A period of openness toward the concerns of lesbians and gays set in, and the city parliament of East Berlin decided to establish a "Lesbians' and Gays' Home." Therefore, our Center for Homosexual Lifestyles became a sought-after negotiating partner both for East Berlin local politicians and for civil servants. The women from the office for sexual equality, created only a few months before, were constant visitors; they came to us for information and took part in meetings organized by the center. The office for sexual equality would be extended to include equality for lesbians and gay men. After the general elections, in which a majority of GDR citizens voted for a unification of the two German states (rather than for a survival of two associated German states), the East Berlin administration was merged with that of the West. The process of integration of two such diverse systems, however, has not yet been completed, and is expected to take several more years.

At another level, a cooperative effort with representatives of East German authorities and womens' initiatives was inaugurated within the so-called working women group of the "regional working committee" for the period of its existence from spring to autumn 1990; it was the group's task to identify problems of integration of the two German states and to submit solutions to them. Many contacts were made at these official meetings, which proved to be useful for later cooperation. On these occasions initiatives and institutions were informed of the situation of lesbian women and, thus, were able to include these aspects in their deliberations and political action.

Another contribution to the integration of the two city halves and the two German states was made by several special events organized by our center, including further education programs in education and meetings on local politics as well as on the subject of "violence against gays." To all those meetings both government representatives and lesbians and gays from East Berlin and the GDR were invited. As much as possible, they were invited to give talks (e.g., at the conference "Aspects of Lesbian and Gay Emancipation in Local Governments"). It was a very time-consuming affair to send invitations and to address letters to the lesbians', women's, and gay magazines, which had not existed before the second half of 1990 (one exception being the newsletter *Frau Anders* [*Ms. Different*] issued by the church). In some cases private accommodation had to be organized for participants. Members of our center held lectures in East Berlin and other GDR cities; attended meetings; and gathered personal information on social conditions, the development of the emancipation movement, and other issues. Our intention was to make it clear that members of our staff also "move around in the East" and approach people; we wanted also to point out that the process of gathering information and support involves everybody and must be a mutual affair.

## ONGOING DEVELOPMENTS

Nineteen eighty-nine and 1990 were years of vast political changes, not only in the GDR but in the whole of Germany. The civil rights movement of the GDR emerged and made itself heard in 1989. In all major cities, "round tables" were established, assembling around them representatives of the civil rights movement and the local administration, who were designing concepts for the reorganization of society and making concrete decisions on certain issues. (For instance, the round table in Leipzig appointed a commissioner for minorities.)

At almost all "round tables," lesbians and gays were represented, since in previous years they had made efforts to organize themselves (Kokula 1988: 133–42). In the open and democratic atmosphere of these round tables, the social position of lesbians and gay men were discussed, and steps to improve their situation were suggested. Unfortunately, however, the decisions taken at the round tables were, later on, often overlooked or ignored when new administrative systems were established. Lesbian and gay activists who founded associations and projects sought the advice of our center. East Berlin and Potsdam have been—and still are—trying to set up equality offices for homosexual women and men, as in the case in the State of Brandenburg. Here, too, members of our center have been actively serving as discussion partners and counselors. As of September 1, 1991, the East German city of Leipzig has had an office for homosexual lifestyles, staffed by one woman and one man. They cooperate closely with our center.

It remains to be seen whether the political upheaval in the former GDR, and its repercussions in the former Federal Republic of Germany, will offer genuine opportunities to gays and lesbians, and whether these opportunities are effectively used. It remains also to be seen whether offices to ensure the quality of homosexual women and men will be created in the future.

## REFERENCES AND BIBLIOGRAPHY

Kokula, Ilse. "The Situation and Organization of Lesbian Women in the German Democratic Republic." *Second ILGA Pink Book: A Global View of Lesbian on Gay Liberation and Oppression.* Utrecht: Interfacultaire Werkgroep Homostudies, 1988, pp. 133–42.

———. "Business as usual. Entstehungsgeschichte, Ziele und Arbeitsschwerpunkte des Referats für gleichgeschlechtliche Lebensweisen der Senatsverwaltung für Frauen, Jugend und Familie in Berlin" ("Business as Usual. The History of the Origins, Goals, and Principal Functions of the Center for Homosexual Lifestyles of the Berlin Senat Ministry for Women, Youth, and Family"). *Zeitschrift für Sexualforschung* 4, no. 3 (December 1990): 364–67.

———, ed. *Aspekte lesbischer und schwuler Emanzipation in Kommunalverwaltungen (Aspects of Lesbian and Gay Liberation in Local Administration).* Berlin: Senatsverwaltung für Frauen, Jugend und Familie, 1991.

———, ed. *Geschichte und Perspektiven von Lesben und Schwulen in den neuen Bundesländern (Past History and Future Prospects of Lesbians and Gays in the New Federal States).* Berlin: Senatsverwaltung für Jugend und Familie, 1991.

Scheiber, Anke. "Grenzen der Verwaltbarkeit homosexueller Lebensweisen am Beispiel des Referats für gleichgeschlechtliche Lebensweisen bei der Berliner Senatsverwaltung für Frauen, Jugend and Familie" ("Limits of the 'Administratibility' of Homosexual Lifestyles Based on the Example of the Center for Homosexual Lifestyles of the Berlin Senat Ministry for Women, Youth, and Family"). Unpublished dissertation in the Department of Political Science at the Free University of Berlin, January 1991.

van der Veen, Evert, and Adrianne Dercksen. Onderzoeksverslag deel I, vijftien jaar discriminatie wegens homoseksualiteit (Research Report Part I, Fifteen Years of Anti-Homosexual Discrimination). Utrecht, 1990.

# 13

# The Development of the Gay Movement in Ireland: A Personal and Political Memoir

## David Norris

My approach to the subject of the development of the gay movement in Ireland and its relations with the international gay movement is, perhaps, idiosyncratic and even, on first glance at least, egotistical. This is an inevitable byproduct of historical circumstances. I was born in 1944 in Central Africa to an English father and Irish mother. Ancestors on both sides of my family had some pretensions to nobility, and my early life and educational background was, to a certain extent, a privileged one.

The date of my birth meant that I passed my adolescence in the Ireland of the 1950s, an era in which sexual ignorance was endemic among heterosexual as well as homosexual people, and the celibate hierarchy of the Roman Catholic Church ruled the private lives of Irish citizens with a crozier of iron in every diocese. Divorce and contraception, regarded by the minority Protestant churches as legitimate options for married couples, were both strictly forbidden; divorce was actually prohibited constitutionally.

Not surprisingly in such a climate, there was no recognition at all of the existence of homosexuality. Any suggestion that 10 percent of the population of the Island of Saints and Scholars (a popularly sentimental title for Ireland during its period of monastic preeminence in the early Middle Ages) might be gay would have come as a profound and traumatic shock to the Irish psyche.

Some incidents from this period stand out with painful clarity. I recall the terror I experienced as a small boy in boarding school when I, with beating heart, was chased around the perimeter of the playing fields by an older boy intent, for some reason then obscure to me, on removing my short trousers. When he ignored my desperate pleas to be left alone over several weeks (during which, like a coursed hare, I only narrowly escaped his fangs), I reported the matter to one of the teachers. Nothing was explained to me; an ominous silence on the subject enveloped the school; and two days later, the unfortunate youth's equally unfortunate elderly father arrived to remove him forever from the establishment. Years later, when I came to realize the meaning of this episode, I felt first shame and then sadness that we should all have been victims of such pressurized ignorance.

As I grew older, there were vague hints of the existence of at least one well-known male couple in Dublin's theatrical circles—Michael MacLiammoir and Hilton Edwards of the Gate Theatre, whose sexual eccentricities were tolerated because of their talent. Nevertheless, in this period all was surreptitious and non-specific; there was little of the erotic in Irish society, at least for homosexual males. Later I was to watch in fascinated amazement the orderly queues of young and not-so-young men—rivaling the length of cinema queues—that would form outside the several notorious *pissoirs* on the Dublin quays at weekend pub closing times. These were virtually the only meeting places for gay men in the fifties and sixties; their popularity, and the fact that the general population passed in apparent unconcern, gave a very clear signal. Society was quite prepared to turn a blind eye and, indeed, be surreptitiously encouraging to compulsive promiscuity as long as it did not become publicly or consciously acknowledged. On the other hand, any attempt to claim for gay relationships the same level of dignity and respect that was held for heterosexual ones would be dealt with mercilessly. A committed monogamous relationship led to visibility and the courts, whereas for the vast majority, who were prepared (if not exactly content) to remain oppressed and invisible, disease and the occasional good scare were the principal hazards.

Homosexuality was still very much the "crime which must not be mentioned among Christians," and the conspiracy of silence thus engaged in by society meant that gay people in Ireland lived in conditions of isolation, fear, and ignorance. Therefore, gay people did not know or recognize each other officially, let alone have a capacity to organize.

At last, in the early 1960s, the first chinks appeared in the wall of silence, due largely to the debate provoked by the British report of Sir John Wolfenden and his Commission of Enquiry into Prostitution and Homosexuality. The resulting laborious parliamentary process in Britain culminated in the passage of the 1967 Sexual Offences Act, a niggardly and parsimonious piece of legislation which did, at least, remove the criminal penalties from a limited area of male homosexual behavior. Thus for the first time, the word "homosexual" started appearing in the newspapers. The law was clearly a major focus of the control of gay people in Ireland, and for this reason it is worthwhile to give a brief historical account of the legal attitude to this form of sexuality in Ireland.

## IRELAND'S HISTORY OF GAY OPPRESSION

In the Celtic period, homosexuality was known but not discriminated against, except to the extent that the homosexuality of a husband constituted, under Brehon Law, a cogent reason for the dissolution of a marriage at the instigation of the wife. Slightly greater knowledge of homosexual practices emerges in the early Middle Ages as a result of Celtic Christianity and the existence of penitentials such as that of Cummean Fada, a ninth-century monk, which goes into specific—even lubricious—detail concerning the precise categories and variations of the sexual act and their appropriate penalties. However, an important point must be made here, and that is that homosexual behavior remained in the realm of sin and within the sphere of operation of the church throughout the medieval period, only coincidentally becoming subject to criminal law in the sixteenth century. This happened as a result of the seizure of the monasteries by Henry VIII in 1533. By so doing, Henry also possessed himself of the ecclesiastical courts under which homosexual behavior had been regarded as a religious offense.

It was thus accidental that the acts known as sodomy and buggery made the transition from sin to crime. Indeed, the etymology of these two words is itself interesting: "sodomy" derives from the story of the cities of the Plain in the Old Testament; "buggery" is a corruption of the term "Bulgar," another name for the Albigensians who were believed to have originated in Bulgaria. Fairly early on, "buggery" also implied sexual deviation. Curiously enough, however, the Act of 1534 punishing "the detestable and abhomynable vice of buggery, commyttid with mankynde or beaste,"[1] was discovered subsequently not to extend to Ireland. This became clear in 1631, when an Irish noble, the Earl of Castlehaven, was charged with committing sodomy with one of his male servants. These charges were brought by the earl's son, who was afraid that the close friendship between master and servant might lead to the loss of part of the son's inheritance. The earl was found guilty of sodomy by a 15-to-12 verdict of his peers and executed. Both the offense and the trial took place in England, thereby underlining the fact that such an act would not have constituted an offense nor obtained such a conviction in the earl's native land of Ireland.

Spurred by this discovery, John Atherton, an Anglican prelate and bishop of Waterford and Lismore, launched a campaign, for political reasons, to have the statute extended to cover Ireland in a manner curiously reminiscent of the recent campaign by the Reverend Ian Paisley to "save Ulster from sodomy."

Atherton's campaign was ultimately successful. "An Act for the Punishment for the Vice of Buggery" was passed by the Irish House of Commons on November 11, 1634. By an irony that it would perhaps be uncharitable to regard as delightful, the first man to be hanged under this act was, in fact, none other than Atherton after accusations of homosexual acts between the bishop and his tithe proctor, John Child, had been laid by Child himself. The accuser was tried at Waterford, sentenced at Cork, and hanged at Bandon Bridge in March 1641. Atherton himself was taken to Dublin, imprisoned in the Castle, and sentenced to be hanged on the gallows green at Dublin on December 5, 1641. On the scaffold Bishop Abbott said: "I am, I thinke, the first of my profession, that came hither to this shameful end, and I pray God I may be the last: you are come hither to see a comedy turned into a tragedy, a miserable catastrophe of the life and actions of a man in this world."[2]

The penalty for male homosexual activity remained death by hanging until 1861, when the present statute involving two sections of the Offences Against the Person Act was introduced.

It is perhaps strange to realize now that this 1861 act was in fact a liberalizing statute, in that it involved a substantial reduction of the sentence. The same could not be said of the La Bouchere Amendment of 1885, which was introduced late at night in the House of Commons as an adjunct to a bill with which it had no connection and upon whose introduction there was no vote, nor any discussion. Thus was passed into law a bill described by Sir John Wolfenden eighty years later as a blackmailer's charter. Perhaps the most serious consequence of the enactment of this amendment was that it criminalized what it termed "gross indecency between males." This very imprecise language meant that the intent of the section was determined only subsequently by case law. It is scarcely surprising that the socialization of gay men in the British Isles remained at a primitive level under these restraints.

It is sometimes incorrectly stated that the reason this legislation did not extend to cover lesbian sexuality was because Queen Victoria could not bring herself to believe that women were capable of such lewdness. The real reason is more instructive, i.e., male legislators in the cultural environment of the nineteenth century were reluctant to believe that women actively experienced anything so unladylike as sexual pleasure, and certainly not if this was to be achieved independent of the imperial, all-conquering penis. A facet of this argument surfaced once more with anachronistic irony when I sued the State of Ireland in the Supreme Court in Dublin. One of our contentions was that the fact that lesbian women were excluded from criminal consideration represented a discrimination on the basis of sex alone. The chief justice, in his wisdom, discovered that the solution to this problem lay in the question of the different capacities of the two sexes, maintaining that whereas women might be capable of indecency, it was not credible that they could, like men, be guilty of gross indecency.

However, I remember feeling, very early on in the gay movement, that, in a paradoxical fashion, gay men in Ireland were lucky in that at least they did have a specific focus of injustice which could be used as a rallying cry for liberal opinion, whereas women were insulted by being simply ignored as usual. Moreover, subsequent experiences have demonstrated that the absence of any mention of lesbianism in legislation does not prevent discrimination against lesbian women; in fact, it is rather the reverse, especially in cases of marital breakdown or the custody of children where the lesbianism of the wife is never neglected by opposing counsel as a negative factor, and is frequently a basis for blackmail by the husband and his advisers.

## THE BIRTH OF THE MOVEMENT

It was not principally an understanding of the precise impact of the law that propelled me into the gay movement at the end of the 1960s, but a more generalized feeling of outrage at the tacit discrimination against people like myself. By the late 1960s, some organizational framework had begun to emerge in America and—closer to home—in England. It was with great excitement that I remember seeing a small box ad in, I think, *The Sunday Times* for an organization calling itself "The Campaign for Homosexual Equality." It advised those who were homosexual (the word "gay" was not then fashionable) to send a stamped addressed envelope to an address which, as I recall it, was 28A Kennedy Street, Manchester. The address has lingered in my mind for over twenty years because it was the first beacon of hope. Against the advice of suspicious straight friends who thought it might be an opening for blackmail, I sent away to the address and received in return some fact sheets on homosexuality.

Dublin, however, in 1971 was entirely unaware of the events of the Stonewall Riots in New York eighteen months previously; so it was without this inspirational lead that I almost accidentally took the jump into what then appeared to be the gay void, in a manner which may give some clue as to how difficult it was for gay people in Ireland at that time to identify with each other at even the most minimal level. At the inaugural meeting of the Southern Ireland Civil Rights Association, a group formed in response to the emerging crisis in Northern Ireland, I listened with increasing irritation as speaker after speaker detailed abuses of the civil rights of Roman Catholics in the north of Ireland, comparing this unfavorably with the treatment of Protestants in the south. I had by now spotted an attractive young Dutch man and had begun to wonder how I could run up a flag of some kind to signal that I was gay and possibly spark his interest. This prompted me to rebuke the speakers for their complacency with regard to discrimination north and south, and to indicate that whatever their smug self-congratulation might suggest to them, there was at least one minority in the south, i.e., homosexuals, who were being savagely discriminated against. My contribution had the desired effect of bringing me into conversation with the young Dutch man who, unfortunately, turned out not to be gay; it also created something of a furor during which I was variously advised to recant, lie low, or pretend I'd had a nervous breakdown for "confessing" that I was gay.

In any case, it made it all the easier for me to be explicit when over the next two years moves began, at first in a very general way, that would lead to the founding of the gay movement in Ireland. This began with a series of conferences sponsored by the student welfare bodies of a number of universities, including my own, Trinity College, Dublin. The atmosphere thus created led to the founding of an umbrella body on an all-Ireland basis called The Union for Sexual Freedoms in Ireland. This had a number of constituent elements, of which the Dublin-based one became known as the Sexual Liberation Movement, or SLM. The SLM consisted of about a dozen people, predominantly male and all homosexual except for one person of undeclared sexuality. A good deal of time was spent in what I quickly came to regard as camouflage activity to demonstrate how conscientious we were, such as letter-writing campaigns to the newspapers advocating access to contraceptives and divorce. A group of us, per-haps the majority, felt that this was quixotic in the extreme, given our own sexual orientation; therefore, I led a move to create a specifically gay organization to be called the Irish Gay Rights Movement (IGRM), which would, in its very title, place our demands and our statements about ourselves unapologetically at the forefront of the organization.

We continued to meet in the rooms of a student society in Trinity College, discussing what had then been the forbidden topic of our sexuality, letting it all hang out in the most delicious orgy of self-revelation and self-acknowledg-ment—what came to be known as consciousness-raising. We also began to organ-ize social events, rather innocent little alcohol-free dances or record hops which ended strictly at 11:30 P.M. How daring and nervous we all felt at the first of these events, but how quickly we became used to them. It also struck a few of us that here was the ideal gay liberation machine in embryo: a simple mecha-nism consisting of two parts: (1) a political/theoretical wing which would do battle with the forces of conventionality and repression in our society, and (2) a much-needed social outlet that would, in turn, generate the funds necessary to sustain the political effort.

Unfortunately, there emerged fairly rapidly within the developing movement some tensions between the political forces on the one hand and social forces on the other, and between the personalities that controlled them. It was perhaps inevitable at this early stage that there should be disagreement with regard to what constituted priorities for the gay community, with competing claims being made for the development of a social life and the achievement of political advances. There were those who felt that increased opportunities for safe contact with others of "like disposition," as the phrase then went, were all that was necessary, and that attacks upon the criminal status of homosexual men would rock the boat, merely drawing attention to a situation that was better left alone.

The workload, of course, was heavy. The strains of being in the front line, and of running discotheques every weekend in order to provide money to fund the building we had now acquired, proved taxing for some. This was, however, compensated for by the buzz of excitement we all felt as pioneers of the gay movement that was traveling ceaselessly to the four corners of Ireland, spreading a message of hope for those who been long oppressed. Indeed, one of the problems to confront the gay movement of the 1990s is how to replace this psychic energy source, now that the pioneers' primitive ideals must be replaced by something more durable and, perhaps, more prosaic. In 1974, our telephone counseling and information service called "Tel-a-Friend" was established, and this survives today, albeit in modified form. Once again this survival is, I believe, largely because the demanding work is stimulated by an individual reward system, in that it provides a practical sense of achievement and value to the participants.

Among the various types of calls coming into the counseling service was a steady trickle of cases indicating the existence of police pressure. This arose partly from the quirks of the laws already referred to; partly from the vulnerability of the gay community to sporadic police crackdowns; and partly from the fact that gay people, being comparatively easy prey and highly likely to plead guilty and obtain a summary conviction to avoid adverse publicity, became an attractive target to any enthusiastic young cop who was not too scrupulous as to how he increased his batting average. Many of the offenses were under the category known colloquially in the gay community as "cottaging."

Groups of us used to attend court dressed in three-piece suits and carrying briefcases, often attended by a valiant young campaigning solicitor, Garrett Shee-han, who, although not gay, was sympathetic and displayed the forensic talents of Perry Mason. Without ever stating bluntly that the police lied or even fudged evidence, he was able to demonstrate in cross examination that much of their evidence was suspect; in fact, every single case in which we represented clients was dismissed. This, together with our political campaigning, led to a virtual end to charges for consensual activity between adults under the criminal law.

Despite the fact that annual data were released in the Garda Report on Crime in such a diffuse and inexact way as to make interpretation hazardous, the figures compiled between 1962 and 1974 suggest that out of nearly 600 cases brought during that period, 75 percent involved offenders who were over the maximum age of consent in any European jurisdiction.[3]

## THE FIGHT TO OVERTURN THE SODOMY LAWS

By 1977, we had become firm in our resolve to remove this pernicious law al-together; The problem, however, was how to achieve this aim. One obvious line of approach was to persuade a member of the public, arrested under one of the obnoxious provisions, to appeal the sentence on constitutional grounds. The difficulty with this approach lay in the very natural human wish, which we found to be universal among defendants, to escape from confrontation with the law with as little publicity as possible. We recognized early on that such a case would, in the Irish context, be very sensational. This being so, we directed our attention to finding a method whereby any such publicity might be turned to our advantage. In pursuance of our aim, we decided to mount a showcase trial in which evidence would be sought on an international basis from leading authorities in such areas of psychiatry, sociology, theology, and medicine. I was charged with the task of mounting this case.

We had decided upon a constitutional action in 1975 and made initial contacts with solicitors. In 1976, we commissioned a legal brief from a leading senior counsel, Donal Barrington. Although Mr. Barrington believed we had an incontestable case intellectually, he was careful to warn us that due to the political complexion of the issues involved, we would face an uphill battle in achieving the judgment we required. Before we got into court Mr. Barrington, having been appointed to the Bench, removed himself from the case. He was replaced by Mrs. Mary Robinson, now President of Ireland, who continued to act in my behalf right through to final victory in October 1988 at the Human Rights Court in Strasbourg. Meanwhile, the division between the political and social sides of the gay liberation movement was becoming critical. The building housing both discotheque and offices was taken over by the group's more socially and less politically conscious members, who proceeded to demonstrate their total incompetence by losing control of the situation they had themselves created: they ceased political activity altogether, closed the discotheque, and abandoned the office.

In these adverse circumstances, a small group of politically committed colleagues, Bernard Keogh, Edmund Lynch, Brian Murray, and I, relaunched the campaign under the banner of "The Campaign for Homosexual Law Reform." Our assets now consisted of one drawer in a filing cabinet and some headed notepaper; therefore, it was rather flattering to be described—as some right-wing Catholic organizations labeled us—an international conspiracy financed by Jewish money from the United States. It was also at this troubled time that I first ran for public office. To be honest, the motivation behind this initial move was largely a propagandizing one. I had discovered that each candidate was entitled to circulate among the entire electorate of his or her constituency an information sheet covering the principal elements of his or her campaign, and the government would pay the postage. I could not resist the idea of a free mail shot to a conservative electorate on so controversial a subject as gay rights. Although I lost by a wide margin, I did receive a few hundred votes.

One reason for my defeat was that I was seen as a one-issue candidate which, at that stage, was a reasonable enough description of my position. However, as I pointed out at the time, the possession even of one issue to which I was passionately committed represented one issue more than most of the other candidates' platforms. This was also the beginning of a much deeper politicization on my part. Like most gay people, I had cut myself off entirely from political involvement of any kind. We had all been brainwashed into believing that we were in some way unreal people because a central reality of our lives was either denied or derided. How then could we be real in a political sense—how could we realize our political identity in any effective form? For me, the experience of being gay, leading inexorably but unexpectedly into increasingly political areas, also served to radicalize me and to force me to identify clearly analogies that existed between my own oppression and that of other minority groups. Paradoxically this radicalizing process broadened both my own political platform and my political appeal, which, I believe, eventually led to my election in 1987 to the Upper House of the Irish Parliament. People by that time had become fully satisfied that there was considerably more than one arrow in my political quiver.

In November 1977, proceedings were finally brought before the High Court seeking a declaration that sections 61 and 62 of the 1861 Act and section 11 of the 1885 Act had automatically lapsed with the passage of the Irish Constitution in 1937, as a result of the conflict between these sections and the provisions of Article 40, sections 1 and 3, guaranteeing the rights of the individual. As already noted, a wide range of expert evidence from all over the world was introduced, and on October 10, 1980, Mr. McWilliam gave his judgment. The success of our aim—to make the hearings a showcase—can be gauged from the fact that McWilliam's judgment is notable for its favorable findings of fact regarding homosexuality as a condition. We were agog with excitement as Justice McWilliam's findings were read out in court. But our excitement was soon dampened when McWilliam indicated that because of the Christian and democratic nature of this State he had to find in the government's favor despite all these findings. At least on this occasion, we had somewhere to go to be with our own. This was because, between 1977 and 1980, not only had the political movement been relaunched but, following the collapse of IGRM, a new organization had been created, The National Gay Federation, with the intention of once more seeking to resolve tensions between the political and social sides of the gay experience.

On one of my rambles through Dublin's inner city I had spotted an abandoned warehouse; in the late summer of 1978, I acquired a lease on these premises —No. 10 Fownes Street, in what has now become known as Temple Bar area. In it we opened the Hirschfeld Centre, where once again we combined social activities, such as a disco, restaurants, coffee bar, and a cinema, with outreach services in the form of a youth group, publications group, and a telephone counseling/befriending service as well as a political campaigning machine. So it was that we trooped back to the Hirschfeld Centre on that day in 1980 to have lunch with an excited—if somewhat disconsolate—group of gay people and to listen to a taped radio interview in which I promised that the fight would continue to the Irish Supreme Court and, if necessary, to Europe until we had achieved our final victory. Our refusal to be downcast drew a resounding cheer from the group assembled in the Centre.

Nineteen eighty-one saw the landmark decision in the European Court of Human Rights regarding a colleague from the old days in the Union for Sexual Freedom in Ireland, Jeffrey Dudgeon. Jeff preceded us to the European Court for two principal reasons. First, his case was taken in response to an actual incident of police harassment, and second, the United Kingdom having no written constitution, he could bypass the requirement to exhaust the domestic remedy and go straight to Europe. Jeff kept us in touch with the progress of his case, and we helped by supplying documents missing from his files—files indicating, for example, covert activities by the Roman Catholic Church to sabotage an earlier attempt to alter the sodomy law in Northern Ireland. The *Dudgeon* judgment, in fact, became available to us during the conduct of my own appeal to the Supreme Court in Dublin; but the court chose completely to ignore the fact that the Irish legislation had been judged to be in violation of fundamental human rights.

This second defeat opened the way to the European Court of Human Rights itself. At Strasbourg the government of Ireland maintained its fine tradition of illogicality, claiming on the one hand that it was vital for the moral welfare of the country to retain the criminal sanction, and on the other hand that the law was never used anyway. Mary Robinson, however, had in the meantime unearthed a couple of cases in family law where couples looking for a separation or declaration of nullity had pleaded the homosexuality of the husband as grounds for the nullity decision. In one of these cases, the presiding judge actually stopped a witness who was about to testify to his participation with the husband in homosexual activities, remarking that if they continued it would be his duty to refer the report of the case to the Director of Public Prosecutions, and that the witness might find himself serving a lengthy term of imprisonment. Ultimately the European Court found in my favor by a very narrow margin; however, as I write almost three years after the court's decision, the Irish government has yet to respond and continues to treat the European Court with complete contempt.

Meanwhile, back at the Senate, I immersed myself in a wide range of political activities, ranging from inner city renewal programs to secretaryship of the Foreign Affairs Committee established by myself and the chairman of the Labour party, Michael D. Higgins, T.D. The experience of working on a daily basis with other members of parliament helped, I think, to demythologize the question of gay liberation for most of the other members of the House; when I came to inserting sexual orientation clauses into government legislation, I found that I rapidly began to have the support of other members of the Senate. Sexual orientation clauses involved merely the addition of the words "or sexual orientation" in any context where the rights of vulnerable groups such as women and racial, religious, or ethnic minorities were concerned. My first outing of this kind was during a debate in the Senate on a bill to institute censorship of videos.[4] This was a bill which I opposed totally in principle, being in fact the only senator so to do. When the bill was passed by an overwhelming majority on the second stage, I took the opportunity of the committee stage procedures to introduce a number of amendments which I had signaled during the second-stage speech. One of these concerned a clause making the Incitement to Hatred on the basis of race, nationality, and religion grounds extend to the banning of video materials. Senator Brendan Ryan and I took the opportunity to seek to amend this by simply adding the clause "or sexual orientation."

A final footnote on sexual orientation clauses. One of my colleagues, Senator Costelloe of the Labour party, attempted to introduce a sexual orientation clause into the Larceny Bill. I was unaware that he was doing this but heard the debate on the television monitor in my office. I rushed over and attempted to make a contribution in support of the general principle, even though Senator Costelloe's amendment was ill advised and would have had precisely the opposite effect to that which he intended. I was but a few sentences into my speech on a remote technical area of the law known as misprision of felony, when the chairman of the Senate indicated that I could not continue as the minister had risen to his feet, thereby automatically concluding that stage of the bill.[5] After the minister's contribution, the chairman put the amendment to the House by a voice vote asking those in favor to say "Ta" (yes). The three of us who were present on the opposition benches all said "Ta." The chairman then said, "I declare the amendment defeated." Senator Costelloe sat down, but I remained standing. I indicated to the chair that he had very properly decided to call a voice vote rather than the formal vote by physical passage of the representatives through the division chambers. I also pointed out that when he asked those in favor to indicate their approval, three of us did so. He had neglected, however, to ask for the vote against the amendment; even if he had done so he could not claim to have heard any voice raised against the amendment since, as I indicated with a gesture, he could see for himself there was not a single government member present on the government benches. Pandemonium broke loose. The law books were sent for, and it was at length determined that the government had been defeated.

## THE NEED FOR INTERNATIONAL COOPERATION

Even in the absence of provisions under an international treaty, convention, or protocol extending the protection of human rights to cover matters such as sexual orientation, it is still possible to persuade government ministers to undertake some serious consideration of their inclusion by citing comparable precedents in the relevant domestic legislation of other countries. The greater the body of such legislative example becomes, and the more easily available it is to individual politicians in their respective countries as an instrument for advancing the cause of civil rights for homosexually oriented citizens, the more effective and persuasive our campaign will be. Ultimately the objective should be to make the inclusion of such a provision a matter of form in as many domestic jurisdictions as possible, so that when pressure is subsequently applied at an international level, they will pass almost automatically into the relevant human rights clauses of international treaties and protocols. I understand, in fact, that the International Lesbian and

Gay Association (ILGA) is, at the moment, seeking to include just such a sexual orientation clause into the supranational structure of the European Economic Community.

The need for information exchange and political cooperation at the international level has long been recognized. The great pioneer of sexual liberation, Dr. Magnus Hirschfeld, was working toward this end through the international petition of 1897; the establishment of the Scientific Humanitarian Committee; the International Congress of Physicians in London in 1913; and the London Congress of World League for Sexual Reform in 1929, which met under Hirschfeld's own presidency. This process was unhappily interrupted by the rise of fascism in the 1930s, but the subject was gradually opened up once more for debate after the Second World War. Particularly important in this regard was the first international gay rights congress held in Edinburgh in 1974, which I attended with other leaders of the emerging gay rights movement in Ireland, and which established a fragile network of cooperation between gay political leaders. This was capitalized upon four years later at Coventry in August 1978, at the International Committee meeting held in conjunction with the annual Campaign for Homosexual Equality Conference. At this meeting a very significant move forward was made in the founding of the International Gay Association, now the ILGA.

I still believe that informational exchange is the most effective way the gay movement can contribute to the development of legislative reform at both national and international levels. For example, in ongoing negotiations with the Department of Justice in Ireland on the question of sexual orientation clauses, I found my personal files relating to the ILGA most useful in indicating to me where the most valuable legislative precedents throughout Europe, North America, and New Zealand can be found. I found also that the information resource provided by ILGA and its constituent organizations was a most valuable source of information, with groups and individuals always ready to respond on short notice to demands for such supporting information. I am glad of the opportunity to express my thanks and appreciation for this very valuable function.

In the early days of the ILGA our imagination was captured by the possibility of such dramatic international actions as that undertaken by Enzo Francone in flying to Teheran to protest against the treatment of gay men under the Islamic fundamentalist regime. I remember, in particular, my excitement at the information secretariat in Dublin as the telephone snowball system was set in operation to secure his release. I now reflect, however, on how naive we were to imagine that such actions, however appealing, would in the long term achieve substantial change in the international perception of the human and civil rights of gay people. Advances can be made—of this I have no doubt—but they will be made by the slow and painful accretion of case histories; precedents; and changes in domestic law, trade union legislation, employment practice, and so on until a moment is arrived at when such changes work their way naturally onto a genuinely international agenda.

This role played by ILGA as part of a networking system proved to be of crucial importance in the next major battle on sexual orientation clauses, that concerning the introduction of an Incitement to Hatred Bill by the then Minister for Justice, Gerard Collins, T.D., now Minister for Foreign Affairs. Mr. Collins, one of the least enlightened members of a rather dim cabinet, freely admitted that this particular legislative item was being introduced as part of a minimalist strategy aimed at allowing Ireland to participate in certain international conventions. He opposed extending the protection of this legislation to a number of groups who were not directly threatened, but steadfastly set his face against extending the provisions of the bill to cover the gay community and the Travellers (the Irish counterpart of European gypsies) who were really at risk; I attempted to counter this move with a series of amendments. With the assistance of the ILGA secretariats, I was able to place on the record a comprehensive list of comparative legislation as well as provide documentary evidence from my own files of threats of arson and murder issued by neofascist groups against the gay community in Dublin (which may have actually played some role in the destruction by fire of the gay community's headquarters there). Even though the minister refused to bow to this pressure, there is no doubt that we won a comprehensive intellectual and moral victory; after the general election of 1989, the new Minister for Justice introduced my amendments himself from the government bench, thus giving Ireland some remarkably progressive legislation for which he has been happy to receive congratulations from his European partners.

## THE MOVE TO OVERTURN DISCRIMINATION IN EMPLOYMENT

Even though legislative change has been slow, there have been some significant positive indicators in the area of discrimination in employment. As an academic, I am a member of a trade union, The Irish Federation of University Teachers (IFUT). In 1980 I placed on the agenda of my local branch a resolution favoring decriminalization and securing the rights of gay workers against discrimination on the basis of sexual orientation. In arguing for this proposal I had the support of useful precedents in the European Trade Union movement, notably documentation from the Scottish Trade Union Congress, made available to me by Ian Dunne of the Scottish Homosexual Rights Group in Edinburgh. After some difficulties this resolution was eventually sent on to, and overwhelmingly passed by, the annual general meeting of IFUT, from which it was sent to the annual general meeting of the Irish Congress of Trade Unions, which, in July 1982, passed an historic pro-gay rights resolution guaranteeing support for decriminalization and equality of job opportunity.[6]

This step, achieved with the assistance of information from trade union groups in other countries, has since formed the basis for a developing program of education and support for gay rights within the Irish trade union movement. Moreover a group operating originally from the Hirschfeld Centre, GLEN (the Gay and

Lesbian Equality Network), among others, successfully lobbied from within the civil service to achieve a remarkable advance in 1988, under which discrimination on the basis of either HIV status or sexual orientation is outlawed.[7]

This document once more highlights the contrast between the conservative desire on the part of Irish authorities to retain out-of-date imperial statutes, and a much more humane approach to the individual in the workplace and in society in general, which is a feature of Irish life.

## RESPONSE TO THE AIDS EPIDEMIC

I recall very clearly in the early days of the gay movement in Ireland a discussion as to whether or not there was such thing as a gay community. I can now say, having witnessed the very remarkable courage and altruism of individuals and groups within the gay movement in confronting the AIDS epidemic, that I have no doubt of the existence of a gay community—indeed, it is a community of which I am very proud to be a member.

In the beginning, many of the organizations responding to the threat of AIDS proliferated out of the Hirschfeld Centre in Fownes Street. After it burned down, these organizations dispersed. They have, however, continued to grow and to make a contribution, although, sadly, the level of discrimination in terms of funding is now such that although virtually all the AIDS organizations have a predominantly gay personnel, they invariably assume a bland, nonsexual cover in order to continue to attract state funding. On two occasions in the Senate there has been a full debate involving all parties in support of a £50,000 grant already sanctioned by the city authorities to go toward the rebuilding of the Herschfeld Centre. Nevertheless, this has been steadfastly refused by the Minister of the Environment, Padraig Flynn, T.D.* This is despite the example of Denmark, where the government contributed 750,000 Kroner to the gay organization's AIDS program and 1,500,000 Kroner to the establishment of a gay center because they understood that such a center operates as an important channel of information about sexual hygiene and safe sex practices, and is one of the most efficient methods of gaining access to an otherwise disparate community. Nevertheless, there are ongoing efforts to restore the Herschfeld Centre, and it is hoped that we will ultimately achieve its rebuilding. In the meantime, a skeleton staff continues to produce a newsletter, *The Gay Community News.*†

---

*Since January 1, 1993, Commissioner of the EC for Social Affairs

†This is, I believe, a most important function within the gay community. In the early days we had an occasional newsletter, which gradually became monthly, called *In Touch.* This was replaced by a more lavish—indeed scholarly—quarterly called *Identity,* which was issued not only to the gay community but placed on sale publicly. This was followed by another partly commercial magazine called *Out,* which has since ceased publication. The importance of these publications lay in the fact that they gave us dignity, as a community, to name ourselves and our own statements. To appear

## CONCLUSION

I believe it is important to acknowledge the necessity of understanding the historical development of the gay movement through the growth of individual consciousness. It is then necessary to discover ways of producing a coherent stratagem for dealing with gay-related issues which would be both socially and politically effective on a national basis.

Finally I believe in the crucial importance of what women's groups call networking—the support of individual and local group effort by information gathering and campaigning groups; for example, National Gay Federation and GLEN domestically and ILGA internationally. It is inevitable that as a result of the way in which the gay movement developed, the early history should be one of strong combative individuals. But it is essential now that this first phase, with its slight flavor of the cult of the personality, should be replaced by a strong and permanent gay infrastructure.

## NOTES

1. Statutes of the Realm, III 441.

2. Anonymous (1711), "Bishop Atherton's case discussed," in A. Clarke (1979), the Atherton file, Decies 11, May 1979, pp. 47–48.

3. "In the Eyes of the Law," *Irish Times,* September 12, 1975.

4. Video Recordings Bill, 1987, Committee Stage, Irish Parliamentary Debates, vol. 117, no. 15, col. 1659–1746.

5. Larceny Bill, 1989, Report Stage, Irish Parliamentary Debates, vol. 124, no. 16, col. 1622 ff.

6. "Conference supports the decriminalization of homosexual behavior between consenting male adults in private, and as a consequence of such support urges affiliated unions to resist any attempts to discriminate against their members in their employment on the basis of their sexual orientation."

7. *Civil Service Policy on AIDS in the Workplace:*

a) Officers who are HIV positive or who suffer from AIDS will be retained in their job for as long as they can perform their duties to an acceptable standard.

b) The normal sick leave regulations as set out in Circular 25/78 will apply to staff who suffer from AIDS.

c) All details of an officer's health record should continue to be treated in the strictest confidence.

in print in our own journal gave, and continues to give, a feeling of reality to our lives. I am glad also to report that even within the shattered building on Fownes Street the newspaper and clipping archive survived and continues to be updated. The maintaining of this kind of fragile record is another important function of gay organizations and should, I feel, be strengthened by international cooperation in, and access to, the collection and preservation of such material.

d) Discrimination on the basis of sexual orientation or medical condition (e.g., hemophilia) will not be tolerated in the civil service.

e) *General*
Nothing in this policy statement is to be interpreted as constituting a waiver of management's responsibility to maintain discipline or its right to take disciplinary measures under normal disciplinary procedures.

# 14

# Male Homosexuality in West Africa

## Gerben Potman and Huub Ruijgrok[1]

Homosexuality is without any doubt a tremendous taboo in West Africa. Being known as a homosexual often means exclusion from family and society. Or, as many of our friends put it: "It will be the end for us." Social oppression of homosexuals is a fact. However, the negative attitude toward homosexuality does not imply that homosexual contacts do not take place nor that West Africa is necessarily a particularly bad place for homosexuals to live.

It is not easy to understand homosexuality and the position of gays in West Africa from a (purely) Western perspective. There are so many differences that a simple comparison cannot be made without an explanation of the differences in definition within a West African context, and the various ways in which love and sex between men actually take place. One of the first things we experienced during our stay in Senegal and Burkina Faso was that the meaning and explanation given to the words "homosexual" and "homosexuality" differed dramatically from the way we tend to understand these concepts in our Western world. "Homosexual" is mainly used in describing a rather queer, feminine man who likes to play the passive sexual role. Homosexuality itself connotes transvestism and transsexuality. Although there are many same-sex partners in West Africa, only a small portion of them will identify themselves as homosexual. Sex between men is not automatically labeled as homosexual behavior. One of us once had a wonderfully romantic and erotic safe-sex night with a Senegalese boy. Next morning, when the word homosexual was used during a conversation, the boy really got upset: "Why do you talk about homosexuality; you are not a homosexual, are you?"

## THE WEST AFRICAN CONTEXT

The way in which people give shape to their sexual lives and identities cannot be discussed without a reflection on their economical, social, political, and cultural circumstances. For this reason we must briefly describe the situation in West Africa.

### Socioeconomic: Restrictions by Dependency

Most West African countries are poor. The state cannot guarantee employment and social security to all its citizens, which implies that most people are highly dependent on family structures. A single source of income has to be divided among many family members. Individual freedom is scarce; moreover, many consider individual liberty to be inferior to the rights of the community, notably the family. Losing the respect, and thereby contact with and/or support, of the family is one of the worst things that can happen to a West African. Loss of family support will lead not only to social isolation but also economic insecurity.

Economic dependency on one's family causes great fear among homosexuals of being recognized as such, and inhibits same-sex lovers from expressing their sexual and emotional feelings and ideas in public. Coming out will mean losing respect and bringing shame to yourself and your family. It can lead to being renounced by your family, and thereby becoming a socioeconomic outcast.

### The Importance of Marriage and Children

Marriage is an important sign of status and prosperity. It does not have to be based on romantic love and partners are not always freely chosen; often they are given in marriage. Not being married at a certain age is regarded as a failure in life. Children are looked on as signs of one's prosperity, a blessing from God, and life insurance for the future.

The importance of marriage and children, therefore, deters people from exploring alternative lifestyles. Consequently, most homosexuals get married; young gays simply take it for granted that they, too, will be wed. Moreover, they do not see marriage as a big obstacle to same-sex relationships; as long as they fulfil the obligations belonging to marriage (food, income, and children) their wife (or wives) and family will not complain. They will have enough opportunities to continue their homosexual activities; indeed, marriage may even enlarge their freedom since it provides a social cover.

### Sex Is the Bright Side of Life and Money Is What Matters

Sex in the West African culture is something enjoyable and, like food, an essential source of well-being. Many times we are told: "If you do not have sex, you will get ill soon." There is nothing unusual at all about people fulfilling their sexual desires. It is generally not surrounded by feelings of fear, shame, and guilt as often happens in European and North American society. Sex is a natural part of life; at the same time it is something private. People do make jokes about sex but they never discuss sexual options and techniques seriously. Kissing and hugging in public is something not done. Sex education is not available. Parents do not talk about sex with their children, and in schools the subject of sexuality— let alone homosexuality—is never covered.

Sexual impotency and infertility are the worst things that can happen to a West African man. It is an enormous taboo that can destroy careers and relationships, and even result in suicide.

Sex and money are often interrelated: money not seldom plays a role in sexual relationships. Within heterosexual contacts, women before marriage demand and receive money, clothes, or other rewards for their sexual favors. This is a very common practice, which has nothing to do with prostitution, although there are, of course, women who do make a living at it.

The attitude of same-sex partners toward their activities reflects attitudes in general. It is something you simply do but do not talk about. In West African society, sex between men may be considered strange, incomprehensible, or disgusting; but having no sex at all is looked upon as even more bizarre and even inhuman. As in heterosexual relationships, money often plays a role. Who is paying or giving presents depends on the relative economic situations of the persons involved.

### Religious: Pragmatic Solutions

Religion plays an important role in the West African society, with its impact extending to social, political, and economic life. For many people, religion is an important part of their personal life as well, influencing decision making and lifestyles. The dominating religions in West Africa (animism, Christianity, and Islam) reject homosexuality.

Despite clearly defined religious guidelines for human conduct, we seriously doubt whether religion has a great influence on the sexual lives of West Africans. People tend to have a very pragmatic attitude toward religious rules: breaking religious taboos is usually not accompanied by heavy feelings of guilt. Sex before marriage, for example, is formally forbidden, but the majority still engage in premarital sex.

For all same-sex partners we know, religious rules did not cause personal problems or dramatically influence their sexual behavior. However, religion does indirectly influence the life of homosexuals by openly disapproving of same-sex relationships and thus influencing the social climate.

**Politics and the Law: A Potential Threat?**

The laws applying to homosexuality vary from country to country. In some countries homosexual acts are strictly forbidden and subject to prosecution, while in others homosexuality is not mentioned at all in the law. Even if there are legal sanctions, these are not always enforced.

Before analyzing the phenomenon of legal oppression, one should know that in West African society there is not a tradition of national politics interfering much with private life. As long as people do not criticize or rebel against the existing (political and religious) elites, they are relatively free to do what they like, especially in the area of sexuality.

We never met homosexuals who mentioned legal oppression as a constraint to their sexual life. Quite often those we met did not even know about the legal situation. Nevertheless, discriminating laws do exist and will be a threat to homosexuals, especially if they intend to organize.

## HOMOSEXUALITY AND LIFESTYLES

Most West African homosexuals live a closeted life. The fear of losing respect and dignity, not to mention the shame they may cause their family, makes them hide their desires and/or activities. There are very few gay men who develop a completely different lifestyle based on their sexual preference. But there are many ways in which their sexual activities influence their lives.

First of all, there is a group of men who have sex with other men but consider it just have a sexual variation. Our friends often said to us, "Love is love and it is all the same thing." Quite often it is a natural outcome of the intimacy and friendship existing between men or boys. In other cases, money may be a motivation. Men belonging to this group will never consider or identify themselves as homosexuals, even if they have sex with other men regularly. Their identity is mainly heterosexual. Nor do their homosexual activities cause them any problems as long as they do not make them public. Generally they do not feel a need to do so.

There is, however, another group of men who do consider themselves homosexual, since they clearly *prefer* homosexual contacts. However, they will never label themselves publicly as homosexual because of the consequences. They therefore hide both their identity and activities; indeed, they often have heterosexual contacts to remove any suspicions about them. Living in a village makes it almost impossible to carry on an overtly homosexual lifestyle, because in such a small society social control is very high. Living in a city creates more opportunities. To avoid social control, gay men often carry on their sexual activities outside their own neighborhood. These men often form a kind of social network that organizes friendships, sexual relations, and amusements. Friends visit each other at bars, cinemas, and cruising areas, and describe their experiences and exchange news.

Within these relationships traditional male/female casting plays an important role. Partners characterize themselves as "the man" or "the woman"; this choice of social roles is reflected also in sexual intercourse, with an active and a passive partner. In fact, gay men often copy heterosexual relationships; sometimes this goes as far as a marriage ritual. One of us took part in a ceremony where two male couples married in front of their friends. Each of the friends delivered a speech and rings were exchanged. The married couples, however, did not have the means to live together in the same house. Only a few rich urban men actually have the opportunity to live together.

Finally, there is a very small group of men who make no effort to hide their homosexual identity, and who have made the choice to deal with social and political oppression. This group consists only of some militant transvestites and other uninhibited types in bigger cities.

## CONCLUSION

A recurring theme of this book is the ways in which lesbians and gay men may organize and gain political power. The cental question remains: How can they improve their lives and turn often unfavorable circumstances—whether political, social, legal, or cultural—to their advantage?

All the gay people we met expressed the need for more individual liberty, more information about homosexuality, and social change. According to our information, no official gay rights organizations exist in West Africa. The only way homosexuals may organize themselves is through informal networks of friends. We did not have contact with persons who could be considered gay activists. Most were only seeking individual solutions for their problems. This strategy includes moving to the city or even abroad, finding a good job and income, and attracting a rich lover.

Such individual solutions are possible without coming out of the closet. Building an organization, however, will mean getting known publicly as a homosexual. For many, the resulting personal disadvantages are considered to be of greater consequence than eventual improvements for the group. Or, as one of our friends put it, "Nobody will have the courage to destroy his own life; if you want to live happily, be discreet about your sex life." Others state that in this way nothing will ever change, and that it is time for homosexuals to raise their voices.

We think that regardless of the ways in which West African homosexuals try to improve their lives, there should be international support. Individual, local, and national initiatives can be supported by information (books, magazines, and international radio programs), legal assistance (against discrimination, censorship, and violation of human rights), and financial support.[2]

## NOTES

1. This article is based on our own experiences during our stay in Senegal and Burkina Faso, and is the result of interviews and correspondence with our African friends. At first we hesitated accepting the invitation from the editors of the *Pink Book* because we had never done any scientific research on homosexuality; it seemed to us much better to engage West Africans themselves to write this article. But within the limited time schedule West Africans willing to write an article were not found. We asked some of our African friends but they were afraid to give their name to such an article. Since information on homosexuality in West Africa is scarce, we decided to share our experiences. Given the "participatory" character of our findings, most remarks concerning homosexuality are related to the situation in Senegal and Burkina Faso. However, we will treat the subject for the whole of West Africa. Regional and ethnic differences surely exist, but the similarities indicated by our friends originating from different West African countries made us decide to generalize for the whole region.

2. The authors would like to express the hope that for the next edition of the *Pink Book,* West Africans will send in many articles in reaction to their views, and invite them to share their experiences and enlarge the diversity and strength of the international lesbian and gay movement.

# 15

# Gathering Strength and Gaining Power: How Lesbians and Gay Men Began to Change their Fortunes in Britain in the Nineties

## Lisa Power and Tim Barnett

Britain has had a visible and vocal movement for gay and (latterly) lesbian rights since the 1960s. From the small lobbying movement which resulted in the 1967 Sexual Offences Act, partially decriminalizing male homosexual activity, it grew through the radical Gay Liberation Front activities of the seventies into a diverse range of groups with varied approaches. Services such as helplines and youth groups were established; cultural activities such as magazines, drama, and publishing houses flourished. Yet, in retrospect, it is clear that in terms of political organization, the British movement failed to develop beyond the early seventies. Indeed, from the mid-seventies it declined and is only now recovering.

This decline was masked by the constant founding of new gay organizations or by the revival of old ones. Each organization was heralded as the way forward, but none involved more than a small proportion of potential movement activists, despite claims to represent the aspirations of all. Each group, if it was at all active, was riven by political disputes in a movement that spent far more time on the issues pulling people apart than on the common enemy of homophobia. These self-destructive tendencies, common to oppressed groups and certainly echoed in the gay movements of other countries, drove many potential lesbian and gay political activists either to label themselves "non-political" or to work only on social groups and helplines.

External factors, such as the rise of AIDS, added to the pressure on our communities as well as to the level of public hatred and misunderstanding of us. But above all other pressures, Britain in the eighties lived under a government that provided an open door for the "moral right": a government that was, whatever its fine public words, contemptuous of human rights and actively hostile to any form of social deviation; a government with an overwhelming majority in Parliament and the support of most of the British press. Since the ruling Conservatives outfaced and overthrew many previously powerful groups, such as the trade unions and municipal authorities, what chance, then, had a small and disunited group of social outcasts? Given the social and political climate of the time, it is not surprising that lesbians and gay men became a scapegoat of the Thatcher government; the real surprise is that we managed to escape their legislative attention for as long as we did.

## MUNICIPAL HOMOSEXUALITY IN THE EIGHTIES

Given such a homophobic and socially repressive government, human rights and minority concerns became associated with the opposition political parties. In particular, socialist groups from the Labour Party leftwards began to take on board the concerns of women, black people, and lesbians and gay men in a very public manner. This approach was particularly pursued by municipal Labour authorities. Local support for lesbians and gay men was provided in the form of community grants, equipment, and premises; inclusion of sexuality in equal opportunities policies and training; and appointment of lesbian and gay officers or even the creation of separate gay and lesbian units within the authorities. It seemed, for a short while, as if lesbians and gay men were finally reaching power.

It took less than a decade to shatter the illusion of a homosexual power base within municipal socialism. Under the Conservatives, local authorities did not mean power. In the face of grossly distorted hostile press coverage, many Labour politicians pragmatically retreated from supporting our rights in hopes of preserving their wider vote. Local authority spending was severely curbed by legislation, forcing many to drop community grants. Municipal authorities, including the Greater London Council (the most generous and widely publicized of all), were simply abolished by an all-powerful central government.

The collapse left much of the lesbian and gay movement in disarray. Many groups that had become dependent on local authority grants folded or went into funding crises. Tellingly, few who had called for the setting up of lesbian and gay units mourned their passing or rushed to their defense; most seemed to feel that they had been run by activists for activists with little reference to the local lesbian and gay population. Political cynicism was rife. Our own organizations had not worked; our jump onto the socialist bandwagon had not worked; central government seemed impervious to criticism. The scene was set, and the victim mentality perfectly instilled, for the first legislative attack upon our few existing rights, when Clause 14 (later Clause and Section 28) was introduced into the Local Government Bill late in 1987.

## THE FAILURE TO PREDICT AND PREVENT SECTION 28

Section 28, as finally agreed, reads in part:

A local authority shall not:

(a) intentionally promote homosexuality or publish material with the intention of promoting homosexuality;

(b) promote the teaching in any maintained school of the acceptability of homosexuality as a pretended family relationship.

The failure to preempt or to persuade parliamentarians to reject this Clause has proved a watershed for the British lesbian and gay movement. Only now, six years later, can we see it as the disaster which pulled us into political reality.

Up until then, we had survived the eighties relatively unscathed. Police entrapment, or "pretty policing," as it became known, had been exposed by the inadvertent and (for both sides) embarrassing arrest of a rising young Conservative MP in a male strip show. Customs and Excise had been forced to withdraw from their attempt to use existing laws to ruin Gays The Word bookshop for importing gay literature. However, attacks in the tabloid press and by extremist Conservative MPs against positive images of homosexuality in the education system had stepped up dramatically. A prototype of Section 28 had been floated the previous year by Lord Halsbury in the House of Lords and tacitly approved by the Prime Minister herself. It should not have come as a surprise and yet, to all but a few, it was.

The insularity of the movement was exposed. Our total refusal to engage with those in power had led us to neglect the impact of legislation and to underestimate the ease with which it could be introduced against us. And although reaction was swift, with hundreds of people mobilizing within days by word of mouth and thousands on the street within a few weeks, the major groupings began to split and fight almost from the start, breaking into factions and caucuses.

The automatic oppositional British politics of left against right meant that from the start, the campaign, rooted in the political left, refused to negotiate with the government in any way. The lobbying of parliamentarians, the only people with the power to change the legislation, was left to a few individuals without support or input from the campaign as a whole. The movement's longstanding rejection of "professionalism" meant that virtually none of us understood the intricacies of the lobby system, or had the contacts to pursue it had we wished to. We just assumed that everybody wrote letters to anybody they could think of who might help. So poor were our links with the parliamentary parties that at the start the Labour and Liberal Democrat opposition political parties were equally unbriefed and failed to comprehend the scope and danger of the proposals.

Despite all talk of alliances and a broad coalition, radical orthodoxy drove many willing helpers to the margins of the campaign. The Gay Business Association, which brought masses of previously apolitical disco queens into the first march against Section 28 with their posters in every gay pub and club screaming "Get Off Your Arses And March!" were hissed and abused when they came to a campaign meeting. Their crime was to have helped train police to be less anti-gay. Though there was a desperate shortage of role models for the politicians and media to relate to as gay and proud, the Arts Lobby attracted considerable criticism and outright jealousy for its use of famous actors to gain attention to the cause.

The campaign, though valiant, revealed our lack of resources. It sometimes felt as if we believed that if we marched enough and told enough people the legislation was unfair, the government would simply back down. There had been a consistent problem of lack of reliable documentation and research into the discrimination we faced and the lives we led. This made it doubly difficult to explain the impact that further discriminatory law would have on us. Financially, we had to start from scratch in raising money, exposing our lack of links with the significant community of wealthy homosexuals, many of whom failed to understand the danger of the legislation or felt alienated by the rhetoric of traditional lesbian and gay campaigning. Although much reliance was put on links with other oppressed communities and the unions, in practical terms we received little support from causes many of us had felt allied with and worked for; there was a lot of lip service but little action. In any case, they were mostly weakened by ten years of Thatcherism and had declining political power. Media coverage of the section was extremely uneven, relying upon arrests and stunts and later individual sympathizers who began to come forward and even, in a few cases, come out.

## LEARNING THE LESSONS

Looking back on Section 28 after it had passed, old and new activists began to draw conclusions from it. The areas where we had been successful were clearly the direct action stunts such as abseiling into the Lords—something that could not directly change the legislation (and was a controversial tactic among parliamentarians), but a gesture to raise our spirits and raise our profile with the media over the issue as a whole. What success we had in reaching government ministers and those in power had come largely through the Arts Lobby's willingness to exploit celebrity connections—it seemed the only people who impressed politicians were those more famous than themselves. Although the campaign had identified sympathetic MPs and civil servants, there had been no focus for their offers of help and often little understanding of them. And, although initially there had been an enormous response from usually apolitical lesbians and gay men, this had faded rapidly in the face of dogma and infighting, with none of the existing organizations understanding how to use their support. There were all-too-common stories from all around the country of hundreds of people turning up at initial campaign meetings, but dwindling to a mere handful after a few weeks.

Yet there remained a residue of newly energized activists, many of them new to the movement and some with influence in the wider world. There was also a new awareness of links with lesbians and gay men around the globe. Demonstrations against Clause 28 had been reported from New York to Sydney, the Norwegian foreign minister had been moved to ask their British counterpart what he thought he was playing at, and there was strongly critical coverage in much of the foreign quality press. Previously heavily closeted groups such as gay journalists and media people had met together, and even discreetly organized, for the first time in many years.

Another problem clarified by the campaign was the tendency for lesbian and gay issues to be co-opted by the politics of the revolutionary left. This had been graphically illustrated by the huge rows between Workers Power, the Revolutionary Communist Party, and much of the traditional movement at the 1987 national conference on legislation. It had remained an undercurrent for much of the campaign, contributing heavily to the factional infighting and the alienation of those who espoused reform over revolution. It had also been a major factor in the decision to refuse to engage with the government and to rely on extra-parliamentary activities, as if by taking to the streets lesbians and gay men would herald the revolution. All it had heralded, however, were a few headlines, diminishing as the number of marches grew. And while headlines were useful, they were not enough in themselves, in Thatcher's Britain, to stop bad legislation.


## MOVING ON FROM FAILURE

The initial response by the lesbian and gay communities to the passing of Section 28 was one of nervous apathy. Would it be Armageddon tomorrow or business as usual? The two major organs of resistance, Stop The Clause and the Organization for Lesbian and Gay Action (OLGA), both descended over the course of the next year into political torpor and financial decay. Clearly, Britain was still not ready to sustain a mass membership lesbian and gay "union." But a number of more modest and tightly targeted initiatives were in the making.

On the one hand, a small coalition of diverse activists and Arts Lobby luminaries who had initially come together to fundraise over the Clause began to meet to make plans for the professional lobby and research organization which had been so badly missed in the campaign. This was unveiled in June 1989 as the Stonewall Group, a small voluntary organization, with paid staff, management, and volunteers. Its intention was to exploit allies from across the political spectrum who had come forward over the Section, to educate politicians, and to provide tools enabling lobbying by all lesbian and gay community groups. It deliberately included people with a range of skills and experience, selected as much for their willingness to work with diversity as for their knowledge, and was structured to be impervious to takeover by any political faction. It was, from the start, dedicated to equality of representation for lesbians.

In that same year, ACT-UP, the U.S.A. direct-action group on AIDS, came to Britain. Its early success in direct actions, which brought media and public attention to the injustices faced by people with HIV and AIDS, absorbed many gay activists. In 1990, a small group of gay journalists borrowed a similar tactic from the other, directly gay (or rather queer) U.S.A. action group Queer Nation, and founded OutRage in London. It worked through weekly open mass meetings and planned dramatic public actions. And although it swiftly became a magnet for the revolutionary socialist arguments rehearsed during the Section 28 campaign, the dedication and anger of its central core of new activists won through them. Like Stonewall, OutRage was determined to espouse no one party and no cause but lesbian and gay human rights.

Another feature shared by both groups was their willingness to learn from and make links with lesbian and gay groups in other countries. While OutRage clearly drew its inspiration, and many of its most successful actions, from Queer Nation in the U.S.A., Stonewall made close links with the International Lesbian and Gay Association and became the lead member on its European Community campaign. It, too, borrowed shamelessly from the style and ideas of American lobbying groups such as the National Gay and Lesbian Task Force, and from successful lobbies on other issues in the U.K.

## GATHERING STRENGTH IN THE NINETIES

The key political event of 1990 was the fall of Prime Minister Margaret Thatcher. The immediate catalyst was conflict within the government about future development of the European Community, the more fundamental reason that her style of government was out of touch with reality. Thatcher's replacement, John Major, had risen through urban politics in a community (Brixton, South London) containing an active lesbian and gay movement. Within a year of taking office, Major held a publicized meeting with Sir Ian McKellen of Stonewall, and influential national newspapers began to call for homosexual law reform. It was a remarkable about-face.

Campaigning in 1991 was dominated by two issues that arose directly from the dying months of the Thatcher government. One was Clause 25 of the Criminal Justice Bill, a basically liberal piece of legislation which contained, as a sop to the right wing, a commitment to increase prison sentences for some people with a history of criminal convictions. One effect would have been to greatly increase the possibility of imprisonment for people convicted of more than one minor (gay) consenting sexual offense. It was either a deliberate attempt to further oppress gay men or an appalling mistake by civil servants who drafted the bill.

The campaign by gay activists to amend the bill was this time largely successful. While OutRage actions drew public attention to the injustices of the legislation, Stonewall lobbyists confronted Conservative parliamentarians and civil servants with the consequences of their actions, and suggested ways to amend it. Both groups successfully exploited their links with the media to obtain sensible coverage. Demands from the revolutionary and libertarian left for total opposition to otherwise reasonable legislation were largely resisted, and there was genuine and informed debate within the gay press on the implications of the Clause. Most remarkably, government ministers and their staff met with Stonewall lesbian and gay activists and, while unwilling to concede to all their demands, did agree to monitor the effects of the amended Clause and to ensure that it would not be used in a discriminatory manner; indeed, they promised that they would amend it further in that case.

One of the good effects of the Section 28 campaign had been the increased involvement of lesbians in what was essentially a legislative campaign. This higher profile for lesbians in mixed activism was put to good use in early 1991, when the Department of Health attempted to introduce childcare guidelines which would have effectively barred lesbians and gay men from becoming foster parents, as part of an overall downgrading of equal opportunities. Paragraph 16, as it became known, was a direct reflection of the views of the Health Minister (Virginia Bottomley, coincidentally also responsible for HIV and AIDS), included in the draft guidelines against the advice of civil servants.

The Stonewall Group, with its high level of lesbian involvement and a commitment to prioritize "family concerns," was the first to take the cause up. National fostering organizations and relevant local authorities were contacted and individually lobbied; the wider implications of the legislation for all equal opportunity measures were emphasized. Experts in childcare and fostering, and researchers into lesbian and gay family life were sought out; briefing papers were rapidly produced for parliamentarians; and personal links with civil servants were exploited. This pressure rapidly led to a meeting with the Health Minister, at which she was faced by a combination of campaigners and "experts" she was known to respect, a lesbian foster mother and an eminent member of the House of Lords who had been brought up in a lesbian household.

Though the issue failed to take priority for a gay press dominated by single male issues, other activists ensured that it received some coverage in the quality press. OutRage organized a postcard protest campaign and demonstration and a number of local groups organized joint 25/16 campaigns. When the final guidelines were published, not only had the offending line barring gays and lesbians from being foster parents been removed, but new clauses protecting the rights of lesbian and gay teenagers to be given sympathetic foster placement had been added.

These were not the only examples of success. A number of London-based groups finally agreed to enter into negotiation with the Metropolitan Police after years of refusal. Within twelve months, the London Gay Policing Initiative could point to pilot projects to monitor anti-gay violence, the training of officers to treat such issues more sympathetically, guidelines on the conduct of police operations against public "cruising" areas, new guidance and training on male rape, and a cautious police welcome for the first Lesbian and Gay Police Association in Britain. A Parliamentary Select Committee of MPs had recommended reform of the Armed Forces prohibition on homosexual behavior, to bring it in line with civilian law after receiving written and verbal evidence from Stonewall. The new Press Complaints Commission ruled against homophobia after a flood of complaints by groups and individuals against one tabloid newspaper, the *Daily Star*. The U.K. government bowed to the threat of further embarrassment before the European Court of Human Rights by promising to impose homosexual law reform on the Isle of Man if it continued to ban male homosexual activity.

This transformation in character was not confined to the new political groups within the lesbian and gay movement. A number of long-standing service groups such as London Lesbian and Gay Switchboard, who provide a 24-hour telephone helpline, reported a growth in numbers of new volunteers coming forward. The proportion of lesbians in many mixed-sex organizations, including Switchboards, grew visibly and in 1992 helplines across the country held their first conference in a decade. New social groups based on a variety of social affinities proliferated, as did the commercial venues available in at least the larger towns. The annual Pride event in June became transformed from a short rally after a march into an enormous carnival. Within HIV and AIDS work, it is no longer impossible to attract support and funding for the explicit gay work which is undoubtedly needed.

Even the popular media, whose neglect of lesbian and gay issues had long been a source of complaint, began to schedule more regular items on gay fostering, the military, partnership, and a range of issues. This continuing higher profile for such concerns in turn has led to further interest from all the major political parties. Although the return of a Conservative government in the 1992 elections and its absolute concentration on economic rather than social issues has postponed criminal law reform on the age of consent, other issues have progressed well and the way in which all parties clearly indicated their understanding of the need to court lesbian and gay votes was a breakthrough. With a more liberal regime now installed in the U.S.A. that will hopefully exert some indirect influence on social policy, the question now centers not on whether it is worth trying to fight for constitutional rights but on what shape those reforms should take.

REASONS FOR CHANGE

We would suggest that these changes occurred primarily because the lesbian and gay movement in the U.K. underwent a fundamental shift of approach and attitudes at the end of the 1980s, in an atmosphere of rapidly improving opportunities for reform. Key reasons were:

- the development of adequately funded, and well-defined and targeted groups prepared to work across diversity solely on specifically lesbian and gay issues;

- a new confidence that we could engage with powerful social forces and the belief that we had the ability to change them. Of particular importance in aiding this was the decline in power of the moral right along with their media and parliamentary friends at the departure of Margaret Thatcher;

- the refusal to tie our needs or cause to any one political party or philosophy. This involved particular rapprochement with elements in the Conservative party. The support of a small group of Conservative backbench MPs was of particular importance through the initial victories of 1991. This, in turn, helped to reduce the political marginalization of the issue of lesbian and gay rights: parliamentarians could be seen working on homosexual law reform without fear of being labeled eccentric;

- a new willingness to deal with and confront the press, even when hostile, and to provide good opportunities for stories. The extent and quality of television and radio coverage improved significantly in this period. Lesbian and gay issues provided good news; audiences for programs such as the "Out" television series were numbered in millions;

- the growth of debate within the movement on political and philosophical issues, leading to a more sophisticated understanding of our struggle for power;

- the appreciation of the need for professional and disciplined ways of working within organizations, promoting consistent policies, and ensuring active involvement by the maximum number of people;

- the fuller integration of lesbians within the mixed movement, especially on legislative issues. Although specifically gay male law reform concerns are likely to dominate the next few years, given the discriminatory state of criminal law, concerns of lesbians are now much more central to the movement;

- the growth in internationalism, particularly European integration, and the parallel increase in contact between lesbians and gays across the continent. British people have seen that there are more humane ways in which society and the law can deal with lesbian and gay concerns, including the creation of links with other countries.


## LOOKING TO THE FUTURE

What comes next? The new intake of members of Parliament with widely varying views on the subject has ensured that lesbian and gay rights are no longer a party political issue pure and simple. Given the precarious position of the government and its absolute determination to cling to power, high profile commitments which risk some public disapprobation (such as reform of the age of consent) are not likely in the short term, but the acceptance of the need for law reform within British dependencies and the refusal to countenance the sort of crude gay-baiting which characterized the mid-eighties augur well. It is widely accepted that chipping away at the legal problems combined with increased openness in society and the media is a valid way forward.

The movement has largely, however reluctantly, accepted the principle that lobby and direct action groups can co-exist. If each can continue to gather strength, particularly through resources for the former and people for the latter, and if they can continue to communicate with each other, however tentatively, then success is much more likely. The more difficult challenge may well be ensuring effective international cooperation as power moves to Brussels and toward Eastern Europe. These changes in the power structures of Europe are leading to a growth of fascism throughout the continent and a rise in racism and anti-Semitism. Since these go hand in hand with homophobia, we must be alert to moves against us in many countries. Our opportunities for legislative change in the U.K. must neither mask the real fear of right-wing backlash nor lead us to neglect other major areas of social justice.

Perhaps, with the growth of a realistic and pragmatic approach by lesbian and gay groups of all kinds in Britain, we can begin to make the networks and alliances across our differences just as groups throughout Europe and the rest of the world have begun to work together in international networks such as the International Lesbian and Gay Association (ILGA). Such networking is essential, indeed crucial; after all, if we don't learn to work together now to gain and hold power over our own lives, we may soon lose the opportunity altogether.

# 16

# Coming Out as an MP in Canada

## Svend J. Robinson

Liberation, pride, exhilaration, freedom . . . all of these emotions and more I felt on the evening of February 29, 1988, when I spoke on Canadian national television in both of Canada's official languages—English and French—to tell the nation that I am a member of Parliament who is a proud gay man. Proud to be a member of a community that has demonstrated enormous courage and dignity in the face of widespread discrimination, hatred, and violence, and incredible compassion and caring in response to the devastating toll AIDS has taken on our community. In the years since coming out publicly, I have continued to feel it a great privilege to be a voice not only for my constituency in Vancouver but also for a truly national and, indeed, international constituency. Whether meeting in someone's living room with a small group of lesbians and gay men in rural Canada or speaking before over twenty thousand lesbians, gay men, and bisexuals from around the world at the opening ceremonies of the Gay Games in Vancouver in the summer of 1990; meeting with a courageous young officer in the Canadian Armed Forces following her interrogation as a criminal and expulsion from the military when it was learned that she was a lesbian; or meeting members of the Supreme Soviet together with representatives of the former Soviet Union's growing lesbian and gay community to urge the repeal of repressive criminal legislation in that country, the challenges are endless.

In confronting heterosexism and homophobia in our societies as openly gay legislators, it is essential that we understand that politics is about power and about priorities. If we are to succeed in breaking down the barriers of fear, of misunderstanding, and of bigotry, we must work closely with those groups and individuals in our communities who daily confront discrimination. We can use the special resources available to us as legislators to work with existing groups and establish new networks to share information.

To remain informed and effective, it is essential that we receive major publications of the lesbian, gay, and bisexual community both from within our own countries and internationally. Close links with the International Lesbian and Gay Association (ILGA) can certainly facilitate this communication. In turn we can widely diffuse information throughout the country by using our mailing privileges. My office, for example, publishes a periodical report that updates the lesbian, gay, and bisexual community in Canada on current developments both nationally and internationally. Wherever possible, we should meet with our counterparts in other countries to share our successes and failures. While traveling internationally and working on issues of global concern, we are able to meet with lesbians and gay men in other countries, and by virtue of our positions, to challenge ruling authorities in those countries to respond to the concerns of our community there. Often we have access to government officials in other countries that would be denied to representatives of the lesbian, gay and bisexual community in those countries.

In Canada there exists no national lobby organization for our community, which makes close working relationships with community-based groups all the more important. For example, I have worked with coalitions on a number of issues, including censorship of our literature and images by Canada Customs authorities and changing laws to end discrimination in areas such as health care, immigration, and abusive broadcasting. On human rights legislation it is particularly important to build coalitions with other historically disadvantaged groups as well as churches, progressive civil liberties groups, and the labor movement.

We must, therefore, continually use our privileged access to the media to confront the invisibility and silence that are the greatest barriers to our equality. We must ensure that the institutions we ourselves work in reflect the values of equality and nondiscrimination that we struggle for in society at large. But at the same time, it is very important for us to understand that, as a group, those of us who do hold public office by no means reflect the remarkable diversity of our community. We are overwhelmingly white middle-class males, as are the elected institutions in which we sit. The barriers confronting women, people of color, aboriginal peoples, and those with disabilities within the traditional political culture are already enormous; therefore, it is not surprising that lesbians and gay men from among these groups in our society are so grossly underrepresented in elected politics. As gay men, we must do far more to help break down these barriers and to work in coalitions with our brothers and sisters in these groups. Just as lesbians have been in the forefront of our common struggle against AIDS and in providing support and care to people living with HIV and AIDS, so, too, must we, as gay men, speak out far more in support of freedom of reproductive choice, at the same time condemning widespread violence against women, sexual harassment, and the terrible underfunding of women's health programs. Our principal objective must be no less than a profound redistribution of wealth and power in a society that celebrates diversity.

In making the decision to come out as an elected representative, it is fundamentally important that there be extensive consultation with and support from one's political colleagues, a base of support within the party, key activists within the lesbian and gay community, and personal love and support from one's family and/or partner. It is these people who will be most directly affected by the intense glare of publicity surrounding the coming out and the subsequent visibility. Since it is already intensely difficult to maintain any semblance of a personal life as an elected politician at the national level, the additional stresses on a relationship which arise from coming out publicly must be realistically weighed and prepared for.

The primary concern of my family—who were totally supportive of my decision—was the possibility of personal violence at the hands of some deranged individual, that same violence that struck down Harvey Milk in his prime. While this concern can certainly not be lightly dismissed (my office windows and door were smashed to bits during my coming out, and I have twice had bullets fired at my storefront office window), we cannot allow this risk to prevent us from taking this tremendously important step. One of the interesting benefits of coming out publicly has been a complete silencing of homophobic attacks in the House of Commons, attacks which were commonplace before I came out. Now those who might be tempted to make such attacks realize they will be reported and vigorously condemned. Therefore, while the homophobia no doubt continues behind closed doors, it has been stopped cold in the House.

Throughout our history, strong and brave lesbians and gay men have broken the silence, have challenged the invisibility, and made it possible for us to feel freer in our own lives. We have a proud history and it's a history that young lesbians and gay men must be taught. We truly stand on the shoulders of giants. Those of us who are privileged to be elected to public office can help break down the barriers of invisibility and silence by coming out in pride. In doing so, we remind not only our communities but ourselves that we are everywhere and we have the right to be everywhere.

# 17

# Two of a Kind, Two Different Kinds: Humanism, Homosexuality, and Emancipation in the Netherlands and Britain

## Petra Schedler

On both sides of the North Sea, two gay humanist groups were founded in 1979 The Dutch group called itself "Homowerkgroep van het Humanistisch Verbond' (Gay Working Group of the Dutch Humanist League = HWG). Its British coun-terpart is the Gay and Lesbian Humanist Association (GALHA). In this articl these two groups' organizations, programs, and agenda are compared. I will ex-amine the connection between the social acceptance of homosexuality anc humanism, and the extent to which each group's agenda mirrors conditions fo: gays and lesbians in its respective society.

SOCIETY: HUMANISM AND HOMOSEXUALITY

Humanism in contemporary society is the pursuit of the right of self-determinatio and relates individual freedom with social responsibility. It begins with th' philosophical principle that people can give meaning to and shape their existenc without relying upon higher or divine authorities (Tielman 1984). The humanis movement in the two countries differs with regard to organization, support, an social establishment.

Although both the Netherlands and Britain call themselves democratic, the way their respective democracies are organized differs. Britain has an electoral system by which the majority rules—a moral majority, which is rather conservative on ethical matters. The Dutch political system is made up of several larger and smaller "minority" parties. The Dutch government consists of a coalition of parties, which seems to offer more opportunities to humanism than a society in which the majority is less used to compromise or does not have to consider the interest of others.

England has no separation of church and state. The role of the churches is reflected in many fields, for instance in politics. Clergymen are appointed members of the House of Lords because of their vocation. Holland does have a separation of church and state. Although the authorities finance institutions such as schools and hospitals on a denominational basis, the government has no responsibility for their policies. Holland is also more secularized than England: 42 percent of the population are non-churchgoing and 49 percent are nonreligious (Felling et al. 1982). Continuation of this trend would, according to some, mean that Christians will make up a minority of the population in the future (Tielman & Sinke 1983: 14).

In Holland, the Humanist League, with its 16,000 members, has, as an established organization, been propagating humanism for over forty years. In the course of its existence, the Humanist League has managed to fight its way into several already allocated fields such as the media, philosophical and spiritual instruction in schools, and the armed forces and prisons. For this purpose, it has developed a distinction between *tendency* and *movement* (Tielman 1986). Research has shown that 23 percent of the Dutch population endorse the humanist principles (Tielman 1983). Along with this existing humanist tendency, an organized humanist movement in which some 100,000 people are actively involved can be discerned. As a result, the distribution code the government uses to subsidize organizations on the basis of ideology and activities in the areas of the media, education, and public welfare has been finally changed in favor of the Humanist League.

There are four humanist organizations in Britain with a total membership that is less than that of the Dutch Humanist League. Of these four, the British Humanist Association (BHA) and the National Secular Society (NSS) are the largest in size and the most influential. The BHA, founded in 1950, has a policy most closely resembling that of the Dutch League. The NSS dates back to the end of the last century, and is more militant and anti-religious than the BHA. The four organizations have monthly discussions in the Humanist Liaison Committee, but humanism is hardly an established philosophy in Britain. The positions held by established religion and the political system leave little opportunity for that.

In the same way the humanists in Britain may envy the situation in Holland, English homosexuals may view the opportunities for gays in the Netherlands with longing (see Cummings 1988). It should be noted, however, that research shows that the much praised Dutch tolerance is often actually nothing but "tolerance at a distance" (Dobbeling & Koenders 1984). Homosexuality is permitted as long as social establishment isn't threatened and one's own surroundings remain undefiled.

Despite clear differences in the legal and social position of homosexuality in both countries (pointed out elsewhere in this volume), it is striking that both the Netherlands and Britain have witnessed an explosive growth in the number of gay and lesbian groups within established organizations such as political parties, churches, schools, and trade unions (Schedler & Vrijhoef 1989). In Britain there are the following organizations: Gay Disabled Group, Lesbian and Gay Christian Movement, Gay Medical Association, Socialist Workers Party Gay Group, and Lesbians and Gays in Education, to name but a few. But unlike the Netherlands, Britain does not have gay studies departments in universities (see Tielman 1988).

Both countries do have a gay group within the humanist movement. These two groups cooperated in research in 1987–1988; and the results of that research are analysed and compared in this study.

## THE FOUNDATION OF THE GROUPS

In the 1970s, a broadening and increase in the gay movement in the Netherlands can be seen. Homosexuality comes more and more into the open (van Steenderen 1987: 21). Self-organization—in this case, of homosexual men and women—becomes an important political device (Meulenbelt 1983: 448). At the same time, the churches are dealing with the question of their homosexual "fellow men." The monopolization by the churches of the ethical discussion concerning homosexuality causes some humanists to investigate the views of the Humanist League on homosexuality (Boelaars 1979: 4).

A few male pioneers tried to track down distinct statements on homosexuality in the archives of the league, but concluded that these were lacking. Although the Humanist League had gradually argued more openly in favor of new, more permissive sexual morals in the course of its existence (van Biemen 1987: 136), homosexuality was hardly a point of discussion until the end of the decade. This has to do not with resistance to homosexuality but, on the contrary, with the attitude that homosexuality should not be made into a problem requiring discussion. Until then, humanists principles such as freedom and equality covered potential differences and ambivalences. When those pioneers placed an ad in the league's monthly, a gay humanist group emerged.

During its biennial congress in 1981, when HWG had already been functioning informally for two years, the General Council of the Humanist League presented budgets for the actual support of a gay working group as well as for a women's and youth group. In this way, HWG was introduced within the new "model of categorical groups." The start of the gay working group and the introduction of this model of categorical groups were, according to some humanists, in conflict with the important principle of equality. The advocates of the new model, therefore, developd a distinction in the principle of equality: people were not identical but equal (Tielman 1982: 19). The formation of separate groups offered the opportunity to give meaning to this dissimilarity (see Schedler 1989).

At the end of the seventies, Mary Whitehouse, known as a notorious busybody among gays and humanists and the spokeswoman of the British Moral Majority (Weeks 1981:280), began legal proceedings against the English newspaper *Gay News,* because it had published a poem "The Love That Dares to Speak its Name," describing the gay love of a Roman centurion for Jesus during the Crucifixion. Her action incited substantial social opposition; according to Whitehouse, even "a humanist gay-lobby." From the records of GALHA one can conclude that at that time there was no such lobby; but the obvious fear such an idea provoked provided the spark that convinced gay humanists that the opportunity being offered to them was too good to miss.

Six men who were involved in both the humanist and gay movements founded a gay humanist group. Hiring a stall at the annual conference of the Campaign for Homosexual Equality (CHE), the national organization for equal rights, in 1979, they inaugurated their group by distributing leaflets on humanism and organizing a fringe meeting attended by twenty-five conference participants. The founding members did not consider starting the group within the humanist movement. Homosexual men and women were expected to be more interested in a gay humanist group than humanists themselves.

So, opposing the religious dominance in the field of homosexuality and morality, two humanist gay groups were founded, in the Netherlands and in Britain. From the beginning HWG organized itself within the humanist movement, whereas GALHA associated itself with the gay movement.

## THE GROUPS' ORGANIZATION

GALHA is an autonomous membership organization and is financed from membership fees and occasional donations. Each year at the annual general meeting, a committee responsible for running the group is formed. GALHA uses the system of honorary presidency, a position held by Maureen Duffy, a well-known lesbian and humanist writer. GALHA also has a number of honorary celebrity vice-presidents, including George Melly, jazz musician and journalist; Claire Rayner, "agony aunt" and TV personality; and Sir Hermann Bondi, president of the BHA. The honorary president and vice-presidents, whose names form part of GALHA's letterhead, have merely symbolic functions and do not interfere with the group's policies. The use of honorary presidents is quite common in Britain. The CHE, which is organized in the same way, served as a model for

GALHA. After a few years, GALHA became a member of the Humanist Liaison Committee.

HWG is not an autonomous organization, and subsequently does not allow paying members. The group usually consists of ten people, one of whom is a representative of the General Council of the league. This is a common organizational principle within the Humanist League as a whole. HWG has at its disposal an annual budget, which is largely used to pay a part-time official for gay issues. In contrast to GALHA, HWG cannot issue its own press releases. The General Council of the Humanist League bears in all cases the ultimate responsibility for the activities of the working group.

The relation of HWG and the General Council has not always been easy. The working group had to do without a professional official for a year because of cuts in funds, which caused a fierce internal correspondence. Sometimes the group feels left out of certain issues, for instance when the General Council determines its position on issues like AIDS or gay parenthood without consulting its own gay working group first. Despite these differences, however, HWG has managed to acquire a position in the "Verbondsraad" of the Humanist League, an advisory and consultative board for the General Council. The group considers its position in the "Verbondsraad" as a recognition of its status, analogous to GALHA's participation in the Humanist Liaison Committee.

## WEEKEND EVENTS

Both groups organize weekend gatherings: GALHA once a year, HWG twice yearly, in the spring and fall. But the organization of the weekend events differs.

The weekend events of HWG have been its most important and time-consuming activity since the group was founded (Verduyn 1986: 224). The organization of the weekend gatherings constitutes a breach with the tradition of meetings, preferably held on Sunday morning, within the Humanist League. At the same time the weekend gatherings continue an established formula used by the gay movement. But HWG's weekend events include humanist components, such as explicit access for all those interested and an introduction to humanism to place the weekend in a philosophical context. Humanist social and cultural workers were used in the past to train the facilitators of the workshops. The participants may choose from different workshops that form the main part of the event. The organization of the workshops is taken seriously, although there is also time for leisure in the evening. The weekend gathering is considered a great success by both HWG and the Humanist League. An average of ninety people, mostly gay men, take part in the weekend event. Very often people have to be put on a waiting list.

The GALHA weekend gatherings, which are of a more recent date than HWG's events, are characterized by a rather different tradition. The weekends are not GALHA's most important or time-consuming activities. About twenty or thirty gay men on average take part. The group visits seaside resorts with a hotel run by and meant for gays, whereas HWG retreats to a training center in the woods. The second weekend gathering organized by GALHA was visited by a delegation of HWG; the following year, a number of GALHA members visited a weekend event in Holland. As a result of these mutual visits, GALHA decided to introduce workshops on Saturday afternoon. The significance of the workshops for the entire weekend is minimal in comparison with the Dutch approach. Drinks, walks through town, visits to a local pub and a gay disco, and excursions make up the main part of GALHA's weekend events.

HWG focuses on the educational function of the weekend gathering, whereas GALHA concentrates on its social function. The Dutch formula nevertheless offers opportunities for entertainment and informal social contacts, while the English organization provides a chance for a serious discussion during Saturday afternoon.

## OPPOSING CHRISTIANITY OR PROMOTING HUMANISM?

Differences in policy and substance between the two groups come to light in their leaflets, magazines, press releases, talks, or discussions with Christian organizations. GALHA and HWG have different interests and opt for different strategies.

The magazines both groups publish—*GALHA Magazine* and *Van 't Zelfde*—have changed from simple publications into respectable periodicals over ten years. The characteristic difference between the two periodicals emerges from the subject the articles deal with. *Van 't Zelfde* concentrates especially on activities and developments in the gay scene, which are then supplied with a humanist commentary. It contains reports of the meetings of the Dutch Association for the Integration of Homosexuality (COC) working group "Religion and Philosophy," in which HWG takes part. This working group is originated by, and forms a part of, the Dutch national organization for equal rights, the COC. While different philosophical and/or religious groups participate, the emphasis is not on the position of the churches on homosexuality. This is, however, an important issue in *GALHA Magazine,* as indicated by the following article titles: "Beware of Evangelic Threat," "Christianity Can Kill," and "Why I Find Religion Impossible." It is impossible to be gay and Christian at the same time, according to GALHA in one of its articles. Both periodicals have lately devoted articles to AIDS, HWG concentrating on humanist views, while GALHA chiefly opposes the view of the churches on AIDS.

The leaflets distributed by the two groups show the same differences. The Dutch group discusses homosexuality as a biological fact and humanism as a philosophy people can freely choose. It also elucidates the qualities of a "humanist homosexual" or a "gay humanist." The British group, on the other hand, is far more militantly anti-Christian as it catalogues the homophobic remarks made by Christianity, including:

> Homosexual acts are intrinsically disordered and can in no case be approved of. (Vatican statement)

> By its very nature homosexuality corrupts all around it. It defiles, it degrades, it contaminates, it ruins innocent lives. (Reformed Presbyterian Church of Ireland)

The GALHA then discusses humanist statements on homosexuality, which mention equal rights, respect, and tolerance. Its leaflet deliberately creates differences between religious and humanist views on homosexuality and highlights these in its layout. The reader is guided through its content and is led inexorably to the conclusion that humanism is more liberal than Christianity toward homosexuality.

The press releases GALHA issues, which are meant especially for gay magazines, also unqualifiedly favor humanism. These press releases often first discuss negative statements on homosexuality made by religious organizations, and then highlight the more positive humanist views. The design and content of these press releases undoubtedly express the idea that a "good" homosexual, by definition, is nonreligious. HWG also tries to promote humanism, but not by opposing Christian views. Its magazine and leaflet—the Dutch group cannot issue its own press releases—exemplify the fact that the group relies more heavily on the strength of humanism.

Both groups are asked to give outside talks, and eagerly seek such opportunities. HWG especially aims this kind of activity at branches of the Humanist League. GALHA concentrates on local gay and lesbian groups. The Dutch organization informs humanists on issues like homosexuality, lifestyles, and relationships. The English group tries to promote the gospel of humanism among gays and lesbians. Humanism offers more opportunities than Christianity to gay men and women, according to GALHA. The discussion of humanist and Christian views on homosexuality has become more or less formalized in the Netherlands. This discussion, for instance, takes place within the COC working group "Religion and Philosophy." GALHA has opted for an open confrontation by way of public debates, in which representatives of GALHA and the Gay Christian Movement try to outdo each other.

## PARTICIPATION BY WOMEN IN HWG AND GALHA

The position of women in the two groups, at least until 1988, was only marginal. GALHA and HWG were founded by gay men and remained primarily male organizations.

The place of women in HWG has repeatedly been a point of discussion.

The formation of a special subcommittee, "Women and Society," was even considered. The organization finally accepted minimal female participation; lesbian women who wanted to participate actively in the working group were advised to start their own lesbian group, which could make use of HWG's facilities. Only one woman tried, unsuccesfully, to start a lesbian working group. HWG does, on the other hand, organize workshops specifically for women on their weekend events. At its tenth anniversary in 1989, the group changed its name to the Gay and Lesbian Working Group, and a small number of lesbians appeared to be active in it for some time.

GALHA has about twelve female members, although its executive committee has almost always been exclusively male. Its weekend events are also almost exclusively visited by men. Only recently the group adopted the name GALHA. Before this it was called the Gay Humanist Group (GHG). Because several British gay organizations consciously began to include the term "lesbian" in their name, the GHG decided to do likewise—hence the Gay and Lesbian Humanist Association. Its hope that this change of name would attract more women has not yet been fullfilled, however. The group thinks that women who want active participation take up such a radical position that humanism would not be sufficiently militant for them.

The Dutch group, therefore, changed its name in response to existing circumstances. The British group's name change is the result of a conscious decision made in the hope of achieving female participation.


## CONCLUSIONS

A preliminary examination of the activities both groups organize shows an apparent resemblance: the organization of weekend events, the publication of a magazine, the distribution of leaflets, and the organization of outside talks. The actual implementation of these, however, is different.

The GALHA weekend events concentrate on the gay aspect in the form of social activities. HWG focuses on workshops and the humanist tradition, which is expressed by the introduction to humanism. The British group seems to characterize itself first and foremost as a gay group, the Dutch group as a humanist one. The way the accesibility to the events is organized deepens this impression. For GALHA's event only members can subscribe; HWG's is thrown open to all those interested, whether homosexual, humanist, or neither. Moreover, the English stay in gay hotels while the Dutch remain in educational centers. As regards the organizational structure, GALHA may be called a gay as well as a humanist group, taking CHE as an example. In this respect HWG is a humanist group, nestled within the Humanist League.

The analysis of the two groups' magazines, leaflets, and outside talks, however, must slightly modify this conclusion. In these activities GALHA presents itself as a humanist organization that wants to provide a humanist alternative for gay men and lesbians. HWG presents itself in this respect primarily as a gay group that tries to make humanism more liberal toward homosexuality. Both organizations have in common the fact that they direct themselves first to the humanist movement in their search for recognition. HWG has representatives in the "Verbondsraad," while GALHA takes part in the discussions among the four humanist organizations. The reasons for their recognition by the humanist movement differ, however. The Dutch group has been accepted into the "Verbondsraad" on the basis of its homosexual nature. The participation of the English group in the Humanist Liaison Committee has been based on its humanist character. The definition of HWG as a gay group and of GALHA as a humanist organization is thus confirmed.

Emancipation groups like GALHA and HWG are usually assigned two functions (Hoekendijk 1980; Veenker 1983): on the one hand, mutual support (for instance, weekend events); on the other, such outreach efforts as the publication of periodicals and the giving of talks. With regard to mutual support, GALHA may be characterized primarily as a gay group and HWG as a humanist group. In the case of the promotion of interests, the roles are somewhat reversed.

The position both of humanism and of homosexuality are not very bright in Great Britain. Why, for instance, does GALHA concentrate primarily on religion as the prevailing philosophy of life, and less on the standard of heterosexuality? The group presupposes the existence of a relationship between the two. By "humanizing" society, the conditions for a liberalization of homosexuality, for the social acceptance of homosexuality as a lifestyle, are created. GALHA considers the four English humanist organizations as allies. Their loyalty is so important that GALHA tries to refrain from criticizing their possible hostility to gays. Together with its kindred organizations, GALHA tries to promote humanism, not merely for humanism's own sake but also to preserve and consolidate the position of GALHA itself. The group is, after all, an autonomous organization, whose continuation depends on its members, mostly from the gay community. The religious tradition in England causes many difficulties for homosexual men and women, and the British gay humanists try to offer help for those with moral dilemmas. GALHA does not seek to attract members from humanist organizations. Their thinking seems to be: You can try to change people into humanists, but you can't turn them into homosexuals.

Homosexuality and humanism are, relatively speaking, quite accepted in Dutch society. Why then does HWG concentrate on gay liberation and not on the promotion of humanism among gays and lesbians? Because of the social acceptance of homosexuality, associated organizations in the humanist movement can be critically tested on their homosexual persuasion. The social establishment of humanism, the organization of the Humanist League, and its relations with other humanist associations offer HWG the possibility to promote its message of emancipation and tolerance among humanist officials in welfare work, the media, and the armed forces. As a working group of the league, HWG can also make use of the various facilities, such as its postal service, professional training for staff members, sociocultural education, and office equipment. The continuation of HWG is discussed every two years at the congress of the Humanist League, where the budget for gay issues is put to the vote. The official for gay issues is paid out of this budget. The explicit promotion of humanist principles is initially left to the Humanist League.

Despite all these differences the two groups are in two respects "two of a kind." First, both GALHA and HWG consider humanism to be a choice, an option, and homosexuality to be a disposition, a "freak of nature." In their view, you can become a humanist at any time and at any age. Homosexuality, on the contrary, is considered to be something you are, whether you like it or not, an inescapable destiny. Homosexuality as a choice—a playful variation, a political statement, a sexual experiment, or a potentiality in everyone   is conceived to be too threatening to vested interests and is considered counterproductive to gay emancipation. Second, the history of these two groups leads one to the conclusion that the formation of gay groups on a humanist basis is a communal affair. In this connection, gay humanists can reach out to each other by boat, by plane, and, in future, by tunnel.*

## REFERENCES

Biemen, T. van. *Het Humanistisch Verbond 1946-1977. Historisch onderzoek naar het denken over liefde, arbeid en emancipatie* (*The Dutch Humanist Union 1946-1977. Historic Research into Thoughts about Love, Labor, and Emancipation*). Dordrecht, 1987.

Boelaars, B. "De houding van het HV tegenover homoseksualiteit" ("The Attitude of the Dutch Humanist Union towards Homosexuality"). *Humanist* (March 1979).

Cummings P., "The Land of Hope and Glory." In *Second ILGA Pink Book: A Global Review of Lesbian and Gay Liberation and Oppression*. Utrecht: Gay and Lesbian Studies Department, Series on Gay and Lesbian Studies, No. 12, 1988, pp. 109-116.

Dobbeling, M., and P. Koenders. *Het topje van de ijsberg. Inventarisatie van tien jaar discriminatie op grond van homoseksualiteit en leefvorm* (*The Tip of the Iceberg: Inventory of Ten Years of Discrimination on the Basis of Homosexuality and Lifestyle*). Utrecht: Gay and Lesbian Studies Department, Series on Gay and Lesbian Studies, No. 3, 1984.

Felling, A., J. Peeters, and O. Schreuder. "Gebroken identiteit. Een studie over christelijk en onchristelijk Nederland." *Archief voor de Geschiedenis van de Katholieke Kerk in Nederland* ("Shattered Identity: A Study on Christianity and Anti-Christianity in the Netherlands." *Archive of the History of the Catholic Church in the Netherlands*) 24 (Nijmegen 1982-1).

Hoekendijk, L. "Functies van de vrijwillige organisaties ten aanzien van de samenleving." In *Besturen in verandering. Handboek voor verenigingen, stichtingen en andere*

---

*Editors' note: In 1992, the Dutch Gay Humanist Group got into difficulties and has since been struggling for its survival.

*vrijwillige organisaties* ("Functions of Voluntary Associations with Regard to Society." *Management in Change. Manual for Foundations, Unions, and Other Voluntary Organizations*). Edited by P. L. Dijk. Alphen aan de Rijn/Brussels, 1980.

Meulenbelt, A. *Brood en Rozen. Artikelen 1975-1982 (Bread and Roses: Essays 1975-1982)*. Amsterdam, 1983.

Schedler, P. E. "Humanisme en Homoseksualiteit, paradox of parallel. De HWG van het Humanistisch Verbond, een casestudy." *Rekenschap. Humanistisch Tijdschrift voor wetenschap en kultuur* ("Humanism and Homosexuality, Paradox or Parallel. The Gay Group of the Dutch Humanist Union, a Case Study." *Account. Humanist Periodical for Science and Culture*) 36, no. 2 (June 1989).

Schedler, P. E., and J. Vrijhoef. "Emancipatie en organisatie. Vrouwenen homogroepen in gevestigde organisaties." *Tijdschrift voor Agologie* ("Emancipation and Organization: Women's and Gay Groups in Established Organizations." *Journal of Andragogy*) 18, no. 2 (1989).

Steenderen, B. van. *Homo worden, homo zijn. Een onderzoek naar de vormgeving van een homoseksuele identiteit bij jongens (Becoming Gay, Being Gay: A Study of the Social Design of a Gay Identity in the Case of Boys)*. Utrecht: Gay and Lesbian Studies Department, Series on Gay and Lesbian Studies, No. 9, 1987.

Tielman, R. A. P. "Anti-humanisme in de sociologie" ("Anti-Humanism in Sociology"). *Rekenschap. Humanistisch Tijdschrift voor wetenschap en kultuur* 31, no. 1 (March 1984).

———. *Homoseksualiteit in Nederland. Studie van een emancipatiebeweging (Homosexuality in the Netherlands: Study of an Emancipation Movement)*. Meppel/Amsterdam, 1982.

———. "Humanisme in Nederland. Stroming en beweging" ("Humanism in the Netherlands: Tendency and Movement"). *Rekenschap. Humanistisch Tijdschrift voor wetenschap en kultuur* 33, no. 1 (March 1986).

———. "Humanisten in Nederland. Een cijfermatige verkenning" ("Humanists in the Netherlands: An Exploration of the Figures"). *Rekenschap. Humanistisch Tijdschrift voor wetenschap en kultuur* 30, no. 1 (March 1983).

———. "International Developments in Gay and Lesbian Studies." In *Second ILGA Pink Book: A Global Review of Lesbian and Gay Liberation and Oppression*. Utrecht: Gay and Lesbian Studies Department, Series on Gay and Lesbian Studies, No. 12, 1988, pp. 55-58.

Tielman, R. A. P., and J. Sinke. "Humanisme in Nederland. Een samenvattend overzicht" ("Humanism in the Netherlands: A Summarizing Overview"). *Rekenschap. Humanistisch tijdschrift voor wetenschap en kultuur* 30, no. 1 (March 1983).

Veenker, J. H. "In de kloof tussen persoonlijke en politieke aanpak. Homohulpverlening na 1971." *Homojaarboek 2. Artikelen over emancipatie en homoseksualiteit* ("The Gap between Personal and Political Approach. Gay Social Work after 1971." *Gay Yearbook 2: Contributions on Emancipation and Homosexuality*). Amsterdam, 1983.

Verduin, M. W. "Humanisme—homoseksualiteit. Een terreinverkenning." In *Congresboek van de vijfde landelijke jaarmarkt voor lesbische en homostudies* ("Humanism—Homosexuality: An Exploration." In *Report of the Fifth National Congress for Lesbian and Gay Studies*). IPSP Publikatiereeks No. 70, Rotterdam, 1986.

Weeks, J. *Sex, Politics, and Society: The Regulation of Sexuality since 1800*. London, 1981.

# 18

# Lesbians and their Emancipation in the Former German Democratic Republic: Past and Future

## Christina Schenk

### HOMOSEXUALS—OUTSIDERS IN GDR SOCIETY

The ways in which society deals with deviancy, with those who are perceived as "different," and especially with homosexuality and homosexuals develop within a historical context and take specific national forms. In the former GDR (German Democratic Republic), the situation was determined by a number of factors. An authoritarian, totalitarian, one-party system exerted central control, resulting in the absence of basic civil liberties. The legal system was so ambiguous that it could be used at any time as an instrument of repression by the ruling political bureaucracy. There were no public fora for debate, the expression and exchange of opinions, or a balance of interests. Significantly, there was a secret service whose function was to "ward off internal enemies."

Nevertheless, after the GDR was founded in 1949, a liberalization of attitudes toward homosexuality took place, albeit very slowly, and it gradually ceased to be a taboo subject. This change was brought about as a result of work by experts in a number of fields, such as medicine, sociology, philosophy, education, sexual research, and law, and by politically active lesbians and gay men who repeatedly tried to draw the problems of homosexual people into public debate. The effect of this development, together with an increasingly prominent international homosexual movement, was to lend encouragement to lesbians and gay men who were no longer prepared to tolerate the existing conditions.

At the beginning of the 1970s, they set up the first private gay and lesbian groups to enable gays to make contact with each other, socialize, work through their personal experiences, and provide support to people who had decided to "come out." It was also the declared aim of the groups to draw public attention to the situation of homosexual people in society and to demand changes. In view of the fact that at that time homosexuality was generally portrayed not only as a pathological condition but also as a crime, and prejudice against homosexuals continued to be endemic, these activities were of great importance for the self-confidence and positive self-image of lesbians and gay men.

In view of the restrictive interpretation of civil law, however, public expression and self-organization were out of the question. The ruling Socialist United Party of Germany (SED) had not concerned itself with the issue of homosexuality and, as a result, there were no clear-cut guidelines for the organs of the state to follow. This led to uncertainty on the part of the authorities, other political parties, and mass organizations, all of which were anxious to remain on good terms with the SED, when they were confronted with the demands of the homosexual groups. The applications of the groups to be registered as official associations were, without exception, rejected on specious grounds; they were told, for example, that registering them would not be "in the interests of the socialist state" and that "special status" was not warranted. The groups found it virtually impossible to obtain the permission necessary to stage public events. The political parties and mass organizations refused to support them in any way, preferring to adopt a cautious approach in view of the SED's own fundamentally restrictive attitude toward "grassroots" movements.

The approach to homosexuality and those people who challenged official attitudes on this issue is just one example of the crudely egalitarian concept of society forming the basis of SED policy, which was shaped through its centralized administrative machinery. Social groups with specific interests did not feature in this view. The voluntaristic concepts of a socialist society, in which social development could be controlled and planned to the point where society would be absolutely classless and free of contradictions, were completely unrealistic. They were also an expression of the fear felt by the founders and proponents of the totalitarian and authoritarian state when confronted with social movements originating independently of the parameters prescribed by the state.

Any activity organized by the groups and developing its own momentum could not be fully controlled by the state, and was therefore unpredictable. As such, it was seen as an intrinsic threat to the state, and was therefore monitored with suspicion. As a rule, such activities were hampered, and finally halted completely, by subjecting the organizers to harassment and persecution.

When specific interests were articulated—for example, by the lesbian and gay men's groups—they met with a negative response and were dismissed as a demand for privileges (!) or for special conditions which could not be justified. Until the late 1980s, calls for public debate of hitherto taboo social issues, and for official recognition of the gay liberation groups, were seen as an implicit criticism of "socialist society" and thus rejected outright.

Efforts to initiate any democratization in social conditions "from below" were persistently blocked by the state; so, too, was any social science research which might have analyzed the situation and suggested ways of bringing about change.

For lesbians and gay men, the situation remained unchanged until the late 1970s, when the Protestant Church in the GDR, witnessing the state's repression of dissidents, increasingly offered its protection and the use of its facilities to anyone who challenged "real existing socialism in the GDR," especially in matters of the ecology, world peace, human rights, and feminist issues. The first church-based opposition groups were formed, from which the opposition movement in the GDR was later to develop. Very few members of these groups were Christians; the Protestant Church imposed no such condition upon the groups seeking shelter. This was the major factor enabling an opposition movement to form on church territory in a country where almost three-quarters of the population were atheist.

In Leipzig in 1982, gay men and several lesbian women founded the first (semi-) official homosexual group in the GDR. Admittedly, the official church viewed the establishment of this and subsequent groups with disfavor, and expressed its views with varying degrees of outspokenness; but thanks to the support of clergy and individual parishes it proved possible to set up the group. Similar groups were soon set up in other cities. This was a major step forward. Neither the authorities nor the state security service had any direct access to church territory, and so, for the first time, the groups were able to work autonomously in an atmosphere relatively free of fear. The state security service did attempt subsequently to infiltrate informers to keep a check on the groups' activities, but it was unable to reduce the groups' new-found effectiveness in drawing public attention to their agenda, or to hamper processes within the groups. The groups themselves were able to make use of the church infrastructure to some extent; the church press could be used for publicity purposes; and the groups were able to raise their profile by participating in well-publicized church events such as the annual church rallies, and to organize their own event which the public could attend.

Over the next few years, the network of gay and lesbian working groups set up under the auspices of the church continued to expand, thus providing a forum for self-help, counseling, social activities, and discussion for the first time, and enabling gays and lesbians to initiate campaigns which attracted public attention.

The groups exchanged experiences on a fairly regular basis and coordinated their campaigns. An annual members' meeting enabled lesbians and gay men from the various working groups to report on their activities and discuss joint action and objectives for the future. Despite many logistical problems and only limited public impact, the foundation stone for a lesbian and gay liberation movement in the GDR had thus been laid.

Homosexual groups were not permitted to exist outside the church until the mid to late 1980s. These groups were founded by lesbians and gay men who did not want to enter into contact with the church on principle, or who did not consider themselves to be in "opposition" to the state. The groups were set up as "clubs for lesbians and gay men" on youth club premises, in municipal cultural centers, or under the auspices of the local "freethinkers" associations which had been established in 1988 in response to instructions "from above." Permission to set up these groups was conditional upon members' proving their conformity to state and system. As a result, the approach and aims of the lesbians and gay men who met in these groups differed radically from those of their counterparts who met under the auspices of the Protestant Church.

The political dimension of being homosexual, combined with criticism of the GDR state, formed the common basis of the church-based groups, which called for the emancipation, democratization, and restructuring of society. The purpose of the homosexual clubs, on the other hand, was to integrate into socialist society, without questioning that society or subjecting it to any form of critical analysis. The aim was to become an invisible part of "normal" society. The clubs demanded equal treatment of homosexuals and heterosexuals by the state bureaucracy at a formal level, and expected their members to make a collective effort to conform to heterosexual standards; for example, by expressing disapproval of promiscuity, anonymous sex in public places, and so on.

These clubs did not recognize, or chose to ignore, the link between the structures and mechanisms of the totalitarian state, on the one hand, and the particular situation of lesbians and gay men in the GDR, on the other. Being different from the "norm" has a political dimension which some people had recognized from the outset; however, the clubs did not address this issue for fear of losing official permission to meet. No activities took place without the blessing of the "appropriate authorities." The strategy was to conform at all costs and to keep in the government's good books. As a result, they assiduously avoided any contact with the church-based lesbian and gay groups. They even attempted to present themselves to the state as the sole representative of the interests of lesbians and gay men. As a consequence, relations between the church-based groups and the homosexual clubs became considerably strained.

Despite all the efforts made by the various groups, however, the lesbian and gay movement never succeeded in attracting the attention of the public at large; nor did lesbian and gay issues become a matter of public debate on different levels. Despite some progress in the GDR, traditional homophobia still colored public attitudes to homosexuality, and archetypical behavioral patterns, i.e., marginalization of gay issues by the public, and voluntary self-segregation by gays themselves, continued unchallenged.

## THE LESBIAN MOVEMENT IN THE GDR:
## FROM FEMALE HOMOSEXUALITY TO A LESBIAN IDENTITY

### Women in the GDR, or: The Difficulties of Becoming a Lesbian

The everyday lives of lesbian women in industrialized countries with patriarchal structures certainly have many common features, but they can only be understood fully within their particular national context.

The significant factors in this respect are the position of women generally in the society in question, the prevailing concepts of "normal" behavior for women (and men), the conditions for self-organization, and, furthermore, social attitudes to hetero- and homosexuality. Examination of these factors in connection with the situation of lesbian women in the GDR revealed a very varied and paradoxical picture.

Throughout the GDR's existence, equal rights for women and men consti- tuted one of the stated political aims of the "leadership of party and state." To this end, important principles were embodied in the country's constitution, family law, and other laws and decrees by the early 1950s. Women were given access to professional training and employment, and over the years a number of social policy measures were taken which, by providing adequate childcare facilities, en- abled mothers to work. During the 1980s almost 90 percent of mothers of working age were in paid employment or full-time education, and, as a rule, had an adequate income. As a result of this "emancipation from above," women were able to use their qualifications and experience to earn their living, and achieved extensive economic independence.

The SED announced in the early 1970s that the "woman question as a social question" had already been resolved. This illustrated that the SED considered the gender conflict largely from an economic perspective. Although progress had been made with regard to the position of women in society, patriarchy persisted unchallenged. At no time was the underlying patriarchal structure of GDR society the subject of debate, and certainly not of policy. The divergence in the social, political, and economic positions of women and men was considered in a purely quantitative sense.

Although women in the GDR had the financial security to adopt indepen- dent and alternative lifestyles, such lifestyles did not conform to the official image of what was normal and acceptable. Although the role model for women did not contain any overtly sexist elements, it nonetheless remained heterocentric. The "normal" woman had professional qualifications; was employed on a full- time basis; was a wife and mother; and, in addition, "played an active role in society." This role model was based on the concepts of a monogamous hetero- sexual relationship and parenthood, which were never challenged or called into question. Other lifestyles were never portrayed in the models used in the socialization process and in daily life. For lesbian women, then, the way to self-awareness was fraught with obstacles that often proved impossible to overcome.

The obstacles to self-awareness posed by the socialization process in the GDR were further exacerbated by the complete absence of a widespread women's network, to say nothing of a lesbian subculture, due to the political situation described at the beginning of this article. There were no women's cafes, women's libraries, or women's centers. For a long time, contact advertisements were either forbidden or permitted only in cryptic form in a few newspapers. There was no public recognition that lesbians existed, and there was absolutely no information provided.

In terms of the officially promoted role model for women in the GDR, a lesbian way of life was a deviation from the norm. It was dismissed by the state as a fringe group phenomenon, a social irrelevance that could safely be ignored; at most, it was treated as a potentially subversive phenomenon that had to be dealt with. There was no objective debate about lesbianism as a legitimate alternative lifestyle, nor was the need to initiate such a debate acknowledged.

### Lesbian Emancipation, or: Variations on the Theme of Gender Conflict

After the first "working groups on homosexuality" had been established during the early 1980s under the auspices of the Protestant Church, and the first "clubs for homosexuals" had been set up outside the church in the late 1980s, lesbians and gay men, joined by the common bond of their homosexuality, began to campaign together for improvements in their situation.

The gender-typical patterns inherent in this situation went virtually unnoticed at first. This was due in part to the nature of the relationship between male and female which, while basically patriarchal, was nonetheless rather less hierarchical and sexist than that in West Germany, for example. It was also due to the impact of the official image promoted by the state, which ignored the difference in the situation of men and women in society or at least portrayed it as unproblematic and idealized. The underlying patriarchal structure of GDR society was not discussed, and society as a whole was not conscious of it. Girls (and boys) and women (and men) lived with the illusion that the issue of sexual equality was essentially resolved. They failed to notice that the reality of the situation was rather different.

In order to recognize the patriarchal elements in the GDR's social structure, a learning process was required which was laborious in the extreme, particularly since the public had no access to the necessary social data.

Given the circumstances just described and the fact that public debate of these issues was impossible, it was hardly surprising that an autonomous lesbian movement took a considerable time to develop in the GDR. It also took time for the homosexual working groups to realize that they had to deal not only with the issue of homosexuality and society, but also with the divergent and conflicting interests of lesbians and gay men. Elements of traditional sex role behavior—particularly in the form of nonverbal dominance and dominant speech patterns—play a part here; so, too, does the fact that in "mixed sex" groups lesbian women are almost always in a minority. Consequently, men tend to dominate and determine the course of events, and it is obvious that the issues and activities of interest to women are largely neglected. In these circumstances there is a particular lack of attention paid to the wishes of lesbians. Lesbian women's needs and expectations—contact with other lesbians, an opportunity to discuss the problems they have in common, self-awareness, and confidence-building— cannot, therefore, be met in "mixed" groups.

By its third meeting, in 1983, the lesbian and gay men's working group in Berlin had already decided to split. From then on, two separate working groups— one for lesbians and another for gay men— existed in Berlin. In the majority of the church-based working groups the lesbians split from the gay men much later, although they did not reject joint action when they felt this was helpful for lesbian women.

This separatist trend clearly increased in the late 1980s; when the GDR ceased to exist, there were eight autonomous lesbian groups in various towns. The close links between these groups justify the term "lesbian movement" in the case of the GDR. An important contribution was made by the lesbian newspaper *Frau Anders* (*Ms. Different*), founded in 1989 and published by women in Jena.

Remarkably, lesbians who joined the "clubs for homosexuals" that were set up independently of the churches did not establish autonomous lesbian groups. This is perhaps not surprising, given that there was a considerable degree of conformity to state and system within these groups, which made it impossible to discuss the continuing existence of the mechanisms of repression, whether traditional or inherent in socialism.

The social status of lesbians and gay men, respectively, in a patriarchal society is unequal, purely on account of their gender. Their homosexuality is a common bond, but it in no way lessens the differing social roles and status of women and men. The tendency to establish a separate and independent lesbian movement, then, may be regarded as a yardstick of women's awareness of the sociopolitical dimension of their position in a patriarchal society, and of their ability to identify their own interests and needs.

## LESBIANS IN POLITICS

The radical changes that swept GDR society in the autumn of 1989 were brought about by the grassroots movement, some of which had sprung from the church-based opposition movement, others coming into being as the peaceful revolution progressed. Although some women were prominent in these movements, they were underrepresented to a considerable degree, and there was virtually no discussion of women's issues or feminism at this time. Many women all over the

GDR realized, or at least suspected, that women had still not achieved social equality with men; and they saw that the emancipation of women (and men) was in danger of being dismissed as a peripheral issue and excluded from the political agenda for social change in the GDR, unless they themselves organized a women's association with feminist demands.

The Independent Women's Association (UFV) was founded at the beginning of December 1989, and it soon acquired a high profile in the political landscape of the GDR.

Lesbian women played an important role in setting up and working within the UFV right from the start. Even at its constituent meeting, attended by women from all over the GDR, lesbian groups and lesbians from mixed groups took the opportunity to voice their opinions. Their demands to participate on an equal footing were accepted, without discussion, as readily as those of the other women's groups. This was unusual in itself, given that for years lesbianism had been a taboo subject and shrouded in silence.

The UFV's program states: "We aim to establish a modern society in which every woman and man is free to choose the lifestyle s/he prefers, without suffering marginalization or disadvantage because of his/her gender, origin, nationality, or sexual orientation." The fundamental aims of the UFV are to ensure that all lifestyles that do not encroach on others' rights to self-determination are accepted as equally valid, and that the relationship between the sexes, based as it is upon power, is fundamentally changed. The UFV used its influence at the Round Table, which governed the GDR from December 1989 until the first democratic elections to the GDR parliament in March 1990, and in the associated working groups, to make sure that a ban on discrimination based on "sexual orientation" was incorporated into several fundamental draft laws, including the draft of a new constitution for the GDR (Articles 1 and 22), the Party Law (§3 [2]), the Unification Law (§2 [2]), and the Electoral Law (§8 [2]). The working groups on "Equality of Women and Men" and "Education, Upbringing, and Youth" issued manifestos stating specifically that all lifestyles, irrespective of sexual orientation, were equally valid; they also expressed the principle of "respecting the dignity of every person, irrespective of age; sex; sexual orientation; nationality; social and family origin; and cultural, political, or religious identity." The UFV was represented not only by lesbians in Round Table talks and its working groups; the principles expressed by the UFV in its policy regarding lifestyles were vigorously supported by the nonlesbian women in the negotiations. There was no sign of the "lesbian-hetero conflict," which has played quite a considerable role in the women's movement in the West.

In mid-1990, representatives of a number of lesbian groups and lesbians from other UFV groups met together for the first time since the political upheavals in the GDR. Their aim was to discuss possible ways of reestablishing the network of contact which had existed prior to the peaceful revolution in the GDR, and to seek ways to raise the lesbian profile in the UFV. It was decided to issue a declaration to the other women in the UFV, stating that lesbianism was a central aspect of their activities within the women's movement, focusing on the role of lesbian women in the UFV and urging other UFV women to lend their support to lesbian policy initiatives in the future. They also demanded that "on appropriate occasions the existence and role of lesbians in the UFV should not be ignored or 'overlooked,' and that they should play a part commensurate with their numbers in the UFV in building up the association and making it effective." It was proposed that "in accordance with the scale of the problems associated with a lesbian lifestyle in a heterocentric, patriarchal society, one of the spokes-women of the UFV could be authorized by the lesbian women in the association to speak out on the situation of lesbian women in the area of the GDR." The association accepted the declaration without debate.

In accordance with its political aims, the UFV selected candidates to stand in the 1990 elections to the local councils, *Land*\* parliaments, and the German Bundestag. On each occasion, it formed an alliance with various other grassroots movements.

The UFV has been represented by two women in the German Parliament of the Federation since December 1990. One of them was elected from the PDS† list, while I myself stood as a candidate for Alliance 90/The Greens.

I am the only member of the German Bundestag who lives openly as a lesbian. My main fields of work are women's issues and lesbian politics, and—as far as this is possible—gay politics. One achievement in the current electoral term is that the words "lesbian" and "gay" may be used in motions and draft laws by the German Bundestag. Prior to this, only the term "homosexual" was permitted. It is important to use the avenues of parliamentary democracy (plenary debates, motions, and draft laws) and make the public aware of these issues in order to combat general ignorance and, if laws are prepared in Parliament which discriminate against lesbians and gays, also to mobilize the lesbian and gay movement. At the time of writing, efforts are being made to abolish Section 175 of the Penal Code.‡ However, the government has no intention of repealing this antiquated law completely; it is merely considering a reduction in the age of consent from eighteen to sixteen. Furthermore, this would apply not only to gay men but also to lesbians. If these ideas are put into practice, it would be possible, for the first time in the Federal Republic of Germany, to prosecute lesbians under the penal code. The lesbian and gay movement is called upon to protest vociferously against such a move.

---

\*Germany is a federal republic. *Land* refers to "Bundesland." There are fifteen such constituent "Lands" with far-reaching autonomy and political powers.

†PDS = Partei des Demokratischen Sozialismus (the Social Democratic Party), the successor of the SED.

‡Under Section 175, a male of eighteen years or older who has had sexual contact with a male under eighteen is punishable for up to five years' imprisonment or is subject to a fine.

## GDR LESBIANS AND GERMAN UNIFICATION

For the women in the UFV and many other grassroots activists, the peaceful revolution in autumn 1989 was a euphoric time. We felt that this was the start of the "third way" for the GDR. The aim was not to unite with the Federal Republic of Germany, but to create a new GDR. The Round Table discussions gave the grassroots movement experience of the feasibility of politics, and the huge numbers of people actively involved in politics at that time marked the end of lethargy and resignation and the dawn of a new era. For the women in the UFV there seemed to be a real hope of establishing new social conditions which would take account of feminist priorities.

The victory of the Conservatives in the elections to the People's Chamber (Parliament) of the GDR in March 1990, showed that the majority of the population failed to recognize the need for a new beginning, or that they did not have the strength to face this challenge. The dreams had faded, and the GDR's *Anschluss* with the Federal Republic under Article 23 of the (West German) Basic Law (Constitution) was inevitable. The women in the UFV were back in the opposition movement. The issues and questions now on the agenda differed radically from those of autumn 1989:

- In a capitalist society on the Federal German model, in which economic pragmatism takes priority over the creation of a society in which the needs of individuals (women and men) and the preservation of the ecosphere are paramount, to what extent is it possible to challenge and change the relationship between the sexes as a social, cultural, economic, and socio-psychological problem?

- To what extent is it possible to remove all the various forms of marginalization in society, and, in particular, what measures will ensure that all lifestyles are acceptable and that marriage no longer recieves privileged status?

- What strategies for success are possible for women in capitalist German society?

The legal formalities of the GDR's *Anschluss* with the Federal Republic were completed with monetary union on July 1, 1990, and accession on October 3, 1990. It amounted to the de facto annexation of the GDR by the Federal Republic; now the way was clear for the virtually wholesale imposition of the West German system on the territory that had once been the state of the GDR.

The complete social transformation that has ensued will be complete in a matter of years. For women and lesbians who lived in the GDR, the graphic differences between the patriarchies of the Federal Republic of Germany and the GDR are becoming only too clear. Until now, there has been no detailed description or systematic analysis of this issue, as this is impossible until the social transformation now taking place in the former GDR is more or less completed. The drastic changes that will directly affect women are outlined below.

## Employment

At present, approximately 50 percent of people of working age in East Germany are out of work. Women now number more than 60 percent of the unemployed. Today, only around 36 percent of women who are able to work have a job, in contrast to a figure of more than 80 percent in the GDR. Admittedly, unemployment, especially among women, may fall once the East German economy has been consolidated as expected in the next few years; but a number of leading politicians have already made it quite clear that the "excessive level of employment of women in the GDR" should be reduced to "normal" levels. At present, women are steadily being eased out of employment.

Women's economic independence, then, which is the prerequisite for an independent lifestyle, is under threat. This thrusts them back into a position of humiliating dependency and makes it particularly difficult for lesbians to find the lifestyle that suits them.

## The Relationship of the Sexes

This process of marginalization will lead to a radical change in the relationship between the sexes in East Germany. Society—and women themselves—will attribute a higher status to men, and women's status will decline accordingly. Men will once more be the "breadwinners" and head of the family, with women primarily assuming responsibility for reproduction and earning a little pin money if they wish. Whereas in the GDR men were increasingly assuming domestic responsibilities, this role will be reassessed and the main burden will be borne by women once more.

Since it will be no longer generally accepted, as it was in the GDR, that every women will have a career as a matter of course, girls' and women's expectations will change. They will now focus once again on men for their economic security, especially in view of the increasing status of men in East German society.

These processes will make it increasingly difficult for girls and women to come out as lesbians.

## Sexism

Sexism is pervasive and omnipresent in the media, particularly in advertising, and is an integral part of "normal" contemporary life in the Federal Republic. This clearly illustrates that patriarchy in West German capitalism has a completely different dimension, with the public image of women and men still being determined by the conventional stereotypes.

The problem of sexism is compounded by the massive attempt now being undertaken by the churches to "re-Christianize" East Germany. In this connection, debates over the status of marriage and abortion are being revived.

## CONCLUSION

With the collapse of the GDR, the social status of women has begun to change dramatically, and these changes directly affect lesbian women.

The coming down of the Wall brought many lesbians in East and West Germany into contact for the first time. It very quickly became clear that forty years of separate development in the two German states had resulted in very different mentalities, approaches, and political intentions. The great challenge now facing the lesbian movements in East and West Germany is to ensure that they draw strength and inspiration from their differences and do not allow their dissimilarities to drive a wedge between them.

Much will depend on the newly won freedoms being used effectively to make the women's and lesbian movements in both the Federal Republic and the former GDR a politically relevant force for the future.

# 19

# Gay Perestroika: The Political Changes in Central and Eastern Europe and their Effect on the Lesbian and Gay Movement

## Andrzej Selerowicz

Perestroika, the Russian term for "reconstruction" coined by former Soviet President Mikhail Gorbachev, has become a symbol of the largest political phenomenon to take place in Central and Eastern Europe in the last several years. Like an avalanche, the Warsaw Pact countries, those states that had militarily terrorized the Western World since the end of the Second World War, and led millions of their own citizens to financial and moral ruin, crumbled at last. While the concept of communism started to become politically incidental, the process of democratization began to take hold and, with this, there arose a gay and lesbian movement in the countries of the former Eastern bloc.

The origin of both developments can be traced to a time before perestroika became a part of everyone's vocabulary. Similar to the establishment of political opposition groups, such as Solidarnosc in Poland and Charta 77 in Czechoslovakia, the first circles of lesbian and gay activists appeared in the mid-1980s, stimulated by the International lesbian and Gay Association (ILGA) and its regional structure, the Eastern Europe Information Pool (EEIP). Chronologically the movement started in the former German Democratic Republic (GDR), and later in Hungary (where the first officially recognized group, "Homeros Lambda," was registered in 1988), Poland, Czechoslovakia, and Slovenia. During the last two years in the former Soviet Union, an activity in the Baltic republics, as well as in Moscow, St. Petersburg, Novosibirsk, and Kiev, has been noticed, despite the inconvenient circumstances, especially in the legal field. In 1990, Bulgaria joined the movement. Later groups were established in Romania, Croatia, and Serbia. For five years annual regional conferences have been taking place where the political coordination of action and exchange of experiences has been allowed to develop.

The legal situation for homosexuals before the beginning of "gay perestroika" can be divided into two categories: In the bloc consisting of Poland, the GDR, Czechoslovakia, Hungary, Bulgaria, and the northern federal republics of Yugoslavia (Slovenia and Croatia), sexual contacts between consenting adults of the same sex were not illegal; in the Soviet Union and the Balkans (Romania, Albania, and the southern republics of Yugoslavia), homosexual relations were criminalized. Ukraine, Latvia, and Estonia repealed their laws after independence. Russia is still in the process of revising its penal code. Apart from these countries, the legal situation for homosexuals, except for a few small changes, has not altered until now. So what caused the change in their living situation, and what has made so many gay men and lesbians come out?

Two main sources of oppression have been lifted: a censorship that tightened all aspects of social life and was responsible for homosexuality being generally taboo, and a conscious effort on the part of the previous governments to unify various parts of the country, destroy all shades of individuality, and to educate an intimidated and obedient society. Forming an organization required official permission; insubordination was very severely punished. Even women's unions, peace initiatives, and groups of ethnic minorities were controlled from above. (Maybe this explains why the authentic feminist movement has not been able to develop fully in these countries, where repression of ethnic interests has brought about the current conflicts.) As the activity of all permitted organizations had as its professed aim the fulfillment of the ideological principles of the Communist party, the spontaneous unification of homosexuals—whose very existence was denied—had to be very suspicious to the officials. There are known cases of attempts by the police to infiltrate the first unofficial lesbian and gay groups in Poland and the GDR. Their leaders were persecuted, sometimes even forced to emigrate. All this has happened within the last few years and should be remembered here to reinforce the contrast with the present situation.

The ongoing process of democratization in this part of Europe has changed the situation rapidly. First of all, the carrying out of political activity and the founding of new organizations and political parties is no longer dangerous.* Under these circumstances, the lesbian and gay groups that worked underground until now became formally legalized in Hungary, Poland, the former GDR, the Czech Republic, Slovenia, Bulgaria, Estonia, Latvia, and Ukraine. The parallel appear-

---

*Editors' note: On the other hand, lesbian and gay activitists in a few countries, notably Russia, face severe forms of mental and physcial harassment.

ance of AIDS also partly influenced the moral and financial support from some institutions. Even in those countries where homosexuality is still criminalized, some lesbian and gay groups have been founded, although their legal status is consequently denied (e.g., the Tchaikovsky Foundation in St. Petersburg and the Moscow group MGLU). The abolition of censorhip, the rise of commercialism, and the privatization of economic activity have caused real gay bars (mainly in Budapest) to appear, magazines and books to be published (six in Poland alone), and even a gay radio station to start up (as in Slovenia).

Is everything going well, then? Unfortunately not!

Due to the evident economic mistakes of the Communist system, the countries of Central and Eastern Europe have to labor under huge financial difficulties. The necessary budget cuts concern mainly the social and cultural fields. Lesbian and gay groups cannot count on their own governments for financial support. The impoverishment of society means that group members are also poor. With nothing but their own membership fees, it is impossible to run a successful organization.

The other new negative aspect is the radical shift in social attitudes. Now when it is allowed to demonstrate one's sexual orientation in public, the voice of bourgeois conservatism also becomes louder and louder. The growing poverty in society and the increase in radicalism, with the loss of many traditional moral values, bring with them a rapid increase in crime. Gangs of skinheads and hooligans see in homosexuals (especially their increasing visibility) an easy victim. The collective harassment of gay bars in East Berlin and Warsaw, as well as robberies and beatings in cruising areas of many cities, are the tangible evidence of this. This escalation results also from the relatively passive role of the police. The state security system and the police are no longer there to contain it, so now the repressed violence can escape. It will get worse because of new social problems: a crisis of identity, of confidence, of authority and security. The violence is showing itself most ominously in sporadic eruptions of neo-Nazism. It might also be called nascent anarchy. Authority in the East, ubiquitous until the revolution, has all but disappeared, and what is left is ineffectual.

As is the case with all authoritative orders of the totalitarian power, atheism was never wholly accepted by society. Everywhere, especially in Catholic Poland and, to a lesser extent, Catholic Lithuania, the church always played a role of political opposition, and therefore enjoyed universal authority over the people. With the abdication of the Communists, this void was filled by new parties which took religious tendencies broadly into consideration in their platforms because they wanted to win over a maximum number of politically disoriented voters. Furthermore, the consequent expansive politics of the Vatican and increasing Islamic fundamentalism have brought it about that nowadays being an atheist is nearly as socially unacceptable as being religious was before. The church's power appears not only in the traditionally religious countries (e.g., Albania and Romania), but also in new ones (e.g., Slovakia). The universal denunciation of homosexuality by conservative religions (it was better in the former GDR with its Protestant Church) is nowadays the biggest danger for gay men and lesbians. The religious institutions themselves have not taken any concrete action against the lesbian and gay movement up to now, but are consciously steering the temper of the people by instigating homophobia. Appeals for a ban on pornography, which is often misinterpreted as sexuality, and for moral cleanliness are alarmingly multiplying. Publications about homosexuality in the mainstream press and actions toward AIDS prevention are being vitiated, as the very people and institutions responsible for social action face the caveat, "What will the church say about this?"

After the loss of political power by the Communists (for most of whom even the formal renaming to socialists did not win sympathy), chaos began to rule the political arena. Before the elections (now free and democratic) about fifty different parties campaign with curious and nearly indistinguishable platforms. For the average voter it is enormously difficult to differentiate between them; it is no less of a problem for lesbian and gay organizations to identify their political allies. Probably for that reason, discussions with the leaders of political parties do not take place. For Germans from the former GDR, it is easy: the political landscape has been completely imported from the Federal Republic. For other countries, the situation is new and completely unclear. Some attempts at questioning the parties have already been undertaken in Poland, Hungary, the Czech Republic, and Slovakia; but the results have remained unknown to the voters. Surprisingly, the candidates from former Communist parties have approached homosexual organizations in order to establish a dialogue and seek support. However, these proposals have been withdrawn because the Communists are humiliated and do not promise any positive results. At this point the lack of experience and serious political interest of some group leaders must be mentioned. An attempt to obtain the concrete point of view of President Lech Walesa of Poland on homosexuality was not properly carried out. The ensuing protest action over Walesa's imagined homophobia, which even reached international dimenions, became a public humiliation because of a lack of evidence. However, when Polish Deputy Minister of Health Kazimierz Kapera made a derogatory statement about homosexuals in a TV interview in May 1991 and therefore initiated a scandal, many progressive groups and persons protested. The ones who did not take a stand and kept silent were, ironically, the Polish gay organizations.

Some groups, however, taking advantage of subsequent opportunities, have established a well-organized operation. These groups have now formed coalitions in the form of national unions ("Stowarzyszenie Grup Lambda" in Poland and SOHO in Czechoslovakia* being the best examples). In March 1993, several small lesbian and gay groups in Ukraine also established a nationwide organization. During

---

*Editors' note: Despite the split of the country into the Czech Republic and Slovakia, gay and lesbian groups seek to continue to cooperate closely.

regular meetings of the delegates from various member groups, general trends of activity and political actions with a national scope are decided upon. Within SOHO, for example, the appointment of gay candidates for the next elections, appeals to Parliament concerning the legalization of same-sex partnerships, and the abolition of "pink files" have been discussed. By ensuring complete autonomy for individual groups, close cooperation within such a structure seems to increase efficiency. In those countries where these structures do not exist, the weak points of the lesbian and gay movement become visible immediately (as in Hungary and the former Soviet Union). As for international cooperation, unions seem also to be the correct form, because they facilitate contacts and the flow of information.

Romania, the southern republics of Yugoslavia, and Albania remain the great unknown area on the map of the lesbian and gay movement. The main reasons for this are their very repressive penal codes and the mentality of the people. In the south, as is the case in many Mediterranean countries, machismo is very prevalent. Sex is treated biologically and is not a point of discussion. All known gay men from this region are or were married, or are keen on getting married quite soon. This habit is popular not only because of the social pressure to be a "real man," but also because they generally want to avoid inconveniences. Having done everything to appear "normal," one can allow oneself some homosexual adventures in complete anonymity. Those who are not able to endure such sexual hypocrisy either emigrate or are forced to do so, or give up their real needs. The best one can do is to join a gay clique that is completely isolated and self-contained. All arguments for coming out and starting sociopolitical activities are dismissed as absurd. For lesbians the situation is even worse. A few isolated positive exceptions are not cogent evidence of an overall positive change.

Aside from the negative factors coming from outside, there are problems in the lesbian and gay movement that arise from homosexuals themselves. One should not forget that leaders do not possess any experience in leading political activities. Mistakes are, therefore, made quite often. The wrong tactics of the leadership of the Hungarian group, "Homeros Lambda," paralyzed the efficiency of the organization for many years. As a result, numerous members left the organization and its efforts, in both the national and international fields, died completely. The frustration among Hungarian homosexuals and bad publicity caused difficulties in starting the work again. The case of "Homeros Lambda" is unfortunately not unique. It is worse when the mistakes coming from the lack of experience are accompanied by consciously destructive acts. As the financial side of the organization is mostly not presented and checked precisely enough, money, especially funds from Western organizations, are sometimes embezzled for private purposes. This is not only a matter of lost money, but one of internal conflicts that develop in such situations and end in disaster for the organization.

Although the appearance of many gay magazines, often published in large circulations, guarantees a good flow of information to the masses, the work of lesbian and gay organizations still remains quite elitist. The hindrance is the lack of real clubs and communication centers, as well as the resulting lack of interesting events for the public at large. The organizing of disco events or the opening of gay bars (in Budapest) is surely a positive development. But the subculture will never be able to fulfill broad political aims and needs.

Although the term "lesbian and gay movement" is being used here, it is necessary to mention that the participation of women is very limited. Almost all existing organizations in Central and Eastern Europe are mixed, but there are only a few lesbian activists. In Hungary, for example, they do not cooperate in the work of the group, even though they are regularly encouraged to do so. In the beginning, probably for tactical reasons, women started by cooperating with men. This is actually being continued and works well, a fact that astonishes many lesbians from Western European countires. Recently, however, a slow tendency toward founding separate groups for women only (in Slovenia, Poland, the Czech Republic, Slovakia, and Moscow) can be observed, even though they remain a part of parent organizations. Sometimes a surprisingly large number of lesbians appear in groups at social events. Those women, who have decided to cooperate with men, are very dedicated and often mediate in quarrels between gay men.

The lesbian and gay movement in Eastern and Central Europe can become, due to its impetus and innovation, a real source of motivation for similar initiatives in the West. The extent of their activities, as well as the process of democratization itself, are very progressive signs. As long as no regression to social conservatism takes place and no substantial tactical mistakes are made, it will surely increase in power and international importance. It is worth paying more attention to this region and investing more work and financial means. The opening of borders and the Eastern bloc's entrance into the European community should additionally accelerate this process.

## BIBLIOGRAPHY

Boczkowski, Krzysztof. *Homoseksualizm* (*Homosexuality*). Warsaw: PZWLek, 1988.

*Diskrete Leidenschaften: homosexuelle Prosa aus Polen* (*Discreet Passions: Homosexual Prose from Poland*). Edited by Wolfgang Jöhling. Frankfurt: Foester Verlag, 1988.

Hale, Keith. *In the Land of Alexander.* Boston: Alyson Publications, 1990.

Nenadál, Radoslav. *My Te zazdíme, Aido* (*Aida, We Will Inmure You in a Wall*). Prague: Interkontaktservis, 1991.

*Rosa Liebe unterm roten Stern* (*Pink Love under the Red Star*). Homosexuelle Initiative (HOSI) Wien Auslandsgruppe Collective. Hamburg: Frühlings Erwachen, 1984.

*Second ILGA Pink Book.* ILGA Pink Book Editing Team. Utrecht: Interfacultaire Werkgroep Homostudies, 1988.

*Sexual Minorities and Society: The Changing Attitudes Towards Homosexuality in 20th Century Europe.* Edited by Teet Veispak. Tallinn, Estonia: Eesti TA Ajaloo Instituut, 1991.

Tatchell, Peter. *Europe in the Pink.* London: GMP, 1992.

# 20

# Coming Out as an MP in the United Kingdom

## Chris Smith

It was in November 1984 that I decided to come out to the world. In the previous year's general election campaign—when I was first elected to the British Parliament—there had been a little sniping from the Social Democrats, talking individually to voters about my sexuality, but nothing had emerged into full public glare. I was, however, conscious that at some stage it would be right to say something in public. It was simply a question of choosing the right occasion and the best time.

When it actually happened, it did so almost by accident. Rugby Council, a Conservative-controlled local authority in the Midlands, had deleted "discrimination on grounds of sexuality" from its list of forms of discrimination in choosing people for jobs. The Council Leader announced to the press that he would not tolerate "men coming to work in dresses and earrings." Anti-gay prejudice was stirring.

A protest march and rally were called, and the organizers contacted me to speak. I agreed; and on the train up to Rugby that lunchtime, I scribbled out a few notes about the right to work and the need for equal treatment in employment: the makings of a worthy if not exactly earth-shattering speech. Yet something inside me told me, as I arrived at the hall packed with people, that this was the time to do something more. I got to my feet and began: "My name is Chris Smith. I'm the Labour MP for Islington South and Finsbury. And I'm gay." The hall erupted. Before I could say another word, I was given a standing ovation for the next five minutes. The rest was something of an anticlimax!

Afterwards I rationalized it all to myself. There was, of course, a logical point to what I had done. The issue at Rugby was all about the ability of lesbians and gay men to do a job just as well as anyone else. Precisely the same, I felt, applied to MPs: it was an important point to make.

I thought the "popular" press in Britain—who have frequently proved themselves to be rabidly anti-gay—would go berserk. They didn't. There have since been a number of articles, some hostile, some supportive; but there was no instant condemnation. There was coverage, yes, but mainly in the more serious papers and in the local media in my constituency. I suspect that when you *are* open about your own sexuality, when you stand up and are prepared to be counted in your own way and by your own choosing, you automatically remove much of the "sleaze" value with which the press loves to invest lesbian and gay issues. No scandal, no story.

There was something else I wanted to do, too, in the immediate aftermath of speaking out. That was to demonstrate to my parliamentary colleagues that I could be every bit as effective as any other MP on a whole range of "ordinary" issues: on the environment, or housing policy, or economics, or indeed the future of the British film industry—which I made a speech on, the following day. I feel passionately that it is vital for lesbian and gay politicians to avoid being "boxed in" to a lesbian and gay corner—being seen as simply single-issue politicians concentrating perpetually on lesbian and gay matters. The message that goes out to the lesbian and gay community from openly lesbian or gay politicians who earn respect over a wide range of issues is so much stronger than that. It helps reinforce the self-evident truth too often ignored by the rest of society: that lesbians and gays are everywhere, and can be effective on behalf of *everyone*.

There have, of course, been issues of particular concern to the lesbian and gay community which have needed pursuing: be it the problems of police entrapment, or the activities of Customs in raiding gay bookstores, or the urgent needs of those with HIV or AIDS, or the issuing of adverse guidelines on fostering and adoption to local authorities. Perhaps most important of all has been the battle over the now notorious Section 28 of the Local Government Act 1989. This is the clause which prohibits local councils from "intentionally promoting homosexuality," and was bounced into the bill by a group of right wing Conservatives, aided and abetted by the government.

The worst thing about Section 28 is not so much what it prohibits, although that is bad enough, but the fact that it has created a climate of self-censorship in local government up and down the country. It is *what it stands for* that is particularly offensive. It labels lesbian and gay men as second-class citizens with a second-class sexuality and second-class relationships. In my speech on the floor of the House of Commons bitterly opposing everything that Section 28 represented, I quoted from the Declaration of Democracy issued by the heads of government of the group of seven leading industrialized nations. Among the values of democracy loudly endorsed in that declaration is a society based on diversity.

The *protection of diversity* was what my opposition to Section 28 was all about. One of the Conservatives propagating the section rose to intervene. In a democracy, he queried, surely the majority must be right. Weren't the wishes of the majority more important than diversity? How wrong he was. Many years ago, I was taught that democracy is about defending and protecting the rights of minorities every bit as much as it is about asserting the wishes of a majority. On lesbian and gay rights, our legislators tend to forget this simple lesson all too often.

Over Section 28, of course, there was a massive protest movement outside Parliament. Thousands of lesbians and gay men organized, petitioned, and marched. Some of them abseiled into the House of Lords, or chained themselves to a television presenter in the middle of the main news bulletin. These protests surged during the whole period of debate over Section 28—and they were very effective. But after it was all over, there was no permanent network left. In Britain, sadly, there is no national lesbian and gay political organization established on a continuing basis. People come together to campaign about a specific issue and then disperse. It makes for fervent campaigning when anything *does* arise, but it means that there is less permanent political clout for lesbian and gay issues than exists elsewhere.

There are two recent exceptions to this general point. The first is OutRage— a highly visible group of activists with an acute eye for media opportunities and an ability to raise issues by carrying out newsworthy direct-action protests. By doing so, they help to set the public agenda. The second is the Stonewall Group, established by a group of prominent lesbians and gay men in the aftermath of the Section 28 debates and dedicated to carrying out sophisticated parliamentary and political lobbying of a detailed and thorough kind. They have already achieved a number of substantial changes in government policy; have brought together a group of sympathetic MPs from all sides of the House of Commons; and have had a major impact on the Labour party's policy making on lesbian and gay rights, too. The success of the Stonewall Group has taught us all the value of having a permanent, consistently good, lesbian and gay voice in the political process. It has certainly made my own task of standing up for lesbian and gay rights in Parliament a much easier one. It is also important to recognize the need for *both* forms of campaigning: OutRage's activism and Stonewall's patient lobbying. It is entirely to the credit of a mature lesbian and gay movement that both have arisen, and are continuing their work.

What we now need to do is to move forward onto *our* agenda of issues. Throughout the Thatcherite eighties in Britain we were on the defensive, arguing against damaging proposals as they arose and campaigning hard to stop them from being implemented. On some, we lost; on others, we made a little progress. We now need to turn our attention to the issues that *we* choose: the inequality of a different age of consent; the discrimination that exists in housing, in immigration practice, in the custody courts, in employment; the position of lesbians and gays in the armed services; the continuing absurdity of our sexual offenses laws in Britain; and the position of gay people who want to foster, or who want to have a formally recognized partnership.

Perhaps most important, the challenge of Europe offers an unprecedented opportunity to British lesbians and gay men. On virtually every civil liberties issues, other European nations are far more progressive than we are; this is true above all of lesbian and gay equality. And as we move into a single European market, and towards a closer Europe-wide integration, the chance to change the status and treatment of lesbian and gay sexuality for the better has to be seized eagerly by us all.

The challenge of European examples, the possibility of forging European-wide networks, the use of European institutions—all of these have to be taken up and developed. That won't however, remove the need to convince a skeptical House of Commons here in Britain that we need some European standards of protection for the lives and needs of lesbians and gay men. I will carry on saying so as loudly and clearly as I can; so will Stonewall and OutRage; so—I hope—will increasing numbers of my parliamentary colleagues. And eventually, we'll make some progress.

# 21

# The Land That Never Has Been Yet: Dreams of a Gay Latina in the United States

## Carmen Vázquez

The U.S. lesbian/gay movement has been and remains divided between those who view the struggle for lesbian and gay liberation through the single lens of oppression on the basis of sexual orientation and those who view it through a prism. For those of us looking through the prism, our standing in and relationship to the rest of the U.S. is best described by the African American poet, Langston Hughes:

> Oh, let America
> be America
> again
> the land that never has been yet
> and yet must be.

The recent confirmation of Clarence Thomas to the Surreme Court of the United States and California Governor Pete Wilson's repeated betrayals of civil rights for people of color, women and lesbians, and gay men are living testimony to an America that never has been. They are not the first but only the latest example of a nation that has failed in its promise of freedom and justice and equality for all. Free America, a just America is the land that never has been yet—not for the peoples of the great nations that roamed this land before any

European ever laid eyes on it; not for African Americans; not for poor people of any color; not for women; and not, definitely not, for queers.

Langston Hughes's cry for fulfillment of America's promise came not only from the ravages visited upon his enslaved African ancestors or his queer poet soul, but from the depths of his own humanity and his longing for the freedom and equality he was never to know in his lifetime.

My own assessment of the U.S. lesbian and gay movement is made within the context of our humanity. I address not the familiar refrains of oppression, not the schisms and the isms they are based on, but the uniqueness of our shared experience as a people, what that experience offers to the collective human experience, and what it can offer to the fulfillment of the promise America has yet to keep for so many of us.

I was born in Puerto Rico forty-three years ago to a couple of very poor people who became part of the great Puerto Rican migration to the United States in the fifties. I arrived at the age of five in a place I thought was the moon but was, in reality, only the city of New York. My dreams of finding streets glittering with silver and gold in the moonlight were replaced by the harshness and poverty of the Lower East Side, Harlem, Welfare, and the Projects. I grew up to learn that poverty is not something you can get out from under by working hard and obeying laws because mami and papi worked their butts off and never got a car or a house or even a full meal for themselves and their seven children on any given night. Fulfillment of the American Dream would come to rest on the shoulders of their children, and especially on those of their eldest daughter— Carmen Idalia Vásquez.

I just was never ready for it. Not then and not now. I was a dyke. I am a dyke. I will die a dyke. And dykes, along with our gay brothers or any other kind of queer, are just not part of the American Dream or mainstream.

But should we be? That depends on who's defining the dream, and on what we understand of our history and heritage as sexual outlaws and as people with power—if we so choose—to join millions of other people in recasting the contours of what privacy, sexuality, women's rights, and political empowerment mean in American society today.

I say we need another dream and we need another stream. If, however, we don't embrace our own humanity; if we don't see where our struggle for equal protection under the law becomes one with all struggles for human liberation; if we don't understand that no one politician or elected office is worth the sacrifice of our humanity and our community's unity; if we don't understand the alluring and dangerous politics of the mainstream, we will be doomed to repeat the mistakes of others who have sought the right to plunge into the great mainstream of the American Dream and, once having got there, found it too much narrow to swim in.

We need another dream and we need another stream.

If we don't learn to embrace our humanity, to love our queerness in the fullness and rich textures of the cultures, national histories, and languages that we collectively come from, we will be ill equipped to form those coalitions and alliances that will win our struggle for civil and human rights, or to heal the divisions that threaten our movement; to be that queer Star Trek crew member, boldly going where no one has gone before.

I believe that the experience of oppression—any oppression—works to dehumanize us, to make us think of ourselves as "other," detached from our families, our communities, and each other. The experience of oppression robs individuals of the ability to see themselves as subjects in the world, of the ability to see and appreciate the uniqueness of their own experience and what it gives to the collective experience we call humanity. The experience of oppression insulates us and creates a deep-rooted fear and mistrust of anyone not like us—and, on the other hand, anyone like us who, even for a nanosecond, wants to be like "them" or acts like "them" or looks like "them."

I do not now—nor have I ever—espoused the notion that being queer is no different from being straight. I believe that when the whole of our story has been told and can be shared without fear or guilt or shame, we will see and celebrate that there is among human beings a "gay difference." Not teeny hypothalamus cells but a sensitivity and sensibility, a capacity for love and lust and friendship with our own sex that is unique to the queer in all cultures. The difference, however, contributes to the whole of human experience; it is not separate from it.

Today in our movement there rages what I call the great "pseudo-debate." Some say that anyone not calling him- or herself "queer" in our movement is a self-loathing assimilationist. Twenty years ago, anyone who did call him- or herself queer was perceived as a self-loathing throwback to the pervert-invert, sick, illegal, and immoral school and an obstructionist to gay liberation.

From my perspective, both positions are absurd because for the majority of human beings whose life experience, whose sense of being alive and conscious is intricately bound up with same-gender love, what the intellectuals or the militants of our movement decide is the current term by which we are to be defined means absolutely nothing.

I did not need the New York Gay Activists Alliance telling me what to call myself in order to know that I was in love with another girl when I was thirteen. I did not need them to know what to do in bed with another girl when I was fifteen. I did not need them to declare my undying love for my high school sweetheart and to ask her to marry me and run away with me forever.

No. What happened to me then, what matters to all our people regardless of what we call ourselves and what will mean liberation, is the day we can leave our dreary or fabulous job, step out the door, kiss our lover or date hello, get in the car, have dinner, go dancing, and then home to make wild passionate love or cuddle, and never once have to think about it. What we dream of is being that Star Trek crew member, or the famous actor, or the great writer, or the brave and good activist. What we dream of is making out on the beaches of Santa Monica or Luquillo or Puerto Vallarta or the Jersey shore with that one person who makes us want to faint every time we see her or him. What we dream of is a home with a fireplace and how we'll spend our old age. What we dream of is living with our sweetheart without fear, without shame, without guilt, without denial.

These are not queer dreams or lesbian/gay dreams or homophile dreams or the dreams of an invert. These are human dreams.

What we call ourselves or what drag we wear—leather drag, executive drag, school drag, rich drag, poor drag, military drag—is irrelevant. What we are debating without necessarily admitting it are two points:

1) Can we achieve the fulfillment of America's promise of justice and equality for our own people in America as she exists today?

2) Can we win the struggle for lesbian and gay civil rights as a separatist movement?

I don't think so.

When I was thirteen, I wrote a simple poem that was very important to me for many years although I did not, in a conscious way, understand why it was important. I just felt it to be true and it made it OK for me to be who I was in the world:

> I am
> a world
> alone
> and I build bridges.

Today, I understand that what I wrote at thirteen was very appropriate to my life then and, in fact, all true. I was a world—a young person in whom Puerto Rican, black, Jewish, and Irish and Italian Catholic cultures converged; a welfare kid in Harlem, seduced by dreams of a Donna Reed, white picket fence future whose emerging sexuality was full of girl dreams, and who couldn't stand the boys with their clumsy hands and shaking thing trying to grab me in the closet during spin-the-bottle games.

And my sense of aloneness was very stark.

So, then, given the confusion of multicultural convergence, of cuchifritos, chitlins, knish, and lasagna; given the limitations of poverty; given the tendency on the one hand to want to knock someone upside their head if they dared to question the righteousness of an independent Puerto Rico and the desire, on the other hand, to learn me some good English and go to college; given this burning desire to kiss girls and only girls . . . what could I do but build bridges?

The little poem was the formula I would use for surviving in a hostile world and bridge building is still very much a part of my survival scheme. In prose we call it coalition work, which I am an ardent believer in for reasons neither altruistic nor idealistic. I believe in coalitions because my understanding of the real world tells me that my survival is dependent on my ability to close the gaps between the different worlds that converge in me, and on my ability to cross over from my queer world or my Puerto Rican world or my women's world and build alliances. It is only on the strength of those alliances that I can be whole—a Puerto Rican lesbian living in a straight, sexist, and racist world.

From my perspective, then, it is not possible to secure passage of a lesbian/gay civil rights bill in a country that denies women the right to choose what we will do with our bodies. The values that celebrate burying Iraqi soldiers alive are the same ones that celebrate gay bashing; the values that support S&L bailouts above national health care are the same that support the quarantine of people with HIV. The value system and the people who think that women invite their own rape haven't any use for us. A country that thinks twelve-year-old black children are expendable fodder for the War on Drugs doesn't give a damn about queer anybody. It never has and it never will—unless we and all the people this country thinks are expendable work together to change it.

The queer experience is not separate from the human experience.

All movements for social change and human liberation have the same ultimate goal: radical change in the structures that limit or deny the possibility for human survival and freedom. The point of radical change rarely comes solely from external pressure. In the case of the government of the United States, I am certain that radical change will not be possible without great internal and external pressure.

What does that mean? It means we need all of us and our allies in order to achieve the kind of change in American government and values necessary to secure our freedom and our right to equal protection under the law. All of us—our lawyers and our lobbyists, our street fighters, our visionaries, our quiet everyday people who do their jobs and send us a check, the ones we all know and the ones we have yet to meet. We need the veterans of civil rights struggles and the newcomers. We need to hold on to what is common to our experience, to an enduring love for each other, if not as individuals, then as a people.

Twenty years ago, on the eve of my graduation from the University of Puerto Rico with a degree in education, I spent the night in a hotel room with a man whom I had spent the better part of a year raging at because he was arrogant and privileged by Puerto Rican standards, because he was the son of a military man, because he looked down on Newyoricans like myself, and because night after night he filled rooms with laughter at the expense of the effeminate men he thought himself better than. But this night, Arturo was in my room because his father had learned of his love for men and had disowned him, removed him from his home. He cried because he felt ashamed. He cried because he was afraid.

I cried with him and I held him because all the differences between us meant nothing that night. I shared his fear and his shame. I was like him.

The history of the lesbian and gay movement since that night in Puerto Rico has been a tapestry woven with militancy, courage, and compassion; with love and vulnerability; with extraordinary organizing; with grief and loss; and with unprecedented political clout. The life of fear and hiding I thought would be my lot never materialized because, long before I knew I was a dyke, there were men and women who dedicated their lives to building the modern lesbian and gay movement that would give me the support I needed to be out, visible, powerful.

As we feel our rage and contemplate our response to the cowards and liars in Washington or Sacramento, as we recoil from the cynicism of our time, we need to remember that we, like so many other people from the fifties through the eighties, have made a significant change in our response to the experience of stigmatization and oppression. Once we sought to disguise ourselves as best we could or separate ourselves from the larger society, or—if we could neither disguise nor separate—plead for sympathy for our "condition." In the second half of this century, we have come out as a people. Disguise or costume has become a shared cultural symbol called drag, not a way of hiding but of celebrating. Our clandestine existence as denizens of the night, whispering passwords for entry into our "private clubs," has opened up into cafes, bars, restaurants, service organizations, and political lobbying groups very much out in the light of day; our pleas for sympathy have become demands for our right to privacy and equal protection under the law. This is a profound transformation of a people's response to their experience brought about in a relatively short period of time. This transformation of what it meant to be gay in America before I was born into what it means today is not yet complete, and it is not a "white only" experience.

We need to understand that our common experience as queers is a bond, not a political road map. We are a people, yes, but a people responding to our experience and trying to take meaningful action in the world as we know it; who have to grapple with a myriad of cultural discourses that guide how we take meaningful action in the world. We must learn to hear each other and to communicate effectively across cultural differences that are thousands of years old.

The struggles for racial equality and women's rights in the United States have a long and proud history with much to teach us. We need to know those histories. We need to honor them. We need to participate in today's civil rights struggle for racial and gender equality, or else the queer struggle for civil rights will not be won.

We need leadership. I know that's a nasty word in the U.S. movement because some of our so-called leaders are hypocrites or bullies or both, but we need elected, appointed, and grassroots leadership. There is an inherent hypocrisy in the cry for "no leaders" when it comes from people shouting the loudest for us to follow them. I know of no movement for civil rights and progressive social change that was able to mobilize masses of people in support of its goals without effective and strong leadership. We need to develop and nurture the capacity for leadership inherent in all of us. We need to develop standards of critical support for those among us who take the risk of leading so that we can engage in constructive criticism without tearing each other apart.

We need to have real dialogue among ourselves about political direction, about the strategies and tactics and actions that will someday realize the goal of full equality under the law for every lesbian and gay man, and get off the simplistic, stand-still arguments that polarize our communities. Assimilation into existing democratic structures and radical militancy are not a contradiction. They are two essential strategies in a very complex dialectic for social change.

The U.S. lesbian and gay movement stands at a critical juncture. The legal strategies we have relied on for the past two decades face an extraordinarily conservative judiciary hostile to civil and reproductive rights, and even the much cherished civil liberties embodied in the Bill of Rights. The survival of the communities we have built, our AIDS agencies, our social service agencies, and our political action organizations are imperiled by a collapsing U.S. economy. We have become a target of a well-organized and virulently homophobic right wing that has placed the reversal of lesbian and gay, reproductive, and civil rights, as well as the economic survival of people of color in the U.S., squarely at the center of its agenda for the last two decades. We cannot fight and win our struggle against the right wing or make real our commitment to ending heterosexism simply by raising a lavender flag over our lavender bubble, where no heterosexual shall touch us or speak to us or work with us.

Historically, our ability to work effectively in political coalition with those who share with us the assaults by the right wing has been hampered both by the single lens focus on oppression based on sexual orientation and by the misguided notion that we can address racism and sexism within our own movement through consciousness raising without a political agenda that specifically addresses racism, sexism, and economic injustice.

Some of us have no choice in the matter. As a Latina and a lesbian, I cannot reduce what I understand about oppression and political repression in the United States to heterosexism. I also find little solace in the tendency on the part of my white lesbian sisters and gay brothers to treat sexism and racism as an abstraction that can be studied and learned in a book or reduced to an interpersonal dynamic between two individuals. Our ability as a movement to act on the premise that oppression is an institutional reality requiring radical change in the cultural and racial makeup of our organizations and leadership lags far behind our consciousness-raising efforts.

I believe the political realities of our time don't afford us the luxury of spending the next twenty years figuring out how to be sensitive to one another. I believe our only real hope for political unity within our movement and political coalition work with other movements for progressive social change hinges on our ability to work in defense of the civil and democratic rights of all people; on our willingness to work for social justice issues such as national health care and the demilitarization of the national budget; and on our commitment to international peace and our openness to anyone willing to sign on to that agenda, no matter how incorrect they look or talk or dress.

Freedom is still in the future. Our ability to build communities, to win anti-discrimination legislation, and to lobby for social services is still very limited. We must understand that the tensions between militant street activists and suit-and-tie activists is not new or even unhealthy if we take care not to treat each other as the enemy. To win our freedom, we must reclaim, in a real and visible way, the love for each other that the continued assaults by bigots on our people sometimes make us forget or become numb to.

The next great leap forward in our struggle as lesbians and gay men, as bisexuals and transsexuals and queers of any color, is to radically alter the prism through which the world views us by radically altering the prism through which we see ourselves. We need to move from "other" and outcast to conscious subjects capable of joining with other progressive people to lead this nation; from gender benders who defy gender constrictions to conscious beings who obliterate gender roles. It is our time to be equal, not other, to be not oppressed but righteously furious. It is our time to say we refuse to respond to the indignity of the question: Why are you gay? We are. Our being needs no justification nor explanation. We are as whole and sacred and worthy of dignity and justice and freedom as any other being blessed with the gift of conscious existence. We are, and we will be, free.

# 22

# Lesbian and Gay Rights in Europe: Homosexuality and the Law*

## Evert van der Veen, Aart Hendriks, and Astrid Mattijssen

The discussion about lesbian and gay rights is an important although complex one. None of the international human rights treaties explicitly distinguishes the recipients of rights and freedoms on the basis of their sexual orientation. Nor is the word "homosexuality" or "sexual minority" mentioned in any of the existing human rights treaties. This may easily lead to the conclusion that lesbian and gay rights are not recognized by these codes. However, on several occasions authoritative bodies and scholars have interpreted human rights provisions in a way commensurate with the demands formulated by the lesbian and gay movement. Indeed, the international treaties seem to contain even more provisions that may potentially offer lesbians and gay men their warranted legal protection.

In Europe the relationship between homosexuality and the law is an old one. The European lesbian and gay movement has traditionally put a lot of energy into trying to influence the (democratically elected) legislature and to alter the interpretation of the existing laws by the ("independent") judge, first to abolish discriminatory laws and later to find official recognition of their specific interests.

*This chapter is an elaboration and update of a 1990 article by E. van der Veen and A. Mattijssen, published in the legal magazine *Ars Aequi* under the title "Homoseksualiteit en mensenrechten" ("Homosexuality and Human Rights"), vol. 39 (September 1990): 535–44.

For self-evident reasons, the protection and promotion of lesbian and gay rights have always been connected to the domain of human rights law. The specific lesbian and gay interests became known (read: were self-proclaimed) as "lesbian and gay rights," being a broad set of claims on the authorities to protect lesbian and gay interests. To a large extent, lesbian and gay rights fully overlap with the internationally recognized human rights provisions, in spite of the sometimes restrictive interpretation given to these by some authoritative bodies and scholars. Some lesbian and gay rights, however, go a bit further. Lesbians and gay men not only demand equality before the law, but at the same time require safeguards to develop their own lifestyles as well as adequate protection against discrimination and other forms of less favorable treatment. As such, these demands do not conflict with international human rights laws, although they do not as yet enjoy full legal recognition. Insistent efforts on the part of the European lesbian and gay movement resulted in the (sometimes reluctant) official recognition by the major European institutions of the existence of discrimination against lesbians and gay men. In this respect the International Lesbian and Gay Association (ILGA) and its strong European network have been instrumental.

In this article we will examine the relevant provisions of the various human rights treaties that were, or potentially can be, invoked by lesbians and gay men to safeguard their rights and dignity. We shall focus primarily on developments at the supranational European level. To that end, special attention will be paid to the European Commission and Court of Human Rights, both established under the European Convention of Human Rights (ECHR) on the one hand; and, on the other, the statements adopted by the Parliamentary Assembly of the Council of Europe and the European Parliament, the latter being the democratically elected forum affiliated with the European Communities. We aim at evaluating the efforts made by the European lesbian and gay movement to reform the law. Prior to this assessment, we will briefly describe the various patterns of discrimination against lesbians and gay men in Europe in conjunction with the human rights of same-sex lovers under the European legislation.

## DISCRIMINATION AGAINST LESBIANS AND GAY MEN

Discrimination against lesbians and gay men is a phenomenon difficult to define. For several reasons, lesbians and gay men are occasionally or systematically less favorably treated if compared with heterosexuals. Thus, the difference in treatment forms the core element of this phenomenon, which arises in very distinct situations. However, different treatment is not automatically worse, and may be perfectly justified. Therefore, besides difference in treatment, discrimination implies that the way people are treated is less favorable for unjustifiable reasons. The core of discrimination is that those who discriminate attribute a negative connotation to such irrelevant criteria as sexual orientation or (sexual) lifestyle.

It has to be noted that nonhomosexuals can also be the victims of anti-lesbian or anti-gay discrimination. This is particularly true in cases where they are erroneously looked upon as homosexuals. The parents, children, friends, and relatives of lesbians and gay men may also become the targets of discrimination.

Discrimination against lesbians and gay men finds its "justification" in the persistent negative views many in society hold about homosexuality, which they still consider as sick, sinful, perverse, unnatural, dangerous, contagious for children, shameful to the family, and so on. Whatever the legitimation, it is regarded as inferior to heterosexuality, particularly since lesbian and gay couples cannot procreate "by nature."

Discrimination against lesbians and gay men takes many forms. It may assume the shape of direct and explicit discrimination. This means that one is discriminated against purely for reasons of sexual preference. Forms of direct discrimination range from "bashing" to exclusion from jobs or military service and denial of certain goods and services, and limitations imposed on the freedom of expression and the right to assembly. For example, in Italy (as in many other countries), men risk dishonorable discharge from the armed forces following sexual contact with another male.[1]

Most prevalent, however, is the so-called indirect form of discrimination, whereby lesbians and gay men experience less favorable treatment due to an interwoven network of legal and social rules presented as "objective." These rules are perceived by many, and thus upheld, as the moral foundations of our society. Consequently, efforts to change these rules usually meet with massive opposition. These moral values, deeply embedded in habits and tradition, dominate various gender roles attached to marriage, public health and decency laws, and so on. All these "neutral" rules are equally applied to lesbians and gay men, who generally experience them not only as inappropriate but as highly discriminatory. For example, in the Netherlands a lesbian who applied for a job at a public transport company was rejected after a negative evaluation by the company's psychologist. The psychological examination "revealed" that the woman's political ideas on sexuality did not fit the company's employment policy.[2]

What is considered discrimination changes from time to time and from place to place. The mechanisms generally remain the same, but the targets and intensity of discrimination may vary. Twenty years ago, no one in Europe would ever have dreamed of assigning equal parental rights to a lesbian couple with children. Nowadays many Europeans favor this idea. We are aware that our notion of discrimination is culturally biased and may, as a consequence, be somewhat different from those of our readers. As far as possible, we will substantiate our views and indicate why we disapprove of certain forms of unequal treatment, while approving of others.

It should be equally noted that there is no universal standard for lesbian and gay lifestyles, let alone the ways lesbians and gay men organize. We must accept that the struggle against discrimination reflects the variety within the lesbian and gay movement itself and depends equally on such environmental factors as the political climate and the legal system.

## HUMAN RIGHTS LAW AND LESBIAN AND GAY RIGHTS

Human rights legislation is supposed to protect individual and collective rights of minority groups of whatever kind. Recognizing that all people have equal rights and dignity forms the core of human rights law.

There are various human rights instruments, each with its own particularities. The most widely accepted human rights standards are laid down in the Universal Declaration of Human Rights (UDHR, 1948), a formally non-binding document almost unanimously adopted by the General Assembly of the United Nations. This declaration, embodying the full range of human rights, is generally considered the "common standard of achievement" for humanity. The rights enumerated in this document became elaborated in the International Covenant on Civil and Political Rights (ICCPR, 1966) and the International Covenant on Economic, Social, and Cultural Rights (ICESCR, 1966), being legally binding documents from which ratifying states are not allowed to deviate unless explicitly foreseen by the treaties themselves. The rights enshrined in these three documents, in combination with the optional protocol to the ICCPR, are now generally known as the "International Bill of Human Rights," and recognized by the vast majority of countries.

Additionally, two major human rights treaties were prepared under the auspices of the Council of Europe. These treaties are the ECHR (1950) and the European Social Charter (ESC, 1961). While the ECHR may be said to be a regional "counterbalance" to the ICCPR, the ESC has more in common with the ICESCR. It should be noted that there is no hierarchical stratification among the various international human rights instruments. These systems are, rather, complementary, with regional systems generally elaborating on the universal principles, being more specific and covering more issues.

If the legal protection offered by the rights embodied in these treaties is considered insufficient, there are generally two channels through which adaptation can be sought. First of all, one can strive to formally amend the treaty and/ or some of its provisions. This can be accomplished only by a treaty drafting body, such as the Council of Europe, after which the contracting parties (the countries) still have to accept this amendment. Experience has shown that instead of amending an existing treaty, it is easier to adopt an additional protocol or to draft an entirely new treaty on a specific issue.

A second channel for seeking legal reform is by way of jurisprudence. By having the body authorized with the binding interpretation of the provisions enshrined in a treaty revise its views, the warranted legal protection may be obtained as well. A way to produce such legal revisions is by preparing test cases. A judgment may then be provoked by bringing a case to court which, in the eyes of the litigants, should lead to legal reform. In this respect, the European human rights protection mechanism, with extensive authority ascribed to the Strasbourg-based European Commission and Court of Human Rights, offers excellent opportunities. Such test cases produce either jurisprudence with which national regulations can be influenced or else they are rejected by the European Human Rights Commission, which exposes the weakness in the protection by human rights laws.[3] Both methods, trying to alter the law and producing test cases, have been used extensively by the European lesbian and gay movement.

## CAN HUMAN RIGHTS BE INVOKED IN THE FIGHT AGAINST ANTI-LESBIAN AND ANTI-GAY DISCRIMINATION?

Article 2 of the UDHR states that each individual can claim all the rights and freedoms set forth in the declaration without distinction of any kind whatsoever. If the rights contained therein grant people equal protection, then it should logically follow that this also holds true for lesbians and gay men. In other words, they should be able to equally enjoy the rights and freedoms as enshrined in the declaration. However, experience has shown that there are deeply rooted structures discriminating against people on the basis of their sexual orientation. Historical, religious, moral, and other values and traditions are invoked to justify the privileges ascribed to heterosexuals. Most societies seem to be centered around the *assumption of heterosexuality,* that is to say, they implicitly assume that everybody is heterosexual. Complex societal structures, therefore, inhibit lesbians and gay men from enjoying equal, not to mention equally privileged, treatment. What lesbians and gay men consider as their human rights, however, have not always been recognized as such in legislation, jurisprudence, or legal literature.

Lesbian and gay rights are not a deviation from "general" human rights law; the core of lesbian and gay rights is that they demand a broader, less heterosexually biased interpretation of the recognized human rights standards. Therefore, the lesbian and gay movement considers its rights to be part of overall human rights, and it is determined to achieve a more just and fair interpretation of the existing provisions.

The international lesbian and gay movement has been, and still is, striving forcefully to convince the international community that fundamental rights for lesbians and gay men need to be recognized as part of international human rights law.[4] Before we describe these efforts, we will analyze the current status of lesbian and gay demands vis-à-vis the human rights treaties currently in force in Europe. We will focus on those fundamental rights that have also been embodied in the ECHR and the ICCPR, aware that some very fundamental lesbian and gay rights will thus fall outside the scope of this study. The following rights will be analyzed:

- the right to respect for private and family life (Article 8 ECHR and Article 17 ICCPR)

- the right to freedom of expression (Article 10 ECHR and Article 19 ICCPR)

- the right to freedom of assembly and association (Article 11 ECHR and Articles 21 and 22 ICCPR)

- the right to marry and to found a family (Article 12 ECHR and Article 23 ICCPR)

- the principle of nondiscrimination (Article 14 ECHR and Article 26 ICCPR).

### The Right to Respect for Private and Family Life

As far as gay men are concerned, the right to private life is, as a result of successful litigation, partly recognized by the European Commission and Court. With regard to lesbians, discrimination in the area of privacy has not yet been petitioned before the Strasbourg court. This is not to say, however, that anti-lesbian discrimination does not exist or that lesbians do not feel a need to enjoy the protection of the right to private life.

The right to lesbian and gay family life, often being perceived as one right, is totally denied.

The right to private life reflects the old liberal idea that the individual should be protected against any undue interferences with his or her private space and autonomy.[5] In addition to the protection of the individual's family life, home, and correspondence, this right also protects the individual's particular identity, integrity, autonomy, private communications, and sexuality.[6] In 1976, the commission explicitly stated that one's sexuality forms an important aspect of one's personal life and that undue interferences with this would amount to a violation of Article 8(1) ECHR.[7]

As a result of the famous *Dudgeon* and *Norris* cases[8] (see chapter 13 of this volume), gay men are now also recognized as a group that can, though only to a certain extent, enjoy the right to private life. After the court had stated in the *Dudgeon* case:

> [T]here can be no denial that some degree of regulation of homosexual conduct, as indeed of other forms of sexual conduct, by means of criminal law can be justified as "necessary in a democratic society,"[9]

it concluded:

> [A]s compared with the era when that legislation was enacted, there is now a better understanding, and in consequence an increased tolerance, of homosexual behavior to the extent that in the great majority of the member States of the

> Council of Europe it is no longer considered to be necessary or appropriate
> to treat homosexual practices of the kind now in question as in themselves a
> matter to which the sanctions of the criminal law should be applied; the Court
> cannot overlook the marked changes which have occurred in this regard in the
> domestic laws of the member States.[10]

From the court's final conclusions it can be learned that it wants to depenalize only certain forms of male homosexual behavior, i.e., sexual acts committed in private between consenting males over twenty-one years of age. Like the minimum age provision,[11] the "privacy" restriction in practice has amounted to a serious limitation of same-sex relationships. In the U.K., for example, hotels and prisons are considered public places. Moreover, according to English Sexual Offences Act, as amended in 1967, homosexual acts in private with more than two persons taking part or present is equally forbidden. According to the European Commission,

> the existence of this legislation does not constitute an interference with his right
> to respect for private life or his home.[12]

Over time, this lowered the initial enthusiasm of the lesbian and gay movement over this verdict, now that the European Court and Commission seem to be unwilling either to nullify discriminatory ages of consent or to eradicate the "privacy" restriction. In spite of this, the success of the *Dudgeon* and *Norris* cases inspired several other lesbian and gay groups in countries with a total ban on homosexual acts to file a complaint with the Strasbourg legal organs. In 1990, the European Commission ruled favorably on the admissibility of Alexos Modinos's complaint against Cyprus.[13] U.K. groups are now considering submission of a similar petition against the authorities of the Island of Man.

The right to lesbian and gay family life is not recognized at all by the European Commission and Court. According to the commission, a family, as referred to in Article 8(1) ECHR, consists of a man and a women with their possible (biological or adopted) offspring. Lesbian and gay couples do not, according to the commission, qualify as a "family" in the same sense. In the case of a Malaysian-English gay couple the commission reasoned as follows:

> Despite the modern evolution of attitudes towards homosexuality, the Commis-
> sion finds that the applicants' relationship does not fall within the scope of the
> rights to respect to family life ensured by Article 8.[14]

The British government did not, therefore, violate the right to family life by denying the Malaysian partner a work permit in the U.K.

Similar problems emerged in the case of a Australian-British lesbian couple in the U.K. with a child conceived by artificial insemination. After the birth of the child, the Australian mother decided to quit her job in order to devote herself to child-rearing. The fact that she had no income made her lose her work permit. After the mothers had petitioned before the Strasbourg organs, the commission eventually refused to recognize this trio as a family under Article 8, paragraph 1. Thus the protection of family provisions, as enshrined in the British immigration law, was denied to the couple and their child.[15]

In 1992, the commission declined the claim of a Dutch lesbian couple to be granted full parental rights over their son.[16] According to the commission, the right to family life cannot be interpreted in such a broad way.

The commission and court are notably more tolerant and willing to interpret the concept of "family life" far more extensively and autonomously when it concerns other than lesbian or gay issues. Over the years, the following extramarital relationships have become equally recognized as family types: brothers and sisters and other relatives,[17] unmarried heterosexual couples with a common household,[18] polygamous family types,[19] and a parent with a child born outside of marriage or after divorce.[20] In other words, according to the Strasbourg organs, the right to family life envisages the protection of all people bound together by satisfactory true bonds.[21] Apparently, in the view of the commission and the court, lesbians and gay men lack the capacity to establish such bonds.

### The Right to Freedom of Expression

Whereas the interpretation of the rights to private life has, reluctantly, found some legitimation in the Strasbourg Commission and Court, this hardly holds true for the right to freedom of expression. The dignity of lesbians and gay men was (and is) definitely at stake now that British local authorities, under Section 28 of the Local Authorities Act, are forbidden to "promote" homosexuality as an accepted form of family life. This type of legislation imposes clear restrictions on the right of lesbians and gay men to express themselves in a positive way. However, the now famous Section 28 has so far never been challenged for review by the Strasbourg organs, probably now that its adversaries anticipate, in line with previous judgments, a very restrictive interpretation by these same organs.

The only positive statement the commission ever made with regard to the expression of homosexuality was when it was petitioned to review the case of a British man imprisoned because of homosexual acts. The applicant alleged that his detention inhibited him from expressing his affection for men. The commission thereby stated

> that there may be an issue under Article 10 regarding his . . . claim that the fact of imprisonment denied him the right to express feelings of love for other men.[22]

In its report however, the commission came to the conclusion that

> the concept of "expression" in Article 10 concerns *mainly* the expression of opinion and receiving and imparting ideas. . . . It does *not* encompass any notion of the physical expression of feelings in the sense submitted by the applicant. (Emphasis added)[23]

The right to freedom of expression was of paramount importance in the case of the Belgian teacher, Eliane Morissens. Morissens was dismissed after she had openly spoken on television about her experiences as a lesbian and the negative repercussions of her sexual orientation on her professional career. The commission stated that the Belgian State could justifiably restrict Morissens's freedom of expression in view of the special responsibilities her profession imposed upon her for the protection of her school and the persons she had mentioned in the program. The commission concluded that dismissal was a "proportional" measure in such cases.[24]

The UN Committee in Geneva, established under the ICCPR, also did not rule favorably in the complaint submitted in the famous SETA case.[25] In this case, five individuals opposed the ruling of the censor of the Finnish state-controlled broadcasting company on homosexual themes. The committee declared that the state should have some freedom of maneuver, as one could not check the negative impact the promotion of homosexuality by radio and TV broadcasts could have on the public.

### The Right to Freedom of Assembly and Association

This right assumes that there is also a right to freedom of organization and the right to affiliate oneself with such entities. Consequently there should be a right to found and to become a member of such groups as political parties, trade unions, and lesbian and gay interest groups.[26] Laws prohibiting the establishment of lesbian and gay organizations, such as the Austrian Penal Code,[27] may actually be in defiance of the right to freedom of assembly and association. Cases such as these, however, have never been brought to the attention of the Strasbourg Commission and Court by the lesbian and gay movement.

### The Right to Marry and to Found a Family

When the texts of the human rights treaties were drafted, probably nobody even thought that the living together of two people of the same sex might be covered by the right to marry. In one of the first cases to challenge the traditional concept of marriage, the so-called *Rees* case,[28] the European Commission and Court, in a unanimous decision, decided that the right to marry guaranteed by Article 12 refers to the traditional marriage between persons of opposite biological sex. This also appears from the wording of the article which makes it clear that Article 12 is mainly concerned to protect marriage as the basis of the family.[29]

The reluctance of the European Court to recognize same-sex cohabitants as a "family" entitled to marriage did not prevent the lesbian and gay movement from finding alternative ways to obtain the warranted recognition of same-sex relationships. Since October 1, 1989, the Act on Registered Partnership has been in force in Denmark. This law bestows on registered same-sex partnerships most of the rights, privileges, and duties traditionally reserved to heterosexual marriage (see chapter 8 of this volume). Norway and Sweden will probably follow soon. In France, a proposal to recognize the *parténariat civil* is presently under discussion. In July 1991, the *Schwulenverband in Deutschland* (German Gay Alliance) launched a proposal for the *nichtehelige Partnerschaft* (non-marriage partnership). In the Netherlands, numerous local authorities recently opened their municipal registration and record offices to same-sex partnerships.

In the *Dudgeon* case the European Court clearly indicated that it is willing to adjust its standing jurisprudence in view of "the marked changes that have occurred in this respect in the domestic law of the [Council of Europe] member states."[30] Thus, by pushing for national law reform, the lesbian and gay movement may eventually achieve a readjustment of the European human rights bill along the line of domestic law changes.

As we all know, there is not necessarily a causal relationship between marriage and procreation. Strong evidence exists that the commission and the court, though probably unconsciously, seem to agree with this statement. In the *Marckx* case the court explicitly stated that the concept of family is not necessarily connected to that of marriage.[31] In the so-called *Cossey* case, Judge Martens, in his dissenting opinion, stated that

> it cannot be assumed that the stated purpose of the right to marry (to protect marriage as the basis of the family) can serve as a basis for its delimitation: under Article 12 it would certainly not be permissible for a member State to provide that only those who can prove their ability to procreate are allowed to marry.[32]

Despite the fact that the Strasbourg organs, as discussed above, have in practice also recognized nontraditional heterosexual relationships as "families," including their rights to procreate and custody over children, so far these privileges have systematically been denied to lesbian and gay couples. It seems, however, that in this respect also the lesbian and gay movement is making progress. While in the Netherlands various commissions have recommended considering same-sex social (i.e., nonbiological) parents as similar to opposite-sex social parents for full parental rights,[33] in the U.K. the lesbian and gay movement succeeded in the spring of 1991 in preventing Parliament from adopting a proposal that would almost automatically take away all parental rights from lesbian and gay parents.

### The Principle of Nondiscrimination

The right to equality and nondiscrimination is enshrined in Article 26 ICCPR. Other universal human rights codes that recognize this principle include the UDHR (Article 2) and the International Covenant on Economic, Social, and Cultural Rights (Articles 2 and 3). This principle also inspired the drafting of specific codes, such as the International Convention on the Elimination of All Forms of Racial Discrimination, the Convention on all Forms of Discrimination against Women, and the Declaration on the Elimination of All Forms of Intolerance and of Discrimination based on Religion or Belief. There is no such code on discrimination against homosexuals, however.

The ECHR contains a provision similar to Article 26 of the ICCPR, but contrary to its ICCPR counterpart and most national constitutional equality provisions,[34] ECHR Article 14 does not have an autonomous status; it only prohibits discrimination with regard to "the enjoyment of the rights and freedoms set forth *in this Convention*" (emphasis added). Therefore, in the legal literature, Article 14 is considered to have an "accessory" or "complementary" character.

Although in neither the universal nor the regional nondiscrimination clauses is homosexuality or sexual preference explicitly mentioned, their scope does not envisage any limitations. The grounds mentioned are not exhaustive, something that is confirmed by the phrase "or other status." This suggests that sexual orientation is also one of the grounds that does not allow any discrimination.

The European Commission in its reports often stresses the broad interpretation that should be given to the anti-discrimination clause.[35] However, none of the gay or lesbian cases brought to the attention of either the European Human Rights Court and Commission or the Human Rights Committee were ever considered favorably. The Strasbourg organs always decided that there were objective and reasonable grounds, serving a legitimate aim, that would justify the different treatment. The major reason still seems to be that the members of these bodies lack the political willingness—and maybe the simple capacity—to discover discriminatory patterns in our society. This should not deter the lesbian and gay movement, however, from consistently addressing these institutions in case malicious governmental practices are being reported in society.

In summary, one can say that as of now the European human rights bodies recognize the right of gay men over twenty-one to a "private life" to be conducted in private. An absolute prohibition of male homosexuality can, according to the European Commission and Court, not be deemed necessary in a democratic society for the protection of morals and health—hereby justifying states to impose other restrictions on homosexuality. Similar cases involving lesbians have not come up yet. All attempts to get other lesbian and gay demands included in the European human rights code have failed so far. There are, however, good prospects that the commission and court may follow the more enlightened European governments and attach more value in the near future to the recommendations of the European Parliament and the Parliamentary Assembly of the Council of Europe. We will now try to analyze the limited success of the lesbian and gay movement so far.

## AN ANALYSIS OF THE REACTION OF THE EUROPEAN JUDICIARY WITH RESPECT TO THE EFFORTS OF THE LESBIAN AND GAY MOVEMENT

Soon after its birth, the European Commission of Human Rights was confronted with a number of cases in which gay men alleged that their fundamental rights had been violated. In the 1950s, the commission received complaints from German civilians, who were charged under Article 175 of the criminal law book. The complainants claimed that their punishments, based on a general prohibition of homosexuality, conflicted with the guarantees laid down in Articles 8 (respect for private life) and 14 (sex discrimination) of the ECHR. The commission rejected the charges, without argumentation, and upheld the German government's reasoning that such a prohibition is necessary in view of the "protection of health and morals."[36] The commission also rejected the claim that discrimination on the basis of gender had taken place. In its report it stated that in the underlying case men and women could be treated distinctly, because homosexual men were a larger social and moral threat to society than women.[37]

It took the commission until 1975 to change its negative, almost hostile, attitude toward homosexuality. The commission dealt with two complaints submitted by British citizens against their government. They alleged that the laws in England and Northern Ireland, criminalizing homosexual acts between men, were discriminatory and a unjustifiable infringement on their right to private life.[38] The English case was rejected. In the *Dudgeon* case the commission, and eventually the court, stated that the Northern Irish law was not in concordance with Article 8 (right to private life) of the ECHR as far as it concerned sexual acts between consenting men over twenty-one years of age and acts committed in private.

In the later *Norris* case[39] the court confirmed this view. Norris complained in 1983 that the Irish Offences against the Person Act (1861) and the Criminal Law Amendment Act (1885) were not in accordance with Article 8. Like the Northern Irish law, the Irish law prohibits "buggery," defined as an "abominable crime . . . committed either with mankind or with any animal" (Section 61 Offences against the Person Act). Although these laws had not been applied for several decades, the existence of these laws as such posed a threat and exposed all male homosexuals to criminal prosecution. Therefore, the commission and the court declared that the sole existence of these laws already caused a breach of the right to private life as guaranteed by the ECHR.

Two important conclusions can be drawn from the Strasbourg case law, notably from the development having taken place between the decisions in the cases of the German applicants in the 1950s and the judgments in the corresponding British and Irish cases in the 1970s and 1980s. First, one can observe an increasing willingness by the commission and the court to recognize anti-lesbian and anti-gay discrimination and to give a more ample interpretation of Article 14 ECHR. Second, lesbian and gay rights and the dignity of homosexuals have been recognized with respect to the right to private life.

In the fifties, gay men were still regarded as posing a moral and social threat to society. In the seventies, the decade in which lesbian and gay groups were mushrooming all over Europe,[40] the commission took a more differentiated approach. In the case of *X* v. *the United Kingdom*, the commission recalled its earlier views; it questioned the state's authority to regulate the private, notably the sexual, life of two consenting adults, considering the societal developments in this area.[41] In the *Dudgeon* case, the commission went even further by stating that beyond doubt the mere existence of a law prohibiting any form of homosexual contact in private was an undue interference with the plaintiff's private life.[42] The court concluded that the moral judgment on male homosexuality in Northern Ireland did not justify such a severe infringement on Dudgeon's private life.[43] These general principles were repeated in the case of Norris, who, unlike Dudgeon, was himself not arrested on the basis of the relevant laws but who claimed that the existence of these laws *threatened* him in the enjoyment of his private life.

Aside from the fact that in terms of lesbian and gay demands, both the *Dudgeon* and *Norris* cases resulted in positive verdicts, it also makes clear to what extent the Strasbourg organs are willing to approve discrimination against lesbians and gay men. So far the commission has dealt with cases on homosexuality only in the context of the right to individual privacy, as distinct from the right to family life not to mention the right to found a family. The rights of lesbians and gay men as a minority group, with a dignity equal to heterosexuals, are not being recognized. Neither have laws impeding lesbians and gay men in the development and fulfillment of their identities[44] been criticized. The core of the *Dudgeon* and *Norris* cases is that sexuality is an important aspect of one's personality and that the state should not be allowed to interfere, unless there is an objective and reasonable ground that serves a legitimate aim. This adapted view reflects the general changes of ideas in medicine and social science.[45]

The reluctant recognition of lesbian and gay rights by the European judiciary corresponds, according to Girard,[46] with the interpretation of sexuality in general. Sexuality is considered an important part of private life and the state should provide the conditions for the optimal development of people's sexuality. For a long time, however, sexuality was exclusively seen as a procreational activity.

Politicians, health educators, and representatives from many other professions still have great difficulty in recognizing the recreational function of sexuality.[47]

The consequence of this narrow vision is that, as yet, the discussion of equal opportunities for lesbians and gay men is not admissible. In the *Dudgeon* case the court declined to give its opinion concerning the admissibility of different ages of consent for heterosexuals and homosexuals. According to the court, this falls within the jurisdiction of the national legislators.[48]

We can learn from this that the fight for equal opportunities should not be restricted to petitioning the Strasbourg Commission and the Court. This is evident not only from the *Dudgeon* case but also from the other petitions made by lesbians and gay men.[49]

If we compare the view of the European Commission and Court on lesbian and gay rights with the current European legal reality, we cannot but conclude that the ideas of the (majority of the) members of the Strasbourg organs are rather conservative.[50] Total bans on (male) homosexuality in theory still remain in force in the Channel Islands, Cyprus, Ireland, the Island of Man, Gibraltar, and the former Yugoslav republics of Serbia, Bosnia-Herzegovina, and Macedonia. In practice, however, these provisions are hardly ever applied.

The real exceptions in Europe are Romania and most of the former Soviet republics,[51] where homosexuality is not only forbidden but where homosexuals, both male and female, are criminally prosecuted for "committing their sin." It seems, however, that in these countries also law reforms are on the way, partially inspired by the jurisprudence of the Strasbourg organs, anticipating closer collaboration with the EC and the Council of Europe.

The Strasbourg Commission and Court can also be said to uphold a completely outdated definition of the "family," denying same-sex couples the right to form a family unit. This not only strongly contradicts the legal traditions of the more progressive countries of Denmark, the Netherlands, Norway, and Sweden, but is now also undermined by the family policy launched by the EC. The European Parliament, Council, and Commission seem to recognize "new family types" besides the "traditional nuclear family," such as "de facto families," "single-parent families," and "reconstituted families."[52] The EC policy reflects, in our view, a far more contemporary and realistic approach than the philosophy of the Strasbourg organs.

It took the lesbian and gay movement a lot of energy and resources to provoke a favorable judgment by the European Court. One could argue whether or not the strategy followed was efficient and effective in achieving its goals. The progress made can be judged, at best, as moderate. On the one hand, one could say that the recognition of homosexuals as entitled to the right to private life is a first and essential step that should lead to the full and integral recognition of lesbian and gay rights. On the other hand one could also argue that the limited interpretation of this right could endanger the other demands of the lesbian and gay movement (e.g., equality and nondiscrimination, and protection of family life). Besides that, the petitions made by self-proclaimed lesbians and gay men made the movement as such more visible, and revealed that patterns of repression of lesbian and gay rights are similar throughout Europe (and throughout the world).

Independent of the outcome of this evaluation, it must be considered a great advantage that the lesbian and gay movement has more diverse aims than legal reform by means of Strasbourg jurisprudence. Many other plans have been set into motion over the past decade. Apart from the European Court and Commission, many other European institutions, such as the European Parliament and the Parliamentary Assembly of the Council of Europe, have been the target of carefully planned lesbian and gay lobbying strategies. Attempts have also been made to draft an additional protocol to the ECHR, spelling out lesbian- and gay-specific rights.

## EUROPEAN POLITICS

As a result of the extensive efforts by the lesbian and gay movement, both the Parliamentary Assembly of the Council of Europe and the European Parliament adopted several pro-lesbian and gay measures.

In 1981, without any form of international precedent, the assembly accepted both a resolution and a recommendation concerning anti-lesbian and anti-gay discrimination. Both pronouncements were based on a report prepared by the so-called Committee Voogd.[53] The assembly, recognizing that everybody has the right to sexual self-determination, expressed its concern about the fact that lesbians and gay men frequently are the subject of discrimination, and sometimes even repression. In its recommendation the World Health Organization (WHO) was urged to remove homosexuality from its International Classification of Diseases (ICD).[54] In one of its resolutions, the assembly made an appeal to ban certain forms of discrimination, specifically: exclusion of lesbians and gay men for certain professions, anti-lesbian and anti-gay violence, and the keeping of files on homosexuals by the police.

How successful the efforts by the lesbian and gay movement were, can be seen in the official text of the assembly's recommendations, which repeat almost verbatim the demands put forward by the lesbian and gay lobby. The recommendation and resolution call upon member states to take appropriate measures in order, first, that all laws and practices that criminalize and brand as "sick" homosexual acts between adults be totally banned; second, that the same age of consent apply to both homosexual and heterosexual acts; third, that discrimination in the areas of employment and salary be eliminated; fourth, that medical acts aimed at changing sexual orientation be prohibited; fifth, that custody, visiting rights, and accommodation of children by their parents not be restricted solely on the grounds of a parent's sexual preference; and, finally, that effective measures to reduce the danger of rape and violence in prisons be introduced.

Actions of this kind are not unsuccessful. Although the Council of Ministers of the Council of Europe was not at all pleased with these actions by the assembly, national governments did turn their attention to these progressive statements. Probably as a direct result of these pronouncements, France adjusted the differences in ages of consent in 1982. When adopting this legal amendment, the French legislature referred to the Council of Europe's resolutions. The Spanish parliament accepted the resolution and recommendation in 1985.

The ILGA is proposing the adoption of an additional protocol to the ECHR to extend the protection of the rights enshrined in the assembly's document to lesbians and gay men.[55] If this protocol is accepted, which, despite an intensive lobbying campaign, has not happened yet, the European Court and Commission will have to revise their case law, paying more attention to the interests of lesbians and gay men.

The Assembly of the Council of Europe has not been the object of a lesbian and gay lobby; similar activities have been directed at the European Parliament. Since 1979, the European Parliament has been working on the shaping of a lesbian and gay emancipation policy. Until now, these efforts have not had a big impact on the overall EC, notably as a result of stubborn opposition by the Council of Ministers (being the most powerful institution within the EC). The reluctance of the council finds its legitimation in the fact that the EC treaty does not contain specific references to the protection of human rights. This, however, does not restrain the council from persistently underlining the importance of full recognition of human rights "both as one of the cornerstones of European cooperation and in the relations of the Community with third nations."[56] Indeed, in 1977 the European Parliament, and the European Council and Commission made a joint statement in which they emphasized the importance they attach to the protection of human rights and declared to respect these rights in the exercise of their power.[57]

To illustrate that times are changing, reference should be made to two projects funded by the Commission of the EC. The first project concerns an inventory on the social and legal situation of lesbians and gay men in the EC. This study, presented to EC Commissioner of Social Affairs, Mrs. Vasso Papandreou, in December 1992, may be an important incentive to revitalize the discussion on a European lesbian and gay policy.[58] The second project concerns a visibility study of lesbians in the various EC countries.[59] Moreover, since 1989 the EC has been funding lesbian and gay exchange study programs in the context of the so-called Erasmus program.

The council's reluctance did not deter the European Parliament from adopting progressive statements. The first resolution of the parliament[60] on lesbian and gay issues was based on a report by the Italian member, Vera Squarcialupi, adopted on February 1, 1984.[61] She prepared a document on anti-lesbian and anti-gay discrimination, following two resolutions by the parliament in 1979 and 1982. Her recommendations were approved by the parliament in 1984 and correspond with the assembly's resolution and recommendation. In its own recommendation, the European Parliament also urges its Legal Affairs Committee to look for ways to end the inequality in EC member states' legislation concerning homosexuality. This recommendation has never been effected, however, despite pressure from several parliamentary members.[62] After the Squarcialupi report many other activities touching upon lesbian and gay issues followed.[63] Some members of the European Parliament were actively involved in setting up ILGA's Iceberg Project, and enabled the project to be presented in Strasbourg on the occasion of a parliamentary session there.

One of the most recent victories is the approval of a new recommendation by the Council of Social Affairs on "Protecting the Dignity of Women and Men at Work: A Code of Practice on the Measures to Combat Sexual Harassment."[64] This code also condemns the harassment of lesbians and gay men in the workplace. The inclusion of this explicit condemnation followed a discussion of the issue of harassment at a meeting between EC Commissioner Papandreou and ILGA representatives in December 1990. In 1992, the European Parliament took the decision to report annually on the state of human rights within the European Community. In the first report and motion for a resolution, prepared by reporter Mr. Karel de Gucht, there were a number of explicite references to issues highly relevant to the lesbian and gay movement. These reports, which are expected to have an unprecedented influence, may offer new opportunities to the lesbian and gay movement to attain its goals.

The Parliamentary Assembly of the Council of Europe and European Parliament are both very progressive in their statements; however, their influence is limited. The lesbian and gay movement has been effective in influencing both institutions and has been able to open and guard communication channels between the movement and these institutions. This may be very important in view of future, follow-up strategies to be decided upon soon.

## CONCLUSIONS

According to the lesbian and gay movement, their rights enjoy insufficient protection under the recognized human rights codes. This is not so much a result of textual shortcomings of the major treaties, as it is the consequence of the rather conservative interpretation of their provision given by the authoritative bodies. Both the European Commission and Court of Human Rights as well as the UN Committee for Human Rights has so far only secured for lesbians and gay men limited protection under the right to private life provisions. The committee and the court show a lack of political willingness in guaranteeing lesbians and gay men appropriate legal protection against infringements on their dignity as well as enabling lesbians and gay men to develop a lifestyle that follows from their sexual preference. The European Parliament, the Parliamentary Assembly of the Council of Europe, and ever more European governments seem to disagree with this stubborn rejection of lesbian and gay rights, and are developing, in response, far more progressive policies. Ongoing pressure is needed to provoke a more liberal interpretation of the human rights treaties that goes beyond the limits of the right to private life.

The strategy of confronting the Strasbourg organs with test cases has been partially successful. The same can be said of the strategy to effect law reform through pressure at democratic fora, such as the Parliamentary Assembly of the Council of Europe and the European Parliament of the European Community. They have proven to be far more sensitive to the demands of the lesbian and gay movement. Their limited powers, however, have restricted the success of their initiatives.

Especially in view of the process of a unifying Europe, with more powers being given to supranational agencies, the question of continued investment of effort by the lesbian and gay movement in the European institutions becomes an issue of paramount importance. Regular evaluation and innovative lobbying strategies need to receive high priority in the ILGA.

## NOTES

1. See Part Two of this volume.

2. Unless otherwise noted, the examples all come from the compilation of cases by the Iceberg Project (K. Waaldijk et al., "The Tip of an Iceberg: Anti-Lesbian and Anti-Gay Discrimination in Europe, 1980–1990," first draft of report [Utrecht: Gay and Lesbian Studies Department, University of Utrecht, October 7, 1991]), with the exception of the Dutch cases, which come from the Centre Anti-Discrimination Homosexuality (CADH) (E. van der Veen and A. Dercksen, "Onderzoeksverslag deel I" ("Research Report, Part I") (Utrecht: Gay and Lesbian Studies Department, University of Utrecht, 1989).

3. P. Ashman, "Homosexuality and Human Rights Law," in *The Second ILGA Pink Book* (Utrecht: Interfacultaire Werkgroep Homostudies, 1988), p. 47.

4. P. Ashman, "Background of the Proposal for a Protocol to Amend the European Convention of Human Rights," CSCE Parallel Activities, Study Conference on the Possibilities of Expanding the European Convention of Human Rights to Eliminate Discrimination Based on Sexual Orientation (Copenhagen: Landforeniging for bösser og lesbiske Forbundet af 1948, 1990).

5. "European Court of Human Rights," *Belgian Linguistic Case* 23, July 1968, Series A., No. 6 (1968), pp. 24–25.

6. See M. Novak, "UNO-Pakt über bürgerliche und politische Rechte und Fakultativprotocol" ("UN Agreement on Civil and Political Rights and Optional Protocol"), *CCPR Kommentar,* Kehl/Strasbourg/Arlington: Engel, 1989, pp. 302 ff.

7. European Commission of Human Rights, Case 5935/72, *X* v. *Federal Republic of Germany,* Yearbook XIX (1976), pp. 277 ff.

8. European Court of Human Rights, *Dudgeon* case, October 22, 1981, Series A., No. 45 (1982), and *Norris* case, October 25, 1988, Series A., No. 142 (1988).

9. *Dudgeon,* p. 20.

10. Ibid., p. 21.

11. In most European countries the age of consent for heterosexuals ranges from twelve to eighteen years. See Part Two of this volume.

12. European Commission of Human Rights, Case 10389/93, *Johnson* v. *U.K.*, D&R 72 (1986).

13. European Commission of Human Rights, Case 15070/89, *Modinos* v. *Cyprus*, December 7, 1990, Council of Europe press release.

14. European Commission of Human Rights, Case 9369/81, *X and Y* v. *U.K.*, May 3, 1983, D&R 32 (1983), p. 221.

15. Case 14753/89, *X and Y* v. *U.K.*, October 9, 1989 (unpublished).

16. Hoge Raad (Dutch Supreme Court), February 24, 1989, Rek. Nr. 737, *Rechtspraak van de Week* (*Jurisprudence of the Week*), 1989, No. 65.

17. European Court of Human Rights, *Marckx* case, June 13, 1979, Series A., No. 31 (1979).

18. European Commission of Human Rights, Cases 7289/75 and 7349/76, *X and Y* v. *Switzerland*, Yearbook XX (1977), pp. 168 ff.

19. European Commission of Human Rights, *Khan* v. *U.K.*, Yearbook X (1967), p. 478. Cf. "Toelatingsbeleid bij polygame huwelijken" ("Admission Policy in Case of Polygamous Marriages"), with a comment by S. W. E. Rutten, *NJCM Bulletin* 16, no. 5 (1991): 430–36.

20. *Marckx*.

21. Ibid., p. 15. Cf. P. van Dijk and G. J. H. van Hoof, *De Europese conventie in theorie en praktijk* (*The European Convention in Theory and Practice*) (Nijmegen: Ars Aequi Libri Rechten van de Mens, 1982, 1990).

22. European Commission of Human Rights, Case 7215/72, *X* v. *U.K.*, Yearbook XXI (1978), p. 374.

23. Report of October 12, 1978, D&R 19 (1980).

24. European Commission of Human Rights, Case 11389/85, *Morissens* v. *Belgium*, May 3, 1988 (unpublished). See also Anonymous, "The Eliane Morissens Affair: A Lost Case," *ILGA Bulletin*, No. 4 (1988): 15.

25. Views of the Human Rights Committee No. 4. 14/61, *Leo R. Herzberg et al.* v. *Finland*, Report of the Human Rights Committee 1982, p. 165.

26. Cf. European Commission of Human Rights, case 1038/61, *X* v. *Belgium*, Yearbook IV (1961), p. 324: "Their right to set up an association or a trade union."

27. Under Article 221 of the Austrian Penal Code, those who establish or belong to an organization that supports "homosexual lewdness" and causes public offense are liable to six months' imprisonment. See P. Tatchell, *Out in Europe* (London and Glasgow: Channel Four Television Publications, 1990).

28. European Commission of Human Rights, *Rees* case, October 17, 1986, Series A., No. 106 (1987), pp. 15–19.

29. *Rees*, p. 19. Cf. European Commission of Human Rights, Case 7654/76, *Oosterwijck* v. *Belgium*, Report of March 1, 1979, par. 57: "A marriage requires the existence of a relationship between two persons of the opposite sex."

30. *Dudgeon*, p. 24.

31. *Marckx*, p. 14.

32. European Commission of Human Rights, *Cossey* case, September 27, 1990, Series A., No. 184 (1990), p. 18.

33. A. Hendriks and L. Markenstein, "Recht als medicijn" ("Law as Medicine"), in M. Moerings and A. Mattijssen, eds., *Homoseksualiteit en recht (Homosexuality and Law)* (Arnhem: Gouda Quint, 1992), pp. 185–214.

34. E.g., Article 6, Belgian Constitution; Article 1, Dutch Constitution; Article 2, French Constitution; Article 3, German Constitution; Article 4, Greek Constitution; Article 40, Irish Constitution; Article 3, Italian Constitution; Article 11, Luxembourg Constitution; Article 13, Portuguese Constitution; Article 14, Spanish Constitution.

35. Among others: *Johnson*, Case 7525/76; *Z. v. U.K.*, March 3, 1978, D&R 11 (1978); Case 7215/75, *X v. U.K.*, D&R 11 (1978); Case 9237/81, *B. v. U.K.*, D&R 34 (1983); Case 11716/85, *S. v. U.K.*, May 14, 1986, D&R 37 (1986).

36. European Commission of Human Rights, Case 104/55, *X* v. *Federal Republic of Germany*, Yearbook I (1955–57), p. 229.

37. European Commission of Human Rights, Case 167/56, *X* v. *Federal Republic of Germany*, D&R 1 (1955–57); European Commission of Human Rights, Case 530/59, *X* v. *Federal Republic of Germany*, Collection of Decisions; Case 5935/72, *X* v. *Federal Republic of Germany*, D&R 3, p. 46.

38. European Commission of Human Rights, Case 7215/75, *X* v. *U.K.*, D&R 11 (1978), pp. 117–32 (cf. n. 8).

39. *Norris;* Ashman, "Homosexuality and Human Rights Law," p. 48.

40. See John Clark, "The Global Lesbian and Gay Movement: Mass Movement, Grassroots, or by Invitation Only" = chapter 4 in this volume.

41. European Commission of Human Rights, Case 7215/75, *X* v. *U.K.*, D&R 11 (1977), p. 43.

42. *Dudgeon.*

43. Ibid.

44. According to the European Commission, in a case considering the right to private life, "the right to establish and develop relationships with other human beings, especially in the emotional field," is conditional to "the development and fulfillment of one's own personality." Case 6959/75, *Brüggeman & Scheuten* v. *Federal Republic of Germany*, Yearbook XIX (1976), p. 414.

45. In the 1970s, the ideas concerning homosexuality altered in Europe. Homosexuality had long been officially seen as a mental disease and was treated as such. After the 1970s, the central problem was the repression of homosexuality. New psychological therapies were developed which no longer tried to "cure" homosexuality, but aimed instead at making the person accept sexual preference as part of his or her personality. In psychiatry and the other branches of medicine, the illness syndrome was overthrown. The main focus of research shifted to social sciences, where the central theme was repression of homosexuality by society (R. Tielman, *Homoseksualiteit in Nederland. Studie van een emancipatienbeweging* [*Homosexuality in the Netherlands: Study of an Emancipation Movement*] [Amsterdam: Boom, 1982]).

46. Ph. Girard, "The Protection of the Rights of Homosexuals under the International Law of Human Rights: European Perspectives," *Canadian Human Rights Yearbook* 3 (1986): 11.

47. A. Hendriks, "Homorechten in de jaren negentig" ("Gay Rights in the Nineties"), in A. Dercksen et al., eds., *Tolerantie onder NAP. 20 essays over homoseksualiteit voor Rob Tielman* (Utrecht: Gay and Lesbian Studies Department, University of Utrecht, 1992);

"The Poltical and Legislative Framework in Which Sexual Health Promotion Takes Place," in H. Curtis, ed., *Promoting Sexual Health* (London: British Medical Association, 1992).

48. Ibid., p. 18.

49. European Commission of Human Rights, Case 7215/75, *X* v. *U.K.;* Case 9237/81, *John Bruce* v. *U.K.;* Case 9721/82, *Richard Desmond* v. *U.K.;* Case 11716/85, *Mary X.* v. *U.K.;* Case 12513/86, *X* v. *U.K.; Johnson,* note 13.

50. A. Hendriks, "Homoseksualiteit in West Europa: een landenoverzicht" ("Homosexuality in Western Europe: An Overview by Country"), unpublished paper, Utrecht, September 1991; "Gay Men and Lesbians in Central and Eastern Europe: A Survey," unpublished paper, Utrecht, September 1991.

51. As of March 1993, Ukraine and the Baltic republics of Latvia and Estonia have repealed the total prohibition on homosexual acts from its Penal Code.

52. European Parliament, Resolution on Family Policy (83/C 184/116); conclusions of the Council regarding family policy (89/C 277/02): Commission document (COM[89] 363).

53. Parliamentary Assembly of the Council of Europe, Thirty-Third Ordinary Session, Recommendation 924 (1981) of October 1, 1981, and Resolution 756 (1981) of October 1, 1981, on discrimination against homosexuals.

54. Eventually effect in late 1991.

55. Draft Protocol of the Convention for the Protection of Human Rights and Fundamental Freedoms concering the elimination of discrimination based on sexual orientation, Study Conference, Copenhagen, 1990.

56. Conclusions of the Council of Ministers, Luxembourg, June 28–29, 1991, Annex V., in *Europa van Morgen,* July 3, 1991.

57. Declaration of April 5, 1977, *Official Journal,* 1977, No. C 103/1.

58. P. Ashman et al., eds. *Homosexuality: A Community Issue: Essays on Why and How to Incorporate Lesbian and Gay Rights in the Law and Politics of the European Community* (Dordrecht and Boston: Martinus Nijhoff, 1993). This volume is a document of the European Commission prepared by the European Human Rights Foundation (Belgium); the European University (Italy); and the Gay and Lesbian Studies Department, University of Utrecht (the Netherlands).

59. The "Lesbian Visibility Project" is currently being carried out by the women's group of LBL/F-48 in Denmark.

60. European Parliament, 1984–1985 Debates (Doc. No. 1–311, 12), Resolution of March 13, 1984. EP Doc. 1–1072/82, PE 87. 477 def.

61. European Parliament, Documents 1983–1984 (Doc. No. 1–1358/83), February 13, 1984, PE 87.477 def. Report for the Committee for Social Affairs and Employment about Sexual Discrimination and Labour (Squarciapuli).

62. E.g, MEP Ien van den Heuven made a proposal for EC action with regard to discrimination against lesbians and gay men. EP Debates, March 13, 1984, No. 1–311/1, at p. 19; also European Parliament, Documents 1982–1983 (Doc. No. 1–1072/82) (Van den Heuven). Cf. H. d'Ancona, *Europese Notities, mensen en andere minderheden in het Europa van morgen (European Notes: People and Other Minorities in Tomorrow's Europe)* (Utrecht and Antwerp: Veen, 1989), p. 88.

63. In a resolution on human rights in the former Soviet Union in 1983, the Soviet government was urged to end the KGB tactic of making dissidents suspicious by accusing

them of immorality and homosexuality, and to end the persecution of homosexuals (Resolution on the Human Rights in the Soviet Union, No. 3 161, pp. 67–70, 1983). In 1986, the European Parliament approved a resolution on the rise of racism and fascism in Europe, in which it called for respect for all men and women. Homosexuality was explicitly mentioned (d'Ancona, p. 89). Also in 1986, a resolution by the former member of Parliament, Hedy d'Ancona (at present Minister of Welfare, Health, and Cultural Affairs of the Netherlands) on sexual violence against women included a call to extend the word discrimination to include sexual preference. Moreover, a call was made to subsidize lesbian self-helf groups (Resolution on violence against women, Doc. A2–44/86).

64. The Code of Practice was approved on November 27, 1991. Cf. Stonewall Press Release, December 6, 1991.

# Part Two

# A Country-by-Country Survey

# 23

# World Survey on the Social and Legal Position of Gays and Lesbians

## Rob Tielman and Hans Hammelburg

PROLOGUE

In 1985, the first country-by-country survey of lesbian and gay liberation and oppression was published in the *First Pink Book* of the (then) International Gay Association (IGA). In 1988, the second worldwide inventory was included in the *Second Pink Book* of the (then) International Lesbian and Gay Association (ILGA). This is, therefore, the third survey of the social and legal position of gay men and lesbians in the vast majority of countries of the world.

Attention is paid to (1): official attitudes and the law regarding homosexuality, (2) social attitudes to homosexuality, and (3) the gay and/or lesbian movements all over the world. Insofar as information is available, a short description of the situation in each country is given. The legal and social situation of gay men is in general better documented than that of lesbians.

The most important sources of information were the 1988 *Pink Book,* the International Lesbian and Gay Association (especially Edwin Udding and Micha Ramakers of the Information Secretariat in Brussels); the Department of Gay and Lesbian Studies of the University of Utrecht (especially Aart Hendriks, Evert van der Veen, and Kees Waaldijk); Swedish and Dutch embassies all over the world; and foreign embassies in The Hague and Brussels (which had the opportunity to comment on the information on their country to be provided in this overview).

Our informants are not responsible for the way in which information is presented in this report; that responsibility rests with the Department of Gay and Lesbian Studies of the University of Utrecht, under whose aegis the research was done. Please let us know about any mistakes, omissions, changes, and additional information: our address is P.O. Box 80140, 3508 TC Utrecht, the Netherlands.

This survey was co-sponsored by the International Lesbian and Gay Association, the International Humanist and Ethical Union, and the Department of Gay and Lesbian Studies of the University of Utrecht.

In the questionnaire, information was requested about the law on sexual contacts between men, between women, and between people of different ages: Are homosexual relationships officially recognized, are openly gay and lesbian people discriminated against, does legislation exist against such forms of discrimination, has research been done to investigate the social position of homosexual women and men, can homosexuality be openly discussed without repercussions for the people involved, are violations of human rights of gay men and lesbians recorded, and do organizations of homosexual women and men exist in the various countries?

Of the 202 countries investigated (as compared to 182 in 1988), we were able to obtain legal data on 178 (in 1988: 124). In those countries where no information could be obtained, we assumed that neither a gay and lesbian movement, nor social support for equal rights for lesbians and homosexuals existed, because otherwise the ILGA and its member organizations would have heard about it.

The main results show that: in 56 countries a gay and/or lesbian movement exists (in 1988: 36), in 15 countries groups are being set up (in 1988: 16), and in 131 countries no movement or group could be found (in 1988: 130). Relatively speaking, the situation was and has remained proportionally the worst in Africa and the best in Europe, as far as concerns the number of countries in which a gay and/or lesbian movement is active. During the last ten years the number of developing countries and former Communist countries with gay and lesbian movements has grown impressively.

At a social level, in 11 countries a majority of the population is in favor of equal rights for lesbian women and gay men, in 47 countries only a minority is in favor. In 144 countries hardly any support for gay and lesbian rights can be found among the population. From a social point of view, the situation is again the worst in Africa and the best in Europe. The growing social acceptance of homosexuality is less impressive than the growth of the gay and lesbian movement worldwide.

In 6 countries (and in some parts of the U.S.A, Canada, and Australia) the law protects gay men and lesbians against discrimination. In 98 countries homosexual behavior is not illegal (although different ages of consent for homo- and heterosexual behavior may exist), but there is no protection against discrimination on the basis of sexual orientation. In 74 countries homosexual behavior is illegal (in most cases between men, but that does not mean that the situation of lesbians is any better). In 24 countries no information is yet available. The legal developments are even slower than the social ones, but the tendency toward equal treatment of gays and lesbians is certainly continuing to take place worldwide, with the exception of most Islamic countries.

Viewed from a legal perspective, the situation is again the worst in Africa and the best in Europe. Another interesting finding is that the 53 countries where homosexual behavior is illegal, where there is no social support for gay and lesbian rights, and where no gay and lesbian movement exists are predominantly Islamic, formerly Communist, or have been part of the former British colonial empire.

From a historical perspective, the English legislation against homosexuality has had (and unfortunately still has) appalling consequences for the legal position of homosexual men and, to a lesser extent, lesbians in the former British colonies. The effects of the former French, Dutch, Spanish, and Portuguese colonial legislation against homosexuality are less severe. In general, nevertheless, Christian-based homophobia has damaged many cultures in which sexual contacts and relationships between men and between women used to be tolerated or even accepted. Recently, Christian puritanism from the West, mixed with Islamic fundamentalism, has attacked homosexuality, even in countries where same-sex contacts had usually been tolerated.

In many countries AIDS has had paradoxical effects: in those countries where the gay and lesbian movements were already relatively strong (such as in Scandinavia, the Netherlands, New Zealand, and some areas in Northern America and Australia), the AIDS crisis presented a challenge to those movements in such a way that they became more influential. In many countries where the movements were relatively weak, the AIDS epidemic seriously endangered their situation. In those countries where no movements existed, AIDS sometimes made it even more difficult to start one, but sometimes stimulated the beginning of a movement (such as in Eastern Europe and many Latin American and Asian countries).

The important changes in the former Communist countries have influenced the position of gay men and lesbians as well. In the past, the gay and lesbian movement was not allowed to organize itself in Eastern Europe (with the exception of East Germany and Hungary). The introduction of democracy supported the right to individual self-determination of gays and lesbians, but it also made visible the underlying homophobia in societies which have never been informed about homosexuality properly.

Generally speaking, the success of gay and lesbian movements is closely related to the capacity for pragmatic cooperation within and outside the movement, and the support of key figures and allies in the general public. Furthermore, wise use of the media can develop a positive image of homosexuality, bring the law to bear to defend the human rights of gay men and lesbians, and to promote the development of a gay and lesbian professional leadership (including lawyers, physicians, teachers, researchers, journalists, politicians, and trade unionists).

Although assimilation or segregation under certain conditions can be effective in counteracting heterosexual oppression, in the long run integration strategies turn out to be more successful. The development of strong and positive gay and lesbian individual and subcultural identities enables the movement to gain political power and social prestige by defending the human rights of an oppressed minority in order to attain treatment on an equal footing with other minorities and the rest of society. Too much isolation leaves the gay and lesbian movement vulnerable in society. Too much assimilation is a denial of gay and lesbian-specific needs and features and makes it unattractive for future generations of gay men and lesbians.

Unfortunately, many gays and lesbians (indeed, all people) tend to look for easy solutions to their individual problems, whereas it is also important to find solutions for the structural oppression of gay men and lesbians. A similar trend can be seen when comparing national movements and their international relationships. For the future of the legal and social situation with which gay men and lesbians have to live, it is essential that the international movement and national movements make clear to their constituencies that no one can survive without cooperation. A look at the situation in the various countries investigated shows how illusory it is to think that some gay and lesbian communities can survive while others are destroyed. International cooperation is as important a form of life insurance as prevention is. In fact, they cannot exist without each other. We hope that this survey will support both goals for the benefit of us all.

## COUNTRY-BY-COUNTRY SURVEY

### Afghanistan

*Official Attitudes and the Law*

Islamic law (*Sharia*) has been reintroduced.

*Society*

The attitude toward homosexuality is very hostile. There is no visible social support of gay and lesbian rights.

### Albania

*Official Attitudes and the Law*

Since 1977, homosexual behavior between consenting adults has not been mentioned in the law as being a criminal offense. However, homosexuality might be considered as being in defiance of "societal morals," according to the Penal

Code, and grounds for imprisonment for a maximum of ten years. The age of consent for both heterosexual and homosexual acts is fourteen. (Sections 98 and 99). Male *heterosexual* acts with minors under the age of fourteen are considered to be more offensive than a similar gay act; sexual intercourse with a girl under the age of fourteen is punishable for up to fifteen years' imprisonment, whereas homosexual intercourse with a boy younger than fourteen is subject to up to five years in jail. This may stem from the Islamic influence, which attibutes special value to female virginity before marriage.

## Society

Homosexuality is considered not to exist. There is no visible support for gay and lesbian rights.

## Algeria

*Official Attitudes and the Law*

Homosexual acts between men and between women are illegal according to section 338 of the Penal Code, and can be punished with a maximum of three years' imprisonment.

## Society

Openly homosexual relationships are not possible and homosexuality cannot be discussed in public. No visible support for gay and lesbian rights.

## Andorra

*Official Attitudes and the Law*

There is no legal information available.

## Society

There is no visible support for gay and lesbian rights.

## Angola

*Official Attitudes and the Law*

Homosexual acts are illegal, described as offenses against public morality.

## Society

There is no visible support for gay and lesbian rights.

## Antigua and Barbuda

*Official Attitudes and the Law*

Homosexuality is prosecuted on the basis of British law.

*Society*

There is no visible support for gay and lesbian rights.

## Argentina

*Official Attitudes and the Law*

Homosexual behavior between consenting adults is not mentioned in the law as being a criminal offense. However, many provinces have *edictos policiales* on the basis of which one can be detained for 30 days for "offenses against morality" and for 48 hours for "documentation controls." These rules are used especially against gay men and make registration of them possible.

In November 1991, the Minister of the Interior recognized that homosexuals are discriminated against, and promised legal recognition of gay and lesbian groups.

In 1992, after three years of attempts to legalize its existence, the country's principal gay rights organization, "Comunidad Homosexual Argentina" (CHA), was granted legal standing.

*Society*

Homosexuality is hardly discussed or seen in public. The society is *machista:* the roles for men and women are very rigidly defined with strong influence from a conservative, anti-homosexual Catholic church. There is no visible social support for gay and lesbian rights.

*The Gay and/or Lesbian Movement*

CHA, and the "Grupo de Acción Gay" and "Grupo Federativo Gay Buenos Aires" (the former "Movimiento Gay para la Liberación") are known as gay groups. An informal group of lesbians (Grupo ISIS) has published the first Argentinian lesbian magazine. In 1990, an attempt was made to make the gay movement illegal. CHA took the case to the Argentine High Court, which ruled unfavorably. Nevertheless, many new gay and/or lesbian groups have been created since.

## Armenia

*Official Attitudes and the Law*

In the former Soviet Union, anal intercourse between men was prohibited. The corresponding section is still part of the present Penal Code of Armenia. Homosexual acts between women are not mentioned in the law, nor is homosexual behavior between consenting adults explicitly included in the law as being a criminal offense.

*Society*

The attitude of society is hostile. Homosexuality is taboo. There is no visible support for gay and lesbian rights.

## Aruba

*Official Attitudes and the Law*

Legislation of the Netherlands Antilles is applied. Homosexual behavior between consenting adults is not mentioned in the law as being a criminal offense.

*Society*

Homosexuality is hardly discussed or seen in public, but closeted homosexuals seem to be tolerated. A minority of the population is in favor of gay and lesbian rights.

## Australia

*Official Attitudes and the Law*

Federal legislation (the Human Rights and Equal Opportunity Commission Act of 1986) confers on the Human Rights and Equal Opportunity Commission the function of investigating and conciliating complaints of discrimination in employment on the grounds of sexual preference. Homosexual relationships are discriminated against in the areas of resident permits, adoption, and foster parenthood.

The Department of Immigration, Local Government, and Ethnic Affairs declared that homosexuality is not a bar to migration to Australia. Since April 1991, new immigration laws have given legal recognition to homosexual relationships. These regulations create a category of "relationships of emotional interdependency" outside the legally defined family links. The ban on homosexuals in the armed forces was lifted at the end of 1992.

In 1992, the Australian government made illegal any discrimination against people with HIV/AIDS, and granted asylum to foreigners facing anti-gay persecution in their native countries, e.g., China.

## Capital Territory

### Official Attitudes and the Law

Homosexual behavior between consenting adults is not mentioned in the law as being a criminal offense. The age of consent is eighteen years for homosexual acts and sixteen years for heterosexual acts.

### Society

A minority of the population is in favor of gay and lesbian rights.

## New South Wales

### Official Attitudes and the Law

Legal protection against anti-homosexual discrimination exists. The Anti-Discrimination Act 1977 prohibits discrimination on the ground of homosexuality in a variety of areas, including employment, accommodation, education, the provision of goods and services, and club membership or benefits.

The age of consent for heterosexual acts is sixteen years; for homosexual acts between men, eighteen years. Homosexual acts between women are not mentioned, nor are homosexual relationships recognized in the areas of housing and insurance.

### Society

The majority of the population is in favor of gay and lesbian rights.

## Northern Territory

### Official Attitudes and the Law

Legal protection against discrimination on the basis of homosexuality exists. Homosexual acts between males were decriminalized in 1981. The age of consent for male homosexual acts is eighteen years, compared to sixteen years for heterosexual acts.

### Society

The majority of the population is in favor of gay and lesbian rights.

## Queensland

*Official Attitudes and the Law*

Homosexual behavior between consenting adults is not mentioned in the law as being a criminal offense. Homosexual acts between males were decriminalized in 1982.

*Society*

A minority of the population is in favor of gay and lesbian rights.

## South Australia

*Official Attitudes and the Law*

Legal protection against discrimination on the basis of homosexuality exists. The age of consent is the same for heterosexual and homosexual acts (sixteen years). The Equal Opportunity Act of 1984 prohibits discrimination on the grounds of sexuality in a variety of areas, including employment, accommodation, and the provision of goods and services.

*Society*

The majority of the population is in favor of gay and lesbian rights.

## Tasmania

*Official Attitudes and the Law*

Tasmania is the only Australian state where sexual acts between men are still illegal. Those between women are not mentioned. Anti-discrimination laws were approved in 1991. The UN Human Rights Committee accepted in 1992 a complaint from the Tasmanian Gay and Lesbian Rights Group, which is trying to decriminalize homosexuality.

*Society*

A minority of the population is in favor of gay and lesbian rights.

## Victoria

### Official Attitudes and the Law

Homosexual behavior between consenting adults is not mentioned in the law as being a criminal offense. The age of consent is the same for heterosexual and homosexual acts (sixteen years).

### Society

A minority of the population is in favor of gay and lesbian rights.

## West Australia

### Official Attitudes and the Law

Homosexual behavior between consenting adults is not mentioned in the law as being a criminal offense. Homosexual acts between consenting adults in private were decriminalized in 1990. The age of consent for male homosexual acts is twenty-one years, compared to eighteen years for heterosexual acts. The "promotion and encouragement" of homosexual behavior is an offense.

### Society

A minority of the population is in favor of gay and lesbian rights.

### The Gay and/or Lesbian Movement

In all states there are active gay and/or lesbian groups. Well known is the gay male magazine *Outrage.*

## Austria

### Official Attitudes and the Law

Homosexual behavior between consenting adults is not mentioned in the law as being a criminal offense. Male and female homosexual acts were decriminalized in 1971. Homosexual prostitution was legalized on the same basis as heterosexual prostitution in 1989. However, there remain three sections in the Penal Code that discriminate against homosexuals:

Section 209 provides for a higher age of consent (eighteen) for male homosexuals than for heterosexuals and lesbians (fourteen). Noncompliance may result in imprisonment from six months to five years.

Section 220 provides for up to six months' imprisonment or a fine for those who advocate or approve of homosexuality (both male and female) or bestiality.

Section 221 provides for up to six months' imprisonment or a fine for those who found or are member of an organization that "favors homosexual lewdness" and thereby causes public offense.

A constitutional complaint against Section 209 was rejected by the Constitutional Court for formal reasons in March 1988. There have been few trials or sentences based on articles 220 and 221, although on several occasions charges have been filed against gay and lesbian activists, which have led to police and court investigation. Almost all charges were, however, eventually dropped by the public prosecutor.

Yet Section 220 was used indirectly by the Supreme Court to substantiate its decision that the representation of homosexual acts is "hard" pornography and, as such, illegal. By the end of 1990, on the basis of Section 220, the Austrian customs authorities confiscated AIDS-information materials from Germany containing explicit (visual) safer sex information for gay men.

Gay asylum seekers, e.g., from Iran, have been granted asylum status, on grounds of their sexual orientation.

## Society

Although the majority of Austrians rejects equal rights for gays and lesbians, they are tolerant of closeted homosexuals.

## The Gay and/or Lesbian Movement

In spite of Section 221, there are officially recognized homosexual organizations in Vienna, Salzburg, Linz, Graz (Steiermark), Innsbruck (the Tyrol), and Bregenz/ Dornbirn (Vorarlberg). Called "Homosexuelle Initiative (HOSI)," they operate independently of one another. Vienna has a gay and lesbian center, the "Rosa Lila Villa." In spite of article 220, HOSI Wien has since 1979 been publishing its quarterly *Lambda-Nachrichten*. It received official press subsidy for the first time in 1987.

## Azerbaijan

### Official Attitudes and the Law

In the former Soviet Union, anal intercourse between men was illegal. This prohibition is incorporated in the Penal Code of Azerbaijan. Homosexual acts between women are not mentioned in the law, nor is homosexual behavior between consenting adults explicitly included in the law as being a criminal offense.

### Society

The attitude of this predominantly Islamic society is hostile toward homosexuality. There is no visible support for gay and lesbian rights.

## Bahamas

### Official Attitudes and the Law

Homosexual behavior is illegal. Sexual acts between men are criminalized under Sections 390 and 530 of the Penal Code, with a maximum of ten years' imprisonment. In 1992, the first case under this law, two men were prosecuted for having had sex in public. The case was dropped after international protest campaigns. Homosexual contacts between women are criminalized under Section 529, with a maximum penalty of two years' imprisonment.

### Society

There is no visible support for gay and lesbian rights.

## Bahrain

### Official Attitudes and the Law

Homosexual behavior is illegal. Islamic laws against homosexuality are applied.

### Society

Homosexuality is taboo. No visible support for gay and lesbian rights.

## Bangladesh

### Official Attitudes and the Law

Homosexual behavior is illegal; Islamic laws against homosexuality are applied. The government's official stance is that homosexuality does not exist.

### Society

Homosexuality is considered to be a perversion. There is no visible social support for gay and lesbian rights.

## Barbados

### Official Attitudes and the Law

Homosexual contacts between consenting adults are illegal but enforcement is lax.

### Society

There is no visible support for gay and lesbian rights.

# Belarus

*Official Attitudes and the Law*

In the former Soviet Union, anal intercourse between men was illegal. This prohibition is incorporated in the Penal Code of Belarus. Homosexual acts between women are not mentioned in the law, nor is homosexual behavior between consenting adults explicitly included in the law as being a criminal offense.

*Society*

The attitude of society is hostile. Homosexuality is taboo. There is no visible support for gay and lesbian rights.

# Belgium

*Official Attitudes and the Law*

Homosexual behavior between consenting adults is not mentioned in the law as being a criminal offense. Section 372 bis of the Penal Code, which prohibited homosexual contacts under the age of eighteen, was abolished on June 8, 1985, making the age of consent sixteen for both homo- and heterosexuals. Since 1985, a proposal for anti-discrimination legislation has been pending in Parliament without being debated upon. Only married foreign partners can obtain a partner-dependent residence permit. Homosexuality is no bar against a person enlisting in the armed forces.

Although society in general is tolerant of lesbians and gay men, this has not led to an equally positive attitude on the part of the authorities. A majority of political parties has declared its support for lesbian and gay rights, but this has not yet been implemented by changes in legislation or official policies.

*Society*

A majority of the population is in favor of gay and lesbian rights. A representative European study shows, however, that 24 percent of Belgians objected to homosexuals as neighbors in 1992 (*European*, July 9–12, 1992).

*The Gay and/or Lesbian Movement*

In Flanders, the lesbian and gay movement is present in most cities, whereas this is not the case in the French-speaking part of the country. Therefore, many Dutch-speaking gay and lesbian groups exists, such as the "Federatie Werkgroepen Homoseksualiteit" (FWH), GOC, and "Roze Aktie Front." There are some French-speaking groups in Liège and Brussels, e.g., "Antenne Rose," where the ILGA Information Secretariat has its offices.

## Belize

*Official Attitudes and the Law*

Homosexual behavior between consenting adults is not mentioned in the law as being a criminal offense. Homosexuality was decriminalized in 1988.

*Society*

Homosexuality is taboo. There is no visible support for gay and lesbian rights.

## Benin

*Official Attitudes and the Law*

Homosexual behavior between consenting adults is not mentioned in the law as being a criminal offense.

*Society*

There is no visible support for gay and lesbian rights.

## Bermuda

*Official Attitudes and the Law*

Homosexual acts between men are illegal and can be punished by up to ten years imprisonment. Attempts at homosexual contacts can be punished with up to five years imprisonment under Section 175 of the Penal Code. Homosexual acts between women are not mentioned in the law. Homosexuals are often subjected to official (police) harassment and violence.

*Society*

There is no visible support for gay and lesbian rights.

## Bhutan

*Official Attitudes and the Law*

Homosexuality is illegal but not persecuted as long as it is closeted.

*Society*

There is no visible support for gay and lesbian rights.

## Bolivia

*Official Attitudes and the Law*

There is no legal information available.

*Society*

The attitude toward homosexuality is very hostile. There is no visible social support of gay and lesbian rights.

## Bosnia-Herzegovina

*Official Attitudes and the Law*

Homosexual acts were illegal in all of the former Yugoslavia until 1977. In 1976, the then federal government delegated the power to the republic to set the age of consent for sexual behavior. Homosexual acts between men are prohibited in Bosnia-Herzegovina under Section 93.2, which imposes a maximum penalty of one year imprisonment.

*Society*

Closeted homosexuality is tolerated, but it remains a taboo. A minority of the population is in favor of gay and lesbian rights.

## Botswana

*Official Attitudes and the Law*

There are no official laws against lesbians and gay men. "While the government does not have an official stand against such individuals [gays and lesbians], the society as a whole looks down on such acts and regards such practices as immoral, but does not necessarily mean it discriminates against those who indulge in them. They are merely regarded as 'perverts.' " (Excerpt of a letter from the embassy of Botswana in Oslo, 1987)

*Society*

There is no visible support for gay and lesbian rights

*The Gay and/or Lesbian Movement*

An informal group has contacts with the gay and lesbian movement in South Africa.

## Brazil

*Official Attitudes and the Law*

The age of consent for both homosexuals and heterosexuals is eighteen years. Homosexual behavior between consenting adults is not mentioned in the law as being a criminal offense, except for Section 235 of the military Penal Code, which criminalizes "indecent acts, homosexual or not," between soldiers. Although homosexuality is not illegal, the police use the pretext of "safeguarding morality and public decency" and "preventing outrageous behavior" to stop, arrest, and bring homosexuals to trial, whereas they would not bother heterosexuals in similar situations. Several cities have adopted anti-discrimination regulations which protect homosexuals.

*Society*

A minority of the population is in favor of gay and lesbian rights. There are, however, reports of more than 320 lesbians and gays being killed in the Bahia in the recent past because of their sexual orientation.

*The Gay and/or Lesbian Movement*

One group, "Grupo Gay de Bahia," has existed since 1983. "Triangulo Rosa" in Rio de Janeiro and "Lambda" in São Paulo are political lobbying groups. There are several other groups, some of which are lesbian. Since 1979, a lesbian information group (GALF) has been active; it publishes a quarterly magazine.

## Brunei

*Official Attitudes and the Law*

There is no legal information available.

*Society*

The attitude toward homosexuality is very hostile. There is no visible social support for gay and lesbian rights.

## Bulgaria

*Official Attitudes and the Law*

Homosexual behavior between consenting adults has not been illegal since 1968, but no legal protection against discrimination exists. Section 157 of the Penal Code, which applies to both gay men and lesbians, imposes some limitations. Homosexual acts with a person under the age of twenty-one, in public, or in a way that "causes scandal or entices others to perversity," are forbidden. Prison terms of up to five years are prescribed, as well as social opprobrium. The legal age of consent for heterosexuals is fourteen (Section 151).

## Society

Homosexuality is taboo. There is no visible support for gay and lesbian rights.

## The Gay and/or Lesbian Movement

Homosexuals started organizing in the context of AIDS prevention. The first group, not exclusively gay, "Stop AIDS," was founded in Sofia in 1991. Other groups are KIS-Contact, GEMINI, and BULGA.

## Burkina Faso

### Official Attitudes and the Law

Homosexual contacts with men or women under the age of twenty-one are illegal under Section 331 of the Penal Code and can be punished by up to three years of imprisonment. The age of consent for heterosexual contacts is thirteen years.

### Society

No public attention is paid to homosexuality. There is no visible social support for gay and lesbian rights.

## Burma/Myanmar

### Official Attitudes and the Law

There is no legal information available.

### Society

The attitude toward homosexuality is very hostile. There is no visible social support for gay and lesbian rights.

## Burundi

### Official Attitudes and the Law

There is no legal information available.

*Society*

The country is governed by the Tutsi tribe, for whom bisexual behavior is common although not discussed. There is no visible support for gay and lesbian rights.

## Cambodia

*Official Attitudes and the Law*

There is no legal information available.

*Society*

The attitude toward homosexuality is very hostile. There is no visible support for gay and lesbian rights.

## Cameroon

*Official Attitudes and the Law*

Homosexual behavior between consenting adults is not mentioned in the law as being a criminal offense. The protection of the rights of homosexuals is not considered part of overall human rights protection. On the contrary, the official attitude both of government and of an unspecified but substantial part of the population is negative.

*Society*

No public attention is paid to homosexuality. There is no visible social support for gay and lesbian rights.

## Canada

*Official Attitudes and the Law*

Canada is a federation of states (called provinces) with a federal parliament and government, and ten provincial assemblies and governments. Federal criminal law applies throughout the country. On January 1, 1988, new sexual offenses sections were enforced in Canada's Criminal Code. "Buggery" was eliminated as an offense; "anal intercourse" became legal between consenting adults of eighteen years and older. A new system based on age and power between the partners was adopted in the defining of sexual offenses.

Canada's anti-discrimination protection at the federal level came largely from the common law system. In 1982, the Canadian Charter of Rights and Freedoms was adopted by Parliament and constitutionally entrenched. Political controversy between the federal government and the provinces had delayed its adoption, the provinces complaining that their powers would be curtailed by such a sweeping piece of legislation.

Although sexual orientation is not specifically listed in the constitutional guarantee of equality, it is likely one of the enlisted grounds of discrimination that this provision forbids. In several court decisions, sexual orientation has been found to be covered by Section 15, although the Supreme Court of Canada has not yet ruled on the question.

On a federal level, discrimination against homosexuals still exists with respect to jobs in the Royal Canadian Mounted Police. In 1992, Canada abolished the ban on homosexuals in the armed forces, and asylum has been granted to several foreigners facing anti-gay persecution in their native countries, e.g., China.

In the provinces of Ontario, Quebec, Manitoba, British Columbia, Nova Scotia, and the Yukon, nondiscrimination provisions for homosexuals exist.

### Society

According to a Gallup poll in 1985, 70 percent of Canadians are in favor of equal rights legislation or nondiscrimination regulations for homosexuals. Quebec seems to be the most liberal province with regard to homosexual rights.

### The Gay and/or Lesbian Movement

In Canada, several active gay and lesbian groups exist, such as the Coalition for Lesbian and Gay Rights in Ontario, and the Pink Triangle Press.

## Cape Verde

### Official Attitudes and the Law

Homosexual behavior is de facto illegal. The Penal Code of 1886, inherited from the Portuguese, allows the imposition on those who perform "acts against nature" of a bail, or surety for good behavior, or freedom under supervision but with bail doubled for a second offense. Imprisonment is possible for repeat offenders. Homosexuals can also be punished for violation of Sections 390, 391, 405, and 406 of the Penal Code: "assaults on public or personal decency, prostitution, or the corruption of minors."

### Society

Homosexuality is ignored. No visible support for gay and lesbian rights exists.

## Cayman Islands

*Official Attitudes and the Law*

There is no specific information available. British legislation is applied.

*Society*

Homosexuality is ignored. No visible support for gay and lesbian rights exists.

## Central African Republic

*Official Attitudes and the Law*

Homosexual behavior between consenting adults is not mentioned in the law as being a criminal offense. The protection of the rights of homosexuals is not considered to be a part of overall human rights protection. The official attitude of the government is negative.

*Society*

Homosexuality is ignored. No visible support for gay and lesbian rights exists.

## Chad

*Official Attitudes and the Law*

Homosexual behavior between consenting adults is not mentioned in the law as being a criminal offense. The protection of the rights of homosexuals is not considered to be a part of overall human rights protection. The official attitude of the government is negative.

*Society*

Homosexuality is ignored. No visible support for gay and lesbian rights exists.

## Chile

*Official Attitudes and the Law*

On August 14, 1989, the Reform Act of the Constitution deleted the old Article 8 of the Constitution, which provided a legal provision for persecution of gays and lesbians. Nonetheless, male homosexual acts are still illegal. Article 365 of the Penal Code sanctions consenting male homosexual activity as a sodomy delict with a penalty of one and a half to three years' imprisonment. The penalty depends on the complaints of the "victim." Lesbian sexual contacts are not mentioned in the law. Homosexuals are often subjected to official and police harassment and violence. A policy exists of compulsory HIV testing of all known gay men.

## Society

Homosexuality is taboo. No visible support for gay and lesbian rights exists.

## The Gay and/or Lesbian Movement

Gay and lesbian groups exist but are illegal. In Santiago, a lesbian group called "Colectivo Ayuquelen" organized the first lesbian and gay meeting in Chile in 1987. In 1988, they received letters from right wing groups threatening to kill them.

## China

### Official Attitudes and the Law

Homosexual behavior between consenting adults is not mentioned in the law as being a criminal offense. There are reports about homosexuals being imprisoned on specious grounds, such as Section 158 of the Penal Code, which penalizes "disturbance against the social order" with up to five years in jail. In the large-scale campaign "against crime" several homosexuals were arrested.

All visitors from Hong Kong, Taiwan, and Macau now have to present a certificate of HIV-negativity before they can enter the country, and reports exist of homosexuals being subjected with electric shock "therapy" to cure them.

In April 1992, the Chinese ministry of public security concluded that there were no legal reasons to separate lesbians who were living together.

### Society

Homosexuality, or *Tongxinglain* (same-sex love), is considered to be a "foreigners' disease," according to press reports. The November 16, 1990, issue of the newspaper *Wen Wei Po* revealed that half a percent of married men in China's cities (as opposed to two percent in rural areas) have had gay sex. No visible support for gay and lesbian rights exists. Homosexual men have fled the country and have been accepted in (e.g.) Australia as political refugees on the grounds of fear of prosecution because of their sexual preference. In 1991, research on homosexual behavior started to take place.

### The Gay and/or Lesbian Movement

In 1992, the first underground gay group was started in Suzhou. In 1993, the first openly gay bar was allowed to open in Beijing.

## Colombia

*Official Attitudes and the Law*

Homosexual behavior between consenting adults is not mentioned in the law as being a criminal offense. A statute, which stated that homosexuality was behavior in contradiction with the dignity of Justice, was overruled by the Supreme Court of Justice as contrary to the Constitution. Theoretically, officials in Colombia can be homosexual. The law authorizes detention for three days without access to a lawyer and without being able to telephone outside. Jailed homosexuals and transvestites are interned in separate facilities to avoid rape and killings.

*Society*

Society in general has a negative attitude toward homosexuality. Reports of violence, kidnapings, and murders have been received. Extremist death squads target homosexuals. No visible support for gay and lesbian rights exists.

*The Gay and/or Lesbian Movement*

The group "Colectivo de Orgullo Gay," which used to edit the publication *El Ambiente,* has reorganized as part of the "Colectivo de 28 de junio." They publish a new magazine called *Urania.* There are also informal groups in Bogotá and Medellin.

## Comoros

*Official Attitudes and the Law*

There is no legal information available.

*Society*

There is no visible support for gay and lesbian rights.

## Congo

*Official Attitudes and the Law*

Homosexual behavior between consenting adults is not mentioned in the law as being a criminal offense. The Embassy of the Congo in Brussels stated on April 13, 1987, that "the practice of homosexuality does not exist in the Congo."

*Society*

Homosexuality is ignored. No visible support for gay and lesbian rights exists.

## Cook Islands

*Official Attitudes and the Law*

Male homosexual acts are illegal. Section 206 of the Penal Code prohibits "buggery," with a maximum penalty of ten years imprisonment. Section 207 criminalizes attempted "buggery" and "indecent assault" among men, with a maximum penalty of five years imprisonment. According to Section 207.2 it is no defense to state that the partner consented. No information on the legal position of lesbians is available.

*Society*

There is no visible support for gay and lesbian rights.

## Costa Rica

*Official Attitudes and the Law*

Homosexual acts are not mentioned in the law as being a criminal offense. Police raids are irregularly reported to take place in San José.

*Society*

Closeted homosexuality is tolerated. A minority of the population is in favor of gay and lesbian rights.

*The Gay and/or Lesbian Movement*

The "Communidad Ecuméncia de Fe" is a group based on the "Theology of Liberation." A lesbian group called "Las Entendidas," a self-help organization, was founded in 1987. In 1993, the "Colectivo Gay Universitario," the ALCS, the GGLFC, and the "Grupo Diferentes" were members of the ILGA. Furthermore, informal gay and lesbian groups exist; openly gay men and lesbians are active within AIDS organizations.

## Croatia

*Official Attitudes and the Law*

Homosexual acts have been illegal in all of the former Yugoslavia until 1977. In 1976, the then federal government delegated the power to the republic to set the age of consent for sexual behavior. In Croatia, homosexual acts between consenting individuals under eighteen years are illegal; among heterosexuals the age of consent is fourteen.

*Society*

Closeted homosexuality is tolerated. Social attitudes toward homosexuality are improving. Homosexuality is dealt with in magazines and newspapers and it is relatively well tolerated. A minority of the population is in favor of gay and lesbian rights.

*The Gay and/or Lesbian Movement*

Several lesbian and gay groups exist in Croatia, such as Klub 1991 and LIGMA ("Lesbian and Gay Men in Action") in Zagreb. There is a magazine called *Revolver*.

## Cuba

*Official Attitudes and the Law*

Homosexual behavior is illegal. Article 303-a of the Penal Code of April 30, 1988, sanctions it as a "public scandal" with three months to one year of imprisonment, or a fine of one hundred to three hundred *cuotas* for "people persistently bothering others with homosexual amorous advances." Homosexuals are often subjected to official (police) harassment and violence.

*Society*

Society is hostile to homosexuality. Many homosexuals try to emigrate from Cuba, because an openly gay and lesbian life is not possible there. There is no visible social support for gay and lesbian rights.

## Cyprus

*Official Attitudes and the Law*

Homosexual acts between women are not mentioned in the law. Homosexual acts between men are illegal under Section 171 of the Penal Code, with a maximum penalty of five years. "Attempts to commit" homosexual acts between men can be punished with three years' imprisonment. There have been prosecutions under this section.

*Society*

Society is very intolerant. The Greek Orthodox archbishop of Cyprus condemned homosexuality in his Christmas message of 1990: he stated that he would excommunicate known homosexuals. There is no visible social support for gay and lesbian rights.

*The Gay and/or Lesbian Movement*

In 1989, the president of the Gay Liberation Movement of Cyprus, Alexander Modinos, challenged Articles 171–174 of the Penal Code in an application to the European Commission of Human Rights in Strasbourg. In 1991, the Commission concluded that the anti-homosexual legislation of Cyprus is a clear violation of Article 8 of the European Convention on Human Rights (the right to private and family life). The Commission has now brought the case before the European Court of Human Rights in Strasbourg.

## Czechia

*Official Attitudes and the Law*

Homosexual behavior between consenting adults is not mentioned in the law as being a criminal offense. The Penal Code Amendment of May 2, 1990, has repealed the provisions of Section 244 of the Penal Code of Czechoslovakia prohibiting homosexual acts with persons under the age of eighteen; this has been applicable to both men and women. Since then, the age of consent for both homo- and heterosexuals is fifteen years (Section 242). Proposals of law to regulate gay and lesbian relationships and to protect against discrimination on the basis of sexual orientation have been made in the former Czech and Slovak Federal Republican Parliament. According to Articles 189 and 190 of the Penal Code, it is an offense to intentionally or unintentionally to spread a life-threatening disease; this has special relevance to the spread of HIV/AIDS.

*Society*

Of the former Communist countries in Europe, the position for homosexuals is probably among the best in Czechia, although still only closeted homosexuality is tolerated. Social attitudes toward homosexuality are improving. A minority of the population is in favor of gay and lesbian rights.

*The Gay and/or Lesbian Movement*

Several gay and lesbian groups exist; "Svaz Lambda" publishes its own magazine. In February 1990, the movement for equal rights for gay men and lesbians, "Hnuti za rovnoprávnost homosexualnich obcanu," organized the first gay and lesbian demonstration in Prague. On June 23–24, 1990, a national body of gay/lesbian groups was formed called SOHO. A gay representative, a member of "Svaz Lambda," was appointed to the National AIDS Committee. In 1991, "Svaz Lambda" organized an Eastern European ILGA meeting to initiate gay and lesbian cooperation in former Communist countries.

**Denmark**

*Official Attitudes and the Law*

Legal protection against discrimination based on sexual preference exists. Since 1976, the uniform age of consent for homo- and heterosexual contacts has been fifteen years. Since 1979, it has been possible for homosexuals to be called up or enlist in the armed forces. Since 1986, homosexual couples have been recognized in inheritance tax legislation. In 1987, the ground of "sexual orientation" was added to the anti-discrimination clause in the Penal Code (Article 266) and to the Anti-Discrimination Act of 1971. According Article 266b of the Penal Code, as amended in 1987, it is illegal "to utter publicly or deliberately, for the dissemination in a wider circle, a statement or another remark, by which a group of people are threatened, derided, or humiliated on account of their sexual orientation." Homosexuality has not been regarded as an illness since 1981, according to the classification of diseases of the Ministry of Health.

Since 1989, it has been legally possible for homosexuals to engage in "registered partnership." This has a status similar to marriage as an institution recognized by the state. This means, for example, that homosexuals can enjoy the same rights of community of property and inheritance as married spouses. The "registered partnership" does not allow the homosexual couple to adopt children, however, and in this respect it has been noted that homosexuals have not yet obtained completely equal status with heterosexuals.

According to article 9(1) of the Aliens Act, a residence permit will be issued to a foreigner living with a person permanently residing in Denmark in a "cohabitation of prolonged duration" of at least two years. This is not required for registered partners, one of whom, however, has to have Danish citizenship.

*Society*

Society is generally tolerant toward homosexuality. The majority of the population is in favor of gay and lesbian rights. According to a representative European study, only 12 percent of the Danish object to homosexuals as neighbors.

*The Gay and/or Lesbian Movement*

Since 1948, there has been a national lesbian and gay organization, now called "Foreningen for bøsser og lesbiske" (Association for Gays and Lesbians: LBL/ F-48), with nine local branches throughout the country. There are also other gay and lesbian groups, especially in the big cities.

## Djibouti

*Official Attitudes and the Law*

There is no legal information available.

*Society*

The attitude toward homosexuality is very hostile. There is no visible social support for gay and lesbian rights.

## Dominica

*Official Attitudes and the Law*

There is no legal information available.

*Society*

There is no visible support for gay and lesbian rights.

## Dominican Republic

*Official Attitudes and the Law*

Homosexual behavior between consenting adults is not mentioned in the law as being a criminal offense. However, laws regarding "offenses against morality" and "corruption of minors" are used particularly against gay men. Homosexuals are often subjected to official (police) harassment and violence.

*Society*

Social attitudes are hostile to homosexuality. Homosexuals in prison are treated badly. A minority of the population is in favor of gay and lesbian rights.

*The Gay and/or Lesbian Movement*

There are two known groups: "Colectivo de Lesbianas Feministas," which started in 1985 and publishes a magazine *Pezones* four times a year, and a mainly male group called "Nosotros," which started in 1987.

## Ecuador

*Official Attitudes and the Law*

Homosexual behavior is illegal. Homosexual acts can be punished with up to eight years' imprisonment, under Article 516 of the Penal Code, eight years for the "aggressor" in cases of force or violence, four to eight years for both parties in the case of consenting adults. Homosexuals are often subjected to official (police) harassment and violence. In 1991, twenty gay men were killed by death squads.

## Society

Homosexuality has been treated in the press in a very hostile manner. An opinion poll held on January 6, 1989, showed that 75 percent in Quito and 52 percent in Guayguil do not tolerate homosexuality. No visible support for gay and lesbian rights

## The Gay and/or Lesbian Movement

Individual gay men and lesbians are organized around the issue of AIDS. SOGA ("Sociedad General Ayuda Inmediata") was founded in 1988. The group is involved with AIDS prevention work and in AIDS education. They are also active political lobbyists.

# Egypt

## Official Attitudes and the Law

Homosexual behavior between consenting adults is not mentioned in the law as being a criminal offense.

## Society

Homosexuality cannot be discussed openly. Traditional standards of marriage and child rearing are valued highly. Still, it is possible to have homosexual contacts, if discretely. There is no visible social support for gay and lesbian rights.

## The Gay and/or Lesbian Movement

Informal gay and lesbian groups exist in Cairo and Alexandria.

# El Salvador

## Official Attitudes and the Law

Homosexual behavior between consenting adults is not mentioned in the law as being a criminal offense.

## Society

In urban areas a more liberal attitude toward homosexuality exists.

*The Gay and/or Lesbian Movement*

There are reports of a gay group and magazine founded in 1991.

## Equatorial Guinea

*Official Attitudes and the Law*

The protection of the rights of homosexuals is not considered to be a part of human rights protection. The official attitude of the government is negative.

*Society*

The majority of the population is against equal rights for homosexuals. There is no visible social support for gays and lesbians.

## Estonia

*Official Attitudes and the Law*

Under Soviet legislation, Article 118 of the Estonian Penal Code prohibited anal intercourse between men. This was repealed by the Estonian parliament in April 1992, establishing an equal age of consent of sixteen for both homo- and hetero-sexuals.

*Society*

Closeted homosexuality is tolerated. The first congress on homosexuality in the former Soviet Union was held in Tallinn in 1990, with support from the Estonian Academy of Sciences. This meeting received large and positive media coverage.

*The Gay and/or Lesbian Movement*

Several gay and lesbian groups exist in Tallinn, such as ELU (Estonian Lesbian Union). Gay men and lesbians have started to organize in the context of fighting HIV/AIDS.

## Ethiopia

*Official Attitudes and the Law*

Homosexual acts between men and between women are illegal under Sections 600 and 601 of the Penal Code, with a penalty of "simple imprisonment" from ten days to three years, with the possibility of increasing the penalty with five years or more. This depends on whether the offender takes advantage of a po-sition of authority in order to exercise influence over the other person, or whether the offender "makes a profession of such activities." The maximum term of imprisonment is ten years where the offender uses violence, intimidation or coercion, trickery or fraud, or if he takes unfair advantage of the victim's inability to offer resistance; where the offender subjects his victim to acts of cruelty or sadism; where the offender transmits a venereal disease with which he knows himself to be infected; where the adult offender commits the offense with a person under fifteen years; or where the victim is driven to suicide by distress, shame, or despair.

### Society

There is no visible support for gay and lesbian rights exists.

### Falklands

#### Official Attitudes and the Law

There is no specific legal information. British legislation is applied.

#### Society

There is no visible support for gay and lesbian rights.

### Fiji Islands

#### Official Attitudes and the Law

Male homosexual acts are illegal. Section 168 of the Penal Code punishes "carnal knowledge against the order of nature" with a maximum penalty of fourteen years' imprisonment, possibly combined with corporal punishment. Section 169 criminalizes "attempts to carnal knowledge against the order of nature and indecent assaults" with a maximum penalty of seven years' imprisonment, possibly combined with corporal punishment. Section 170 prohibits acts of "gross indecency" between males in private or public with a maximum penalty of five years' imprisonment, also possibly combined with corporal punishment. No information on the legal position of lesbians is available.

#### Society

There is no visible support for gay and lesbian rights.

## Finland

*Official Attitudes and the Law*

Homosexual behavior between consenting adults is not mentioned in the law as being a criminal offense. The age of consent for homosexual acts is eighteen years, whereas that for heterosexual acts is sixteen years.

Officially there is no discrimination against homosexuals. However, Article 9 (as amended in 1971) of Chapter 20 of the Penal Code reads as follows:

> If someone publicly engages in an act violating sexual morality, thereby giving offense, he shall be sentenced for publicly violating sexual morality to imprisonment for at most six months or to a fine.
>
> If someone publicly encourages unchastity between persons of the same sex, he/she shall be sentenced for incitement of unchastity between members of the same sex as mentioned in Subsection 1 for at least six months and at the most four years.

With respect to social security, the government recognizes (in some cases) homosexual relationships in the area of social benefits. Meanwhile, as regards the law of inheritance, the death duty is three times higher than for married persons.

Since 1991, a renewal of the Finnish criminal law has been under discussion in Parliament. Part of this renewal concerns discrimination on the basis of sexual orientation.

*Society*

According to an international comparative study done by Gallup Fennica (1990) about "world values," in September 1990, 33 percent of the Finnish population disapproved of homosexuality, as compared with 56 percent in 1981 and 53 percent in 1986. Still only a minority of the population is explicitly in favor of gay and lesbian rights.

*The Gay and/or Lesbian Movement*

The Finnish national gay and lesbian organization is called SETA.

## France

*Official Attitudes and the Law*

Since 1982, homosexuality has not been mentioned in the Penal Code. Legal protection against discrimination of homosexuals exists: on July 25, 1985, the prohibition of discrimination (Articles 187-1, 187-2, 416, and 416-1 of the Penal

Code) was expanded to discrimination on grounds of "moral habits," which includes homosexuality. In 1986 and 1990, the Code of Labor Law was amended to prohibit discrimination on similar grounds (Articles 122-35 and 122-45), including the civil service and armed forces. On July 12, 1990, such AIDS-related topics as "state of health" and "handicap" were added to the Penal Code as revised in 1985.

*Gai Pied,* France's major gay magazine, was banned in May 1987 on the grounds of a 1949 law for the protection of minors, but the ban was reversed in the face of public outcry. Reports have been received about secret services tapping telephones and infiltrating the gay movement in connection with the murder of Pasteur Doucé, a gay activist, in 1991.

In the spring of 1991, conservative members in the Senate tried to raise the age of consent for homosexual contacts from fifteen to eighteen years, "as part of AIDS-prevention." This was strongly put down in the Assemblée (House of Representatives). Only married foreign partners can obtain a partner-dependent residence permit. There is a growing tendency to recognize same-sex couples living together, the *certificat de concubinage,* which can be obtained from the local authorities. In Parliament proposals for "contracts of civil partnership" were introduced in 1990 and 1991.

## Society

On the basis of public opinion polls, society can be said to be tolerant, with the majority of the population being in favor of gay and lesbian rights. According to a representative European study, 24 percent of the French objects to homosexuals as neighbors.

## The Gay and/or Lesbian Movement

There are several groups active on both a national and local level. Groups organized along professional (architects, physicians), religious (Christians), or political (socialists, liberals) lines also exist. The "Mouvement d'Information et d'Expression des Lesbiennes" (MIEL) is mainly active in Paris. There are active professional gay organizations, e.g., the radio station *Fréquence Gai;* the AIDS organization AIDES; the lobby group "Projet Ornicar"; and the weekly magazine *Gai Pied,* which, however, ceased to exist at the end of 1992. *Lesbia* is the largest lesbian magazine. In July 1992, participants in the world conference of the ILGA demonstrated in front of the Mexican Embassy to demand investigations into the murders of gay activists taking place in Mexico; the Paris police used force to break up the demonstration.

## French Guyana

*Official Attitudes and the Law*

There is no specific legal information. French legislation is applied.

*Society*

There is no visible social support for gay and lesbian rights.

## French Polynesia/Tahiti

*Official Attitudes and the Law*

There is no specific legal information. French legislation is applied.

*Society*

In this group of islands there is a social phenomenon known as *mahu*: a man, only one in each village, who is raised as a girl and acts like a woman. The Christian church has vigorously opposed this, but the tradition remains. Since the 1950s there have also been *raeraes,* male transvestite prostitutes, who emerged when the tourist industry started. A minority of the population is in favor of gay and lesbian rights.

## Gabon

*Official Attitudes and the Law*

Homosexual behavior between consenting adults is not mentioned in the law as being a criminal offense.

*Society*

The attitude toward homosexuality is very hostile. There is no visible social support for gay and lesbian rights.

## Gambia

*Official Attitudes and the Law*

There is no legal information available.

*Society*

The attitude toward homosexuality is very hostile. There is no visible social support for gay and lesbian rights.

## Georgia

### Official Attitudes and the Law

In the former Soviet Union, anal intercourse between men was illegal. This prohibition is still incorporated in the Penal Code of Georgia. Homosexual acts between women are not mentioned in the law, nor is homosexual behavior between consenting adults explicitly included in the law as being a criminal offense.

### Society

The attitude of society is hostile. Homosexuality is taboo. There is no visible support for gay and lesbian rights.

## Germany

### Official Attitudes and the Law

Homosexual behavior between consenting adults is not mentioned in the law as being a criminal offense. The age of consent for homosexual acts between men was eighteen in West Germany (the Federal Republic of Germany, FRG) according to Article 175 of the Penal Code. The maximum penalty for violation was five years' imprisonment. The general minimum age for heterosexual and lesbian sex was fourteen years according to Article 176 of the Penal Code. The age of consent in East Germany (The former German Democratic Republic, GDR) was, since 1989, fourteen years for everybody according to Article 148 of the Penal Code of the former GDR. Since October 3, 1990, when the territory of the former GDR was integrated in the FRG, the GDR laws on homosexuality have remained in force (for the time being) in the eastern part of the country, and the FRG laws on homosexuality in the western part. The government of the united Germany announced plans to introduce a new general age of consent of fourteen years.

While the former GDR Parliament (*Volkskammer*) was still willing to discuss the possibility of having a gay and lesbian partnership law, this has been given very low priority in the Federal German Parliament (*Bundestag*). In the meantime, unmarried cohabitation (*nichteheliche Lebensgemeinschaft*) of same-sex couples has been recognized for various legal purposes. A foreign same-sex partner may obtain a residence permit according to the Aliens Law of 1991 if "necessary to avoid extraordinary hardship."

The 1992 constitution of *Land* Brandenburg (surrounding Berlin) mentions sexual orientation as one of the forbidden grounds for discrimination. Homosexuals are allowed to serve in the military, but are not considered to be suitable for senior positions in the armed forces. Landlords are allowed to refuse same-sex couples as tenants, but cannot terminate a tenancy contract on the grounds that a partner of the same sex has moved in to live with the tenant.

In August 1992, more than 250 gay and lesbian couples submitted marriage applications in over 50 German cities in an attempted mass wedding, but all the applications have been rejected.

## Society

On the basis of public opinion polls, society can be called moderately tolerant. The majority of the population is in favor of gay and lesbian rights. However, there is a sharp increase in physical violence against gay men and lesbians in the *Länder* of the former GDR, related to growing support for neofacist and ultranationalist groups. According to a representative European study done in 1992, 34 percent of the Germans objects to homosexuals as neighbors.

## The Gay and/or Lesbian Movement

Currently there exist about fifty gay and lesbian groups, especially in the big cities. There are two national homosexual organizations, called "Bundesverband Homosexualität" (BVH), and "Schwulenverband in Deutschland" (SVD). Many universities have gay and lesbian student groups "ASTA Lesben- und Schwulen-referat." The city of Berlin has a department for gay and lesbian affairs, and supports the "Magnus Hirschfeld Institut" named after one of the most important founders of the international gay and lesbian movement. Religious gay men and lesbians founded the organization "Homosexuelle und Kirche" (HuK). One of the most important German gay magazines is *Magnus.*

# Ghana

## Official Attitudes and the Law

Homosexual behavior is illegal. Homosexual acts between men are punishable under sections concerning assault and rape, if one of those involved makes a formal complaint. Homosexual acts with minors are always punishable. In 1992, reports reached us of torture and imprisonment of gay men.

## Society

The Ghanese seem to look at sexuality without considering it a taboo. If partners are discreet, homosexual contacts are tolerated. There is no visible social support for gay and lesbian rights.

## The Gay and/or Lesbian Movement

GLG (Gay Liberation Group) is thought to be the first group in West Africa.

## Great Britain and Northern Ireland

*Official Attitudes and the Law*

Homosexual behavior between consenting adults is not mentioned in the law as being a criminal offense. Homosexual acts between women are not mentioned in the law. Homosexual acts between men are permitted, only if they take place privately, between not more than two men, outside the armed forces and the merchant navy, and between partners who are over twenty-one. In *England and Wales,* this is provided for in the Sexual Offences Act of 1967. In *Scotland,* this is stated in the Criminal Justice Act of 1980. In *Northern Ireland,* this is regulated in the Homosexual Offences Order of 1982. *The Channel Islands and the Isle of Man* decriminalized homosexual acts between consenting adult men in 1983 and 1992, respectively. *Gibraltar* still has a total prohibition on homosexual acts between men, despite the judgments of the European Court of Human Rights in Strasbourg in the *Dudgeon* (1981) and *Norris* (1988) cases. The age of consent for heterosexual and lesbian acts is sixteen.

The Army Act 1955, Section 66; the Air Force Act 1955; and the Naval Discipline Act 1957 allow for a penalty of two years for "disgraceful conduct of a cruel, indecent or unnatural kind." The police use agents provocateurs to entrap gay men and charge them with "soliciting" or "gross violation of public decency." In 1988, a new discriminatory law was passed (Section 28 of the Local Government Act of 1988): it states that local authorities shall not "intentionally promote homosexuality" and shall not "promote the teaching in any maintained school of the acceptability of homosexuality as a pretended family relationship."

According to immigration rules, a homosexual partner cannot be allowed to enter or to stay in the country, on the basis of his or her relationship with a U.K. citizen. In 1990, an effort to restrict the access of lesbians to artificial insemination failed in Parliament. A proposal in spring 1991 to take away legal parental rights of homosexual parents has been rejected in Parliament. Fostering by gay and lesbian couples is legally possible and dependent on social services departments of local authorities.

In 1992, the government announced that it would stop enforcing the criminal laws against homosexuality in the armed forces. However, homosexuality continues to be a bar to employment in the armed forces. Until 1992, homosexuality was also a bar to appointment to senior positions in the Civil Services and to diplomatic positions.

Prime Minister John Major announced a change in policy in 1992: homosexuals should no longer be excluded from official positions. The Home Office wrote in April 1992: "The Government's view is that discrimination against any minority is unacceptable and this is reflected in its policies on employment in the Civil Service. However, the Government is not persuaded of the need for specific legislation in this area, nor does it directly monitor discrimination of the grounds of sexual orientation."

In 1992, the court of appeals in London upheld the convictions against five men found guilty of sadomasochistic sex with consenting adults and sentenced to up to four and a half years in prison.

## Society

The general attitude is still intolerant. A minority of the population is in favor of gay and lesbian rights. According to a representative European study done in 1992, 31 percent of the British and 48 percent of the Northern Irish object to homosexuals as neighbors, the latter being the second-highest percentage in Western Europe.

## The Gay and/or Lesbian Movement

There are national organizations in England ("Campaign for Homosexual Equality," CHE), Scotland ("Scottish Homosexual Rights Group," SHRG) and Northern Ireland ("Northern Irish Gay Rights Association," NIGRA). Other nationwide organizations are the Gay and Lesbian Humanist Association (GALHA) and the gay and lesbian lobby group, "Stonewall." There are also several other local groups. The main periodicals are *Gay Times* and *Capital Gay*.

## Greece

### Official Attitudes and the Law

Homosexual behavior between consenting adults is not mentioned in the law as being a criminal offense. Since 1987, the age of consent for homo- and hetero- sexual contacts has been fifteen years. Several articles of the Penal Code indirectly refer to homosexuality (e.g., Article 347). Homosexuals are not allowed to serve in the navy. In 1981, a bill called "Protection against Venereal Disease" was passed, containing the clause that homosexual men should have themselves regularly examined. There are reports that this law has been used to harass homosexuals.

### Society

The media is changing its attitude toward homosexuality, which means that the negative tone is slowly disappearing. There are no police raids any more in gay/ lesbian meeting places. A minority of the population is in favor of gay and lesbian rights.

*The Gay and/or Lesbian Movement*

There are gay and lesbian groups in the big cities. The best known are **AKOE** and **EOK**. In Greece two gay magazines are published. In 1991, the editor of *Amphi* was sentenced to five months in jail for publishing "indecent materials."

## Grenada

*Official Attitudes and the Law*

There is no legal information available.

*Society*

There is no visible support for gay and lesbian rights.

## Guadeloupe

*Official Attitudes and the Law*

There is no specific legal information. French legislation is applied.

*Society*

There is no visible support for gay and lesbian rights.

## Guatemala

*Official Attitudes and the Law*

Homosexual behavior between consenting adults is not mentioned in the law as being a criminal offense. Homosexuals are often subjected to official and police harassment and violence.

*Society*

Homosexuality is seen as a "moral deficiency, abnormal, and unnatural." There is some social support for gay and lesbian rights.

## Guinea

*Official Attitudes and the Law*

There is no legal information available.

*Society*

The attitude toward homosexuality is very hostile. There is no visible social support for gay and lesbian rights.

## Guinea Bissau

*Official Attitudes and the Law*

There is no legal information available.

*Society*

The attitude toward homosexuality is very hostile. There is no visible social support for gay and lesbian rights.

## Guyana

*Official Attitudes and the Law*

Homosexual behavior is illegal. Section 351 of the Criminal Law Offenses Act criminalizes acts of "gross indecency" in private or public, and attempts to enforce this with up to two years' imprisonment. Section 352 punishes "attempted buggery" with ten years' imprisonment, whereas "buggery" itself is punishable with life imprisonment, under Section 353 of the same Penal Code. Homosexuals are often subjected to official (police) harassment and violence.

*Society*

There is no visible support for gay and lesbian rights.

## Haiti

*Official Attitudes and the Law*

Homosexual behavior between consenting adults is not mentioned in the law as being a criminal offense.

*Society*

Homosexuality is taboo. There is no visible social support for gay and lesbian rights.

## Honduras

### Official Attitudes and the Law

Homosexual behavior between consenting adults is not mentioned in the law as being a criminal offense. According to Section 60 of the Honduran constitution, every citizen has equal rights and every act of discrimination violating human dignity is punishable. In the Penal Code of March 1985 there is no mention of homosexuality. The Honduran Embassy in The Hague stated March 20, 1987, that "no legal protection of homosexuals is necessary."

### Society

There is no visible support for gay and lesbian rights.

## Hong Kong

### Official Attitudes and the Law

Homosexual behavior was illegal until 1991. "Buggery" was punishable under the English law of 1885, with life imprisonment. The law of 1861 provided for "other abominable or unnatural offenses," with a maximum penalty of ten years' imprisonment. The Hong Kong Legislative Council voted 31 to 13 in July 1990 to lift penal sanctions on homosexual relations between consenting adults.

### Society

Harsh police enforcement has been reported. No protection existed against being dismissed from one's job for being gay. There is no visible social support for gay and lesbian rights.

### The Gay and/or Lesbian Movement

A gay group exists, called "Hong Kong Ten Percent Club." The Hong Kong gay and lesbian film festival is well known.

## Hungary

### Official Attitudes and the Law

Homosexual behavior between consenting adults is not mentioned in the law as being a criminal offense. Between 1961 and 1978, the age of consent for same-sex relations was twenty. Since 1978, Section 199 of the Penal Code has stipulated a (higher) age of consent for gay men and lesbians (eighteen) than for heterosexuals (fourteen, according to Section 201). The prison term warranted for a violation of Section 199 is as much as three years. In March 1992, the Budapest police confiscated several lists with names of homosexuals during a raid on the gay magazine *Masok*. Pink files are reportedly being administered by the police, and are perceived as instrumental in the context of contract tracing policies.

## Society

Closeted homosexuality is tolerated. Society is predominantly intolerant toward homosexuality although the situation is improving. The Hungarian government was the first of the Central and Eastern European countries to officially recognize a gay and lesbian association, "Homeros Lambda," in 1988. Only a minority of the population is in favor of gay and lesbian rights.

## The Gay and/or Lesbian Movement

In January 1988, a spokesman of the Ministry of Health and Social Affairs announced that the authorities would allow the founding of a gay and lesbian organization. This group, called "Homeros Lambda" (Homoszexuálisok Szabadidós és Egészségvédó Egyesülete = Homosexual Association for Leisure and Health Protection), had applied for official recognition in October 1987. In May 1988, the group's constituent general assembly took place. However, after initial success, disagreements inside the group caused it to fall apart. At the moment there are several groups in Budapest, in Györ and Veszperem, but contact between them is rare.

There is, however, a degree of tolerance and understanding in regard to the AIDS crisis: men who have had homosexual contacts are not obliged to be tested on HIV-antibodies and the AIDS group in Budapest, "AIDS-Segély (AIDS-Help), is very successful in the fields of medical advice and professional counseling. However, gay men are allegedly being forced to undergo an HIV-antibodies test in the context of tracing programs.

## Iceland

### Official Attitudes and the Law

The Icelandic Parliament legislated in July 1992 an age of consent of fourteen years for all its citizens, replacing the age of consent of eighteen for male homosexual acts (the Icelandic Criminal Law No. 19/1940, Art. 203, 204, and 207), and sixteen for lesbian and heterosexual acts.

### Society

Only a minority of the population is in favor of gay and lesbian rights, although this social repression of homosexuals is decreasing. According to a representative European study, 20 percent of the inhabitants object to homosexuals as neighbors.

*The Gay and/or Lesbian Movement*

Since 1978, there has been a national organization for homosexual men and women, called "Samtöking '78," which publishes a magazine. Another (monthly) magazine, *Bleikt & Blatt* (*Pink and Blue*), is also being published.

## India

*Official Attitudes and the Law*

Homosexual acts between men are illegal under Section 377 of the Penal Code, which criminalizes "carnal intercourse against the order of nature with man, woman, or animal," with a maximum penalty of life imprisonment or a fine. There are reports of raids by the police in Bombay, with homosexuals being arrested for no other reason than that they "look like" homosexuals. The punishment is a 25 rupee fine and/or a beating with laths on the road outside the police station.

*Society*

Open homosexuality is not accepted, although tolerated are the homosexual transvestites (*Heiras*) who act as dancers and entertainers in the major cities. There is no visible social support of gay and lesbian rights.

*The Gay and/or Lesbian Movement*

Lib India has groups in New Delhi, Bombay, and Calcutta. In Bombay there is a fairly well organized gay scene, and a gay magazine *Bombay Dost.* In Calcutta, the magazine *Gay Scene* is published. Most lesbians prefer to join feminist groups, but in New Delhi a lesbian group started in 1992, called SAKHI.

## Indonesia

*Official Attitudes and the Law*

Homosexual behavior between consenting adults is not mentioned in the law as being a criminal offense. The Indonesian Embassy in The Hague replied to our questionnaire on March 13, 1987, that "there is not any mentioning of homosexuals, lesbians, or heterosexuals concerning Indonesian legislation." Nevertheless, there are reports of police raids and violent police actions against homosexual men.

*Society*

The (Islamic) majority of the population is very hostile to open homosexuality, but closeted homosexual acts are tolerated. A more positive attitude toward closeted homosexuality can be found on the island of Bali. A minority of the population is in favor of gay and lesbian rights.

## The Gay and/or Lesbian Movement

There is a federation of lesbian and gay groups in Indonesia, called "Lambda Indonesia." The group KKLGN/GAYA publishes the magazine *Nusantara*. In 1992, the "Indonesian Gay Society" was founded in Yogyakarta.

# Iran

## Official Attitudes and the Law

Homosexual behavior is illegal. The Embassy of Iran in The Hague replied to our questionnaire on March 27, 1987, that "homosexuality in Iran, treated according to the Islamic law, is a sin in the eyes of God and a crime for society. In Islam generally, homosexuality is among the worst possible sins you can imagine."

In the Islamic Republic of Iran the *Sharia* (Islamic law) is applied. The government is forced to punish "unwanted attempts," e.g., to undermine sexual norms. Homosexuality is considered a sin which has to be punished severely. It is not necessary that a complaint be put to the authorities; a judge is allowed to take action by himself.

The Islamic Penal Code, which came into force on August 25, 1982, deals with homosexuality in Articles 139–156. Two concepts are used often in the articles:

1) *Hodood,* in Islamic Law "as an order of God," exactly describes punishments, e.g., whipping, chopping off of hands and feet, and stoning.

2) *Ta'zir* (*Ta'azirat*), are punishments that do not fall under the Sharia. A judge is authorized to decide on what sentences to the prosecuted person. Examples include imprisonment, fines, and whipping. The punishments are less severe than those of the *Hodood*. A distinction is made as to age and different forms of homosexuality. A minor will receive a *Ta'zir* while an adult (if homosexual intercourse is proven) will be sentenced to death. If sexual acts without intercourse are proven, the punishment will be 100 lashes. If the crime has been repeated, the accused will be sentenced to death after being convicted for the fourth time.

There are three ways of introducing evidence in an Islamic court of law:

1) The accused (if of sound mind) can declare four times that he was involved, voluntarily and intentionally, in homosexual acts.

2) Four "eyewitnesses" can declare that they have seen the accused engaged in homosexual acts.

3) The judge can decide upon the evidence that lies before him.

The first two forms of evidence, which are in practice difficult to obtain, are typical examples of a traditional Islamic furnishing of proof. The "knowledge of the judge" as evidence in a *Hodood* is new. This was probably created to obtain more "evidence" if the first two methods were not enough.

According to Article 156, if the accused "regrets" his acts before personal evidence is given, the *Hodood* is not applied; if "regret" comes afterwards, then this is not possible.

Possibilities for appeal are reduced substantially in the Iranian law system; only if the court was not authorized to handle the case in the first place, is appeal possible.

Defending the accused was dangerous, in the first few years after the revolution, for the advocate involved. It is unclear whether this has changed in recent years.

In practice, people are rarely prosecuted solely for being homosexual. Evidence is very difficult to get. The number of times one actively demonstrates homosexual feelings decides whether society and the authorities will prosecute or not.

At present, there is no active prosecution policy by the Iranian government, although prosecution of homosexual identity and/or acts is possible, and did take place more systematically in the first years after the revolution.

### Society

The social position of gay men, lesbians, and women in general conflicts with the human right of self-determination. There is no visible social support for gay and lesbian rights.

## Iraq

### Official Attitudes and the Law

Homosexual behavior between consenting adults is not mentioned in the law as being a criminal offense. Section 393 of the Penal Code imposes a maximum penalty of fifteen years' imprisonment for men or women who commit homosexual acts without the consent of the partner.

### Society

Homosexuality is taboo. There is no visible social support of gay and lesbian rights.

## Ireland

### Official Attitudes and the Law

Male homosexual behavior is illegal. Homosexual acts between women are not mentioned in the law. Male homosexual acts are criminalized by the Offences against the Person Act of 1861 and the Criminal Amendment Act of 1885 ("gross indecy with another male person"). The maximum penalty for such "indecent" behavior with a consenting adult is two years' imprisonment.

In a judgment delivered in October 1988, the European Court of Human Rights in Strasbourg found that the above laws were in breach of the European Convention on Human Rights, in that they unjustifiably interfered with the right to respect for private life of the Irish Senator David Norris under Article 8.1 of the Convention (right to private and family life).

In 1989, the Irish Law Reform Commission recommended legalizing homosexual acts between men, and introducing equal ages of consent for hetero- and homosexual sex. The government promised to introduce legal proposals regularly, taking into account the European Court's judgment; but no proposal reached the Irish Parliament before 1993. In 1993, the new Irish government promised to do so very soon. Since 1974, no prosecutions of consenting homosexual adult men have taken place.

According to Irish ministerial guidelines, it is illegal in the civil service to discriminate on the basis of sexual orientation. In November 1989, the Prohibition of Incitement to Hatred Act was passed, making it a criminal offense to incite hatred on the basis of sexual orientation. The original proposal for this law only covered incitement on the basis of race, color, religion, and ethnic or national origin. An amendment introduced by Senator David Norris to add sexual orientation was adopted by Parliament.

Only married foreign partners can obtain partner-dependent residence permit. The Adoption Act of 1952 does not allow adoption of a child by a single person or an unmarried couple.

## Society

Closeted homosexuality is tolerated. Homosexuality is usually ignored in education; mention of homosexuality (if at all) in schools, is only to deny its possible acceptance. Social attitudes toward homosexuality are improving, however. A minority of the population is in favor of gay and lesbian rights. According to a representative European study, 33 percent of the Irish object to homosexuals as neighbors.

## The Gay and/or Lesbian Movement

There is a national lesbian and gay organization, the "Gay and Lesbian Equality Network" (GLEN). There is also a Campaign for Homosexual Law Reform, as well as other gay and lesbian groups, bars, and social clubs, mainly in Dublin.

## Israel

*Official Attitudes and the Law*

Legal protection against discrimination on the basis of sexual preferences exists. Until 1988, male homosexuality was punishable under Section 351 of the Penal Code, with up to ten years' imprisonment. There was already a policy of non-prosecution under the old law. The Israeli parliament, the Knesset, accepted in 1988 a bill to cancel Section 351. Homosexuality is not a reason for dismissal from the armed forces. There are no legal provisions regarding homosexuality between women.

In January 1992, the Knesset approved a law safeguarding equal opportunities in jobs, stating that employers shall not discriminate between employees or applicants for jobs because of their sexual preference.

*Society*

The majority of the population is in favor of gay and lesbian rights. The chief rabbinate and religious groups and parties condemn homosexuality. There are reports about gay men and lesbian women leaving the country for the United States or the Netherlands, because they are hardly accepted by their family in Israel.

*The Gay and/or Lesbian Movement*

The "Society for the Protection of Personal Rights" (SPPR), founded in 1975, is a gay and lesbian rights organization. Another group, "Claf," has been organized by lesbian feminists. An independent gay magazine, *Magaim*, is published. In June 1989, the first Gay Pride Week was held.

## Italy

*Official Attitudes and the Law*

Homosexual behavior between consenting adults is not mentioned in the law as being a criminal offense. The age of consent of homo- and heterosexual contacts is fourteen. Sexual contact with a person between fourteen and sixteen years, however, is punishable in the case of "sexual ignorance" or "moral purity" of the young person. Laws concerning "public decency" are used on a large scale against gay men. Homosexuality is mentioned as an "imperfection" which renders men "unfit" for military service (Law 1008 of 1985). The police department of Rome maintains a list of (supposed) homosexuals.

No explicit legal recognition of lesbian and gay partnerships exists; but in an attempt to give legal rights to unmarried heterosexual couples, the Italian government also inadvertently opened the door to de facto legal recognition of gay and lesbian couples when it issued new regulations for municipal registration and record offices in 1989. It defines a family as "a group of cohabitating persons tied by bonds of affection," and did not specify that the partners have to be of the opposite sex. Bologna was the first Italian city to allocate public housing for gay and lesbian couples (in 1989), based upon this law.

*Society*

Closeted homosexuality is tolerated. Social attitudes toward homosexuality are improving. A minority of the population is in favor of gay and lesbian rights. According to a representative European study, 39 percent of the Italians object to homosexuals as neighbors.

*The Gay and/or Lesbian Movement*

There are groups operating under the names of "FUORI!" and "ARCI-GAY" in the big cities. Most organizations are concentrated in the northern part of the country. Well known are the gay and lesbian archives of Turin and the gay magazine *Babilonia*.

## Ivory Coast

*Official Attitudes and the Law*

Homosexual behavior is not mentioned in the law. Although there is no direct punishment on the grounds of homosexual acts, e.g., by arrest or harassment, it is not socially accepted.

*Society*

The press does not mention homosexuality, since it is described very seldom in publications about sexuality in general, other than in factual reports, or information or scientific publications. The content of these reports, however, is sometimes questionable. There is no visible support for gay and lesbian rights.

## Jamaica

*Official Attitudes and the Law*

Homosexual behavior is illegal. Sections 76 to 79 of the Penal Code make homosexual intercourse between men a crime, punishable with imprisonment and hard labor for up to ten years. Anyone attempting to commit homosexual acts or an "indecent assault" upon any male person is liable to imprisonment not exceeding seven years, with or without hard labor. There are not many charges known, however, and the law has not been strictly enforced. Still, gay men have been arrested frequently on the charge of "loitering."

## Society

Although public homosexual behavior is still not tolerated by Jamaicans, there is more open discussion of homosexuality in the media. A minority of the population is in favor of gay and lesbian rights.

## The Gay and/or Lesbian Movement

Gays and lesbians are most visible in the island's big cities.

# Japan

## Official Attitudes and the Law

Homosexual behavior between consenting adults is not mentioned in the law as being a criminal offense. There are no legal provisions against homosexuality.

## Society

The *Kodansha Encyclopedia of Japan* (Tokyo, 1982, part 3, pp. 217–18) is positive about male homosexuality (*doseiai*) and mentions the long tradition of *nanshoku* (love between men) in the history of Japan. The encyclopedia regrets that there is no information about female homosexuality, but explains this as the result of "the male perspective in the Japanese language about sexuality." The encyclopedia states that "many homosexuals feel a definite lack of freedom to express their homosexuality openly and without fear, especially at their workplaces. As a result, much homosexual activity remains hidden. Since the stigma attached to homosexuality is not as great as that in the West, the international gay rights movement has had little effect in creating a separate homosexual consciousness for Japanese men and women."

Closeted homosexuality is tolerated. A minority of the population is in favor of gay and lesbian rights.

## The Gay and/or Lesbian Movement

In Tokyo there are active groups of gays and lesbians with many periodicals. Since 1986, the gay group OCCUR has been active in claiming equal treatment for homosexuals. In 1987, an active lesbian group, "Regumi Studio Tokyo," was founded, which publishes a monthly newsletter. The ILGA Secretariat for Asia is established in Tokyo.

## Jordan

*Official Attitudes and the Law*

Homosexuality is illegal.

*Society*

The attitude toward homosexuality is very hostile. There is no visible social support for gay and lesbian rights.

## Kazakhstan

*Official attitudes and the law*

In the former Soviet Union, anal intercourse between men was illegal. This prohibition is still incorporated in the Penal Code of Kazakhstan. Homosexual acts between women are not mentioned in the law, nor is homosexual behavior between consenting adults explicitly included in the law as being a criminal offense.

*Society*

The attitude of this predominantly Islamic society is hostile toward homosexuality. There is no visible support for gay and lesbian rights.

## Kenya

*Official Attitudes and the Law*

Male homosexual behavior is illegal. Although homosexual acts between women are not mentioned in the law, the government opposed any discussion of lesbian issues during the 1985 UN Women's Conference. Homosexual acts between men are illegal, under Sections 162 to 165, which criminalize "carnal knowledge against the order of nature" and attempted homosexual acts.

*Society*

The attitude toward homosexuality is very hostile. There is no visible social support for gay and lesbian rights.

## Kiribati

*Official Attitudes and the Law*

Homosexual behavior is illegal. Section 153 of the Penal Code punishes "buggery" with a maximum penalty of fourteen years' imprisonment. Section 154 criminalizes "attempts to buggery and indecent assaults" with a maximum penalty of seven years' imprisonment. Section 155 prohibits acts of gross indecency in private or public, with five years' imprisonment.

### Society

There is no visible support for gay and lesbian rights.

## Kuwait

### Official Attitudes and the Law

Homosexual behavior is illegal. Islamic laws are applied against homosexuality. In 1992, the National Assembly criminalized knowing transmission of HIV. Foreign residents are forced to be tested for HIV-infection; foreigners with HIV are expelled.

### Society

While homosexuality is taboo, closeted homosexuality is tolerated. There is no visible social support for gay and lesbian rights.

## Kyrgyzstan

### Official Attitudes and the Law

In the former Soviet Union, anal intercourse between men was illegal. This prohibition is still incorporated in the Penal Code of Kyrgyzstan. Homosexual acts between women are not mentioned in the law, nor is homosexual behavior between consenting adults explicitly included in the law as being a criminal offense.

### Society

The attitude of this predominantly Islamic society is hostile toward homosexuality. There is no visible support for gay and lesbian rights.

## Laos

### Official Attitudes and the Law

No legal information is available. In 1992, arrests and isolation of homosexuals were reported.

### Society

The attitude to homosexuality is very hostile. There is no visible social support for gay and lesbian rights.

## Latvia

*Official Attitudes and the Law*

Under Soviet legislation, Article 121 of the Latvian Penal Code prohibited anal intercourse between men. The Latvian parliament decriminalized homosexuality in March 1992, establishing an equal age of consent of sixteen for both homo- and heterosexuals. One member of the national parliament was appointed liaison person for sexual minorities.

*Society*

Only a minority of the population is in favor of gay and lesbian rights, although social repression of homosexuals is decreasing.

*The Gay and/or Lesbian Movement*

Since November 1990, a gay and lesbian group organization in Riga, called the "Latvian Association for Sexual Equality" (LASE), has existed.

## Lebanon

*Official Attitudes and the Law*

Homosexual behavior is illegal. The Lebanese Embassy in The Hague replied to our questionnaire on March 20, 1987, that "homosexuality is not accepted in Lebanon." Legislation is based on Christian and Islamic laws.

*Society*

There is no visible support for gay and lesbian rights.

## Lesotho

*Official Attitudes and the Law*

Homosexual behavior between consenting adults is not mentioned in the law as being a criminal offense.

*Society*

The Ambassador of Lesotho in Brussels states in his letter of December 13, 1990, that "homosexuality is scorned and there is no awareness of gay or lesbian identities." There is no visible social support for gay and lesbian rights.

## Liberia

*Official Attitudes and the Law*

Homosexual behavior between consenting adults is not mentioned in the law as being a criminal offense. The Ambassador of Liberia in Brussels wrote on March 17, 1987, in answer to our questionnaire: "We are unable to furnish you with any information concerning this matter because the number of homosexuals in my country is so microscopic that not much is known about them."

*Society*

There is no visible support for gay and lesbian rights.

## Libya

*Official Attitudes and the Law*

Homosexual behavior is illegal. *Sharia,* the Islamic law, which punishes homosexual acts, is enforced severely. Section 407, par. 4 of the Penal Code punishes homosexual acts with three to five years' imprisonment. Section 114 of the Military Penal Code of 1974 punishes each soldier, who attempts or perform homosexual acts, with up to five years' imprisonment.

*Society*

Closeted homosexual behavior exists on a large scale, though it is a religious and social taboo. There is no visible social support for gay and lesbian rights.

## Liechtenstein

*Official Attitudes and the Law*

Homosexual behavior is illegal. According to Section 129 of the Penal Code of 1852, both male and female homosexual acts are illegal, with a maximum penalty of five years' imprisonment, sometimes combined with severe conditions. In 1989, law reform was introduced to decriminalize homosexuality; however, there were adopted at the same time the anti-homosexual laws of the present Austrian Penal Code (see under "Austria").

*Society*

Social attitudes toward homosexuality are intolerant. There is no visible social support for gay and lesbian rights.

## Lithuania

*Official Attitudes and the Law*

Under Soviet legislation, Article 122 of the Lithuanian Penal Code prohibited anal intercourse between men. This section is still incorporated in the Penal Code of this republic. Homosexual acts between women are not mentioned in the law. Homosexual behavior between consenting adults is not mentioned in the law as being a criminal offense. Since Lithuania regained its independence in 1990, seven men (including one minor) have been sentenced to three to eight years' imprisonment for male-male sexual acts.

*Society*

The attitude of society is hostile. A 1991 study showed that 71 percent of the Lithuanians were opposed to homosexuals teaching in schools. There is no visible social support for gay and lesbian rights.

*The Gay and/or Lesbian Movement*

Since 1992, an informal gay and lesbian group has existed.

## Luxembourg

*Official Attitudes and the Law*

Since August 1992, the age of consent for all sexual contacts is sixteen years, according to the new Section 372 of the Penal Code.

*Society*

Closeted homosexuality is tolerated. Social attitudes toward homosexuality are improving, with a minority of the population in favor of gay and lesbian rights.

*The Gay and/or Lesbian Movement*

There are only informal gay and lesbian groups. The organization called "Initiatives Groupes Homosexuelles" no longer exists.

## Macau

*Official Attitudes and the Law*

Portuguese legislation is applied.

*Society*

There is no visible support for gay and lesbian rights.

## Macedonia

*Official Attitudes and the Law*

Homosexual acts were illegal in all of the former Yugoslavia until 1977. In 1976, the then federal government delegated the power to the republic to set the age of consent for sexual behavior. Homosexual acts between men are prohibited in Macedonia under Section 101.2, which imposes a maximum penalty of one year's imprisonment.

*Society*

Closeted homosexuality is tolerated. Social attitudes toward homosexuality are improving, with a minority of the population being in favor of gay and lesbian rights.

## Madagascar

*Official Attitudes and the Law*

Homosexual behavior between consenting adults is not mentioned in the law as being a criminal offense.

*Society*

There is no visible support for gay and lesbian rights.

## Malawi

*Official Attitudes and the Law*

"Unnatural offenses" are illegal according to Article 153 of the Penal Code. In the past, Europeans committing homosexual acts with Malawis were prosecuted under laws concerning "public decency" (Article 156); they were also expelled as undesirable aliens.

*Society*

Homosexuality is viewed as "unnatural." There is no visible support for gay and lesbian rights

## Malaysia

*Official Attitudes and the Law*

Homosexual behavior is illegal. Section 377 of the Penal Code punishes whoever voluntarily has "carnal intercourse against the order of nature with any man, woman, or animal," with a maximum penalty of twenty years' imprisonment and a fine or whipping. Section 377a of the Penal Code prohibits "the act of gross indecency," in private or public, between two men, with a punishment of two years' imprisonment.

There have been prosecutions under these sections, particularly that having to do with sodomy. Since all prosecutions of a criminal nature are carried out by the police, a formal complaint has to be made. Consenting adults will not make such reports, hence prosecutions are few. With regard to lesbians, Section 377 of the Penal Code covers any offenses of that nature. There are no known prosecutions of lesbians.

*Society*

The (Islamic) majority of the population is hostile toward homosexuality. There is no visible social support for gay and lesbian rights.

*The Gay and/or Lesbian Movement*

Since 1992, a gay and lesbian group called "Pink Triangle" has started to become active.

## Maldives

*Official Attitudes and the Law*

There is no legal information available.

*Society*

There is no visible support for gay and lesbian rights.

## Mali

*Official Attitudes and the Law*

There is no legal information available.

*Society*

There is no visible support for gay and lesbian rights.

## Malta

*Official Attitudes and the Law*

Homosexual behavior between consenting adults is not mentioned in the law as being a criminal offense. There are no legal provisions dealing with homosexuality. The de facto age of consent for homosexual contacts is eighteen, as it is for heterosexual contacts. In June 1991, a debate in and outide Parliament took place on homosexuality related to the new Sexual Offenses Bill, which is not likely to change the position of gays and lesbians.

*Society*

Homosexuality is completely ignored. There is no visible support for gay and lesbian rights.

## Martinique

*Official Attitudes and the Law*

There is no specific legal information. French legislation is applied.

*Society*

There is no visible support for gay and lesbian rights.

## Mauritania

*Official Attitudes and the Law*

Homosexual behavior is illegal. Homosexual acts between men and between women are illegal according to the Islamic law.

*Society*

Homosexuality is taboo. There is no visible social support for gay and lesbian rights.

## Mauritius

*Official Attitudes and the Law*

Homosexual behavior is illegal. According to the High Commissioner in his letter of March 11, 1987, homosexuality has been an offense ever since it was introduced by the French colonial authorities.

## Society

There is no visible support for gay and lesbian rights.

## Mexico

### Official Attitudes and the Law

Homosexual behavior between consenting adults is not mentioned in the law as being a criminal offense. There is a difference between heterosexual "abuse of minors," which carries a maximum penalty of five years' imprisonment, and homosexual "abuse of minors," with a maximum penalty of ten years. In 1991, the local authorities of Guadalajara inhibited the annual ILGA conference from taking place, forcing the organizers to move the venue of the conference to Acapulco. In 1992, many killings of gay activists by death squads took place, and the police raided gay bars in Tijuana.

### Society

Closeted homosexuals are tolerated. A minority of the population is in favor of gay and lesbian rights.

### The Gay and/or Lesbian Movement

In Mexico City, the most active groups are CALAMO, "Colectivo Sol," "Círculo Cultural Gay," RUIIDHO, and MULA for lesbians. Four groups—GOHL, "Communidad Triángulo Rosa," "Projecto Azomalli," and "Grupo Lésbico de Guadalajara"—are active in the city of Guadalajara. In the north of Mexico, "Grupo Y Qué" and "Grupo Polen" (a youth group) are the most important. In Mexico City a group of lesbian mothers made its first public appearance in 1987. There is a magazine called *Hermes*.

## Moldova

### Official Attitudes and the Law

In the former Soviet Union, anal intercourse between men was illegal. This prohibition is still incorporated in the Penal Code of Moldova. Homosexual acts between women are not mentioned in the law, nor is homosexual behavior between consenting adults explicitly mentioned in the law as being a criminal offense.

### Society

The attitude of society is hostile. Homosexuality is taboo. There is no visible support for gay and lesbian rights.

## Monaco

*Official Attitudes and the Law*

French legislation is applied.

*Society*

There is no visible support for gay and lesbian rights.

## Mongolia

*Official Attitudes and the Law*

There is no legal information available.

*Society*

The attitude toward homosexuality is very hostile. There is no visible social support for gay and lesbian rights.

## Montenegro

*Official Attitudes and the Law*

Homosexual acts were illegal in all of the former Yugoslavia until 1977. In 1976, the then federal government delegated the power to the republic to set the age of consent for sexual behavior. In Montenegro, sexual acts between consenting adults (over eighteen) are legal.

*Society*

Closeted homosexuality is tolerated. Social attitudes toward homosexuality are improving. While homosexuality itself remains taboo, a minority of the population is in favor of gay and lesbian rights.

## Morocco

*Official Attitudes and the Law*

Homosexual behavior is illegal. Homosexual acts between men and between women are illegal under Section 489 of the Penal Code with a penalty of six months to three years' imprisonment and a fine of 120 to 1,000 dirhams.

*Society*

Despite the fact that homosexual acts are illegal and can be prosecuted, a lot of Moroccan men seem to have homosexual contacts which are condoned. Islamic fundamentalists have become more aggressive toward gays in recent years; this is no doubt due, in some degree, to prostitution, which is rigorously combatted.

Some male foreigners settle temporarily or permanently in Moroccan cities, because of the possibility of homosexual contacts. Assaults against tourists have become more common.

There is no visible social support for gay and lesbian rights.

## Mozambique

*Official Attitudes and the Law*

Homosexual behavior is illegal. Male homosexuality is illegal according to Sections 70 and 71 of the Penal Code, with a maximum penalty of three years' imprisonment in an institution for reeducation, where forced labor is used to make the accused change his "bad behavior." Female homosexuality is not mentioned.

*Society*

There is no visible support for gay and lesbian rights

## Namibia

*Official Attitudes and the Law*

Namibia still has the laws against homosexuality introduced under South African ruling in the Criminal Act, in which homosexual acts are described as "unnatural sex crimes" and are liable to prosecution.

*Society*

Until recently, no public support for gay and lesbian rights could be given. In 1992, a television program was shown on homosexuality.

## Nauru

*Official Attitudes and the Law*

There is no legal information available.

*Society*

There is no visible support for gay and lesbian rights.

## Nepal

### Official Attitudes and the Law

Homosexual behavior is illegal. Foreigners involved in homosexual contacts can be expelled.

### Society

Homosexuality is taboo. There is no visible support for gay and lesbian rights.

## Netherlands

### Official Attitudes and the Law

Discrimination on the basis of homo- or heterosexual orientation is prohibited by Article 1 of the Dutch constitution. In February 1992, new anti-discrimination provisions in the Penal Code came into force covering discrimination on the basis of "hetero- or homosexual orientation," including anti-homosexual libel and incitement. In February 1993, the Second Chamber of Parliament adopted the General Equal Treatment Act, which will outlaw discrimination "on the sole ground" of homosexuality in the private sector.

The age of consent has been sixteen for both homo- and heterosexual contacts since 1971. Homosexuality has not been mentioned in the Penal Code since 1971. Since 1991, the law has only allowed the prosecution of someone who has had sex with someone between twelve and sixteen, if a formal complaint has been made by the youngster, by either parent, or by the Child Welfare Council (Articles 245 and 247 of the Penal Code). No distinction is made between homo- and heterosexual acts.

Since 1986, the government has regularly published reports on homosexuality and government policy, with proposals for (among other things) continuing prevention of aggression against homosexual women and men, and for integration of homosexuality into the educational system.

Hardly any distinction is made between hetero- and homosexual cohabitation. In an increasing number of areas (e.g., rent protection, income tax, social security, and parenthood) the law does not discriminate between marriage and unmarried cohabitation (defined as permanently having a joint household). Since 1991, many local authorities have started official registration of gay and lesbian partnerships. So far, this has only a symbolic meaning. A foreigner who has been living in a permanent nonmarital relationship with a Dutch national for at least three years, can acquire Dutch nationality if he or she has been living in the Netherlands for at least three years (Article 8.4 of the Dutch Nationality Act of 1984). However, lesbian and gay couples still have no automatic access to all pension, inheritance, tax, and adoption rights attributed to married couples.

They need additional contracts to be made by a public notary to obtain access to some of these rights.

## Society

The vast majority of the Dutch population (90 percent) is in favor of equal rights for homosexual women and men, and for homosexual relationships. Many well-known Dutch artists, politicians, officials, teachers, and sports personalities have come out and offered positive images to young gay men and lesbians. Homosexuals are considered to be just another minority. According to a representative European study, 12 percent of the Dutch object to homosexuals as neighbors (together with Denmark being the lowest percentage in that study). In 1992, a Dutch Catholic bishop ordained an openly gay man.

## The Gay and/or Lesbian Movement

There is a national lesbian and gay organization called "Nederlandse Vereniging tot Integratie van Homoseksualiteit COC" (Dutch Organization for the Integration of Homosexuality COC), with more than fifty branches all over the country. The most important lesbian organization is called "Groep 7152."

There are other local, regional, or national organizations for gay and lesbian Catholics, humanists, Jews, Protestants, teachers, disabled, members of the armed forces or police, sportsmen and women, youth, the elderly, and members of ethnic groups. Similar groups exist for parents of gay and lesbian children, partners of married homosexuals, and homosexual couples parenting children. Gay and lesbian caucuses are active within political parties, trade unions, churchs, educational institutes, and the media. The national Gay and Lesbian Switchboard, the Gay and Lesbian Documentation Center "Homodok," and the gay and lesbian memorial "Homomonument" are situated in Amsterdam. Finally, several gay and lesbian organizations for medical and psychological counseling, and for gay and lesbian studies in several universities exist. Many of them are (partly) state funded.

The most important gay and lesbian magazines are the biweekly *De GAY-Krant*, the COC's monthly *XL*, the cultural monthly *Homologie*, the youth monthly *Expreszo*, the lesbian monthly *Lust en Gratie*, and the pedophile monthly *Martijn*.

## Netherlands Antilles

### Official Attitudes and the Law

Homosexual behavior between consenting adults is not mentioned in the law as being a criminal offense. Section 255 of the Penal Code prohibits homosexual contacts with minors under the age of sixteen, with up to four years' imprisonment. Heterosexual contacts with minors under the age of sixteen are criminal only under certain conditions. However, as far as is known, Section 255 is not applied.

*Society*

Closeted homosexuals are tolerated. A minority of the population is in favor of gay and lesbian rights.

*The Gay and/or Lesbian Movement*

Some informal groups linked to the Netherlands exist.

## New Caledonia

*Official Attitudes and the Law*

There is no specific legal information. French legislation is applied.

*Society*

There is no visible support for gay and lesbian rights.

## New Zealand

*Official Attitudes and the Law*

Homosexual behavior between consenting adults is not mentioned in the law as being a criminal offense. In 1986, the Penal Code was amended with the adoption of the Homosexual Law Reform Act, so that consenting males over sixteen years old were no longer criminally liable when having homosexual contacts. An exception was made for men in the armed forces and the police. A bill to prohibit discrimination against homosexuals was withdrawn.

*Society*

The majority of the population supported the law reform. However, the Salvation Army and other religious groups strongly opposed the 1986 amendment. The Coalition of Concerned Citizens offered a petition of 817,000 signatures to the parliament, demanding the withdrawal of the Homosexual Law Reform Bill. Later it appeared that large numbers of the signatures occurred more than once or were falsified. The majority of the population is in favor of gay and lesbian rights.

*The Gay and/or Lesbian Movement*

New Zealand has an active gay and lesbian movement. *Out* is the national gay magazine.

## Nicaragua

*Official Attitudes and the Law*

In 1992, a proposed penal code reform was approved by the national assembly, which punishes with one to three years' imprisonment any individual who "induces, promotes, propagandizes or practices in a scandalous matter, sexual intercourse between people of the same sex." This law has been criticized internationally. The bill is to be scrutinized by the Constitutional Court. Before 1992, homosexual behavior between consenting adults was not mentioned in the law as being a criminal offense. Prostitution, including male prostitution, is illegal.

*Society*

Closeted homosexuality is tolerated. Recently the situation of gays and lesbians has deteriorated. The new right wing government is less supportive than the previous Sandinista regime. A minority of the population is in favor of gay and lesbian rights.

*The Gay and/or Lesbian Movement*

A lesbian and gay group exists (MFLHM). The first gay and lesbian march took place on July 19, 1989. A women's organization (AMNLAE) maintains contact with gay and lesbian organizations in the United States.

## Niger

*Official Attitudes and the Law*

There is no legal information available.

*Society*

There is no visible support for gay and lesbian rights.

## Nigeria

*Official Attitudes and the Law*

Homosexual acts between men are illegal, and homosexual acts between women are not mentioned. According to Article 214 of the Penal Code every person who has "carnal knowledge of another person against the order of nature," or who permits a male person to have "carnal knowledge of him (or her) against the order of nature," is guilty of a felony and liable to imprisonment for fourteen years. Section 217 of the Penal Code criminalizes attempts at, and actual acts of, "gross indecency," with a maximum penalty of three years' imprisonment.

Furthermore, the assault with intent to have "carnal knowledge with a man (or woman) against the order of nature," is a felony and carries a maximum penalty of fourteen years' imprisonment, under Section 352 of the Penal Code, whereas unlawful and indecent assaults on a male person can be punished with up to three years' imprisonment.

### Society

There is no visible support for gay and lesbian rights.

### The Gay and/or Lesbian Movement

In 1989, a gay group called "the Gentlemen Alliance" was formed.

## Niue

### Official Attitudes and the Law

Homosexual behavior is illegal. Section 170 of the Penal Code prohibits "buggery," with a maximum penalty of ten years' imprisonment. Section 171 criminalizes "attempts to buggery" and indecent assaults among men, with a maximum penalty of five years' imprisonment.

### Society

There is no visible support for gay and lesbian rights.

## North Korea

### Official Attitudes and the Law

There is no legal information available.

### Society

The attitude toward homosexuality is very hostile. There is no visible social support for gay and lesbian rights.

## Norway

### Official Attitudes and the Law

Legal protection against anti-homosexual discrimination exists. Since 1972, the age of consent for homo- and heterosexual contacts has been sixteen years. Since 1981, a law has been in force which prohibits discrimination against gay men and lesbians. Section 135a makes it illegal to publicly "threaten or deride, or to incite to hatred, persecution or contempt against" persons on account of their "homosexual inclination, lifestyle, or orientation." The maximum penalty is two years' imprisonment.

Section 349a makes it an offense "in business or similar activities" to refuse to give goods or services (on the conditions applicable to others) to a person because of his or her "homosexual inclination, lifestyle, or orientation." The maximum penalty is six months' imprisonment.

Business firms intending to discriminate against gay men or lesbians, reconsidered their policies after being threatened with proceedings under these sections.

Homosexuals are allowed to serve in the armed forces.

The Norwegian government is preparing a law on homosexual relationships similar to the Danish partnership law.

### Society

Social attitudes may be defined as tolerant: public opinion polls showed that less than 20 percent of the population opposed equal rights for gay and lesbian relations. According to a representative European study, 20 percent of the Norwegians object to homosexuals as neighbors.

### The Gay and/or Lesbian Movement

There are two national lesbian and gay organizations: "Det Norske Forbundet av 1948" (DNF-48) and "Fellesraadet for Homofile Organisasjoner i Norge" (FHO).

## Oman

### Official Attitudes and the Law

Homosexual acts between men and between women are illegal under Section 32 of the Penal Code, with a maximum penalty of three years' imprisonment.

### Society

Closeted homosexuality is tolerated. There is no visible social support for gay and lesbian rights.

## Pakistan

### Official Attitudes and the Law

Homosexual behavior is illegal. Section 377 of the Penal Code prohibits "carnal intercourse against the order of nature with any man," with a punishment of two years to life imprisonment, which may be extended to include corporal punishment of 100 lashes. The Embassy of Pakistan in The Hague replied on June 2, 1987, to our questionnaire:

> In Pakistan homosexuality and/or sexual contacts among women and men are treated as immoral acts. There is no legal protection against discrimination of homosexual women and men in Pakistan. The homosexual individual is not accepted as a decent individual, and homosexual acts constitute an offense punishable with imprisonment for life or with imprisonment of either description for a term which may extend to ten years. The recorded cases are very few. This fact by itself shows that the offense of this nature is not frequent.

*Society*

Homosexuality is taboo. When homosexual acts become known, the people involved will become social outcasts. There is no visible social support for gay and lesbian rights.

## Panama

*Official Attitudes and the Law*

Homosexual behavior between consenting adults is not mentioned in the law as being a criminal offense.

*Society*

There is no visible support for gay and lesbian rights.

## Papua New Guinea

*Official Attitudes and the Law*

Homosexual acts between men are illegal.

*Society*

There is no visible support for gay and lesbian rights.

## Paraguay

*Official Attitudes and the Law*

Homosexual behavior between consenting adults is not mentioned in the law as being a criminal offense. Homosexuality is not mentioned in the legislation except where specific charges of "corruption of minors" and "offenses against public morals" can be brought.

## Society

There is no visible support for gay and lesbian rights.

## Peru

### Official Attitudes and the Law

Homosexual behavior between consenting adults is not mentioned in the law as being a criminal offense. Homosexual acts, in private and among consenting adults, are not illegal. An exception is made for the military and police forces, where the performance of "dishonorable acts of carnal knowledge against the order of nature" with a person of the same sex can be punished with sixty days to twenty years' imprisonment, in some cases with discharge from the forces (Section 269 of the Military Penal Code of 1980).

Furthermore, the Civil Code states that a marriage can be annulled if one of the spouses has been ignorant of the homosexuality of the other. Homosexuality is also a ground for separation or divorce. Laws referring to "public morality" are often used against gays and lesbians. In April 1991, the police raided an AIDS benefit meeting and arrested several people who were set free later.

In 1993, President Fujimori fired 117 top civil servants because of their alleged homosexuality.

### Society

In general, the attitude toward homosexuality in society is hostile. The terrorist group, "Sendero Luminoso" (Shining Path), killed many gay men for "corrupting youth." A minority of the population is in favor of gay and lesbian rights.

### The Gay and/or Lesbian Movement

The "Moviemento Homosexual de Lima" (MHOL) was founded in 1983. Since 1984, a group of lesbians (GALF) has existed. In 1987, a violent police raid of a lesbian bar took place, which was shown on TV. On March 8, 1988, a lesbian information stand received, for the first time, a great deal of positive TV and radio publicity.

"Contramano," a cultural association formed in November 1989, works for the well-being and integration of the gay community in Lima. In May 1990, this group held a seminar on human sexuality.

## Philippines

### Official Attitudes and the Law

Homosexual behavior between consenting adults is not mentioned in the law as being a criminal offense. Laws referring to "public morality" are used against gays and lesbians. The Philippines' immigration minister has declared a "war against pedophiles," particularly in Manila. Foreigners are to be expected to be the first targets of the campaign. The government banned the radical women's group, "Gabriella," on November 7, 1988, as part of the government counterinsurgence program, "for having possible ties to some underground leftists."

### Society

Closeted homosexuality is tolerated, but "sex tourism" has a negative impact on the social position of homosexual men. A minority of the population is in favor of gay and lesbian rights.

### The Gay and/or Lesbian Movement

A group exists called the "Movement for Social Equality and Recognition of Homosexuals." In the AIDS center, "The Library," many open gays are active.

## Poland

### Official Attitudes and the Law

Homosexual behavior between consenting adults is not mentioned in the law as being a criminal offense. The general age of consent has, since 1932, been fixed at fifteen. In 1991, the Polish Vice-Minister of Health, Mr. M. Kapera, stated that "AIDS is limited, above all, to homosexuals, being according to our convictions a degeneration." He was immediately dismissed from his post. Thereupon the country's primate, Cardinal Glemp, stated that the main means of HIV transmission was sin and asked whether a state official should "be forced to wear an ideological mask."

### Society

Due to the strong influence of the conservative Catholic church, homophobia is widespread. The topic of homosexuality, however, has received broad media coverage since the end of the 1980s. A minority of the population is in favor of gay and lesbian rights.

*The Gay and/or Lesbian Movement*

Since 1986, a gay and lesbian magazine called *Filo* has been published. In June 1988, Professor Mikolaj Kozakiewicz, a famous sexologist and member of Sejm, the Polish Parliament, announced that he had been informed by the deputy Minister of Public Health that gay and lesbian associations would be legally recognized in Poland. This happened in January 1990. LAMBDA is an association of groups that publishes three gay magazines. They were legally registered in February 1990, and have local branches in, among other cities, Warsaw, Krakow, Wroclaw, and Czestochowa.

Pink Service is an "agency for gays and lesbians." They distribute gay newspapers and condoms, organize Gay Pride Day, and operate the gay cafe "Fiolka." Other informal groups exist: ETAP in Wroclaw, "Amiko" in Lódz, "Inicjatywa Gdanska" in Gdansk, and "Warzawski Ruch Homoseksualny" (Warsaw Homosexual Movement = WRH) in Warsaw. WRH organized the second meeting of activists from Eastern and Southeastern Europe in Warsaw in 1988, which played an important role in organizing the gay and lesbian movement in (post)Communist Europe.

## Portugal

*Official Attitudes and the Law*

Homosexual behavior between consenting adults is not mentioned in the law as being a criminal offense. The age of consent for homo- and heterosexual contacts is fourteen years. According to Article 211 of the Penal Code, a person who has sex with a girl or a boy between the ages of twelve and sixteen can only be prosecuted on the basis of a formal complaint by the youngster involved or by his or her parent or guardian.

However, Section 207 of the Penal Code states that an adult who seduces (*desacaminhador*) a minor younger than sixteen to perform "an act in contradiction to good morals with himself or another person of the same sex" can be punished with a maximum penalty of three years' imprisonment.

Article 222 of the Law on Military Service excludes from the armed forces those who have been involved in "offensive acts." Other laws have been interpreted by courts to deny lesbian and gay parents access to and custody of their children following divorce. Only married foreign partners can obtain a partner-dependent residence permit.

*Society*

Society is hostile toward openly homosexual behavior. The conservative Catholic Church strongly rejects homosexuality, but closeted homosexuals are tolerated. A minority of the population is in favor of gay and lesbian rights. According to a representative European study, 50 percent of the Portuguese object to homosexuals as neighbors: the highest percentage in Western Europe.

### The Gay and/or Lesbian Movement

There are some lesbian and gay groups. In Lisbon, a gay magazine called *Organa* is published.

## Qatar

### Official Attitudes and the Law

Homosexual behavior is illegal. Islamic laws against homosexuality are applied.

### Society

Homosexuality is taboo. There is no visible social support for gay and lesbian rights.

## Reunion

### Official Attitudes and the Law

No specific legal information is available. French legislation is applied.

### Society

There is no visible support for gay and lesbian rights.

## Romania

### Official Attitudes and the Law

Homosexual acts between men and between women are illegal under Section 200 of the Penal Code, which provides for prison terms of one to five years. Even an attempt to engage in homosexual acts is forbidden (Section 204). The age of consent for heterosexuals is fourteen years. There are reports of the persecution and arrest of homosexuals (particularly under the Ceaucescu regime). Gay men were put in prison for long periods and sometimes tortured, forced to work as secret informants, and/or castrated. Despite rumors echoed by the Ministry of Health, there is no indication that the laws regarding homosexuality will be changed. There is a (minor) discussion going on about decriminalizing homosexuality, but this has no priority for the government.

*Society*

Romania is the most homophobic country in Europe. Homosexuality is considered to be an illness. There is no visible social support for gay and lesbian rights, and it looks as if the December 1989 revolution hasn't changed the position of homosexuals that much.

*The Gay and/or Lesbian Movement*

In 1991, an informal gay student group called "Total Relations" started at the University of Bucharest.

## Russia

*Official Attitudes and the Law*

After a short period of liberal legislation (1917–1934), Stalin reintroduced in the former Soviet Union the criminalization of homosexuality in 1934. Since then, Article 121 of the Penal Code has prohibited male homosexuality (though in fact the article prohibits only anal intercourse between men). Yearly about 1,000 gays were arrested under Section 121. Similar sections were incorporated in the penal codes of the other republics of the former Soviet Union.

In today's Russia, homosexual acts between women are not mentioned in the law. Homosexual behavior between consenting adults is not mentioned in the law as being a criminal offense. Proposals have been made by the authorities to change the law prohibiting anal intercourse between men, but since the end of the Soviet Union in 1991, nothing has happened. In 1992, a proposal was made to create new ages of consent for both hetero- and homosexuals.

*Society*

The attitude of society is hostile: homosexuality is taboo. There have been improvements recently, however. A minority of the population (30 percent) is in favor of gay and lesbian rights. A slightly larger minority (33 percent) favors killing homosexuals.

*The Gay and/or Lesbian Movement*

There have been informal groups in Petersburg (e.g., "Gay Laboratory," created in 1983, one of the first openly gay groups), Moscow ("Moscow Union of Lesbians and Gay Men" [MULGM], created in 1990), and other cities. A gay magazine, *Tema,* has been published since 1990 by the MULGM. *Tema's* office was cleaned out by "burglars" on September, 21, 1990. Also in 1990, the "Tchaikovsky Foundation" started in St. Petersburg, which was involved in organizing the first congress on homosexuality in the former Soviet Union in Tallinn (see "Estonia"). In 1991, a more radical group was founded called RISK ("Rawenstwo, Iskrennost, Swoboda, Kompromiss" = Equality, Openness, Freedom, Tolerance). Also in 1991, the first Gay and Lesbian Pride Festivals took place in Moscow and St. Petersburg, and a human rights conference was organized during the meeting in Moscow of the Conference of Security and Cooperation in Europe (CSCE). The CSCE was urged "to take measures to eliminate and prevent discrimination against persons based on their sexual orientation." The Russian government was called upon to repeal Article 121 of the Penal Code and to free all gays and lesbians held in prisons and psychiatric institutions because of their homosexuality or their activities in the gay and lesbian movement.

In 1992, the second national gay and lesbian conference took place, and many new groups were starting, such as ARGO, EGO, "Newskije Bezega," "Novokuznetsk," and "1/10." Lesbian issues are not frequently written about in the gay press, but there are plans to start a magazine about lesbian literature. In 1992, a new magazine called *Sibirskij Variant* was published.

## Rwanda

### Official Attitudes and the Law

There is no legal information available.

### Society

The attitude toward homosexuality is very hostile. There is no visible social support for gay and lesbian rights.

## Saint Lucia

### Official Attitudes and the Law

Homosexual acts between consenting adults are illegal. Homosexuals are often subjected to official and police harassment and violence.

### Society

There is no visible support for gay and lesbian rights.

## Samoa, Western

### Official Attitudes and the Law

Homosexual behavior is illegal. Section 58b of the Crimes Ordinance of 1961 criminalizes "indecent acts" performed by a woman over twenty-one with a girl under the age of sixteen, with a maximum penalty of five years' imprisonment.

Section 58c prohibits sexual activities by a man over the age of twenty-one with a boy under the age of sixteen, with seven years' imprisonment. Section 58d punishes "indecency between males," with a maximum penalty of five years' imprisonment. Section 58e criminalizes "sodomy" with a female or a male under the age of sixteen, if the male is over twenty-one; it carries a maximum penalty of seven years' imprisonment, with five years in other cases of sodomy. Section 58g punishes attempts to commit "sodomy," with a maximum penalty of five years' imprisonment. According to Section 58j, the keeper, manager, assistant manager, tenant, lessee, occupier, lessor, or landlord of any premises, which are knowingly used as a place of resort for the commission of "indecent acts" between males, is liable to imprisonment for up to of seven years.

## Society

In Western Samoa there is recognized a woman-like man, called *fa'afaafine.* Other men may even cohabit with a *fa'afaafine;* as long as they assume the traditionally male role, they are not likely to be accused. Casual homosexual relationships between males and between females are tolerated, if they behave otherwise in public according to their respective gender roles. There is no visible social support for gay and lesbian rights.

## The Gay and/or Lesbian Movement

There are two organizations of *fa'afaafines:* one in American Samoa (the "Tamua Starts"), and one in Western Samoa (the "MY girls").

## San Marino

### Official Attitudes and the Law

According to Article 274 of the Penal Code, homosexual acts are an offense if they provoke public scandal. Homosexuality can be punished with imprisonment and with exclusion from certain political rights and public offenses.

### Society

There is no visible support for gay and lesbian rights.

## Sao Tome and Principe

### Official Attitudes and the Law

There is no legal information available.

*Society*

No visible support for gay and lesbian rights exists.

## Saudi Arabia

*Official Attitudes and the Law*

Homosexual behavior is illegal. Under Islamic law all homosexual acts can be punished with the death penalty.

*Society*

The growing influence of Islamic fundamentalism implies more attacks on homosexuality. There is no visible social support for gay and lesbian rights.

## Senegal

*Official Attitudes and the Law*

Homosexual behavior between consenting adults is not mentioned in the law as being a criminal offense.

*Society*

Homosexuality is taboo. There is no visible social support for gay and lesbian rights.

## Serbia

*Official Attitudes and the Law*

Homosexual acts were illegal in all of the former Yugoslavia until 1977. In 1976, the then federal government delegated the power to the republic and the autonomous provinces Vojvodina and Kosovo to set the age of consent for sexual behavior. Homosexual acts between men are prohibited in Serbia under Section 110.3 of the Penal Code, which imposes a maximum penalty of one year in prison. In Vojvodina, sexual acts between consenting adults (over eighteen) are legal. In Kosovo, homosexual contacts between men are illegal under Section 81.2 of the Penal Code.

*Society*

Closeted homosexuality is tolerated. Social attitudes toward homosexuality are improving, although homosexuality remains taboo. A minority of the population is in favor of gay and lesbian rights.

*The Gay and/or Lesbian Movement*

In 1991, the homosexual rights organization "Arkadia" in Belgrade was refused state registration, which means it cannot hold public meetings.

## Seychelles

*Official Attitudes and the Law*

Homosexual acts are illegal.

*Society*

There is no visible support for gay and lesbian rights.

## Sierra Leone

*Official Attitudes and the Law*

There is no legal information available.

*Society*

The attitude toward homosexuality is very hostile. There is no visible social support for gay and lesbian rights.

## Singapore

*Official Attitudes and the Law*

Homosexual behavior is illegal. Section 377 of the Penal Code punishes "carnal intercourse against the order of nature" with ten years to life imprisonment. Section 377a prohibits "gross indecency" between males, in public or private, with a maximum penalty of two years' imprisonment. Under the Interpretation Act, Chapter 1, all words in the masculine gender also include females. Hence, Sections 377 and 377a of the Penal Code apply as well to lesbians.

In 1988 the Public Entertainments Licensing Unit issued a circular to all entertainment spots, advising them to disallow transvestites and gay visitors from patronizing their establishments. The action was seen as part of vice enforcement and control of AIDS, since homosexuality is still a penal offense.

In spring 1990, in a major undercover move to flush out homosexuals from the city's park, seven men were arrested in Singapore. A few days later, the men's names were published in the *Straits Times,* Singapore's most widely circulated newspaper. The men were also tested to see whether or not they were HIV-infected. The arrest followed a two-week operation involving young undercover officers posing as homosexuals in and around the park near the central business district.

*Society*

Singapore is a multiracial and multicultural society, where moral values and customs vary greatly among the respective ethnic groups. There is no visible social support for gay and lesbian rights.

## Slovakia

*Official Attitudes and the Law*

Homosexual behavior between consenting adults is not mentioned in the law as being a criminal offense. The Penal Code Amendment of May 2, 1990, has invalidated the provisions of Section 244 of the Penal Code of the former Czech and Slovak Republic, prohibiting homosexual acts with persons under the age of eighteen; this has been applied to both men and women. The age of consent for homo- and heterosexuals is now fifteen years (Section 242). Proposals to regulate gay and lesbian relationships and against discrimination on the basis of sexual orientation were made in the parliament of the former Czech and Slovak Federal Republic.

*Society*

Only closeted homosexuality is tolerated. Social attitudes toward homosexuality are improving, with a minority of the population being in favor of gay and lesbian rights.

*The Gay and/or Lesbian Movement*

Gay and lesbian groups exist in Bratislava and Kosice called "Ganymedes." In 1992, "Ganymedes" organized the conference of the "International Gay and Lesbian Youth Organization" (IGLYO) in Bratislava.

## Slovenia

*Official Attitudes and the Law*

Homosexual acts were illegal in all of the former Yugoslavia until 1977. In 1976, the then federal government delegated the power to the republic to set the age of consent for sexual behavior. In Slovenia, homosexuality is not discriminated against by the Penal Code. The general age of consent is fixed at sixteen.

*Society*

Closeted homosexuality is tolerated. Social attitudes toward homosexuality are improving. In Slovenia, homosexuality is more often dealt with in magazines and newspapers, and it is relatively well received. A minority of the population is in favor of gay and lesbian rights.

### The Gay and/or Lesbian Movement

There are gay and lesbian groups ("Magnus" and "Lilit") in Ljubljana, which are affiliated with the Student Cultural Center. The groups have been organizing gay and lesbian cultural weeks in Ljubljana since 1984. Since 1988, there has another lesbian group in Ljubljana called "Lezbiska Sekcija," which runs a telephone line for women in Slovenia and publishes a magazine called *Lesbozone.*

## Solomon Islands

### Official Attitudes and the Law

Homosexual behavior is illegal. Section 153 of the Penal Code punishes "buggery," with a maximum penalty of fourteen years' imprisonment. Section 154 criminalizes "attempts to buggery and indecent assaults," with a maximum penalty of seven years' imprisonment. Section 155 prohibits acts of "gross indecency" in private or public, with five years' imprisonment.

### Society

There is no visible support for gay and lesbian rights.

## Somalia

### Official Attitudes and the Law

There is no legal information available.

### Society

The attitude toward homosexuality is very hostile. There is no visible social support for gay and lesbian rights.

## South Africa

### Official Attitudes and the Law

Homosexual acts between men are illegal; those between women are not mentioned in the law. Homosexual men are convicted of "sodomy" and "indecent assaults." Gays and lesbians are not permitted in the armed forces, or on the staffs of airports, harbors, and railways. In the context of defining a new constitution, there is a discussion going on about giving gays and lesbians (equal) rights.

*Society*

Homosexuality is often seen as a psychiatric and a security problem. A minority of the population is in favor of gay and lesbian rights.

*The Gay and/or Lesbian Movement*

There are several organizations, among them the "Gay Association of South Africa" (GASA), OLGA, and within the "African National Congress" (ANC) there is a gay and lesbian pressure group. In 1990, there was the first Gay Pride March ever organized in South Africa.

## South Korea

*Official Attitudes and the Law*

Homosexual behavior between consenting adults is not mentioned in the law as being a criminal offense. All Korean employees who work for special entertainment facilities, such as low-class hotels, saunas, nightclubs, and bars, are required to be checked regulary for HIV-infection.

*Society*

The main problem facing the gay community in Korea is the family tradition. No matter how strongly the government recognizes gay and lesbian rights, the Confucianist beliefs of strict adherence to family tradition will not accept this. Generally, Korean people did not have too strong an opinion about gays and lesbians before the AIDS crisis, as long as it did not affect other people. But now AIDS and homosexuality seem to be everybody's business. There is no visible support for gay and lesbian rights.

## Spain

*Official Attitudes and the Law*

Homosexual behavior between consenting adults is not mentioned in the law as being a criminal offense. Homosexual acts have been decriminalized since 1978; since then, the age of consent for both homo- and heterosexual contacts has been twelve years (Article 429 of the Penal Code). Sexual relations with people between twelve and sixteen are an offense if the younger partner is tricked or pressured into having sex, and if their parents subsequently complain to the police.

Article 14 of the Constitution is supposed to guarantee equal treatment for all citizens, including gay men and lesbians, but this has not been made explicit yet. According to Section 352 of the Military Code of Law, sexual acts between soldiers on duty inside barracks, are punishable with imprisonment for up to six years and discharge from the military service.

For a long time gay and lesbian groups have been asking the government to propose a "real" anti-discrimination law. Proposals from members of Parliament to recognize homosexual relationships, have no significant support from society. Homosexuals have no right to marry, but there are proposals to extend some of the legal effects of marriage to same-sex couples. In 1993, a country-wide campaign against intolerance, including homophobia, was launched. Gay and lesbian groups were the main initiators of this campaign.

## Society

Acceptance of homosexuality has improved significantly during the last few years. According to an opinion poll for the "Asociación pro Derechos Humanos" in Madrid, a minority of 25 to 45 percent of the population rejects homosexuality. Still only a minority of the population is in favor of gay and lesbian rights. According to a representative European study, 32 percent of the Spanish object to homosexuals as neighbors.

In 1992, a Madrid city councilor tried in vain to close down the Gay Center of Madrid.

## The Gay and/or Lesbian Movement

Several groups are active, mainly in Barcelona and Madrid, but also in Valencia, Euzkadi, Galicia, and other parts of Spain. At least once a year, there is a meeting of groups from all over Spain. In 1980, the FAGH (Gay Liberation Front of Catalonia) was the first organization in Spain to be recognized by the government. Since 1991, the FAGH has been composed of the (larger) CGB (Gay Collective of Barcelona) and the (smaller) remainder of the FAGH. Other organizations in Barcelona are "Casa Lamda" and CGL; in Madrid, the COGAM (Gay Collective of Madrid) and the "Radical Gai"; in Valencia, the "Colectivo Lambda"; and in Euzkadi, the EHGAM (Gay Liberation Front of Euzkadi).

## Sri Lanka

### Official Attitudes and the Law

Homosexual behavior is illegal. Section 365a of the Penal Code criminalizes homosexual acts between men, with a maximum of ten years' imprisonment. The Embassy of Sri Lanka in The Hague replied to our questionnaire on March 27, 1987: "We do not have legal protection against discrimination on grounds of homosexuality; nor do we have any laws protecting the rest of society from homosexuals."

*Society*

Closeted homosexuality is tolerated, but "sex tourism" has had a negative impact on the social position of homosexual men. There is no visible social support for gay and lesbian rights.

## Sudan

*Official Attitudes and the Law*

Homosexual behavior is illegal. Since the introduction of Islamic law (*Sharia*) on January 1, 1991, the legal position of homosexuals has worsened.

*Society*

There is no visible support for gay and lesbian rights.

## Surinam

*Official Attitudes and the Law*

Homosexual behavior between consenting adults is not mentioned in the law as being a criminal offense. According to Section 302 of the Penal Code, homosexual acts with minors under the age of eighteen can be punished with imprisonment for up to four years. (Heterosexual acts are legal from the age of sixteen years.) Section 302 is hardly enforced, however.

*Society*

Closeted homosexuals are tolerated. A minority of the population is in favor of gay and lesbian rights.

*The Gay and/or Lesbian Movement*

In the Netherlands an informal group of Surinam homosexual women and men exists.

## Swaziland

*Official Attitudes and the Law*

Homosexual behavior between consenting adults is not mentioned in the law as being a criminal offense. No legislation on homosexuality exists. In 1992, two lesbians were legally married according to an ancient practice. A Swaziland judge ruled the marriage had legal value.

*Society*

There is no visible support for gay and lesbian rights.

## Sweden

*Official Attitudes and the Law*

Legal protection against discrimination of homosexuals exists, although there is no anti-discrimination clause among the basic provisions of the constitution.

The age of consent for homosexuals has been the same as for heterosexuals (fifteen) since 1978; and since 1979, homosexuality is no longer classified as a disease, and homosexuals are free to serve in the armed forces.

There was a parliamentary commission (1978-1986) on homosexuality, which recommended a political agenda to eliminate "all remaining discriminations against homosexuals." In 1987, two important laws were passed:

1) Commercial organizations are forbidden to discriminate on grounds of homosexuality.

2) It is a criminal offense to make derogatory remarks about a person's homosexuality (as it is with race, color, national or ethnic origin, and religious belief).

Since 1988, gay couples living together in a quasi-marital relationship have been protected under the new cohabitation law, giving them some of the same rights as heterosexual partners living together.

Following the AIDS debate, a law has been passed to forbid clubs which encourage sexual acts on their premises; thus, all gay saunas in Sweden were closed in 1987. Discussions in Parliament are going on to make, after the Danish example, a homosexual partnerships law. A homosexual refugee can be permitted to stay in Sweden on the basis of "humanitarian reasons" (Article 31 of the Aliens Regulation).

*Society*

The Swedes have traditionally been supportive of the "less fortunate," and gay men and lesbians are often considered under this category. Schools are encouraged to teach about homosexuality, and open discrimination against gay men and lesbians is not tolerated within this "liberal" society. Where discrimination exists, it tends to be carried out in a more discreet manner. The majority of the population is in favor of gay and lesbian rights. According to a representative European study, 18 percent of the Swedes object to homosexuals as neighbors.

## The Gay and/or Lesbian Movement

There is a national organization, RFSL, with 24 branches over the country. In addition, there are the RFSL-U (youth group), EKHO (Christians), "Gay Moderaterna" (conservatives), and "Homosexuella Socialister," which are all national organizations funded by the state. RFSL played an active role in supporting the beginning gay and lesbian movements in the Baltic states and Russia.

## Switzerland

### Official Attitudes and the Law

Homosexual behavior between consenting adults is not mentioned in the law as being a criminal offense. In December 1990, the House of Representatives voted in favor of reforming the law on sexual offenses (Art. 191 et seq. of the Penal Code). On May 17, 1992, 73 percent of the voters accepted in a national referendum the reform of the Swiss federal legislation on sexual offenses, including the elimination of all discrimination against homosexuality from the Penal Code.

According to the new provisions, a young person under the age of fourteen is deemed not to be criminally responsible for such sexual behavior, and thus no offense is committed if both persons are under fourteen. When one of the persons is at least fourteen, but under sixteen years, such behavior is no offense as long as the older person is not more than four years older than the younger. At the age of sixteen or older, no special conditions apply under the new law.

In the old legislation, adult men were forbidden to "seduce" young men between sixteen and twenty into having sex with them (Art. 194[1] of the Penal Law). The old Article 191 did forbid male prostitution, but permitted heterosexual prostitution.

Since 1992, the age of consent for homo- and heterosexuals is sixteen under the new law. Homosexual acts in the army have been decriminalized.

### Society

Closeted homosexuals are tolerated. The majority of the population is in favor of gay and lesbian rights.

### The Gay and/or Lesbian Movement

There has been a national lesbian and gay organization, "Schweizerische Organisation der Homophilen" (SOH). In addition, there are now more radical groups of gay men united on a national level in the "Homosexuelle Arbeitsgruppen der Schweiz" (HACH). Local groups are active in many cities, such as "Dialogai" in Geneva.

## Syria

*Official Attitudes and the Law*

Homosexual behavior is illegal. Section 520 of the Penal Code criminalizes any "carnal knowledge against the order of nature," with a maximum penalty of three years' imprisonment.

*Society*

Homosexuality cannot be admitted openly. There is no visible social support for gay and lesbian rights.

## Taiwan

*Official Attitudes and the Law*

Homosexual behavior between consenting adults is not mentioned in the law as being a criminal offense. Homosexual acts between consenting adults in private are not an offense in Taiwan. The age of consent for homosexual acts is twenty-one. Taiwanese soldiers who have been "converted" to homosexuality face the death penalty.

*Society*

There is no visible support for gay and lesbian rights.

*The Gay and/or Lesbian Movement*

There exists a lesbian group in Taipei. The first gay march was held by about 100 gays in March 1988.

## Tajikistan

*Official Attitudes and the Law*

In the former Soviet Union, anal intercourse between men was illegal. This prohibition is still incorporated in the Penal Code of Tajikistan. Homosexual acts between women are not mentioned in the law, nor is homosexual behavior between consenting adults explicitly included in the law as being a criminal offense.

*Society*

The attitude of this predominantly Islamic society is hostile toward homosexuality. There is no visible support for gay and lesbian rights.

## Tanzania

*Official Attitudes and the Law*

Homosexual behavior is illegal. Homosexual acts between men are illegal, according to Sections 154 to 157 of the Penal Code, with a maximum penalty of fourteen years' imprisonment. However, prosecution occurs very rarely. Homosexual acts between women are not mentioned.

*Society*

The attitude toward homosexuality is hostile, although this can differ among the various tribes that exist in the country. There is no visible social support for gay and lesbian rights.

## Thailand

*Official Attitudes and the Law*

Homosexual behavior between consenting adults is not mentioned in the law as being a criminal offense. The age of consent is fifteen years for both sexes. If a man has someone between the ages of fifteen and eighteen, who is not his own child, spending the night with him, he can be charged with kidnaping, unless he has a legal document from the parents of the child granting permission. In 1992, the police of Bangkok raided gay prostitution bars.

*Society*

The attitude toward homosexuality is fairly tolerant. A minority of the population is in favor of gay and lesbian rights.

*The Gay and/or Lesbian Movement*

New groups of gays and lesbians are active in Bangkok, such as FACT and ALN, and several gay magazines are published. The gay movement has been active in developing AIDS prevention activities.

## Togo

*Official Attitudes and the Law*

Homosexual contacts are illegal, and can be punished with up to three years' imprisonment. Homosexual acts are often prosecuted as assault or rape.

## Society

The attitude toward homosexuality is very intolerant. There is no visible social support for gay and lesbian rights.

## Tonga

### Official Attitudes and the Law

Homosexual behavior is illegal. Section 126 of the Penal Code prohibits "the abominable crime of sodomy committed either with mankind or with any animal": the offender shall be liable "at the discretion of the court to be imprisoned for any period not exceeding life and such animal shall be killed by a public officer." Section 127 criminalizes attempts to "sodomy and indecent assaults" upon a male, with a maximum penalty of ten years' imprisonment. Partners' consent is explicitly stated not to be a defense.

### Society

In Tonga, a long tradition exists of transvestite males, called *fakaleiti,* who (unlike the *mahu* in French Polynesia) are not very well tolerated. There is no visible social support for gay and lesbian rights.

## Trinidad and Tobago

### Official Attitudes and the Law

Homosexual behavior is illegal. According to Section 13 of the Sexual Offenses Act of October 1986, "buggery" (defined as anal intercourse) can be punished with life imprisonment, if committed on a minor; or ten years if committed on an adult (eighteen years or older) by another adult; or five years, if committed by a minor on an adult. Section 16 on "serious indecency" discriminates against homosexual acts between men and between women, with a maximum of twenty years' imprisonment.

According to Article 8 par. 18/1 of the Immigration Act, homosexual men and women are not allowed to enter the country.

Homosexuals are often subjected to official (police) harassment and violence.

### Society

There is no visible support for gay and lesbian rights.

## Tunisia

*Official Attitudes and the Law*

Homosexual acts between men and between women are considered to be illegal under Section 230 of the Penal Code.

*Society*

Despite the fact that homosexual acts are a criminal offense, closeted homosexual relationships between men do exist, especially in tourist centers. There is no visible social support of gay and lesbian rights.

## Turkey

*Official Attitudes and the Law*

Homosexual behavior between consenting adults is not mentioned in the law as being a criminal offense. The Turkish Embassy in The Hague wrote on January 18, 1991:

> In Turkey there exists no rule forbidding homosexuality; the Turkish Constitution does not permit separation based on a sexual reason. With an amendment to the Turkish Civic Code made in 1988, it is free to change sex. According to the Turkish Penal Code, to act in public in a lewd or indecent manner is a crime. People acting in this manner are punished, but this law applies to everyone regardless of their sexual preference. Homosexuals face no difficulties in enjoying public benefits and employment. Since there exists no legal problem, the need to protect homosexuals has not risen. There are no restrictions on homosexuals to establish or participate in an association or political party.

Nevertheless, homosexuals can be persecuted under general regulations on indecency (Articles 419, 547, and 576 of the Penal Code). Article 10 of the Law of Associations can be used to make gay organizations illegal. In 1989, the publishers of *Yesil Baris,* the newspaper of the Turkish Radical Green Party, were charged with "spreading homosexual information" following their publication of a series of articles about lesbian and gay issues.

*Society*

The attitude of the population is hostile toward open homosexuals. There is no visible social support for gay and lesbian rights.

*The Gay and/or Lesbian Movement*

A radical gay group called "Anthoriset" was founded in 1992.

## Turkmenistan

*Official Attitudes and the Law*

In the former Soviet Union, anal intercourse between men was illegal. This prohibition is still incorporated in the Penal Code of Turkmenistan. Homosexual acts between women are not mentioned in the law, nor is homosexual behavior between consenting adults explicitly included in the law as being a criminal offense.

*Society*

The attitude of this predominantly Islamic society is hostile toward homosexuality. There is no visible support for gay and lesbian rights.

## Tuvalu

*Official Attitudes and the Law*

Homosexual behavior is illegal. Section 153 of the Penal Code punishes "buggery" with a maximum penalty of fourteen years' imprisonment. Section 154 criminalizes "attempts to buggery and indecent assaults" with a maximum penalty of seven years' imprisonment. Section 155 prohibits acts of "gross indecency" in private or public, with five years' imprisonment.

*Society*

There is no visible support for gay and lesbian rights.

## Uganda

*Official Attitudes and the Law*

Homosexual acts between men are illegal under Section 140 of the Penal Code, which criminalizes "carnal knowledge" between men, with up to fourteen years' imprisonment. Section 143 prohibits any act of "gross indecency," in public or private between men, with up to five years' imprisonment. There is seldom a prosecution on the basis of these provisions, however. Homosexual acts between women are not mentioned.

*Society*

There is no visible support for gay and lesbian rights.

*The Gay and/or Lesbian Movement*

A gay and lesbian group called "The Good Samaritan Project" was founded in 1992.

## Ukraine

*Official Attitudes and the Law*

In the former Soviet Union, the Penal Code prohibited anal intercourse between men. The Ukranian parliament decriminalized homosexuality at the end of 1991.

*Society*

The attitude of society is hostile.

*The Gay and/or Lesbian Movement*

A Kiev-based gay and lesbian group called "Two Colors" was founded in 1991. In March 1993, a nationwide association was constituted.

## United Arab Emirates

*Official Attitudes and the Law*

Homosexual behavior is illegal. Homosexual acts are considered as "unnatural offenses" that can be punished with a maximum of fourteen years' imprisonment. Open homosexuality is considered to be "conduct at odds with public morality." Those "obscene acts" can be punished with a fine or imprisonment for a maximum of two years.

*Society*

Homosexuality is taboo. There is no visible social support for gay and lesbian rights.

## United States of America

*Official Attitudes and the Law*

Legal protections against discrimination on the basis of sexual orientation exist now in California, Connecticut, New Jersey, New York, Massachusetts, Vermont, and Wisconsin.

Before 1961, every state criminalized anal and oral sex between persons of the same gender. During the 1950s, a Model Penal Code was developed by the American Law Institute, in which all nonviolent consensual sexual activities between adults in private were decriminalized. The following 24 states have adopted the Model Penal Code or otherwise decriminalized homosexual acts (from East to West Coast): Maine, New Hampshire, Vermont, Connecticut, New York (State Court decision), New Jersey, Pennsylvania (State Court decision), West Virginia, Ohio, Indiana, Illinois (the first, in 1961), Wisconsin, Iowa, North Dakota, South Dakota, Nebraska, Colorado, New Mexico, Wyoming, Washington, Oregon, California, Alaska, and Hawaii.

All anal/oral sex (regardless of the gender) is illegal in: Massachusetts (not prosecuted if in private), Rhode Island, Delaware, Maryland, the District of Columbia (a Reform Bill was overridden by the federal Congress), Virginia, North Carolina, South Carolina, Georgia (the Supreme Court upheld in 1986 the ban on sodomy), Florida, Kentucky (the state's highest court struck down this law in 1992), Tennessee, Alabama, Mississippi, Louisiana, Missouri, Michigan, Minnesota, Idaho, Utah, and Arizona.

States that criminalize anal/oral sex only between persons of the same gender are: Arkansas, Kansas, Oklahoma (the state's highest criminal court decided in 1986 that application to heterosexual sex was unconstitutional), Texas, Montana, and Nevada. In 1992, the third court of appeals in Austin decided that the Texan sodomy law infringes on the laws of the United States and is therefore illegal.

According to the Department of Defense Directive 1332.14 (October 1, 1982), "Homosexuality is incompatible with military service." The implementation of this directive can be found in the Army Regulations 635-100 and 635-212; the Air Force Regulation 39-12; the Secretary of Navy Instruction, 1900-90; and the Marine Corps Separation and Retirement Manual 6016-6018. These regulations have often been applied to enforce dishonorable discharges of members of the military. The General Accounting Office reported in 1992 that the ban on gays and lesbians in the military has cost 500 million U.S. dollars during the last decade. In 1992, a gay Navy serviceman coming out on TV and being fired because of that, was reinstated by federal judge orders. In 1993, President Clinton moved to lift the ban on homosexuals in the military.

Under the terms of the Family Unity and Employment Opportunity Immigration Act, passed through the U.S. Congress on October 27, 1990, homosexuality itself is no longer grounds for barring someone from entering the United States. The Department of Health and Human Services now has the power to remove HIV and AIDS from the list of restricted diseases, but did not intend to do so until 1993. The 1992 International AIDS Congress moved from Boston to Amsterdam because of the U.S. entry and immigration restrictions. The National Commission on AIDS stated in 1992 that "President Bush and the Department of Health and Human Services have failed to meet fully their responsibility in leading the national response to the epidemic."

In 1992, progress was made in the legal fight for recognition of gay and lesbian parenthood: a New York City court approved the adoption of a six-year-old boy by his mother's lesbian lover.

The 1992 presidential election was the first in which anti-gay attacks backfired: the gaybaiting at the Republican National Convention in Houston in August 1992 failed to give the intended boost in the polls. On November 3, 1992, anti-gay initiatives in Oregon and Portland, Maine, failed; two openly gay members of the U.S. Congress, and nine gay state legislators were reelected. The election and inauguration of President Clinton had many pro-gay aspects; openly gay and lesbian politicians have been appointed.

In Colorado, however, an initiative was accepted to preempt any attempt to guarantee civil rights to gays and lesbians in that state; a boycott of the state began and the preemption was under judicial review.

### Society

The attitudes of the U.S. population toward homosexuality differ enormously. In some metropolitan areas like New York, San Francisco, Los Angeles, San Diego, and Boston, and in some smaller towns with large gay and lesbian communities, the majority of the population supports equal rights for homosexual women and men. In many parts of the United States, however, this is not the case.

### The Gay and/or Lesbian Movement

Compared with smaller countries the American gay and lesbian movement tends to be less cooperative due to an enormous number of factions in the communities and the distances between them. Topic- or issue-oriented cooperation can, however, often be established on very short notice, and can be extremely impressive (such as the marches on Washington in 1987 and 1993).

Some internationally well known organizations are the "AIDS Coalition To Unleash Power" (ACT-UP), "Dignity" (gay and lesbian Catholics), the (educational) "Fund for Human Dignity," the "Gay and Lesbian Alliance Against Defamation" (GLAAD), the "Human Rights Campaign Fund," the "International Gay and Lesbian Human Rights Commission," the "Lambda Legal Defense and Education Fund," the "National Gay and Lesbian Task Force," the "National Lesbian and Gay Health Foundation," the "North American Man/Boy Love Association" (NAMBLA), and the "Universal Fellowship of Metropolitan Community Churches" (MCC). Some internationally well known publications are *The Advocate, Christopher Street, Empathy,* and the *Journal of Homosexuality.*

## Uruguay

### Official Attitudes and the Law

Homosexual behavior between consenting adults is not mentioned in the law as being a criminal offense.

*Society*

Since the restoration of democracy at the beginning of 1985, the social position of homosexuals has improved. A minority of the population is in favor of gay and lesbian rights.

*The Gay and/or Lesbian Movement*

There are reports on the formation of gay and lesbian groups in Montevideo, such as "Grupo Somos," "Al Filo del Sartén-Homosexuales," and "Homosexuales Unidos."

## Uzbekistan

*Official Attitudes and the Law*

In the former Soviet Union, anal intercourse between men was illegal. This prohibition is still incorporated in the Penal Code of Uzbekistan. Homosexual acts between women are not mentioned in the law, nor is homosexual behavior between consenting adults explicitly included in the law as being a criminal offense.

*Society*

The attitude of this predominantly Islamic society is hostile toward homosexuality. There is no visible support for gay and lesbian rights.

## Vanuatu

*Official Attitudes and the Law*

Homosexual behavior between consenting adults is not mentioned in the law as being a criminal offense. A law commission is working on a unified legal code for Vanuatu. In the past Vanuatu was administered jointly by the United Kingdom and France. The legal system made a division between British and French subjects, who were liable only on the basis of their own national law and to be tried only by their own courts. Homosexual acts between men, therefore, were only illegal for residents of British nationality.

*Society*

There is no visible support for gay and lesbian rights.

## Vatican City

*Official Attitudes and the Law*

Homosexual behavior between consenting adults is not mentioned in the law as being a criminal offense; in practice, however, homosexual acts are forbidden. In 1991 and 1992, the Vatican issued several statements justifying people involved in homosexual contacts to be discriminated against. Homosexuality was described as "an objective disorder," and compared to mental illness. In 1992, the Vatican urged in a letter to bishops in the United States actively to oppose efforts to outlaw anti-homosexual discrimination.

*Society*

Homosexual behavior is taboo. There is no visible support for gay and lesbian rights.

## Venezuela

*Official Attitudes and the Law*

Homosexual behavior between consenting adults is not mentioned in the law as being a criminal offense. However, gay men and lesbians are not admitted into the armed forces. Homosexuals are often subjected to official (police) harassment and violence.

*Society*

Social attitudes are hostile, but relatively more tolerant than in other Latin American countries. A minority of the population is in favor of gay and lesbian rights.

*The Gay and/or Lesbian Movement*

In Caracas a gay and lesbian group exists.

## Vietnam

*Official Attitudes and the Law*

There is no legal information available.

*Society*

The attitude toward homosexuality is very hostile. There is no visible social support for gay and lesbian rights.

## Yemen

*Official Attitudes and the Law*

Islamic laws are applied; homosexuality is illegal.

*Society*

There is no visible support for gay and lesbian rights.

## Zaire

*Official Attitudes and the Law*

Homosexual behavior is illegal. Homosexual acts can be punished under the Sections 168, 169, 170, and 172 concerning "crimes against family life." The first two sections criminalize assault against a person, with a maximum penalty of six months to five years' imprisonment. Section 170 punishes rape, with a maximum penalty of five to forty years. Section 172 criminalizes, as "a break of public morals," assaults on minors, with a penalty of three months to five years' imprisonment and a fine.

*Society*

Homosexuality is taboo. There is no visible support for gay and lesbian rights.

## Zambia

*Official Attitudes and the Law*

Homosexual behavior is illegal. Homosexual acts between men are illegal under Sections 155 to 158 of the Penal Code, with a maximum penalty of fourteen years' imprisonment. Homosexual acts between women are not mentioned.

*Society*

There is no visible support for gay and lesbian rights.

## Zimbabwe

*Official Attitudes and the Law*

Homosexual behavior between males is a criminal offense. Lesbian contacts are not mentioned in the law. For acts between consenting male adults there is a penalty of a fine; and for those between non-consenting male adults or minors there is a penalty of three years in prison. In practice, very few homosexuals have been arrested or brought to trial.

## Society

The social position of whites and blacks is different: homosexual activities among whites are tolerated up to a certain degree; among blacks it depends upon tribal traditions. There is no visible social support for gay and lesbian rights.

## The Gay and/or Lesbian Movement

A group called GALZ ("Gays and Lesbians in Zimbabwe") is active.

# Selected Bibliography

## BOOKS

Adam, B. *The Rise of a Gay and Lesbian Movement*. Boston: G. K. Hall & Twayne, 1987.

Altman, D. *The Homosexualization of America*. Boston: Beacon Press, 1982.

Duberman, M. B., M. Vicinus, and G. Chauncey, eds. *Hidden from History: Reclaiming the Gay and Lesbian Past*. London: Penguin Books, 1991.

Dynes, W., ed. *Encyclopedia of Homosexuality*. New York: Garland, 1990.

The Gay Teachers' Group. *School's Out. Lesbian and Gay Rights in Education*. London: The Gay Teachers' Group, 1987.

Hinsch, B. *The Male Homosexual Tradition in China*. Berkeley and Los Angeles: University of California Press, 1990.

HOSI Auslandsgruppe. *Rosa Liebe unterm roten Stern* (*Pink Love under the Red Star*). Hamburg: Frühlings Erwachen, 1984.

Kidron, M., and R. Segal. *The New State of the World*. New York: Simon & Schuster, 1984.

Mann, J., D. Tarrantola, and T. Netter. *AIDS in the World*. Cambridge, Mass., and London: Harvard University Press, 1992.

Plummer, K. *The Making of the Modern Homosexual*. London: Hutchinson, 1981.

Sisley. E. L., and B. Harris. *The Joy of Lesbian Sex*. London: Mitchell Beazley Publishers, 1977.

Tatchell, P. *Europe in the Pink*. London: GMP Publishers, 1992.

Tielman, R., M. Carballo, and A. Hendriks, eds. *Bisexuality and HIV/AIDS*. Buffalo, N.Y.: Prometheus Books, 1991.

Tielman, R., and E. van der Veen, eds. *Second ILGA Pink Book*. Utrecht: Gay and Lesbian Studies Department, 1988.
Waaldijk, C., and A. Clapham, eds. *Homosexuality—A Community Issue*. Dordrecht: Nijhoff, 1993.
Weeks, J. *Coming Out*. London and New York: Quartet Books, 1977.

## MAGAZINES AND JOURNALS

*The Advocate*. Los Angeles, U.S.A.
*Capital Gay*. London, U.K.
*Gay Hotsa*. Bilbao, Spain
*Gay Krant Best*. The Netherlands
*Gay Pied Hebdo*. Paris, France
*Gay Times*. London, U.K.
*ILGA Bulletin*. Brussels, Belgium
*Journal of Homosexuality*. San Francisco, U.S.A.
*Lambda Nachrichten*. Vienna, Austria
*Lesbia*. Paris, France
*Magnus*. Berlin, Germany
*Sek/XL*. Amsterdam, the Netherlands

# Index of Contributors

**Barry D. Adam** is professor of sociology at the University of Windsor, Ontario, Canada. He is the author of *The Rise of a Gay and Lesbian Movement* and *The Survival of Domination*. He is currently doing work on the impact of HIV on personal, family, and work relationships.

**Dafna Argov** is an Israeli anthropology student who is writing her Ph.D. dissertation on lesbian activism in Argentina at the Universidad Nacional de Buenos Aires, Argentina.

**Frank Arnal** studied history at the University of Strasbourg, France. In Paris, he received a diploma from the French Press Institute. He had been dealing with lesbian and gay issues, both on a national and an international level, from 1975 onwards. He was involved with the foundation of *Gai Pied* in 1979, and eventually became editor-in-chief from 1981 to 1988. He authored numerous articles on homosexuality, published both in France and abroad. He died on January 11, 1993.

**Tim Barnett** was the first executive director of the Stonewall Group from 1989 to 1991, for which he set up lobbying networks in both the United Kingdom and other European countries and networked with other lesbian and gay organizations. He was previously a local authority politician in London and worked in the volunteer movement. He now lives in New Zealand.

**Vern L. Bullough** is SUNY Distinguished Professor Emeritus at the State University College of New York at Buffalo. He has written and edited about forty books and over one hundred scholarly articles. His major work in the field of sex is *Sexual Variance in Society and History* (1986). His most recent book is *Cross Dressing, Sex, and Gender* (with Bonnie Bullough), 1993.

345

**John Clark,** born in the United States, has lived in Vienna, Austria, for the last nineteen years. He holds a degree in German literature from the University of Southern California. He is presently a member of the Board of Directors of the "Homosexuelle Initiative (HOSI) Wien" and was one of the founding members of the International Lesbian and Gay Association (ILGA) Eastern European Information Pool. He was elected co-secretary general of the ILGA in 1990.

**Mike Coutinho** (pseudonym) is a sociolinguistic researcher and gay activist with South African ancestors and Canadian citizenship. He studied sociolinguistics at McGill University in Montreal, Canada, and at the University of Harare, Zimbabwe. He is currently based in South Africa. Due to his alien status in this country, he has to use a pseudonym.

**Jomar Fleras** studied business administration at the University of the Philippines. He works as a journalist, playwright, and filmmaker. He is also the founder and director of the "Reach Out AIDS Education Foundation," a community-based AIDS prevention project in Manila. He is winner of seven literary awards in the Philippines and the author of two books.

**Ilse Fuskóva-Kornreich** is an Argentine lesbian feminist of Czech ancestry. She came out as a lesbian in 1985 after having been married for more than thirty years. Her main interest is lesbian feminist activism.

**Hans Hammelburg** studied law at the Universities of Amsterdam and Barcelona. He has been affiliated with the Gay and Lesbian Studies Department of the University of Utrecht and the International Humanist and Ethical Union (IHEU).

**Bent Hansen** has been the head of the secretariat of the National Danish Organization for Gays and Lesbians (LBL) since 1984, a member of the governing body of LBL from 1977 to 1984, and deputy chairman from 1978 to 1984. He was also coordinator of LBL's international work from 1978 to 1984.

**John Hart** is lecturer in the Department of Social Work and Social Policy at the University of Sydney, New South Wales, Australia. His Ph.D. research, "A Genuine Relationship? An Investigation into Some Results of the Use between 1983–89 of Ministerial Discretion and the Migration Act of 1958," was an investigation into ministerial discretion in relation to the Australian Migration Act (1958). He is the author of four books on sexuality. His current research interests are education about, and care of, persons with HIV in Thailand.

**Aart Hendriks** is a lawyer and political scientist who graduated from Leiden University, the Netherlands. He has been working for a number of institutions, both in the Netherlands and elsewhere, in the areas of human rights, international relations, HIV/AIDS, and lesbian and gay issues. He was affiliated with the Gay and Lesbian Studies Department of the University of Utrecht between 1989 and 1992. He currently works for the Department of Health Law, the University of Amsterdam.

**Henning Jørgensen** was a member of the governing body of LBL from 1975 to 1986. He was LBL's national chairman from 1977, and was appointed chairman of LBL's internal partnership committee. In addition, he was one of the two LBL members on the Commission to Elucidate the Social Circumstances of Homosexuals in Denmark. He participated in all ILGA annual meetings and European meetings between 1979 and 1986, and was involved with ILGA's financial secretariat between 1981 and 1986.

**Madiha Didi Khayatt,** born in Egypt, is presently working as coordinator of the Women's Studies Programme and as assistant professor at the Glendon College, York University, in Toronto, Canada. She is author of *Lesbian Teachers: An Invisible Presence,* State University of New York Press (1992).

**Ilse Kokula** works in the Center for Homosexual Lifestyles of the Berlin Senate Department for Youth and Family Affairs in Berlin. She studied social sciences (pedagogics and sociology) and earned her doctorate in 1982 from Bremen University. She was the first holder of the Belle-van-Zuylen Chair at the University of Utrecht in the Netherlands on "Socialization and Social History of Lesbian Women" during 1985–86.

**Astrid Mattijssen** studied law at the University of Utrecht and works as a legal research associate for the Gay and Lesbian Studies Department. She conducts research into the legal aspects of anti-gay and anti-lesbian discrimination with respect to employment. Since 1992, she has worked as well for the Clara Wichmann Institute in Amsterdam, an institute for women and law.

**David Norris** is one of the founding fathers of the Irish lesbian and gay movement. He challenged the Irish legislation completely outlawing male homosexual acts before the European Court of Human Rights. In 1987, he was elected a member of the Upper House of the Irish Parliament.

**Gerben Potman** studied tropical forestry at the Agricultural University of Wageningen in the Netherlands. He spent six months as an intern in Senegal, where he wrote a diary that was published under the title *Lonely in Senegal (Eenzaam in Senegal).* Later he worked for eight months in Burkina Faso. He is currently affiliated with the International Humanist and Ethical Union (IHEU) in Utrecht, the Netherlands.

**Lisa Power** was co-secretary general of the ILGA from 1988 to 1992. She has been out as a lesbian since 1976 and a volunteer with London Lesbian and Gay Switchboard, for whom she is an ILGA delegate, since 1979. She was a founding member of the Stonewall Group, Britain's first professional lesbian and gay lobbying group.

**Svend J. Robinson,** a member of the Canadian national Parliament since 1979, comes from Vancouver, British Columbia. He is Opposition Spokesperson on

Foreign Affairs and International Human Rights, and enjoys cycling, skiing, kayaking, dancing, and fomenting revolutions, bearing in mind Emma Goldman's words, "If I can't dance, I don't want to be part of your revolution."

**Fang Fu Ruan** is a Chinese physician who came to the United States in 1987. He works at the Chinese medical school (which practices traditional Chinese medicine) in California. He has written several articles on sexuality in China.

**Huub Ruijgrok** studied tropical forestry at the Agricultural University of Wageningen in the Netherlands. He spent six months as an intern in Senegal. Later he worked for six months in Suriname. At present he works as a video producer. He has produced a video on the social life of partners of Dutch development workers in Zimbabwe.

**Willemien Ruygrok** worked until 1993 as a staff member for the Netherlands Association for the Integration of Homosexuality COC in Amsterdam.

**Petra Schedler** studied adult education at the University of Leiden, the Netherlands. She is currently affiliated with the Department of Andragology at the same university and is working for the center for adult education and public information. She wrote her doctoral dissertation on women's and gay groups within established organizations.

**Christina Schenk** studied physics at the Humboldt University in former East Berlin. Before she became a member of the German Parliament in 1990, she was attached to the GDR Academy of Sciences and worked as sociological researcher affiliated with the Humboldt University. Since 1985, she has been an active member of the Berlin lesbian group that organized under the auspices of the Protestant Church. In 1989, she was co-founder of the Independent Women's Association, the same organization she is now representing in the German Parliament.

**Andrzej Selerowicz,** born in Poland, lives in Vienna. He works on a volunteer basis with the "Homosexuelle Initiative (HOSI) Wien." As an ILGA coordinator for Eastern Europe he maintains regular contacts with lesbian and gay groups in this region. He contributes to a number of lesbian and gay magazines in Austria, the Czech Republic, Slovakia, and Poland. He was one of the co-authors of the book *Rosa Liebe unterm roten Stern* (*Pink Love under the Red Star*).

**Chris Smith** is a Labour Member of the British Parliament for Islington South and Finsbury. His special political interests include housing, local government, civil liberties, finance and economics, and the environment. He is shadow secretary of state for environmental protection.

**Rob Tielman** is professor of Humanist Studies at the University of Utrecht and co-chairperson of the International Humanist and Ethical Union (IHEU). He was secretary general of the Dutch Association for the Integration of Homosexuality COC (1971–1975), chairperson of the Dutch Humanist Association (1977–1987), and head of the Gay and Lesbian Studies Department of the University of Utrecht (1981–1991).

**Carmen Vázquez** obtained a master's degree in education from Richmond College, City University of New York. She is a member of the Board of Directors of the National Lesbian/Gay Task Force, coordinator of Lesbian/Gay Health Services of the San Francisco Department of Public Health, and a member and co-chairperson of the Lesbian Agenda for Action.

**Evert van der Veen** was an active member of the ILGA from 1985 to 1991 while working at the Gay and Lesbian Studies Department of the University of Utrecht. His research interests include anti-gay and anti-lesbian discrimination and violence, homosexuality and the police, and the gay and lesbian press. He has produced various publications on gay and lesbian issues and was the co-editor of the *Second ILGA Pink Book.* He is presently conducting research into care for the dying at the Netherlands Institute for Care and Welfare, NIZW.